D0087638

DISCARDED

University of Winnipeg, 515 Portage Ave., Winnipeg, MB. R3B 2E9 Canada

FOR WHOM
DO I TOIL?

STUDIES IN JEWISH HISTORY
Jehuda Reinharz, General Editor

Other Volumes Are in Preparation

RJ
5052
G6Z86
1988

FOR WHOM DO I TOIL?

Judah Leib Gordon and the
Crisis of Russian Jewry

Michael Stanislawski

New York   Oxford
OXFORD UNIVERSITY PRESS
1988

Oxford University Press

Oxford New York Toronto
Delhi Bombay Calcutta Madras Karachi
Petaling Jaya Singapore Hong Kong Tokyo
Nairobi Dar es Salaam Cape Town
Melbourne Auckland

and associated companies in
Berlin Ibadan

Copyright © 1988 by Oxford University Press, Inc.

Published by Oxford University Press, Inc.,
200 Madison Avenue, New York, New York 10016

Oxford is a registered trademark of Oxford University Press

All rights reserved. No part of this publication may be reproduced,
stored in a retrieval system, or transmitted, in any form or by any means,
electronic, mechanical, photocopying, recording, or otherwise,
without the prior permission of Oxford University Press.

Library of Congress Cataloging-in-Publication Data
Stanislawski, Michael, 1952–
For whom do I toil?
Bibliography: p.
Includes index.
1. Gordon, Judah Leib, 1830–1892. 2. Poets, Hebrew—Biography.
3. Haskalah—Soviet Union.
4. Hibbat Zion. I. Title.
PJ5052.G6Z86 1988   892.4'14 [B]   87-31284
ISBN 0-19-504290-5

2 4 6 8 9 7 5 3 1

Printed in the United States of America
on acid-free paper

To Margie

אל קולך כי ערב מה נפשי כלתה

Acknowledgments

Living with Judah Leib Gordon for the past five years has not always been an easy task, but it was made immeasurably more pleasurable by the assistance and support of the following persons and institutions. The Social Sciences Research Council of Columbia University provided financial resources for several summers of studying Gordon and for a crucial research trip to Jerusalem. Dr. Mordecai Nadav and his staff at the Archives of the National and University Library at the Hebrew University opened their offices to me with their customary warmth, allowing me to dig deeply into the Gordon materials in their collections and granting me permission to reproduce the archival material cited herein. Most of my research was conducted in the luxury of the new Library of the Jewish Theological Seminary of America; I am most indebted to Dr. Menahem Schmelzer, former librarian of the seminary, for his unparalleled hospitality to me. Thanks are due, as well, to Miss Dina Abramovitz of the YIVO Library and to the staff of the Hebrew Union College in Cincinnati.

My friends and colleagues Marc Raeff, Ruth Wisse, and Jehuda Reinharz graciously interrupted their own work to read this manuscript and saved me from many errors and potential embarrassments. To Jehuda Reinharz I am grateful as well for his unstinting support as editor of this series. Over the last several years I have lectured about Gordon to a large number of academic audiences across the United States; every one of these occasions forced me to hone ever sharper my ideas and my presentation. During the course of this project I was most encouraged by the enthusiasm for my work exhibited by the current chancellor of the Jewish Theological Seminary of America, Ismar Schorsch, and by my senior colleague in Jewish History at Columbia, Yosef Hayim Yerushalmi.

Of course, my greatest debt is to my wife, Marjorie Kaplan, who alone knows her contribution to this book, and to whom it is dedicated. She and now our son Ethan Lee have taught me never for a moment to doubt "for whom do I toil."

Contents

Illustrations follow page 128

FOR WHOM
DO I TOIL?

For whom do I toil and deprive myself of joy?
This also is vanity, yea, it is a sore travail.

ECCLESIASTES 4:8

1

Introduction

In the winter of 1891 a graying, elegantly attired gentleman wearily climbed the stairs to the St. Petersburg offices of the great Russian encyclopedia, the Brockhaus-Efron *Encyclopedic Dictionary*. This noble attempt to summarize for the Russians all the knowledge known to man was, perhaps fittingly, a joint effort of the Leipzig firm founded by the famous German Enlightenment encylopedist F. A. Brockhaus and the Vilna-born Jewish publisher Ilia Efron. Efron had hired as an editorial assistant a sixty-year-old native of his hometown, Lev Osipovich Gordon. Every morning Gordon, slowly dying of cancer, trudged through the sleet and bracing winds of St. Petersburg to perform his tasks for the encyclopedia. At first, the work was captivating and important—editing all articles relating to the history and culture of the Jews. But soon Gordon was relieved of this duty and was retained, to his substantial embarrassment, merely to act as translator from and into the German language.

Undoubtedly, few of Gordon's co-workers knew that their sickly but dignified colleague was one of the pivotal intellectual and cultural figures in Russian-Jewish history: not simply the Honorary Citizen Lev Osipovich Gordon, but also Judah Leib Gordon, the most important Hebrew poet of the nineteenth century. In essence, Judah Leib Gordon—known by his Hebrew acronym Yalag—was the most prominent and most passionate exponent of the Jewish Enlightenment movement in Russia; the creator, beyond his Hebrew verse, of an innovative body of Hebrew prose that helped shape the Hebrew language into a modern literary idiom; a reluctant but important dabbler in Yiddish poetry; the author of a vast number of scholarly, polemical, and literary articles in Hebrew, Russian, and German journals at home and abroad; the former editor of the major Hebrew newspaper in the world and director of the Society for the Promotion of Enlightenment among the Jews of Russia; and the onetime secretary of the St. Petersburg Jewish community.

And yet this man who had enjoyed fame, power, and prestige throughout the Jewish world was now doing petty clerical work on a Russian encyclopedia. Gordon did need the slim income the encyclopedia work yielded him, but this was not

3

the primary reason for his current plight. He had, in fact, voluntarily retreated from Hebrew letters and Jewish journalism—the two sources of his previous income—despite desperate pleas to return. He announced that he had ceased writing "from right to left" and would now only write in the reverse direction, in Cyrillic.

This was not the first time that Judah Leib Gordon recoiled in agonizing doubt and moral exhaustion over the fate of Jewish culture and Jewish politics in Russia. Twenty years earlier he had asked, in one of the poems that made him famous and was known by heart by thousands of readers,

> For whom do I toil, I mere mortal,
> For the handful of remaining lovers of Hebrew
> Who have not yet mocked her and scorned? . . .
> O, who can foresee the future, who can say
> Am I not the last of Zion's poets
> And you, the last readers?[1]

Now, recasting the query a bit, he pondered, "For whom and for what should I toil?" I am tired, he wrote to a close friend, I need rest; shall I again pore out my wrath and weep over the days of darkness in which we are mired? What purpose will be served if I add two more tears to the great sea of distress? I withdraw from the battle—my voice shall no longer be heard. *"Die Ideale sind zerronnen!"*—all my dreams have been laid waste, all my hopes have been in vain, and God has not revealed Himself to me in any new dreams. Should I return to fight with the rabbis, on the one hand, and the anti-Semites on the other? Both are obtuse and, like deaf vipers, shut their ears to logic and sense. Our disease is incurable! I, therefore, shall remain aloof and silent. Don't remind me that I was an author in Israel; perhaps I'll be able to forget the shame and live in peace.[2]

Gordon did not long maintain this self-imposed silence. Within a few months he was once more writing sharp, sarcastic Hebrew poems denouncing his enemies. But the decades of internecine warfare had taken their toll. The proud standard-bearer of Jewish liberalism saw the world around him, Gentile and Jewish, denounce and betray the virtues and values that he had taken to be both self-evident and invincible. He had believed for nearly half a century that the liberation of the Jews of Russia, as well as the West, was imminent if they but joined the inexorable march of culture and progress that had begun in Paris in 1789. The stations of this journey were clearly marked: religious reform, economic modernization, linguistic acculturation, loyalty to monarch and state, legal emancipation, social integration. Along the way, the excess baggage that had been yoked to the shoulders of the Jewish people by medieval prejudice and superstition would, of course, be discarded, but without the loss—indeed, with the rejuvenation—of a vibrant Hebrew culture and authentic Jewish faith. In the late 1880s and early 1890s, Gordon's vigilant moderation seemed increasingly archaic and irritatingly naive to a political culture that demanded unflinching identification either with a new type of nationalism that he rejected as reactionary or with a socialist radicalism that he branded a betrayal of both Judaism and Western humanitarianism. As a chorus of dissonant voices in Russian, Hebrew, and Yiddish proclaimed in unison, if in radically different keys, that the dream of Jewish integration into bourgeois European society was not only hopeless but also evil, Gordon swayed unsteadily on the edge of depression and despair.

To the end, he refused to succumb; he persisted in his irremediable fidelity to a vision of Western humanism blended with Jewish dignity. This stubbornness, however, earned him not only the scorn of contemporaries, but, in large measure, also the fate of being deemed irrelevant by future generations, except as an embodiment of an anachronistic ideology. Virtually no one actually reads Gordon these days, and indeed most of his polemical writings in Hebrew and all of his works in Russian, German, and Yiddish have never been reprinted or collected and remain strewn about the disintegrating residue of the nineteenth-century Hebrew, Russian-Jewish, and German-Jewish press. Only a small band of professional students of Hebrew literature periodically return to Gordon to examine his contributions to the history of Hebrew letters. Beyond these rarified circles, any self-respecting history of modern Jewry will, to be sure, make passing reference to Judah Leib Gordon as an important Hebrew poet and may well cite his famous call to arms "Awake, My People!," usually in the form of its almost universally misunderstood catchphrase, "Be a man in the street and a Jew at home." Perhaps his long mock-epic "The Tip of the [Letter] Yud" may be noted as the best-known literary attack on the obscurantism of the rabbis and call for the emancipation of the Jewish woman. And then the paragraph will end, the narrative proceeding to the next subject.

At the heart of this lapse of interest in Gordon lies a phenomenon that strikes at the very core of Jewish ideological and cultural history in the modern world: the accepted appraisal of the death of the Jewish Enlightenment movement, the Haskalah, in the last decades of the nineteenth century.

We have an image of the ideological development of East European Jewry as a neat case of doctrinal succession: traditional Judaism yielding to the Haskalah, whose naive, optimistic view of the world crashes on the shores of anti-Semitism and radicalism and is transmuted into the more realistic and long-lived ideologies of modern Jewish nationalism and socialism. While Western Jewry remains committed to assimilation and integration, the more authentic East European Jewry rejects these naive goals and instead is torn between the conflicting demands and solutions of Zionism, socialism, and their intersection.

The problem with this paradigm is that the vast majority of the Jews in Russia until 1917 (or in Poland to 1939) never became Zionists or Bundists or Autonomists or any other "ists." They were not politicized in the sense of actively belonging to or even identifying with any political party or ideology. Exactly what they did believe is extremely difficult, perhaps impossible, to gauge; to say the least, all judgments are still inexorably clouded by the prejudices of the observer.

But it does seem fair to generalize that vast numbers of Jews in Russia to 1917 or in Poland to 1939 were living with one foot in their tradition and the other outside of it, striving—at times tentatively, at times stridently, more often than not unselfconsciously—to reconcile the way of life of their parents with the attractions and challenges of modern existence. Central to this quest was the overarching dilemma of how to cope with the mundane demands of daily life in a dignified fashion; how to be productive, or at least self-sustaining, members of society-at-large without attempting to escape from or revolutionize that society; how to communicate in the muddle of linguistic options available to them; and, not least of all, how to preserve or transform the faith of their mothers and the observances of their fathers.

This does not mean that the majority of the Jews in Eastern Europe ever became adherents of the Haskalah; only that the essential issues articulated by the Haskalah, its basic quest for the educational, social, and religious reform of the Jews, continued to occupy center stage in the lives of many, if not most, East European Jews until the end.

For a rather simple reason, this picture of the inner life of East European Jewry does not find its way into our history books. All the major historians of this society have been dedicated advocates of one of the dominant political ideologies—Zionism or socialism or autonomism, or a mixture of the three—which claimed to have rendered irrelevant the issues listed above. The notion that a Western-style embourgeoisement, in both the cultural and the economic senses of the term, would solve the Jewish problem in Eastern Europe was rejected by the largest part of the Jewish intelligentsia, despite its mass appeal, and appeared more and more erroneous as East European Jewry was overwhelmed by the forces of evil and of madness.

It is therefore not surprising that Judah Leib Gordon and other proponents of a gradual, liberal, sanguine transformation of the life and culture of the Jews of Eastern Europe have been all but forgotten, ignored, or misrepresented. For Gordon does not fit into the paradigm: a Hebrew poet—or rather *the* Hebrew poet—of the middle and late 19th century who never became a Zionist or a socialist, but persisted in his faith in the future of Jews in bourgeois society even after 1881 and insisted on the need for the Jews to reform themselves in a moderate, Western fashion.

Perhaps his contemporaries and the later consensus were correct. Perhaps Judah Leib Gordon was simply too shortsighted or narrow-minded to behold the lessons that seemed so clear to his opponents on all fronts. The goal of this biography, however, will be to demonstrate that a close study of Gordon that deliberately strains to withhold retrospective ideological judgment can unearth in his life and work a clarity of vision and understanding that has been obscured by the blinders of passion and politics. Precisely because Gordon did not follow the expected path, he illuminates his age and its dilemmas in a new light and challenges us to reconstruct Russian-Jewish society without succumbing to the stereotypes and orthodoxies that have long prevailed.

This is a biography of a poet, and much of Gordon's poetry will be discussed and cited in these pages. But this is, quite self-consciously, not an exercise in literary history or literary criticism. Rather, it is an attempt by a cultural historian to chronicle and analyze the central role played by a poet—as well as a politician, journalist, *intelligent,* feuilletonist, short story writer, communal leader, and intellectual broker—in the cultural and political life of Russian Jewry in some of the most critical hours of its history. Judah Leib Gordon defined himself, to be sure, first and foremost as a poet, and that has been how he has been identified through the generations. But although Gordon held his poetry in greater esteem than his other writings, and Hebrew in greater esteem than his other tongues, to understand his cultural and intellectual views and his activities—or his poetry, for that matter—one must attempt to integrate all layers and facets of his writings while remaining sensitive to their relative position in his aesthetic and linguistic hierarchies. In other words, and contrary to the prevailing method of most studies of the Jewish Enlightenment, this biography will treat all of Judah Leib Gordon's writings, in whatever genre and in whatever tongue, as equally valid and accessible (and equally problematic) sources to his life, thoughts, and times. This assumption, of course, in no way denies the undoubtable truth that Gordon's poetry and his other literary creations had a life of their own, susceptible to specialized literary analysis, and possibly meanings of their own of which their author might even have been unaware. But this study will attempt to resurrect what Judah Leib Gordon himself meant in his works, his own explications of his texts, in the hope of reconstructing and analyzing this vital chapter in the cultural history of modern Jewry.

Out of this effort, it is hoped, the life of Judah Leib Gordon will emerge as a fascinating drama that at once symbolized and summarized his times. That life, quite appropriately, began in the hothouse of East European Jewish cultural discourse through the centuries, in Vilna, the "Jerusalem of Lithuania."

2

From Vilna to Enlightenment
1830–1855

Vilna, a modest East European city rarely visited by foreigners, has loomed mega-lopolitan in the consciousness of three distinct cultures and peoples. To the Lithuanians, the city known as Vilnius is the ancient capital of a proud and fierce nation, a free Baltic race that resisted German, Polish, and Russian imperialism before succumbing to the Soviet juggernaut. The Poles, who constituted the majority of its population until very recent times, venerated Wilno, a Jesuit jewel that boasted thirty-five Catholic churches, dozens of aristocratic homes, and a famous university, where the national poet Adam Mickiewicz studied under the idealist historian Joachim Lelewel. For centuries Jews around the world revered Vilna as one of the main centers of rabbinical learning, Hebrew printing, and Jewish piety; legend had it that when Napoleon arrived there in 1812, he was so taken by the number of Jews in its midst that he exclaimed, "Gentlemen, I think we are in Jerusalem!"—thus yielding the honorific "Jerusalem of Lithuania."

In many respects Vilnius-Wilno-Vilna was three different cities whose inhabitants traded with one another, communicated when necessary in a melange of dialect and gesture, but lived entirely apart, "as if on separate planets," as Czeslaw Milosz was to put it in his eloquent memoirs of his hometown.[1] When Judah Leib Gordon was born there on December 7, 1830 (according to the Russian calendar), Vilna's population of roughly thirty thousand Poles, twenty thousand Jews, and a few thousand Russian bureaucrats and Lithuanian peasants was even more divided than usual by ethnic, religious, and political cleavages. A day earlier, the Polish proto-parliament in Warsaw had declared revolution, transforming the tiny band of conspirators who had attacked Belweder Palace a fortnight before into the avant-garde of Polish national liberation. The tsar's rule over all of the lands of former Poland was condemned as a "political monstrosity" and a breach of the Congress of Vienna. Poland would be free once more, whatever the cost.

The motley inhabitants of Vilna kept a fateful watch as, within a few weeks, rebellion mounted into war. Warsaw declared that the tsar was dethroned as king of Poland; Nicholas I responded that either Russia or Poland would have to perish, and dispatched a massive army to effect his choice. Military stalemate yielded to negotiations that yielded to even more bloodshed. Lithuanian partisans entered into the fray, ultimately gaining control over most of Lithuania except for the capital. For months the frenzied battles raged back and forth over an increasingly decimated terrain, but there was never much hope that this particular David could vanquish its Goliath. By late summer, the predictable end was at hand: *finis Poloniae.* The Kingdom of Poland lost its semiautonomous status in the tsarist realm; the intellectual, cultural, and ideological elite of Poland emigrated to the West; Nicholas's government rededicated itself to severing all links between the Lithuanian, Belorussian, and Ukrainian provinces of the Russian Empire and their former Polish tutelage. The future was to be governed by St. Petersburg, and all vestiges of the Polish past were to be effaced.

For the Jews of Vilna (as well as the rest of the old Polish-Lithuanian Commonwealth) the "November Uprising" of 1830 held little attraction. Despite the patriotic pleadings of later polonized Jewish historians, it seems clear that most Jews at the time remained neutral in the battle between Warsaw and St. Petersburg. Their political universe was predicated on a rather simple premise, well honed over centuries of acute—and quite sophisticated—analysis: support of whatever government was in power. Retrospective judgments of whether the Jews fared better in independent Poland or under the tsars were both unavailable and of little interest to Jewish leaders who knew that when the dust settled they would still have to bear tribute to local authorities, who would extract the same bribes whatever the design of their uniforms. What was important was not to get embroiled in the temporal quarrels of Gentile powers in any way that might possibly threaten the delicate balance that governed Jewish existence in Exile. The Jewish elders could not yet know that the time would soon come when this ancient strategy would no longer be sufficient or, for that matter, acceptable to their flock. On the one hand, the Russian government would begin to view the insularity and autonomy of the Jews as but one of the unacceptable hangovers of Polish rule and would thus seek to impose itself into the internal life of the Jews in an unprecedented manner. On the other hand, many Jews would soon rebel against the authority and politics of their spiritual and lay leaders in the name of new ideologies that hailed not only from St. Petersburg and Warsaw but from Berlin, Paris, and London as well.

But through the 1830s these travails were, at best, in embryo. Vilna shone as one of the brightest stars in the constellation of Jewish life in Eastern Europe. Most important, Vilna was home to the tradition of Elijah ben Solomon Zalman, the Vilna Gaon (1720–1797), one of the major intellectual and spiritual figures in Judaism and the predominant representative of Rabbinism in the eighteenth century. To know Jewish Vilna, and thus the context in which Judah Leib Gordon was reared, it is essential to understand at least the barest outlines of the Vilna Gaon's approach to God and the Jewish tradition.[2]

At the heart of that approach was an unrelenting intellectuality, a boundless determination to reach truth through a rigorous and untrammeled study of all of the classics of Judaism. This belief in the supreme religious worth of study was expressed in Rabbi Elijah's quasi-ascetic regimen—he was reported to sleep only two hours a night and to forbid talk not devoted to the Torah—and, more fundamentally, in his dedication to acquiring all the skills and information essential to an elucidation of the sacred texts. Thus, at variance with contemporary practice, although buttressed by precedent and authority, the Gaon opposed the practice of explaining textual problems in the Talmud through an overly liberal use of the hermeneutic techniques of *pilpul*. Instead, he insisted on a thorough study of all the cognate sources, especially the Jerusalem Talmud, long neglected in favor of the Babylonian redaction. On the basis of his mastery of classic Rabbinics, but without access to manuscript variants, he was able and willing to suggest a large number of emendations and corrections in the Talmudic text, many of which resulted in contradicting the interpretations of post-Talmudic masters. This approach may be viewed as critical, and indeed modern scholars have dubbed the Gaon "the father of the criticism of the Talmud."[3] But Rabbi Elijah's source criticism was grounded in and defined by an assumption of the infallibility of the Torah. Similarly, following the example of a small minority of Ashkenazic sages through the ages, he taught himself mathematics, astronomy, geography, and anatomy through the medium of medieval Hebrew science and, at least in one case, approved the further transmission of scientific knowledge to traditional Jews by encouraging a student to translate Euclid into Hebrew. But for the Vilna Gaon, such scientific knowledge—like textual emendations—were permissible only as ancillary tools in exegesis, not as competing sources of authority. The Talmud and subsequent Jewish law could only be explicated by these devices, never overruled; indeed, the point of the endeavor was to demonstrate the eternal veracity of the canon as a whole, the possibility of understanding God's purpose through a life of uninterrupted study of His words.

This theological stance led the Vilna Gaon to spearhead the opposition to the new form of Jewish religiosity that emerged in his time, Hasidism. His vehement denunciation of the new movement was in no way based on a rejection of mysticism on the part of a rigid rationalist, as it has often been portrayed. Quite to the contrary, the Gaon was a profound student of Kabbalah who enjoyed an exceptionally vivid visionary life that included mystical graces and revelations that were consciously constrained from interfering in his legal and scholarly functions. But the Gaon believed that true charisma inhered only in the Torah, not in its teachers, and that the popularization of mysticism was inherently dangerous because of the potential for antinomianism. He therefore was scandalized by the presumption of both grace and authority on the part of the Hasidim. They had no right to usurp the prerogatives of the kabbalistic elite that had been strictly controlled and limited by rabbinical leadership over the centuries. Following these principles, Rabbi Elijah signed a writ of excommunication against the Hasidim in 1772, and under his direction Vilna became the center of anti-Hasidic propaganda and activity. It was only after his death in 1797 that the breach between the two camps of traditional Jewry in Eastern Europe could begin to be healed.[4]

But even then Vilna and Jewish Lithuania as a whole retained a fierce resistance to Hasidism that was unmatched in the rest of Eastern Europe. There were, to be sure, some important Hasidic enclaves in this region, but here alone Hasidism failed to enlist a majority of the Jews, and the terms "Litvak" (a Lithuanian Jew in the broad geographic sense that included Belorussia) and "mitnaged" (opponent of Hasidism) became synonymous in the popular culture of East European Jewry. The rabbinic leadership of non-Hasidic Jewry was vouchsafed to the disciples of the Gaon—men, like Rabbi Ḥayim of Volozhin, who attempted to translate their master's teachings into a pedagogic theory that was actualized in a number of innovative yeshivot founded in Lithuania at the beginning of the nineteenth century. In order to counter the attractiveness of Hasidism, the academies at Volozhin, Mir, Vilna, and Minsk were imbued with a new theology of the "mystification of Talmudic study," which was supposed to lead not only to virtuoso scholarship but also to increased spirituality and heightened awe of the divine.[5] On a more popular level, the intellectual ideology of the Lithuanian school was diffused by a small coterie of ḥeder teachers, most often alumni of the new yeshivot, who insisted on the study of Hebrew grammar and the Bible as prerequisites to immersion in the Talmud and attempted to emphasize the plain meaning of the Talmudic text rather than find recourse in complicated hermeneutics. In addition, many of these teachers, and the parents who employed them, saw no evil in a very mild exposure of children to the barest rudiments of practical education—the Russian or Polish alphabets and arithmetic.

The very same educational devices—the word "reforms" implies a far stronger consciousness of innovation than is appropriate—were the central planks in the platform of the Jewish Enlightenment movement, the Haskalah, as it traveled eastward from Germany in the last years of the eighteenth century and early decades of the nineteenth century and entered the Russian Empire along the northern frontier from East Prussia and the southern border from Galicia. But neither the Lithuanian *melamdim* nor their charges' fathers were particularly aware of this confluence of pedagogic ideology until the 1840s, when the Haskalah in Russia truly emerged into the open as a result of the support of the government of Nicholas I.[6] In the 1820s and 1830s there was as yet no clear meaning or parameters to the category of maskilim, adherents of the Haskalah, followers of Moses Mendelssohn. It was entirely possible for Jews reared in the cultural universe of Lithuanian non-Hasidic society to entertain some of the ideas of the Haskalah without a public, or even a private, declaration of allegiance to a new system of thought. Even the few obscure Hebrew writers in Vilna and other towns in the Russian realm who were identified subsequently as the first important maskilim in Russia did not yet define themselves in opposition to the prevailing consensus of their society.

The Vilna in which Judah Leib Gordon was born at the end of 1830, then, was rather blissfully poised on the edge of the dramatic transformations that would overtake Russian Jewry from within and without in the next several decades. The family that Gordon was born into was rather typical for its time, place, and material circumstances.[7] His father, Asher, was born in 1796 in a small provincial town in Lithuania that belonged to the Radziwiłł clan, and was married off at the age of thirteen to a girl he barely knew and grew to hate. The birth of a daughter did not improve the relations between husband and wife, and Asher soon sued for divorce and married another woman, whom he loved dearly. This cavalier display of romanticism apparently earned Asher a bit of a reputation for heterodoxy, which he proceeded to aggravate by teaching himself the Russian and Polish languages so well that no Yiddish accent could be detected in his speech. This linguistic dexterity and yearning for broader horizons endeared Asher to a local Jewish entrepreneur, who had become wealthy by supplying the Russian army during the Napoleonic Wars, and in 1813 Asher moved to Vilna to serve as a bookkeeper and supervisor in his mentor's concern. Here, in line with the tsar's decree that Jews adopt surnames, Asher took on the name Gordon, which for some reason was rather popular among the Jews of Vilna, including some well-heeled relatives of his wife who treated him munificently. The happy young couple had a daughter, but their idyll was short-lived. His boss lost his fortune, and Asher was left without a job; soon thereafter his bride died suddenly. The young widower was unemployed and alone in the big city. He had one brother whom he despised and with whom he was not on speaking terms and a sister who was desperately poor and could not assist him in any way. Unable to raise his child on his own, he settled on a third wife for whom he had little affinity. Freyda Drosniss, a young, childless widow from a little town near Grodno, prided herself on her genealogy as the daughter of a ritual slaughterer and the sister of four brothers who were successful merchants in Vilna. The match between Freyda and Asher was far from heavenly. She was haughty, strong in body and spirit, pious, adept at business; without being able to write in any script, she could read her prayers in Yiddish and conduct business in Polish and Russian and do sums at a pace that impressed all her customers. He was bookish, meek, senti-mental, given to recalling with great sadness and in great detail his recently deceased beloved second wife.

Together, Freyda and Asher earned their keep in one of the classic occupations of East European Jews through the centuries—innkeeping. For many years they kept a tavern and hostel in various locations in Vilna that appealed primarily to Polish noblemen and yielded the Gordons quite a respectable income for their hard work. They gave birth to a daughter and, after the lapse of six or seven years, to a son, whom they named Judah Leib. Probably too busy at the inn to nurse her child herself, Freyda hired a wet nurse (also named Freyda but married to a tailor) who raised "Leibinke" in her own home for the first two years. The child's only recorded reaction to this substitution of Freydas was to become wildly obstreperous when his wet nurse left him even for a short while, calming down only after he was fed bread dipped in honey and liquor. Upon his return home he was weaned from this combination by his mother in such a way that he remained a teetotaler the rest of his days. (Gordon's retelling of this tale of abandonment and withdrawal, penned over fifty years after the fact, is replete with dark hints of resentment and anger at his mother, who appears only very rarely in his writings, in sharp contrast to his father and siblings, who are mentioned rather frequently. Unfortunately, the absence of any further information about this tantalizing aspect of Gordon's personality provides rather thin grist for even the most eager psychoanalytic mill.)[8]

The child was taught how to read and write the Hebrew alphabet by a tutor, and how to distinguish left from right by his father, who also took care to instruct Leib on how properly to articulate the sounds "s" and "sh" so as to avoid the com-mon Lithuanian-Jewish confusion of sibilants that produced an idiosyncratic Yid-dish dialect and a greatly stigmatized version of Russian. Soon, young Leib was spared what he would later consider to be a far worse fate—a typical ḥeder edu-cation. At the age of four and a half, he was sent to a ḥeder run by Reb Lippa, a disciple of Rabbi Ḥayim of Volozhin who had as a youth actually served the Gaon of Vilna in person. Lippa was a brilliant student at the Volozhin yeshivah and was therefore snapped up by a wealthy patron as a perfect son-in-law. After continuing his studies for several years, Lippa met a fate similar to that of leagues of *melam-dim* throughout East European Jewish history: he tried his hand at commerce, traveled to Brody and other mercantile centers, was soon left a widower with a child, married another woman, who bore him two daughters before she died, lost all his money, and was forced to turn to elementary education in Vilna as his last resort. Lippa's second wife was a relative of Asher Gordon, who hired the poor fellow with impressive credentials to instruct his tender young son, and two other well-off boys, in the basics of Judaism.

The student would remain deeply grateful to the teacher for the rest of his life. Lippa turned out to be a remarkably gifted guide to the basics of the Jewish curriculum, which he introduced to his pupils in line with the pedagogic traditions of the Gaon and Volozhin, as described above. Thus, young Gordon was led carefully through the Pentateuch once, and then again with the aid of the traditional Rashi commentary, and only thereafter was he slowly brought to the study of the Talmud. At the same time, Lippa took care to teach his students Hebrew calligraphy and the rudiments of Hebrew grammar, which he made into a game by inscribing rules of conjugation and vocalization on long scrolls of paper that became the children's toys. This strategy appears to have been remarkably successful, at least in the case of Gordon, who developed a peerless mastery of Hebrew grammar and an elegant hand in all scripts. Lippa also insisted that his students spend a good deal of time on the parts of the Bible not typically regarded as particularly worthwhile or suitable for schoolchildren. He thus instilled in young Leib a love for the Prophets and Writings that would later have a significant impact on the course of Hebrew letters. At the age of seven, Gordon's attachment to the Bible was consolidated by the lavish praise he received at a large party celebrating his startling memory for biblical stories and interpretations and, a year later, when his father presented him with a luxurious edition of the Bible that became his favorite after-school entertainment.

While important parts of Gordon's future intellectual makeup were being determined, his special place in the family as only son and precocious baby was undermined by the birth of a sister in 1837 and a brother in 1838. From now on he would bear substantial burdens as the responsible older sibling. Meanwhile, he left the ḥeder run by his beloved Reb Lippa with an excellent command of the Bible, a good grasp of the Hebrew language, and a firm footing in elementary Talmud studies. His father could not find a suitable instructor to continue Leib's education at the next level, and the boy flitted from one ḥeder to another unhappy with his tutors. Later, Gordon would recall that even Reb Lippa, for all of his pedagogic innovation, had little idea of what was appropriate for children to learn, confounding his nine-year-old pupils with parts of the Talmud dealing with sexual and biological processes that were both incomprehensible and confusing to them. A few years later, in another ḥeder, Gordon would be taught the facts of life from an eighteen-year-old fellow student who, already engaged to be married, tricked Leib into asking their teacher for an explanation of Talmudic passages that the groom was eager to understand.

As his eyes were being opened to the complex world of adult relationships, an event occurred that would have a lasting effect on Gordon's psyche, though he never publicly examined its implications. On the Friday night before Passover of 1839, the Gordon clan was awakened at midnight by an insistent knock on the door of their flat and a rude, loud voice commanding that the door be opened. Freyda recognized the tones of the local chief of police and hastily rushed to the door trying not to awaken the servants. There stood fully armed a barrage of policemen, soldiers, and armed civilians, all ready for attack. Freyda was obviously frightened by the sight, but not sufficiently so to desecrate the Sabbath by kindling a light. As she searched in the dark for a candle to hand to the police officer, young Leib watched in frightful excitement as the band of warriors entered the dim front room and finally demanded that Asher appear before them. Minutes later, the meek, drowsy older Gordon was taken away by the armed band, to the shrieking wails of his wife. Leib's married sister, who lived nearby, rushed over to console her mother and help sort out the situation. Both women were convinced that Asher must be accused of a serious crime if so many guards were required to take him away. As the first light of dawn descended, Freyda sought out a friend who was known to have clout with the authorities, and he promised to seek counsel when business hours began later in the day. Finally, at about eight in the morning, the door opened again and in walked Asher unhurt and free. The explanation slowly unraveled: around the corner from the Gordon inn the police had discovered a den of Polish émigré conspirators who had come to Vilna with the recently executed revolutionary Szymon Konarski. Asher, probably because of his vast acquaintance with the Polish nobles of Vilna, had been requisitioned to join the police in the sweep through the neighborhood, so as to be able to identify those arrested. Forty years later, his son would relive this scene as once more the middle of a Sabbath night at the Gordon home was disrupted by police searches and arrests caused by charges of disloyalty to the tsar and the Russian state.[9]

In 1839, though, the most immediate consequence of external politics on the life of Judah Leib Gordon was his father's progressive loss of income, caused by Nicholas I's repression of Vilna's Polish elite and hence of Asher Gordon's business. The family, which had grown with the birth of another son, would be forced to move from one part of town to another in search of hotel clientele and would soon be embroiled in debts that led to a messy lawsuit and a general decline of their previous comfortable existence.

The disruption of young Gordon's universe was paralleled by the invasion of threatening thoughts and values in the person of a new brother-in-law. In 1839, Judah's sister Neḥama was engaged to Mikhl Gordon, the sixteen-year-old grandnephew of the government rabbi of Vilna. In the style of the day, after a three-and-a-half-year engagement the couple was married and Mikhl came to live with his wife's family, remaining there supported by his father-in-law for seven full years. Mikhl, however, was no ordinary middle-class Vilna Talmud scholar living off his in-laws' dedication to Jewish learning. Rather, he was a fledgling poet in Hebrew and Yiddish who spent his days in the company of the small coterie of Jewish intellectuals that emerged in Vilna in the late 1830s and early 1840s.

Led by the prose writer Mordekhai Aaron Ginzburg and the poet Ada"m Ha-Kohen Lebensohn, this collection of self-educated, self-styled enlighteners began to meet together regularly to plot the cultural rejuvenation of the Jews. Judah Leib Gordon would later characterize these pioneers as a group of pseudointellectual dilettantes who learned no subject well, mastered no living tongue in any way, and were even incapable of earning a living by any respectable trade.[10] This evaluation was more than a little harsh and self-serving, but it is undoubtedly far more on the mark than later, romanticized accounts that lionize the presumed early gods of the pantheon of modern Hebrew literature.[11] In fact, the revolutionary platform of these early Vilna maskilim was a tame call for a minimum of secular education and a moderation of rabbinical stringency; their greatest rebellion consisted in their still subtle turn away from the Talmud as the sine qua non of Jewish intellectual stimulation and erudition. Scraping together a passive knowledge of German, they began to leaf through the pages of Goethe and Schiller and to identify their travails with those of young Werther. Taking a fateful—if not entirely self-conscious—leap from the Gaon's very limited approbation of scientific knowledge as a tool in exegesis, they began to read, and to translate into somewhat awkward Hebrew, summaries of natural science textbooks, popular histories of Napoleon, and thirdhand renditions of Homer. They began to preach a cult of the Holy Tongue in a hazy rhetorical style that hesitated on the borders of a secularized Romanticism without knowing what either term signified. Emulating in theory the style and ideological stance of Moses Mendelssohn and the Berlin maskilim, they remained in practice entirely observant East European Jews fearing the censure of the rabbis; framed in full beards and sidelocks and clad in caftans and ritual fringes, for example, they advocated the banning of the traditional Jewish garb but were unwilling to shave or cut their cloaks.

At the beginning of the 1840s, however, the circle of early Vilna maskilim that included Mikhl Gordon did produce two crucial cultural prototypes that were to outlast their conservative creators. The first was a modern Jewish school: in 1841, two separate and apparently competitive academies were founded in Vilna, transferring to Lithuania and to the stronghold of European Rabbinism the model of Haskalah education first put into practice in Prussia and from there established in Galicia, Riga, and Odessa. Both schools had the same curriculum—Bible with Mendelssohn's translation and commentary, Hebrew grammar, Talmud, Jewish religion, Russian, German, arithmetic, and calligraphy. Together, the two schools were reported to have enrolled about eighty students.[12] Strongly opposed by the rabbinical establishment, these schools were the first tangible and easily identifiable dens of modernist Judaism in Vilna. In the same year, the Vilna Jewish enlighteners published *Pirhei Zafon* (Flowers of the North), the first Hebrew literary periodical in the Russian Empire. This very modest collection was planned as an annual conduit of Haskalah prose and poetry, but had so measly an audience that it collapsed after two issues. Still, it set an important precedent as the first example of what would soon become the dominant vehicle of Jewish Enlightenment in Eastern Europe.

There is no evidence that Judah Leib Gordon was aware of these concurrent developments at the tender age of eleven and twelve, when Mikhl Gordon first came to live in his home. What the keen-eyed youngster did sense from his brother-in-law was the existence of a semiclandestine world of adults that did not follow the strictures of his heder teachers but experimented with "outside" reading and even that strangest of all crafts, poetry writing. To the rest of the world, Mikhl seemed to live in line with the customs and culture of traditional Vilna Jewry; he was the one, for example, who was commissioned by the family to accompany the twelve-year-old Judah Leib to a new heder, in a suburb of Vilna, in which the sole preoccupation was a rigorous immersion in the "sea of the Talmud" that lasted from nine o'clock in the morning until nine at night. At the same time, however, Judah Leib knew that Mikhl was surreptitiously hiding Haskalah tracts in various corners of their home and was discussing curious topics with the secretive friends who would gather in his rooms on a regular basis. In his few free moments away from his new school and remarkably strict teacher, Judah Leib would plant himself at the door of Mikhl's apartment or search out the stashed contraband. The older brother-in-law was not pleased by this attention. At the beginning, it is likely that he was simply irritated by his wife's younger brother poking about in his things and asking questions that were potentially embarrassing and even dangerous. Soon, however, Mikhl seems to have become aware that Judah's curiosity masked a penetrating intellect and potentially even a literary sensitivity that far outpaced his own. Three decades later, when he was a middle-aged ne'er-do-well moving from one unsuccessful job to another while taking great public pride in his presumed role as first mentor of the famous poet Judah Leib Gordon, Mikhl would recall with much nostalgia

> the early days, the days of the first blossoming of my love for your late sister, when in your face I beheld the features of my beloved, which therefore remain superimposed and etched in my memory till this very day—you with two thick sidelocks covering half your cheeks, and a forehead half obscured with bangs beneath which there shone two black eyes, bright and pure.[13]

At the time, however, Mikhl appears to have attempted to subvert Judah Leib's first experiments in Hebrew prose and verse and to have shamed his young brother-in-law with public mockery and private scorn.[14]

Mikhl Gordon was not the only one to discourage Judah Leib from his increasingly clear attraction to aesthetic diversions. One day at ḥeder, he was caught reading one of Mikhl's Hebrew poems and was subjected to severe castigation and embarrassment. Moreover, as a result of this grave lapse, Judah Leib was rejected as a potential suitor for the teacher's daughter—a position for which he apparently was being groomed because of his intelligence and successful studies. (He would later remark that this was probably the only favor Mikhl ever did for him in five decades!)[15]

Meanwhile, the child Leib became the young man Judah as he reached the age of thirteen in December 1843. At his sumptuous bar mitzvah celebration, he began to deliver a learned Talmudic discourse written by his ḥeder teacher, but was interrupted by a choking fit on the part of a friend. Panic ensued, until sturdy Freyda Gordon slammed a loaf of bread against the back of the victim, causing him to eject the bone from his throat. The calamity resolved, Judah Leib attempted to pick up where he had left off, but could not regain the attention of the guests, who had already wholeheartedly resumed their devotion to their meals. After this debacle, Gordon sincerely attempted to begin his adult life as a pious Jew. The first time he donned his phylacteries, he resolved to repent for his previous sins and began to pray in humble devotion and loud pleas for mercy from the Lord. As fate would have it, however, Mikhl had planted himself behind the young penitent; as soon as Judah Leib reached the peak of his emotional plea, his brother-in-law exploded in an obscene curse, and the bubble of piety burst.

Soon after Judah Leib's attainment of the age of religious independence, he was granted the opportunity of developing other aspects of his independence as well. A year after his bar mitzvah he ceased to attend formal classes, as his father was satisfied that Judah Leib was competent enough in Talmudic study to sit in one of the rooms in his home and work up sections of the Talmud on his own. Curiously, Asher permitted his son to do this in the same room in which a young female relative spent her days sewing and doing other household chores. Judah Leib later admitted to considerable distraction as a result of this proximity. In this same period, he received daily lessons in the Russian language from a private tutor named Heiman. Perhaps Asher realized that he was being too liberal with his son, for the next year Judah Leib was required to attend another very strict ḥeder in order to advance his Talmudic training. But in 1844 his father relented, and Judah Leib was permitted to study alone in the classic manner of reliable Eastern European adolescents, setting himself up every morning in one of the study halls in the neighborhood.

In the several years that followed, Gordon did raise his store of Talmudic knowledge to a very respectable level, but he also began to take advantage of his lack of supervision to delve into the mysteries his brother-in-law had teased him with but withheld from him. Like thousands of other Jewish adolescents in Eastern Europe, he began to cradle in the large tomes of his Talmud books that were not part of the prescribed curriculum—first, Hebrew works of philosophy and moral guidance that were firmly ensconced within the parameters of traditional Jewish culture; then the staples of the Hebrew Enlightment literature of the day, from the poetry of Hartwig Wessely to that of Ada"m Ha-Kohen Lebensohn; and, finally, literature actually written in non-Jewish languages.

Gordon had to look over his shoulder not only in fear of his father, who, for all his liberalism, would never have approved of this diversion from Talmud study, but also in fierce competition with his brother-in-law. Since Mikhl was known to be adept in Hebrew grammar, Judah Leib set himself the task of mastering Aramaic as well. If Mikhl claimed competence in German, Judah Leib decided to learn both the tongue and French. The older maskil did not take kindly to the mounting erudition of his erstwhile inferior and consistently attempted to cut Judah Leib down to size and to convince him of his negligible accomplishments. In 1846, for example, when Sir Moses Montefiore visited Vilna, Mikhl was approached by many Jews to pen petitions in Hebrew to the famous British notable. One time Mikhl was not at home when a petitioner arrived, and young Judah Leib wrote out the requested message. When Mikhl returned and discovered what had happened, he subjected his rival's version to riotous criticism. In the following year, desperately seeking information to ratify his emerging identity, Judah Leib asked his brother-in-law about the origin and source of poetic talent and inspiration. Mikhl answered that these could not be acquired but came only from God, and quickly added that it was certain that the younger Gordon had not one whit of this divine gift.

The discouragement did not work. Judah Leib persisted in his explorations and soon reached the most important realization of his life. At the age of seventeen, he later recalled,

> the mask that veiled my eyes fell off, and I turned around and beheld myself and my setting and saw that I was a wild Asiatic in the midst of enlightened Europe. . . . I therefore resolved to correct what had been distorted by others, to repair the damage

they had done, and I set myself to learning Hebrew grammar properly, as well as the Russian, Polish, German, and French languages and all the knowledge required of man. . . . I was on my own, with no one to help me, no teacher, no guide, no instructor, and I wandered about like a bird on the loose, from book to book, to whatever came into my hands. I studied and read a good deal, and learned a bit.[16]

The lessons thus inculcated would remain with Gordon for the rest of his life. The image of the wild Asiatic struggling to emulate the cultivated European by perfecting his Hebrew as well as Western languages would guide Gordon through personal and ideological thickets for his entire adult life. The charge to correct what others had distorted—in other words, to redress the faults and lapses of traditional Jewish society—would soon be transferred from the personal realm to the public, from the improvement of the individual Judah Leib Gordon to the reform of the Jewish people as a whole.

To be sure, Gordon was more than slightly disingenuous in claiming that he reached this revolutionary conclusion and strategy all by himself, without any teachers or comrades. In fact, the mid- and late 1840s, the critical years of his late adolescence and discovery of self, were precisely the years of the maturation of the Haskalah in Russia. From a loose conglomeration of disjointed individuals clustered in tiny enclaves scattered throughout the vast reaches of Jewish Russia, the Haskalah grew to a well-coordinated movement of several hundred committed adherents preaching their gospel in a coherent and persuasive manner. Intimately connected with this transformation was the unprecedented involvement of the Russian government in Jewish cultural life. From the early 1840s, the minister of education, S.S. Uvarov, began actively to aid and subsidize the purveyors and purposes of Jewish Enlightenment in Russia. In dedicating so much time, energy, and resources to the reeducation of the Jews, Uvarov hoped to reproduce in Russia the social and intellectual metamorphosis that had taken place among Western European Jewry. Espousing a confused and simplistic mixture of Jansenism, Romanticism, and Russian Orthodoxy, Uvarov attempted to effect a "rapprochement" between the Jews of Russia and their Christian compatriots on a moral, intellectual, and ultimately political level. To this end, he committed his ministry, and hence Nicholas I's government, to a thoroughgoing alliance with the Russian maskilim. First, Uvarov invited the German liberal rabbi Max Lilienthal to begin the educational reforms deemed necessary for Russia's Jews; after Lilienthal's departure from Russia, local maskilim were hired to help establish a substantial network of primary and secondary schools, planned and regulated by the Ministry of Education and staffed with teachers of Hebrew language, Jewish history, and Judaic law from among the Russian maskilim themselves. Despite the intense opposition of the traditionalists, and hence the modest enrollments, these schools, and the rabbinical seminaries established in the late 1840s in Vilna and Zhitomir, had a significant and long-lived impact on Russian Jewry. They educated the bulk of the next cohort of Russian-Jewish writers, thinkers, scholars, and ideologues and set into motion the creation of an indigenous Jewish culture in the Russian language. At the same time, these schools provided the maskilim with employment opportunities and financial security. Confident of their eventual victory and hence the liberation of all Jews, the maskilim emerged in the late 1840s and early 1850s as a self-conscious and self-confident intelligentsia, dedicated to restructuring the life, culture, and politics of Russia's Jews.[17]

Although Gordon left no account of his contemporary response to the cultural revolution of the 1840s, his later writings reveal him as a lifelong admirer of Uvarov who firmly believed that the Russian government from Nicholas I's time on sincerely and profoundly desired to benefit the Jews through a Westernization of their education, faith, and social structure. Even after external events forced him to abandon his trust in the Russian government of the late 1880s, Gordon steadfastly held to his previous evaluation of the beneficence of earlier regimes.[18]

In the late 1840s, of course, Gordon was still too young to participate actively in these dramatic transformations. But at this time he did become intimately involved with the younger members of the group of Vilna maskilim whom he had first met through his brother-in-law. In this circle Gordon befriended several writers and intellectuals with whom he would maintain warm relations until the end of his life, and here he drew very close to Ze'ev Kaplan, who would become his closest confidant throughout his adult life. But undoubtedly the most important friend Gordon made among the Vilna maskilim was the most talented of the lot, a young poet who stood alone among all Haskalah poets for his passionate lyricism—Micah Yosef Lebensohn.

The son of the tyrannical and pedantic mentor of the Vilna maskilim Ada"m Ha-Kohen Lebensohn, Micah was groomed to become a Hebrew poet from the moment of his birth in 1828. But the young Lebensohn's life did not quite follow his father's plan, for at the age of seventeen Micah developed the first signs of the tuberculosis that would progressively debilitate him for the remaining seven years of his life. In Vilna, and then in Berlin and the various German spas to which he repaired in an ultimately hopeless search for a cure, Lebensohn displayed a remarkable poetic sensitivity that far outdistanced his contemporaries' rather heavy-handed and didactic notion of versification. Alone among Hebrew poets of the age—and, for that matter, the next two generations—Micah Lebensohn truly shared in the European literary culture of his day, not only reading and copying but thinking in step with Heine, Mickiewicz, and the lesser poets of the late Romantic age. One of his first efforts, the poem "Brotherhood," written to his brother Noah in 1845, testifies to the spirit of this engagement, in its rather primitive but still evocative proclamation:

> How pleasant and how sweet to our ears
> The sound of the word "brother."
> How dear to the spirit and the soul the notion of brotherhood!
> A flare of divine fire from the heavenly light
> Shines down from the glorious seat above
> To the heart of mortal man, cast in mud and matter.
>
> O you, envious and fearful, devoid of heart and wisdom
> Who find faults in your fate and descent
> And seek solace in strangers' ways,
> If you have a brother what more can you seek?
> And if not, why yearn for a fortune
> If without brotherhood, all is nothingness and nil.[19]

Soon, noble fraternity would give way to love and death as the focus of Lebensohn's soul and art as he recast in Hebrew, through Schiller's German adaptation, Virgil's tale of the fall of Troy and, probably based on an early German translation, part of Vittorio Alfieri's drama *Saul*. Lebensohn read and discussed these early works with his close friends and admirers, among whom Judah Leib Gordon figured prominently. In 1849, Micah left Vilna for Berlin and treatment of his illness. In the West, he was inspired by the two giants of Jewish scholarship, S. D. Luzzatto and Leopold Zunz, to turn more forcefully to bibilical themes and Jewish history in his search for epic devices, a charge that he followed brilliantly in his subsequent narrative poems. Yet Lebensohn was all the while able to avoid the hackneyed portrayal of biblical figures and Hebrew heroes common to the works of his father and other Haskalah poets. Perhaps as a result of the lessons he gleaned from Schelling's lectures that he attended at the University of Berlin, Lebensohn sought the inner psychic truth of his heroes' dilemmas rather than their external or even theological purpose.[20] Although from time to time tilting to a Romanticized version of Jewish beliefs, Micah seemed to be guided for the most part by a radically different faith, which he confessed to a correspondent in a breathless explosion of German in the midst of a Hebrew letter discussing his imminent death: "Ich habe keine Religion! Mein Bruder die Menschheit! Die Welt mein Vaterland! Meine Religion die Tugend!" (I have no religion! My brother is mankind! The world is my fatherland! My religion is virtue!)[21] Returning to Vilna uncured, the dying young poet poured out his pain, as well as his love for a nameless woman, in a series of marvelous poems completed before his death in the winter of 1852, eleven days before his twenty-fourth birthday.

Micah's influence on Judah Leib was less literary or intellectual than psychological and personal. Lebensohn was far more radical in politics, agnostic in faith, and modernist in poetic sensibility than Gordon would ever be. But the friendship served as a critical turning point in Gordon's life, allowing him intimately to witness the life of a true poet in the person of a mentor who still shared in the same passions, fears, and hopes as the struggling young Gordon himself. Twenty-five years later Gordon would recall:

> Those were for me the days of the first budding of the blossom, the first hesitant steps of the nestling just barely out of the shell. A ray of light had broken through, beckoning me to emerge into the world, but I had not yet raised my wing or poked my beak outside. The walls of the Talmudic study house had started to topple, and I was standing with one foot in the Tradition and the other in the living world, trying to set off in search of light with buckling knees and unstable gait. I had no guide and no support, until I came upon this joyful and righteous, but still young fledgling who had already spread his wings and determined his course, and he opened my eyes to see the truth. Together we walked—he in front, guiding my way, I closely in his wake, until our stride was blocked by blood.[22]

The tragic interruption of this crucial bond, however, brought young Gordon into close touch with the other important influence in his personal and professional development, Micah's father, Ada"m Ha-Kohen Lebensohn. In 1849, when Micah first left Russia, his father asked Gordon to help copy and prepare Micah's poems for a surprise publication. Gordon hastily agreed, despite his substantial fear of his idol's imperious father. He was ecstatic when the elder Lebensohn praised his copying and editing skills as indicative of an impressive mastery of Hebrew grammar and a fine ear for rhyme and rhythm. Thus, from the most famous Hebrew poet of the day the nineteen-year-old Judah Leib Gordon heard what his jealous brother-in-law had valiantly tried to hide from him—that he possessed the basic credentials of a Hebrew poet. The moment was not to be forgotten.

A short time after this inspirational episode, however, Gordon was diverted to a calling rather distant from poetry. Undoubtedly at the urging of his father, Judah Leib set about traveling through the Pale of Settlement in order to take care of Asher's financial affairs. If his later semifictional descriptions of these episodes are even moderately autobiographical, as is most likely, Gordon did not display much talent for business and even less sophistication as a nineteen- or twenty-year-old out in the world for the first time.[23] His longest trip was to the city of Pinsk, where he spent several months in what turned out to be an utterly unsuccessful attempt to recoup debts owed to his father. But it was here in Pinsk that Gordon first discovered in himself a talent that would serve as his means of support for the next two and a half decades. In order to keep himself fed during the long months of negotiations, he tried his hand at teaching, serving as private tutor in various wealthy homes. The income from these lessons was measly, but Gordon apparently enjoyed the experience. Upon his return to Vilna he prepared for the examinations at the teacher's training branch of the state Rabbinical Seminary.

Slowly but clearly, the adult Judah Leib Gordon was emerging into the open. When his old wet nurse came to see him upon his return to Vilna, she fell upon him weeping, "Leibinke, what has become of you? I know that you could have been a great rabbi in Israel!" Gordon's reply—at least as reported by him twenty years later—was, "Mother, you are a good woman, but the rabbis are evil and sinful, hurting their flock. Therefore, every morning instead of praying 'Thank the Lord for not making me a woman' I thank Him 'for not making me a rabbi!'"[24]

At the same time as Gordon's ideological and professional makeup was being established, his literary self was maturing as well. He began to work, in a style reminiscent more of Ada"m Ha-Kohen than of Micah, on a biblical epic based on various episodes in the life of King David that would take him some five years to complete. But Micah's death—and thus, the meaning of life itself—served as a focus of Gordon's emotional world as reflected in his earliest preserved works. His first poem, entitled "Unwillingly you live!" was written in 1852 and based on an incident that occurred shortly after Micah's death: Gordon was sleeping in a house that caught fire, and he narrowly escaped death by being awakened by alert family members. In simple and rather moving tones, far less grandiloquent than those of the epics he was mulling over at the same time, Gordon wrote:

> For several moments I stood at the bridge
> That stands as the border between life and death
> Already my soul took flight like an eagle
> My body gripped by the shadow of death.
>
> My heart dried up, my senses dulled,
> I felt not a thing, forsook all that was.

The wheels of life stopped whirling and churning
One step more, and I would be as nought.

Was this death, before whom we quiver?
Was this the pit so despised by man!
My friends, we fear a lie so vain
There was no fear in death, no terror in dying. . . .

As my feet already treaded on the road of death
And the door of my grave opened wide,
As I started to enter—
A mighty roar called me back.

The voice of my housemates, o how vain!
Forced me back to the grip of life.
Fools! The rewards of life you cannot grant me
Why then shut before me the gates of heaven?[25]

Soon after completing this poem, Gordon left the scene of this brush with death, the city of his youth, never to live there again. In 1853, he was certified to teach at one of the elementary schools run by the government for Jewish children and assigned to the small Lithuanian town of Ponevezh, where he would spend the next seven years of his life.

Ponevezh—now known by its Lithuanian name of Panėvežys—is located some 150 kilometers northwest of Vilna, in the Kovno province. In 1847, it had an official Jewish population of 1,447; ten years later, its total population was reported as 5,900. In 1840, a school for the children of nobles was moved to Ponevezh from a nearby town; in 1858, it was reorganized as a gymnasium, but was closed five years later after the Polish Uprising of 1863. The government-sponsored Jewish elementary school in which Gordon taught remained open until the revolution of 1917.[26] With his means of support assured, the twenty-two-year-old Gordon took another crucial step: in the late summer of 1853 he married Bella L'vovna Orinshtam, six years his junior. Very little is known about this woman, with whom Gordon would live until his death. From the fact that the match was accompanied by a dowry of several hundred rubles, it seems that Bella came from a well-heeled, if not wealthy, family; from the poem that Gordon later wrote for his father-in-law's tombstone, the impression emerges that the deceased was a generous and pious Jew.[27] Through the years, Gordon would mention his wife sporadically in his letters, but almost always in connection with her ill health and travel to foreign spas and doctors. The few scanty contemporary descriptions of Bella depict her as a kind, if simple, woman who barely knew Russian, understood no Hebrew, and remained cut off from and slightly befuddled by the literary, intellectual, and political interests of her husband.[28]

In the first few years of their life together in Ponevezh, Gordon was still working on his Davidic epics, studying Tasso and Ariosto and Zhukovsky and Pushkin, but he was all the while consumed with the memory of his deceased mentor and beloved friend. On the first anniversary of Micah's death, Gordon wrote a hyperbolic elegy expressing ceaseless mourning for the great poet and admiration for his words, ending with the query "Even were my eyes the windows of Heaven/ My thoughts clouds, my words buckets of rain/ Could I shed sufficient tears over this boundless loss?"[29] On the second anniversary, he set to paper a strange fantasy about Micah's death and ascent to heaven written in the form of a short one-act drama. In the first scene, Micah bravely bids farewell to his family and nation from his deathbed, urging fidelity to the Hebrew language and the goals of the Enlightenment. The second scene opens "in the heavens above, the Hebrew language in the form of an old woman who has fainted; her hands are on her head, her head on her heart, and the heavenly host surround her on her right and her left." The angels fret over her until she awakes, realizes that she is in heaven, and launches into a soliloquy mourning her strange destiny as one who neither dies nor lives, the sole survivor of a land plundered by armies and a nation ravaged by history. Once a proud and productive tongue, in Exile she has been devastated by the burden of sanctification:

> My dry bones were taken along with the exiles,
> In the ark of the covenant and the heart of scholars,
> They called me "Holy Tongue"
> For they placed me in the asylum of holiness,
> Forgotten, almost dead to the living word.
> False authors and evil writers flourished
> While frivolous verses mocked me
> And countless liturgists devoid of taste
> Buried my holy soul in heaps of sand
> Debasing my splendor, abusing my glory,
> Disgracing my honor with words without sense.[30]

Hope appeared: a new generation arose dedicated to retrieving her honor, her beauty, and her future. But the grandest bearer of that future, the most talented of her potential saviors, was cut down without mercy while still a youth. Desperate, the Hebrew language appeals to the archangel Michael, who then appears with a bolt of lightning, bearing a message from God. In the cadences of Isaiah, Michael pledges divine grace for the Hebrew language:

> Do not sob, cease your despair
> A new generation will give birth to sons
> Who will not traduce you though in foreign lands
> But will embrace you with their entire being
> And find eternal deliverance in you alone.[31]

With the promise that her latest prophet will join the ranks of Moses, Solomon, Samson, and Judah Halevi, the scene dissolves, and on the stage appear lesser angels accompanying a young man on his ascent to heavenly rest. When they reach the middle spheres, they are greeted by the souls of Moses, Solomon, Samson, and Judah Halevi and by the Hebrew language herself. In unison the delegation welcomes the new arrival with cries of victory, and the Hebrew language counsels him not to fear, for "I am your mother—the Hebrew tongue/ In my bosom you exulted all of your life. . . . I am the mother, too, of all your brothers/ All the exiled from Zion and Jerusalem."[32] In me, she declares, the Jews will find solace, truth, and divine inspiration, not in the desiccated manner of medieval pseudopoets, but once more in the spirit of the true prophets and muses of the Jewish people. As the Hebrew language takes one ray from the aura surrounding Moses's face and weaves it into a wreath for the young poet's head, he is given his rightful and eternal place in the pantheon of Hebrew creativity. Moses and his aides lift the young poet in their arms and they are all enveloped in a cloud that bears them to the upper heavens. The curtain falls.

This juvenile exercise remained in its author's drawer for several decades, until his poetic reputation was sufficient to permit its publication. But in this first extended piece, for all its obvious and awkward naiveté, Gordon was able to sustain a fluidity of language and rhyme and an impressive dexterity at interlacing biblical images with new and sometimes arresting allusions. Equally important, at this early stage Gordon enunciated a poetic stance that clearly and emphatically placed itself in opposition to the received tradition of medieval Hebrew sacred verse and the culture it embodied. Boldly proclaiming an identification of the poetry of Micah Yosef Lebensohn with that of Moses, Solomon, Samson, and Judah Halevi, he struggled with a still inchoate notion of the Hebrew language as the savior of Jewish creativity and honor.

In 1854, then, the stage was set for the transformation of an obscure teacher in an isolated provincial town into the most vocal and savage critic of traditional Jewish culture in the name of enlightened Hebrew creativity. That transfiguration would slowly evolve, as Judah Leib Gordon published his first works at the same time as Jewish society in Russia was engulfed by tides of enthusiasm hailing a new king and a new era.

3

The Beginnings of a Career
1855–1861

On February 18, 1855, Jews gathered together throughout the Russian Empire and celebrated their good fortune: Tsar Nicholas I was dead. Only the small community of self-styled enlighteners had admired the ruler who presided over the conscription of Jewish children, the debilitation of Jewish communal autonomy, and the devastation of the economy and social structure of the Pale. Indeed, even the maskilim were shaken in their resolve to love this tsar in the last three years of his reign, when in a mad rush to win a mindless war he had subjected all his subjects, and particularly the Jews, to preposterous recruitment duties and outrageous restrictions on normal life.[1]

The accession to the throne of the twenty-seven-year-old crown prince brought new hopes to all segments of the empire's tattered population. The Crimean War was still raging, Allied forces were still occupying Russian soil and laying siege to Sebastopol, but the new tsar nonetheless demanded the repeal of some of his father's most noxious orders, such as prohibiting Russians from traveling abroad or limiting the number of students at university. When he formally acceded to the throne and brought the war to an end, Alexander II broadly hinted that his reign would bring fundamental changes to Russia, perhaps even to the basis of Russian society, serfdom itself.

For the Jews, Alexander brought almost immediate relief. In the first months of his reign he outlawed the conscription of children, banned the baptism of minors without their parents' consent, and significantly eased the censorship rules. Soon, even the walls of the Pale of Settlement itself began to totter, as Alexander II permitted several categories of Jewish businessmen, professionals, and students to reside in the interior of Russia.[2]

The Jews responded to this liberalization with unbridled enthusiasm. Particularly ecstatic, of course, were the maskilim, who saw their beliefs tangibly confirmed from day to day. As a result, in the late 1850s and early 1860s, Haskalah was on the rampage in Russia. New journals and periodicals in Hebrew, Russian, and Yiddish began to appear in large numbers; books, poems, plays, pamphlets, novels, and scholarly tracts were written and published at a dizzying pace. Jews began to flock to the state-sponsored schools, to the gymnasia, even to the universities. More and more Jews were learning and speaking and even thinking in Russian. Liberation—emancipation!—seemed but around the corner; the only question was its strategy, its timing, its wording.

This explosion of hope and creativity has been almost universally misrepresented as the result of a sea change in the ideology and sensibility of Russian Jewry. Historians of the era, blinded by the rays of hope that flickered in this euphoric, if all too brief, intermezzo between bouts of oppression, have drawn a sharp dividing line between the Haskalah before and after 1855. "From the darkness of the Middle Ages in which they were steeped until the time of Alexander II," begins the first book-length study of the Russian Haskalah, the Russian Jews "emerged suddenly into the life and light of the West."[3] Other, more sober scholars described a subtler but equally dramatic turn, from a conservative ideology modeled on the Berlin Haskalah before 1855 to a radical, ultimately assimilationist Russian version thereafter.[4]

This distinction and periodization cannot be supported by the evidence, as a close examination of the views of the Russian maskilim either before or after 1855 makes abundantly clear. All adherents of the Hebrew Enlightenment under Nicholas I had believed that the evils plaguing the Jews would disappear if they themselves would only shed some outmoded customs and superstitions and behave like civilized, modern Europeans. But beyond this basic credo, already in the 1840s and 1850s the Russian-Jewish intelligentsia did not share one view of Judaism or one strategy for its reform. On the fundamental issues of language, religious behavior, and even relations with the government there was substantial diversity of opinion, though open debate was not feasible, given the repressive censorship rules of Nicholas's police. Still, the issues that would dominate Jewish intellectual and political discourse in Russia for decades to come were all adumbrated, debated, and elaborated during the reign of Nicholas I.

The protagonists of the opposing positions did not suddenly choose their sides and develop their views in response to the liberalization of Alexander II. On the contrary, the new tsar's actions merely reaffirmed the maskilim in their fundamental faith. After all, in his coronation manifesto Alexander had expressed the hope that, with the aid of Providence, Russia

> would be strengthened and improved, that justice and mercy would prevail in the courts, that the desire to learn and to perform useful labor would spread and grow everywhere and that every man would enjoy the fruits of his honest toil in peace, under the protection of laws offering equal justice to all.[5]

Was this not, in essence, the very program of the Haskalah extended to all inhabitants of Russia, now articulated by the emperor himself?

Alexander II's assumption of the throne in 1855 did not, in fact, result in any shock to or radical change in the political and intellectual premises of the Russian-Jewish intelligentsia. Such a shock would come—perhaps ironically—later, in the last years of Alexander's reign, when it began to seem that emancipation was not forthcoming; educational advance without political betterment, it turned out, belied the bases of the Haskalah more than did repression. But Alexander's liberalization of censorship ordinances and his general lifting of restraints in the years following 1855 did allow views previously held in silence to be expressed in public, and the result was exhilarating as well as deafening. In this cacophony, the voice of Judah Leib Gordon began as a soft, barely audible chant that slowly grew into a roar.

Gordon left no record of his response to the news from the capital. Perhaps he was too embroiled in his own personal affairs to reflect on global events. In the course of 1855 he was stricken with a serious heart ailment that his doctors deemed incurable. During a slow and painful recovery, he received the news that his father had just died in Vilna, leaving a widow and three young children who would have to be supported by the eldest son, Judah Leib. Soon, life improved: Bella gave birth to a daughter, named Wilhelmina (called Minna in the family); two years later, another daughter was born, known in Russian as Nadezhda and in Hebrew as Nehama, after Judah Leib's sister, who had died in 1849. Gordon's pay as teacher of Jewish law at the government school in Ponevezh was approximately 225 rubles per annum, barely enough to sustain one family, not to speak of three adults and four or five children. To supplement his salary, Gordon took on private pupils, invested his dowry in a business concern, and did some clerical work for the Jewish community.[6] Meanwhile, he continued to work frantically on his poetry, which he hoped would bring him fame and even fortune as well. While the second goal was still far off (for decades his literary work required far greater expenses than the royalties could bear), recognition as a Hebrew poet was within sight.

A sonnet celebrating a pleasurable visit to friends at a summer resort bears witness that Gordon kept on writing incidental poetry at this time,[7] but it is clear that his major efforts went into completing the cycles of epics based on the life of King David that he had been struggling with for several years. The first part of the cycle, completed in 1855, was "David and Barzillai,"[8] based on a short scene in II Samuel 19:32–41 in which a wealthy Transjordanian named Barzillai feted and supported the king during his battle with Absalom but refused to cross over into Judea due to his old age. Gordon wisely decided not to risk his literary debut with this piece, which failed as both a pastoral evocation of the hills of Gilead and a dramatization of a revealing incident in the life of David. Viewed in retrospect, it is most interesting for its deflection of the center of attention from the actions of its presumed hero, David, to the emotions of the secondary character. This shift of dramatic emphasis would continue in the second part of the David trilogy, *The Love of David and Michal,* which was approved by the censor in Vilna on October 8, 1856, and published there in 1857.[9]

Quite appropriately, the first edition of Judah Leib Gordon's first published work bears, in addition to its Hebrew title page, a back cover presenting "L'amour de David et Mical, poème romantique de l'écriture sainte, par Leon Gordon, maître de la Religion à l'école hebraique à Ponives" over a citation from the Song of Songs, "Que tu es belle, et que tu es agréable,/ Amour délicieuse." The work itself is preceded by a long dedicatory poem to Ada"m Ha-Kohen Lebensohn, which asks the senior poet to recommend the novice to the reader and introduces the new poet with the remarkable dedication: "I am a servent to Hebrew forever and ever/ All my senses I indentured to her/ I shall till her soil with sweat on my brow."[10]

This rather overstated pledge is followed by a lengthy, pedantic, and all-too-earnest introduction that pays obeisance to a pious view of God's working in history and attempts to justify the narrative's departure from the Scriptures by alluding to various traditional exegeses of the Book of Samuel. It would have been impossible to predict from this ponderous preface that its author would very soon produce some of the most supple, ironical, and heterodox prose in the Hebrew language.

The Love of David and Michal covers some eighteen hundred lines, divided into twelve cantos. From a lyrical description of the young princess who scorns many swains because she is in love with the shepherd-boy David, the narrative proceeds slowly and rather elliptically as David arrives in Saul's palace, falls in love with Michal, romances her, defeats Goliath, slays two hundred Philistines, escapes through Michal's window, and mourns the death of Jonathan and Saul. Meanwhile, back at the palace, the young wife remains ever faithful to her beloved, if exiled, hero, even after her father forces her to betroth another man, whose love she spurns. As fate would have it, the lusty new king loses his passion for Michal in the course of his travails, and he shuns her upon his triumphant return to Jerusalem. The noble Michal retreats to a life of celibacy and good deeds; David, in his old age, redeems his past by means of his celestial poetry. After the king dies, his erstwhile wife passes from this world and his lyre is heard no more.

As critics have noted from the late nineteenth century on, this first of Gordon's narrative poems is a largely unsuccessful attempt at infusing new force into a tired form.[11] Suffused with numerous digressions on God's role in history and superfluous recastings of psalms, the poem is far too wordy to sustain its dramatic intent, not to speak of the interest of any but the most patient reader. Yet, as several sensitive readers have noted, *The Love of David and Michal* is by no means a complete failure. It does manage quite often to erupt in convincing, and sometimes even lilting, language that sets it apart from contemporary Hebrew verse. At the same time, it breaks entirely new ground in Haskalah poetry by taking as its main subject not the heroic deeds of David, but the mutual love between him and Michal. For a good part of the poem, it is Michal who commands the attention of the poet and the reader. This focus on the romantic needs of a woman is an important first trumpeting of what will become a central theme in Gordon's life and work—the profound concern for the lot of women in Jewish society.[12]

Thus, in the third canto, Michal's declaration of her love for David is introduced with these words:

> While the stillness of the quiet engulfed him
> Swiftly, as the glory of the moon lit up the azure skies
> Its ivory glistening as a window to the world,
> A beautiful voice spake to him:
>
> "Forsooth, innocent lad, cease your lament,
> The longing of your soul is mine too.

From the day you appeared in my father's home
My heart was won and I was yours.

I sought out secrecy, I lived in silence,
My senses frozen, I still could not love;
In the aura of your face I saw great light
I awoke—and could rest no more.

If I swear to forget you, I grow faint. . . .
Wherever I go, your face is there.
Why should I evade the truth, avoid the words:
Your love, David, is better than wine."[13]

Later in the poem, Gordon's lionization of Michal as a model for the contemporary Jewish woman becomes overt, as the narrator, touched by the constancy of her love, cries out: "Women in love come listen to my tale/ Daughters in love, give me your ears!/ And may you, daughter of a king, be an emblem for them."[14]

In its unprecedented theme, then, as well as its aesthetic innovations, *The Love of David and Michal* rose above its deep-seated structural and conceptual flaws to effect what the later, radical Hebrew writer Y. Ḥ. Brenner termed "a revolution" in Hebrew letters.[15]

Gordon quickly dispatched copies of the book to all the luminaries of Hebrew literature in Russia and abroad. The response was positive, if far from enthusiastic. In Leipzig, the prestigious *Allgemeine Zeitung des Judentums* included *The Love of David and Michal* in a survey of contemporary Jewish literature and gave it a generally favorable review that noted that "the gallant author, who makes his literary debut with this work, commends himself well to the public as a Hebrew author."[16] Interestingly, though, Gordon's description of David's bedding of Michal after his victory over the Philistines is decried as far too sexually explicit—indeed, as writing "à la George Sand."[17] Similarly, in Padua the aging warrior of the Italian Haskalah Samuele Davide Luzzatto praised Gordon's talents but confessed that in regard to the poem itself he was of several minds. He did not quite take to romances and to stories that departed from the scriptural truth, even if in a good cause; Gordon's Hebrew is rich, pleasing, and grammatical, but his rhymes, which play on the Ashkenazic, and particularly the Lithuanian, pronunciation of Hebrew offend the Italian ear and the rules of Hebrew prosody. Most disturbing about the poem, however, was its depiction of the love between its protagonists as romantic and sexual, which—Luzzatto admonished—is not in accord with the Judaic ethic but is

a Greek drama, unworthy of mention in the community of the Lord or for that matter in the realm of lovers of truth. And even worse than this is the confusion between the love of fathers and mothers for their children and the love between males and females—this is a muddle of the sacred and the profane.[18]

Luzzatto concluded by expressing his warm regards for the young poet, along with the hope that "your heart be bound with mine in ties of love unknown to the poets of Greece and of France."

Perhaps the most revealing response to Gordon's solicitations of praise from Hebrew writers in the West was a series of letters (which remain unpublished) from the important Viennese Hebrew author and journalist Meir Letteris. Letteris wrote Gordon a friendly letter lauding the book and praying that it would find discerning readers capable of understanding it. Based on his own experiences in Galicia and Vienna, however, he was most pessimistic about the future of Hebrew as a literary medium. To help the struggling young Gordon, Letteris agreed to accept on consignment ten copies of *The Love of David and Michal,* so long as he did not have to pay the postage fees, which he could not afford. Later, Letteris wrote to Gordon that not one copy of the book had been sold.[19]

At the same time as Gordon was trying to sell his book and spread his fame as a poet, he targeted a much larger audience in a different genre. He began to send out large numbers of articles to the major Jewish periodicals of the day, published in Hebrew and in German. In August 1857, his ambitions were rewarded as his first article, entitled "From Lithuania," appeared in *Ha-Maggid* (The Herald), the first Hebrew newspaper in the world, founded just over a year earlier in the small town of Lyck in eastern Prussia. Gordon's short piece transmitted a report printed in a major Russian journal to the effect that Jewish teachers in government schools were for the first time permitted to wear the official uniforms of the Russian Ministry of Education. In rapturous tones Gordon praised the beneficence of Alexander II, who "in the majesty of his heart and the purity of his lofty soul does not distinguish between the multitude of nations that live under his protection, and will not shame the people of Jacob." This small act of tolerance encourages the hope that the gracious emperor is preparing even greater improvements for the Jews of Russia. May God grant Alexander and his ministers the strength, courage, and wisdom to help the Jews, who for their part

> have the duty to obey in all sincerity his orders and desire, and to be faithful and eager servants, so that the friends of the Jews will not be swayed from their course.[20]

Here, in his first published article, Gordon set forth the crux of the political faith he would adhere to in the decades to come. The Russian government—or, at the very least, its liberal and humanitarian elements—is ready and willing to come to the aid of the Jews, in line with the dictates of progress and civility that define the nineteenth century. The amelioration of the status of the Jews, however, does not depend solely on the rational will of the state, but equally on the readiness of the Jews to be loyal and dedicated subjects of the tsar. Thus, from the very beginning of the debate on the contours of Jewish emancipation in the Russia of Alexander II, Judah Leib Gordon resolutely took the position that had a long pedigree among campaigners for Jewish rights in the West—that the self-reform of the Jews is a necessary precondition to their political liberation.[21]

But Gordon, even at this stage, was not merely repeating the cliches of earlier maskilim but was struggling to understand and articulate exactly what cultural and social changes were to be required of the Jews of Russia. Thus, his next article, called "Words of Peace and Truth" [*Divrei shalom ve-'emet*] in obvious emulation of the path-breaking pamphlet of the same name written by Hartwig Wessely in

1782, challenged head on the views of modern Jewish culture expressed by two formidable representatives of the German-Jewish elite and of the new *Wissenschaft des Judentums* movement.[22] In a review of a recent anthology of Hebrew poetry, the historian Isaac Marcus Jost had advanced the notion that the quality of Hebrew poety had disintegrated dramatically since the Middle Ages. The works of Joseph Kimchi, Judah Halevi, and Moses Ibn Ezra were resplendent creations of virtuosi of the Hebrew tongue, Jost explained, and in the eighteenth century Wessely and Shalom Ha-Kohen had vied with the classics. Since them, however, Hebrew verse had become terribly artificial and mediocre. This is not coincidental, for poetry is not simply a philological exercise but also a calling by the muse. When inspired, a poet should create in his mother tongue, and not in a foreign or dead language. In Latin, Greek, Arabic, or Hebrew, one can make pretty verses that resemble true poetry but are really only artifically stitched-together lines, not true poetic out-pourings of the creative soul. Such poems, therefore, ought not be included in any respectable collection of Hebrew verse.

Jost's restatement of the standard Romantic pieties held by his generation threw Judah Leib Gordon into a frenzy: Jost clearly was an inveterate enemy of the Hebrew language who dared to speak of the Holy Tongue as a dead language like Latin or Greek. That is patently false, Gordon steadfastly insisted. Hebrew is the living bond that links Jews all around the world who have no other means of communicating with one another. Unlike Latin, Greek, or even Arabic, Hebrew is not simply studied by adults at universities, but is also infused into millions of children virtually with their mothers' milk. In Russia, even artisans and simple folk can read and understand Hebrew. How dare Jost declare, then, that all contemporary Hebrew poetry is drivel? Perhaps that is true of what passes for Hebrew literature in the German lands, but not of the wonderful poetry produced in Hebrew elsewhere. Age is not a guarantee of worth, and Hebrew literature is not something to be found in dusty old libraries, but a vibrant source of inspiration in the here and now.

In a similar vein, but in even more vituperative tones, Gordon lambasted the suggestion by the German-Jewish bibliographer Moritz Steinschneider that Hebrew newspapers and translations of such works as Eugene Sue's *Mysteries of Paris* were less authentic and important than high-level *Wissenschaft*.[23] To Gordon, these comments were insults that stemmed from snobbery, cruelty, and ignorance. The achievements of *jüdische Wissenschaft* in Germany were eminently laudable, he acknowledged, but what were the Jews of Russia and Poland to do in search of enlightenment and revitalization? Pleading that "all those countries everywhere who master our Holy Tongue, love our people, and have Jewish blood flowing in their veins" disregard the comments of Jost and Steinschneider, Gordon concluded:

> Don't you see what they really want? They want to ban our Hebrew language from the land of the living and to turn it into one of those desiccated tongues and ancient artifacts that demand respect only due to their antiquity, just like all the other arche-ological discoveries of the ancient Near East . . . But you must preserve our language because it alone is your wisdom and your knowledge and the only remnant surviving from our cherished legacy.[24]

To be sure, at the heart of Gordon's venom against Jost and Steinschneider was the cultural divide between the Germanized Reformers and the Hebraizing maskil. But this was not, as was later claimed, a debate between "nationalists" and "assimilationists" in the terms that dominated Jewish political discourse in the last years of the nineteenth century.[25] As became clear in the series of letters between Gordon and several correspondents that ensued on the pages of *Ha-Maggid* for months after the publication of his piece, the thrust of Gordon's attack was not against the substance of German-Jewish scholarship per se or even its applicability to the plight of Russian and Polish Jews. What angered Gordon was what he identified as a threefold syndrome in German-Jewish culture: the intelligentsia's ignorance of Hebrew and the basics of Jewish law and literature; condescension toward the East European maskilim, who were clearly far more at home in classic Jewish texts; and a radical "atheistic" tendency that claimed Spinoza and Uriel de Costa as its heroes. When the conservative editor of *Ha-Maggid* took Gordon to task for his sweeping condemnation of German Jews' religious radicalism and ignorance of Hebrew and the Talmud, Gordon quickly apologized, admitting that in the heat of the moment he had overgeneralized by referring to all German-Jewish scholars rather than only some of them. Of course he did not in the least mean to deprecate the knowledge or the accomplishments of men such as Meir Letteris, Leopold Zunz, Abraham Geiger, or Heinrich Graetz. He had gone too far in his attack and he was sorry.[26]

After this public embarrassment, no article by Judah Leib Gordon appeared in *Ha-Maggid* for the next year and a half. Since the publication of his book, however, he had been working on at least three simultaneous poetic projects that left him little time to ponder his lapsed journalistic career. First, he returned to the epic cycle on David and wrote three excruciatingly long and wooden introductory chapters of a poem entitled "The Wars of David and the Philistines." But Gordon could not bring himself to complete the third, and what he had originally planned to be the longest, segment of the trilogy, Instead, he abandoned the project as a whole and never allowed the unfinished work to be published during his lifetime. Before his death he recovered the forgotten manuscript and noted that it ought to be burned or thrown into the Dead Sea.[27] Wisely deciding that he had exhausted the poetic potential of the epic, he set to work on shorter poems on incidental themes that either emerged from his own experiences or from works by Schiller, Byron, and other masters.[28]

The shift to shorter verses and classical forms other than the epic was most noticeable and productive in Gordon's major project of this period, a collection of one hundred fables that he wrote in the hope that it would be accepted by the Ministry of Education as a textbook in the state schools for Jewish children. Gordon began to work on this compendium immediately after the publication of *The Love of David and Michal* and completed it in the late summer of 1858.[29] As soon as the work was ready, he dispatched letters to a large number of maskilim at home and abroad, asking for letters of recommendation to the Russian government. In addition, he had the publishers (the noted Romm press in Vilna) send advance copies of the book to the various officials in St. Petersburg who would rule on its acceptability as a textbook.

For months he waited impatiently for word from the capital. A kind letter from

Professor Daniel Chwolson, the distinguished Orientalist at the University of St. Petersburg and important counselor to the government on matters Judaic (as well as the most noted Jewish convert to Russian Orthodoxy), raised Gordon's expectations that his work would be accepted by the ministry. At the end of February 1859, however, he received the crushing news: the Jewish experts at the Ministry of Education had ruled that although the work was excellently executed, it was not suitable for use in the government schools because of "the use by the author of too caustic criticisms of the Jews."[30] The minister noted that if the work were nonetheless printed without a subsidy by the state, he would recommend it to the government schools "in order to aid the author in his scholarly endeavors." After negotiations with the censorship board over several minor allusions in the text, *The Fables of Judah* [*Mishlei Yehudah*] was approved by the government censor on June 29, 1859, and was published in Vilna.

The book opened with two laudatory prefaces written by the reigning giants of the Russian Haskalah, Isaac Ber Levinsohn and Ada"m Ha-Kohen Lebensohn, extolling Gordon in the hyperbolic style of the day. These are followed by a long introduction, by Gordon, on the history of the fable in classical, modern, and traditional Hebrew sources. What is most compelling about this essay on the fable is the honesty and clarity of its tone, at once naive in its self-importance and sophisticated in its presentation of evidence, garnished from Greek, French, and German sources. Thus, Gordon began by distinguishing his collection of fables from his previous work: the latter was the product of a youth's idle playfulness and was meant merely as entertainment; because it nonetheless attained attention and praise from distinguished readers, its author was emboldened to embark on this second venture, which is not simply a diverting collection of playful verses but a compendium of fables with great moral seriousness. "This is a work of great utility," he proclaimed, "that will be most beneficial to the reader by imparting to him wisdom and ethics; those attuned to language will delight in the felicity of its diction; those seeking moral guidance will heed its lessons." This, indeed, is the eternal mission of the fable, to be pleasant-tasting medicine. For this reason, Plato advised nursemaids to recite fables while feeding their charges, so that the infant could imbibe justice and morality along with his milk. The fable, therefore, is obviously most suited to the instruction of the young, for in one fell swoop they can learn from it three important things: proper morality, the language in which it is written, and useful information about the world as a whole. Adults, too, can learn much from fables, especially since age does not necessarily guarantee either intelligence or moral sense.

This argument is followed by a lengthy, and reasonably learned, survey of the fable from Aesop through the Latin and Arabic writers to La Fontaine and Krylov. Special notice is given to the Russian fabulist who had died in St. Petersburg only fifteen years earlier. But the genre of the fable, Gordon was quick to point out, originated not with Aesop, but with the Hebrew Bible: the fables of Jotham, the son of Gideon the Judge, and Jehoash, king of Israel, are recorded in the Books of Judges and II Kings. The biblical fable, as distinct from the far more common scriptural parable, is therefore the oldest known version of the genre. Moreover, the Jews did not abandon the fable in the postbiblical period. In Mishnaic and Talmudic times, the rabbis absorbed the Aesopian tales along with other aspects of

Greek culture and reintegrated this mode of teaching into their literary works. In their wake came the medieval and modern Jewish fabulists, and Gordon himself, who placed his own fables squarely in the tradition of this creative mix. Most of his one hundred fables, Gordon explained, were translated freely from La Fontaine and Krylov, and others were located in other superior collections; to this he added fables found in the Talmud and Midrash and many others that were products of his own imagination. All of the fables are presented in clear and easily understood rhymed verse in the certainty that, despite the doubts of experts such as Lessing, fables can indeed be successfully molded into poetry, as Socrates himself advised. To effect this union, Gordon admitted, he had to abandon the traditional metric scheme of Hebrew verse and to use postbiblical diction to convey his thoughts and images.

This introduction is most interesting in its mirroring of the typical Haskalah attempt to reinfuse Jewish culture with European content by claiming that the Gentile models had themselves originated with the Jews and were thus only being reabsorbed after an unfortunate hiatus. In this way, the literary genre or scholarly subject could be presented to a potentially hostile Jewish audience not only as an authentic mode of Jewish creativity—such an argument had been used by medieval Jewish thinkers to justify recourse to Greek thought—but also as a perfect symbol of the beneficial interaction of Jewish and Christian societies in the present.[31] The introduction to *The Fables of Judah,* then, provides the first glimpse of a vitally important part of Judah Leib Gordon's intellectual persona: the pensive but passionate advocate of Jewish cultural revivification pursuing his goal by means of a careful, *wissenschaftlich* refraction of European values and concepts in an enriched Hebrew language. This, perhaps, is what Gordon had attempted to achieve in *The Love of David and Michal,* but the very choice of an anachronistic and problematic medium had subverted the message. In the fable, by contrast, Gordon found an appropriate vehicle for the combination of humanist ethic and Hebraic authenticity that was to be his hallmark for the rest of his days.

In a series of letters to his close friend Ze'ev Kaplan, who was also trying his hand at fables, Gordon described the method and the purpose of his collection. First, he explained, "succinctness is the very lifeblood of the fable," which like a sharp sword must be thrust with one neat jab directly into the heart of a man.[32] While all poems must strive to be taut, the fable must be brief not only in its wording but in its plot as well. While some classic fables may appear to be long, upon closer examination they are composed of many brief, discrete, parts, each of which has its own moral.[33] Clearly, the failure of Gordon's relentlessly prolix Davidic epics had taught him a valuable lesson about brevity as the soul of poetry.

But the secret of a successful fable, Gordon continued, was more than technical skill. Equally important was the ability to mask an ethical or political message in a seemingly naive animal tale. For example, the point of his original fable "The Eagle and the Mountain Goat" was to demonstrate

how our people has been persecuted by many nations through the centuries and has been prevented from joining in the inheritance of the rights of man. But now that the age of rejuvenation has arrived, emancipation is imminent, slowly but surely.

Many enemies and detractors try to block this movement to the better, but the truth shall prevail.[34]

At first, Gordon confessed, this fable had too openly identified its hero, an aging eagle who is able to recoup his strength and fly once more, with the Jewish people, and the mountain goats, who vainly condemn the eagle as superannuated, with those who persecute the Jews. Realizing that this would never pass the Russian censors, Gordon revised the fable to make it seem as if the eagle symbolized the Hebrew language and the goats its detractors; the result would doubtless pass inspection.[35] In other words, in the political culture of nonofficial imperial Russia, in which writing in "Aesopian language" became a habit, if not a cliche, Gordon cherished the fable as the perfect medium for conveying subversive messages that the authorities would otherwise interdict. Interestingly, as has already been noted, the Russian censors of the late 1850s were almost as certain to excise harsh criticisms of traditional Jewish society as those leveled against the Russian state. For Judah Leib Gordon, as loyal to the tsar and respectful of Russian traditions as any censor, subtlety and double entendre would be far more necessary in crafting didactic barbs at Jewish customs and leaders.

Not all hundred *Fables of Judah,* to be sure, were aimed at targets in the traditional world of Russian Jewry. Many of Gordons's tales adhered to the moral messages advanced by Aesop, La Fontaine, Krylov, or the other sources of Gordon's inspiration. Some of his fables related to his own personal experience or to stock situations such as relations between parents and children, the old and the young, the sick and the healthy. But even the fables on universal themes such as these are Judaized in Gordon's presentation by his deliberate—and often very funny—co-optation of biblical images and Talmudic expressions. Thus, La Fontaine's "The Little Fish and the Fisherman"—whose classic moral is "a bird in the hand is worth two in the bush"—is preceded in Gordon's version by the Talmudic motto "a peck from the ground and not a bushel from the roof."[36] More insidious is the reworking of the fish's protest: in La Fontaine, the little captured carp merely begs for clemency, promising that when it grows up, it will yield a better price for the fisherman. Gordon's fish, by contrast, preposterously inquires: "Am I a fish that you pay me heed?/ Or a dragon that you set a watch over me?"—an ironic allusion to Job's anguished lament "Am I the sea or the Dragon/ That you have set a watch over me?" Several lines later, the imagined future consumer of the fish becomes the biblical chief steward, the warden of Joseph's prison.[37]

This same technique is even more blatant in the many fables that bear a clear Haskalah thrust. "The Mice in Council" savagely mocks the passive and fearful rodents who think up the clever device of tying a bell around the collar of the cat persecuting them, but cannot produce one volunteer brave enough to put this strategy into effect. In Gordon's retelling, the mice are personalized into obvious surrogates of the Jewish communal leaders in Eastern Europe. The assembly, the officers, the cries of woe are all cruelly stylized in mock-biblical cadences, deliberately employed to ridicule the failure of courage and of honesty in Jewish leadership—a leitmotif of Gordon's emerging critique of traditional Jewish society in Russia. The polemic is sharpened by another subtle technique, a shift from the third person in the La Fontaine version to the second person in Gordon's. Thus, the moral of the story is directed at the readers themselves:

> Mice! Wisdom and courage for the fight!
> If you haven't in your midst one hearty man
> Who will take action without fear
> What use all your meetings and councils?[38]

Some of Gordon's fables single out for attack not the traditional leaders and the rabbis, but supercilious enlighteners who mislead the masses. His tale "The Boy and the Old Man," for example, recasts the classic fable "The Boy and the Schoolmaster" in a fascinating manner. The original version relates the story of a boy who falls into a river and hangs between life and death clutching onto a willow branch until there approaches a solemn schoolmaster, who first berates the boy for his recklessness and then saves him from drowning. The moral here is obvious: "prudes, windbags, and pedants" are pests who foam at the mouth and think only of how to exercise their lungs instead of taking immediate action.[39] In Gordon's rendition, the schoolmaster becomes a generic old man—perhaps to preserve the integrity of the author's profession—and the message is significantly broadened:

> Thus the perverse lecture their friends,
> Point out their wrongs and faults,
> Pass judgment without correcting flaws,
> Heep scorn without lending a hand.
> Impetuous one! Keep your tongues still,
> Understand, help, and only then give advice![40]

For all his elitism and hatred of the plebeian, Gordon refused to countenance the position of the author or critic removed from the fray; he both preached and practiced the stance of the engagé poet and vehemently denounced ideologues' dreams not rooted in the reality of Jewish life in Eastern Europe. Soon, this fundamental aspect of his artistic and personal ethic would engulf him in endless bitter controversies with foes whom he regarded as analogous to the perverse old man in his fable of the drowning boy.

The Fables of Judah, then, represent a major step forward both in Gordon's mastery of the craft of poetry and in his ability to articulate through his writings deeply felt convictions about the reform of Jewish life in Russia, For Gordon, there was absolutely no conflict between the poetic and the didactic thrusts of his work— to his mind, good poetry and effective preaching were inexorably intertwined, if not synonymous. At this stage he did not yet dwell on the theoretical problems of this aesthetic; his artistic self-image was not yet challenged by the canons of the new "radical criticism" being developed in Russia at precisely this time. Before he would confront that criticism, he would mature substantially as an artist and a thinker. But the voice that Gordon first found in his modest animal tales—superbly controlled plot and deft manipulation of the multiple resonances of the Hebrew lexicon in the service of social satire and humanitarian imperatives—would stand by him throughout his literary life.

The Fables of Judah did not significantly advance Gordon's literary career, however. On the contrary, his second book received even less critical notice than the first. After a year had passed without any review of the book, Gordon took matters into his own hands and rashly dispatched a letter to the *Allgemeine Zeitung des Judentums* proclaiming the importance of this work and recommending that all Jewish schools in Germany ought to buy it "as a useful primer in Hebrew stylistics." He concluded by suggesting that the editors of the paper review this major book.[41] There is no record if Gordon was embarrassed by the fact that this self-recommendation was printed several months after the *Allgemeine Zeitung* had published a review of the book written by one of Gordon's close friends.[42]

Beyond the disappointing critical reaction to the book, Gordon suffered from its commercial failure, admitting to a correspondent that he gave free copies to acquaintances who could not even read Hebrew and that he spent much more money on mailing the book to friends than he ever received in royalties.[43] In his correspondence he angrily revealed that the representatives of schools run by the Karaites of Crimea and the Caucasus had purchased thirty-two copies of his fables in a Vilna bookstore to use at their schools, but that he had seen no profits from this sale. In addition, in Germany, Moritz Steinschneider—whom Gordon had recently maligned as an enemy of the Hebrew tongue—selected eight of Gordon's fables from the copy he had received as a gift from the author and reprinted them in a collection of Hebrew fables he compiled for use in the Jewish schools of India founded by the Sassoon family; the bibliographer had neither asked Gordon for permission to use the poems nor reimbursed him for their republication.[44]

After all the energy expended on the fables, the lack of critical or commercial acclaim left Gordon in an acute state of postpartum depression. In letters to friends in Russia and abroad he repeatedly bemoaned his lot as a destitute teacher in a remote provincial hole in the backwater of Europe. His attempt at lifting himself out of his financial rut by embarking on a business venture had ended in complete failure. He could not even afford to subscribe to journals on his own and had to seek out co-subscribers to share the cost. His only sources of additional income and public exposure were the reports on significant occurrences in Russia—especially laws that benefited the Jews—which he continued to submit to the *Allgemeine Zeitung des Judentums*.[45]

In the quiet of his study, though, he continued to expand his literary horizons by experimenting with new genres. Thus, in 1859 he wrote his first short story, entitled "Two Days and a Night in an Inn," which remained unpublished for a decade.[46] Drawing on the fund of experiences he had accumulated growing up in an inn, Gordon was able to produce a modest but somewhat successful variation on the classic tale of the stranded author's encounter with strange fellow travelers. This clearly autobiographical story describes a young author trying to return to his wife and two daughters in a small Lithuanian town after visiting Vilna to publish a Hebrew book. On his way home, he is forced by the lack of available horses to spend the Sabbath in an inn. During these twenty-four unhappy hours, he witnesses scenes that touch all bases of iniquity and possibility in Russian-Jewish life. On his way to the inn, the author is treated rudely by several Jews, who reserve the externals of civility only for Gentiles, before whom they are disingenuously obsequious. In the hostel, a group of Jews gluttonously feast and drink in a lavish party, which turns out to be hosted by an unscrupulous and ignorant communal leader trying to buy his election by feting his constituents. The innkeeper, dressed in the filthy rags that Jews have inherited from the inglorious Polish past, feigns sympathy with the narrator's disgust; soon, however, the host's putative enlightenment is belied by his kowtowing to a sodden Polish noble who spouts anti-Jewish invective, to the dismay of his wife, a fine French lady who instructs her daughter to be tolerant of all faiths. Meanwhile, the narrator is accosted by two sorts of beggars: he agrees to give money to the first, an old Jew collecting charity for the pious Jews of Palestine, without realizing that he is only continuing the hopeless cycle of ignorance and ignominy that condemns the Jews in the Holy Land to a life of destitution. But the narrator angrily spurns the requests of two women seeking alms to marry off the poor eighteen-year-old daughter of a Jew who spends his days in study and prayer rather than providing for his family; the two women are shocked by the suggestion that the poor girl might be better off working as a servant to a rich family than marrying another unproductive loafer.

Then the author observes the true scourge of Jewish society in Eastern Europe, a folk preacher who travels from town to town spreading superstitions and fear of the outside world to his innocent audience, who are astonishingly ignorant of the basics of their faith and cannot even read their prayers and Bibles with anything approaching accuracy. Back at the inn, the cultural and spiritual level of the local Jews is shockingly exposed when the innkeeper proudly displays his son to the guest, boasting that the boy's amazing accomplishments in Talmud study have earned him fame and probable fortune, since he will go on to the Volozhin yeshivah and find a rich bride. Upon examination, however, the boy is woefully unable to decode a simple Hebrew text and is of course utterly ignorant of German or Russian. Dismayed and distressed by all he has seen, the narrator escapes from the town and goes off to commune with nature in the hills and dales of the surrounding countryside. Upon his return, he meets a Russian army officer who, displaying the modesty, honesty, and hospitality of his nation, eagerly agrees to take the narrator home, offering to wait until the Sabbath is over so that his comrade's religious scruples can be observed. On his way back to the inn to gather his things, the narrator is caught up in a crowd of Jews scurrying about in disarray, frantic with shocking news: one of the Talmud students had passed out and died in the synagogue during the preacher's sermon; when the congregants opened the student's shirt to try to resuscitate him, they discovered, of all things, that the student was a girl masquerading as a boy in order to receive an education closed to her because of her sex. The hubbub over this discovery is joined by a loud cry of anguish on the part of a merchant who had been swindled by the supposedly holy preacher, and our hero returns home, embraces his wife and daughters, and tries to forget all the sorrows he has witnessed during his two days and one night in a typical Jewish inn in Lithuania.

The story's structural faults and cliches are legion, but they are at least in part mitigated by Gordon's surprisingly light touch and easy pace in recounting his alter ego's discoveries and observations. Gordon was quite obviously still struggling to find a way to convey a biting critique of Jewish mores in a medium at once entertaining and enlightening. In the years after the composition of this story, he would produce a dozen or so other short stories that ultimately enjoyed some commercial

University of Winnipeg, 515 Portage Ave., Winnipeg, MB. R3B 2E9 Canada

success. But Gordon never did master control of the two essentials of this genre, plot and characterization. He was far more adept as a raconteur than as a dramatist, and his incisive observations of human foibles were not matched by an ability to flesh out a character's entire personality. In time, he would settle on a division of labor more suitable to his talents. His limited narrative skills were deftly diverted into poetry, where allusion and ellipsis could substitute for sustained plot; his marvelous skill at transforming personal experience into cutting comic sketches would be more successfully manipulated in the feuilleton.

The poems of this period reveal Gordon struggling with the lessons he had learned while writing his fables. In his first fling at a nonscripturally based narrative poem, he began to write about a young couple who fell madly in love despite their parents' objections and fled to America, where they married, became rich, and lived happily ever after, ultimately even bringing their families to join them. Gordon did not get very far with this story, completing only the first section, which was a rather wooden paean to the bounty and freedom of America. This snippet—published by Gordon in 1892 as a tribute to the four hundredth anniversary of Columbus's discovery of the New World—is only interesting in its very early adumbration of Gordon's lifelong (and later very controversial) admiration of the United States as the world's premier den of freedom and democracy, suitable for Jewish emigration.[47]

Far closer to home—and the most important poem of the lot—was "The Way of My People" [*Derekh bat 'ami*], Gordon's first attempt at sounding a trumpet call in praise of the age of enlightenment in Russia and the West. After the citation of Exodus 10:23—"all the Israelites enjoyed light in their dwellings"—the poem lists the various criticisms that were made of the Jews in the long debate over the emancipation: the Jews are not fit to be citizens because they are mired in obscurantism, dishonest in trade, unfit for manual labor, too cowardly for military service, and too corrupt for public office. These charges, the poet admits, had some weight in the past, though not through the fault of the Jews but that of their oppressors. But all these charges are no longer apt, for

> Now the dawn has broken through, the sun shines forth,
> Folly has fled, darkness has departed,
> Light has reached everywhere, and here too.[48]

Throughout Europe, Jews have become loyal subjects of their kings, useful citizens of their states, and productive developers of all sectors of the economy and intellectual world. The new age has even reached Russia, where a wise ruler has opened schools for Jews, allowed them to publish their own newspapers, and permitted them to move outside the Pale in order to pursue new callings. The Jews have responded in kind, learning the language of the land and feeling love for its inhabitants, without in the process suffering any detriment to their faith. Turning directly to his audience, the poet calls for fortitude and determination, ceaseless study, and boundless loyalty both to Russia and to the Jewish tradition. This combination will inevitably result in liberation, he is sure: when the emperor, in all his wisdom and grace, "will give laws to his people as the Lord on high/ He will remember that we, too, are his children."

This poem clearly reveals Gordon inching gradually along to the hortatory style he would perfect in the middle 1860s. But he still had a good way to go, unable as yet to attain in the didactic poem the degree of compression that he knew was essential to good poetry and that he had mastered, to a large extent, in his fables. While he was searching for the forms most appropriate to his literary calling, he continued his attempt to advance his journalistic career as well. In the *Allgemeine Zeitung des Judentums,* beginning in the spring and summer of 1860, he began to reach out beyond simple reportage of legal milestones to describe cultural news and to impart his particular reading of events. Thus, in May he concluded a standard report on education with the following bizarre incident: a thirteen-year-old boy had come to Ponevezh to have a second circumcision, since "the traces of the first were accidentally effaced."[49] In a tone new to his journalistic pen, Gordon added: "By the way, this case is not an isolated one in these parts, where Judaism has not yet been shaken from its ancient principles." Two months later, he wrote a bold piece that launched into a bitter attack on a radical maskil in Zhitomir who had written an article declaring that the Russian Jews ought to be forced into enlightenment. Gordon retorted that castigating blind adherence to the old on the part of the "Orthodox Jews" is justified, but any attempt to force Jews to become enlightened is itself medieval and reminiscent of the Inquisition. In addition, denouncing the Talmud as unsuitable for civilized readers—as the radical modernizer had done— is inappropriate and counterproductive; if one is truly interested in uprooting un-civilized aspects of Judaism, Gordon noted, one might as well begin with the sac-rificial service in the Bible itself. As he had done in *Ha-Maggid* two years earlier, Gordon struck out angrily at a colleague whom he considered to be a dangerously radical reformer of the Jews. But now, as if to remedy the damage caused by his unfortunate debut in Hebrew journalism, he made a point of referring with great respect to both Jost and Steinschneider, the objects of his previous ire.[50]

Soon after this subtle but noteworthy maturation of his journalistic style, Gor-don's third career underwent a major change as well. In October 1860, he was trans-ferred to the government Jewish school in the town of Shavli (Šiauliai in Lithu-anian). Located some fifty miles northwest of Ponevezh, Shavli was a more important city with a larger population, both Gentile and Jewish. In 1861, Shavli reported 5,824 residents, among whom there were over twenty-five hundred Jews. The seat of an ornate seventeenth-century Roman Catholic cathedral that held up to four thousand worshipers and a synagogue established by Polish royal charter in 1701, Shavli had a public boys' gymnasium in addition to the Jewish school founded by the government in 1851.[51]

Gordon was rather unhappy with this move to a new town where he knew no one. His financial plight remained acute, since there was no way he could support his family on the salary he received from the state. Soon after he arrived in Shavli, moreover, burglars sacked his home and made off with his entire fortune—the pal-try sum of seventy-five rubles.[52] In order to make ends meet, he once again began to take on private pupils, tutoring them in both Hebrew and French. Soon, he opened a school for Jewish girls, a move that served to increase his disfavor among the traditionalist Jews of the town.[53]

The dislike was mutual. In early January 1861, Gordon dispatched a long report to the *Allgemeine Zeitung des Judentums* in which he vented for the first time, and in great detail, his hostility to traditional Jewish culture in Eastern Europe.[54] He began by informing his readers—presumably enlightened German Jews—that they might be misled by the news from Russia of the progress of their coreligionists. It is true that the Russian government has done much to advance the cultural level of its Jews—supporting schools, newspapers, rabbinical commissions, and the like—but it would be dangerous to infer from this that the Jews throughout the length and breadth of Russia have made considerable progress on the road to "civilization." On the contrary, while small pockets of Russian Jewry, particularly among the affluent, have made great strides in this direction, the masses remained mired "in the good old Middle Ages, with all its Asiatic resonances." Walk along any Jewish street, eavesdrop in any prayer house, and you will find that here time has stopped in its tracks. Or worse: since the government cast its lot with the enlightened, the communal and rabbinical leaders have declared a war on modernity. They have opened more and more schools in which "Talmud-absolutism" is disseminated to the ignorant; in the north, "musar" academies aimed at extending the lock of the blind tradition on the masses have been established; in the south, Hasidism continues to ensnare most Jews in its trap and the Hasidic masters continue shamelessly to exploit their hapless disciples; everywhere ignorant itinerant preachers pack in huge audiences whenever they open their nonsensical mouths. The new schools exist, that is true, but most parents refuse to send their children to them. Newspapers flourish, but the bulk of their potential audience has not even heard of them and would care less if they had.

The impatient humanitarian could tolerate, if he must, a Bedouin retaining his old way of life on the seamless sand of the desert or an Eskimo not feeling the warm ray of light breaking through the freezing cold. But

> when a Lithuanian Jew, a hardworking tradesman or smooth merchant comes into contact through his commerce with places and persons influenced by the Enlightenment; when he rides on trains, sends cables, and makes use of all the institutions and products of science but returns home without the slightest intention of promoting science or even letting his children benefit from progress—then even the most disinterested observer cannot ward off an involuntary shudder of astonishment, and can only explain this indifference to the outside world by understanding the thousand-year-old exclusion that has led to this state.[55]

The hopes of the Enlighteners, Gordon continued, are pinned almost exclusively on the creation of a modern rabbinate in Russia, that is, on the graduates of the government-sponsored rabbinical seminaries. But the experience of these rabbis does not bode well as a harbinger of change in a resistant community. The foes of modernity are simply too strong. Only when the Orthodox themselves decide to exchange their Asiatic clothes, manners, and ways of thinking for those of modern Europe will Western-educated rabbis have the opportunity to lead their flock in the correct direction. In the end, there is still hope: it will obviously take time for habits thousands of years old to die out. But it is important to note that even by the end of the fifth decade of the nineteenth century the Russian Jews have not yet lived up to the promise of progress.

The tension between the cynicism and gloom of this article and the shining optimism of "The Way of My People," written only a few months earlier, is the first example of a critical, difficult, and often misunderstood aspect of Gordon's life and oeuvre: at many points his poems, essays, stories, and letters would alternate between unbridled hope and near despair. As a result, commentators could all too easily pick up on either side of the emotional equation and misrepresent Gordon's mood or point of view. But a judicious reading of all of his works renders a different judgment: the tightrope leading from traditional Jewish culture to Gordon's idealized view of the future was remarkably strained and susceptible to a host of hostile winds; even the steadiest foot, like Gordon's, would often hesitate, quiver, and just about slip before regaining composure and proceeding.

A few weeks after writing this first pessimistic account, however, Gordon was confronted by a shattering incident that would herald even more serious challenges to his vision of inevitable progress. In late January 1860, a peasant girl disappeared in the village of Shavliany (Sialenai), in the outskirts of Shavli. As it happened, two Jewish grain dealers from nearby towns were traveling on that day through the hamlets surrounding the village. Apprised of this coincidence, the local police jumped to the conclusion deemed most logical by their instincts and training—the Jews had kidnapped and murdered the girl in order to use her blood for ritual purposes. The two Jewish merchants were thereupon arrested and imprisoned, pending investigation. The police also raided the local synagogue, seizing its wine to check if it was actually blood.

Gordon learned of this affair while stopping at an inn not far from where the events took place, and he immediately sent word to the rabbi of Shavliany that it was important to seek counsel of the more enlightened Jewish community in the main district town. The rabbi came to Shavli and informed the local leaders of the potentially disastrous ritual-murder charge. Gordon decided to take immediate action on his own. First, he dispatched a story to the *Allgemeine Zeitung des Judentums* in which he carefully reported on another case in the news. In Novo-Alexandrovsk, Kovno province, a Jewish girl had allegedly been baptized under duress. The press in Russia and abroad had seized on this rumor and had compared this case to the recent infamous Mortara scandal—the abduction in Bologna, with the approval of the Holy See, of a six-year-old Jewish child, Edgardo Mortara, who had secretly been baptized five years earlier. With patent precision, Gordon noted that the Russian government had appointed its top Jewish experts to investigate the Novo-Alexandrovsk case, and they had discovered that the girl in question, who was in fact fourteen or fifteen, and not nine years old as originally reported, had not been forcibly baptized but had voluntarily converted to Christianity. Gordon concluded that it was inspiring to know that the Russian press was sensitive to potential injustices against Jews and he hoped that such vigilance would not be diminished by the outcome in this case. At the same time, he called on the Jews themselves to realize that unjustified panic and appeals to world opinion before the facts are established in any situation could be very detrimental to their cause.[56]

Very soon thereafter, Gordon learned that the body of the young girl in Shavliany had been discovered buried in the snow behind her parents' hut. He then hurried off three versions of a detailed story of the false ritual-murder charge: in German, he wrote to the *Allgemeine Zeitung;* in Hebrew, to the recently founded *Ha-Meliz* (The Advocate) in Odessa, a journal that promised to be more enlightened than its predecessors; and to *Razsvet* (The Dawn), the Russian-language Jewish newspaper that had also just begun to appear in Odessa, he submitted what would be his first published piece in the Russian tongue.[57] In each of these versions he first detailed the facts of the Shavliany case and then explained that despite the discovery of the body, it was not yet clear what the results of this obnoxious calumny against the Jews would be. However, he felt compelled to report the matter far and wide, certain that in so doing he was "fulfilling, for my part, my duty as a man and as a Jew, sincerely sympathizing with the undeserved suffering of neighbors and coreligionists."[58]

Indeed, even though the body was found, the case was not shut. The Polish noble who owned the estate on which the death had occurred was unhappy with the police's conclusion that there obviously had been no ritual murder. His major piece of evidence that something was amiss, and that it involved the Jews, was the fact that Lev Osipovich Gordon, the Shavli Jewish schoolteacher, had reported the discovery of the corpse a week before the official police inquiry held that the body had been found. This discrepancy demanded a special investigation from the Ministry of Justice in St. Petersburg into the actions of said Gordon and the rabbi of Shavliany, as co-conspirators in a cover-up of a ritual murder. To Gordon's good fortune, this accusation was deemed not credible by the provincial officials, and it languished for several years in the files of the ministry until it was formally dismissed as untenable. In the meanwhile, Gordon discovered what had actually happened: the body had in fact been found on the day he reported in his articles, but it was then removed to a shed to protect it from the pigs on the farm. The police officer in charge of the case, however, was out of town for several days, and when he returned he ordered that the corpse be restored to its original location so that no one could be accused of tampering with the evidence. Only a week after the original discovery did the police return to the scene of the death and formally record their findings. The Jews had learned the truth as soon as it came to light and had conveyed the news to Gordon, who reported it immediately to the press.[59]

To say the least, the timing of this crisis is instructive. Gordon became embroiled in the Shavliany ritual-murder charge precisely at the time that all of Russia was consumed with the most exciting and most important event in nineteenth-century Russian history. On February 19, 1861, Alexander II proclaimed the emancipation of the serfs. On this day, even the most heartfelt enemies of tsarism rejoiced: in London, as is well known, Alexander Herzen joyfully saluted the emperor with the exuberant declaration "Man of Galilee, you have triumphed!" But in Shavli, on the very same day, Judah Leib Gordon had no time to reflect on the glorious news from the capital. He was putting the final touches on his literary debut in the Russian language, his first report to *Razsvet,* which began: "Just how widespread the most monstrous prejudices against the Jews are here in our poor Lithuania may be seen from the following case."[60]

The contrast between Herzen's and Gordon's exclamations and preoccupations on that February day is not simply a matter of ironic coincidence and juxtaposition. Rather, it reflects the deep-seated lack of synchronism between Russian and Russian-Jewish societies that complicated their relations and interactions at every moment. Judah Leib—or rather Lev Osipovich—Gordon had not only mastered the Russian tongue, but he also spoke and wrote Russian with grace, wit, and much affection. In the years to come he would become one of the most passionate advocates and practitioners of a Russification of the Jews that would be coterminous with their national rejuvenation. But from his very first public utterance in Russian to his last, Gordon had to steel his commitment to Russian culture against a wall of hostility that appeared to be all but impenetrable. Judah Leib Gordon believed wholeheartedly that the resistance could be breached with goodwill, hard work, and mutual respect. It was only one of the tragedies of his life that he was, as usual, overly optimistic.

4

"Awake, My People!"
1861–1865

As the Shavliany blood libel receded into memory and into the litterboxes of the tsarist bureaucracy, Judah Leib Gordon renewed his trust in the possibilities of progress in Russia. Had not the truth overwhelmed the dark shadows of medieval prejudice and superstition? Was this not an emblem of the inexorable tide of enlightenment and reason that was unleashed when man became free? Some unfortunate residues of servitude and hatred might still appear from time to time, but the march of civilization would go ever forward, promising a glorious future of liberty and ever-increasing knowledge.

With this faith, Gordon rather cheerfully continued to divide his time and energy between his multiple roles as Hebrew litterateur, German-Hebrew-Russian journalist, and schoolteacher in the service of the Haskalah and the tsar. In addition to his regular work in the government Jewish school in Shavli, he continued to run a school for Jewish girls. To its fifteen pupils the academy taught the standard Haskalah curriculum, modified for girls: the basics of Bible and of Hebrew grammar, Russian, German, Polish, arithmetic, calligraphy, and needlework; optional classes were also given in music, dance, and French. At the same time, Gordon volunteered several hours a week of Russian lessons in the local *talmud-torah*—the public elementary school of the Jewish community, which usually taught the children of parents who could not afford a private ḥeder. As Gordon himself noted, this was the first time that Russian-language lessons were offered in such a setting in the whole Lithuanian region.[1]

Gordon's general mood of optimism and accomplishment was undoubtedly buoyed by a more private event: on Yom Kippur 1861, Bella gave birth to a son, whom Gordon named Asher in memory of his father. Significantly, the boy was never called by his Hebrew name, or by Osip, the Russian name that Gordon used in his patronymic. Rather, the child was registered in the town rolls as Oscar Gordon and was always referred to by that Western European appellation.[2]

In the months after his son's birth, Judah Leib Gordon returned to his research on the history of the fable and reworked the introduction to *The Fables of Judah* into a scholarly essay in Russian entitled "The History of Fables among the Jews." He attempted to have this study published in either a Russian or a Russian-Jewish periodical, but was unable to counter the opposition of the government censors.[3] At the same time, he outlined a proposal for a Hebrew-language journal that would include belles lettres, scholarship, and current affairs. This project, too, never saw the light of day.

Despite these failures, Gordon's own literary efforts were still in demand. A new Hebrew periodical, *Ha-Karmel* (The Carmel), founded in Vilna by the rather old-fashioned maskil Samuel Joseph Fin, published a variety of Gordon's short pieces, including reworkings of poems by Byron, Leopold Scheffer, and various French authors. Perhaps most interesting of these efforts was a short poem that mourned the passing of *Razsvet,* the first Russian-language Jewish periodical, which expired after only one year of publication for want of a sufficient audience and a coherent editorial line on how best to deal with the reform of the Jews.[4] The question that had confounded the defunct *Razsvet* was the everlasting dilemma of whether to air dirty Jewish laundry in public. The Haskalah clearly and forthrightly located the ills plaguing the Jews in their own rejection of European civilization. This diagnosis was controversial even when trumpeted solely among Jews, in their own publications, journals, and languages. But the controversy mounted when the same analysis was presented in a European language, accessible not only to those sincerely anxious to improve the lot of the Jews but also to those seeking to harm them. For this reason, many Jews who were committed to the goals and even to the politics of the Haskalah opposed the articulation of its principles in the Russian language. Thus, the journal *Ha-Maggid,* stalwart in a conservative interpretation of Enlightenment that already had resulted in a clash with Gordon, took him to task for his elegy on *Razsvet,* asking, "Poet, why do you cry?"—why mourn the passing of something that hurt the Jews?[5]

Gordon responded with an eloquent poem called "This Is Why I Cry," which went one step farther than "The Way of My People" in advancing his attempt to merge the poetic medium with the message of the Haskalah. Here Gordon presented three defenses of the Russian journal. First, every gracious act of the government in regard to the Jews is attacked by many Russian newspapers, and it is essential that the Jews be able to respond forcefully to these attacks in the Russian language itself. Second, Jews around the world—from Bologna to Damascus to St. Petersburg—are besieged by enemies, and *Razsvet* proudly defended Jewish honor; that alone is sufficient reason to mourn its passing. Finally and most important, *Razsvet* alone among Jewish journals had the gumption to stand up against the basic evil confronting the Jews:

> We have been indentured to those lacking wisdom,
> To cruel treasurers and foolish syndics,
> Stringent rabbis and ignorant teachers.
> The first are chosen by bribes and drink;
> The second line their pockets and neglect their work;
> The teachers thrash around like blind men without guides;
> The rabbis rule harshly, ignoring the results.[6]

After the demise of *Razsvet,* however, Jewish journalism in the Russian language was not dead. Another publication was quickly launched with basically the same purpose (and, as soon became apparent, the same irresoluble problems) as its predecessor. This weekly, entitled *Sion* (Zion) and edited by two Odessa Jewish physicians, Emanuel Soloveichik and Leon Pinsker, tried to strike a more scholarly tone than had *Razsvet,* in order to avoid the acid polemic over Jewish identity that was the inescapable leitmotif of Russian-Jewish politics. Very quickly, however, the inevitable debate resumed: ought the Jews in Russia follow the lead of the Jews of the West? If so, how? If not, were they to assimilate into Russian society or remain isolated in the traditional web of East European Jewry? What ought to be the medium of culture and enlightenment for the Jews—Russian, Yiddish, Hebrew, German?

Gordon threw his hat into this contentious ring with an article entitled "The Hebrew Language Among Russian Jews," published in *Sion* in late October 1861.[7] The essay began with the general observation that while all intelligent people agree to the proposition that significant events inevitably influence the character and development of individual persons or entire nations, they beg the question when they turn to the reasons for the sad contemporary state of Russian Jews. But it is obvious that the historical persecutions of the Jews and their ghettoization are entirely at fault for their present isolation as well as for their fear of contact with the outside world. What has happened is simple: what was once forced upon the Jews has over the centuries become natural to them. Thus, for example, Jewish women must originally have bewailed the loss of their hair upon marriage; now the attempts at outlawing such barbarous practices are looked upon with alarm by the Jews themselves. Similarly, for centuries Jews were excluded from European schools and universities; as a result, they are terribly suspicious of modern educational institutions and methods.

Any rational analysis of the Jews' estrangement from Western culture must conclude that this is simply the result of historical circumstances, Gordon continued, and in no way a natural and inevitable attribute of the "national Jewish character." There is such a thing as a "national Jewish character," but that has always been entirely open to beneficial influences from the outside world. This receptivity is amply documented in all phases and products of Jewish creativity: The later Prophets demonstrate the integration by the Jews of Babylonian theological concepts and culture after the first Exile. The Jewish sects of the Second Temple era were clearly based on Hellenistic models, as was Philo's philosophical system and the Septuagint, which resolutely demonstrated the influence of rationalistic Greek philosophy on a Jewish world eager to respond to changing times in dramatic ways. The Mishnah, Talmud, and Midrash are infused with the spirit of ancient Rome and Persia as well as countless borrowings from their languages. The Spanish Jews' creativity in all branches of human culture is testimony not only to their openness to non-Jewish civilization but to their fluency in the Arabic language as well. Similarly, the Jews of Italy were able to maintain their ancient patrimony while immersing themselves in the splendors of their environment. And, of course, as soon as the Jews of Western Europe were permitted to shed their insularity, they became a vital part of civilization as a whole.

Indeed, even the very symbol of Ashkenazic Jewish separateness, the insipid dialect that East European Jews persist in speaking to the disgust of all educated Jews, is itself evidence of the receptivity of the Jewish people to external influence. For Yiddish—which Gordon referred to in the standard terms of the day as the "German-Jewish jargon"—is in and of itself a perfect mirror and source of Jewish history in Exile. While a complete archeology of the Yiddish language is still unavailable, it is abundantly clear that every degradation suffered by the Jewish people, every expulsion, every persecution is embodied in one layer or another of their daily language. But even the blackest cloud has a silver lining, however tattered: the isolation of the Jews, symbolized by their jargon, caused them to dig even deeper into the wellsprings of their own culture, their own religious truths. Yiddish, for its part, contributed to the preservation and development of the Hebrew language.

This is the main point: the Hebrew language is essential to every Jew, in all segments of society, on every level of education. Every Jew requires knowledge of the tongue spoken by his ancestors, prophets, and kings (whom Gordon refers to in Russian not with the standard word for king, *korol'*, but with the more evocative *tsar'*.) Hebrew is crucial to a correct understanding of Jewish liturgy and jurisprudence and, most important, to a precise comprehension of the Bible. Any translation of the Scriptures invariably results in foreign admixtures, forcing the Jews to rely on possibly biased interpretations. A self-respecting Jew must be able to approach the Scripture without a Christianized medium.

But, Gordon continued, Hebrew must not only be preserved for antiquarian elucidation: it must be advanced as the key to continuous Jewish cultural enrichment. The Russian intellectual world, which is beginning to welcome Jews into its midst, rightly demands that they not come empty-handed, but bring with them the treasures of their two-thousand-year culture. The spiritual and literary gems of the Talmud and Midrash, of Maimonides, Ibn Gabirol, Ibn Ezra, and Judah Halevi are entirely unknown to the Russian world, as are Hebrew liturgical and secular poetry. It is correct to demand of educated Jews wishing to enjoy the benefits of European culture that they contribute to the general good the fruits of their own history and literature.

Moreover, it is the duty of educated Jews to devote themselves to the enlightenment of Jewish society as a whole, to "lead the masses of their people to contemporary civilization." This cannot as yet be done in Russian, for most Jews do not have that tongue, and should not be done in Yiddish, which is by its very nature detrimental to enlightenment. Hebrew is the only effective means to enlightenment and must be enlivened in the battle. But Hebrew must not be cultivated solely as a temporary instrument of education, Gordon insisted. On the contrary,

in the interests of our religion and our nationality, and in the fight against ever-growing indifference, do we not have the duty to preserve the means of spiritual unification of our brothers in faith spread across the entire globe? If Latin preserved the unity of the educated world for centuries and in fact still keeps the unity of the Catholics intact, then it is even more correct to regard Hebrew as the only means to the maintenance of our national-spiritual unity.[8]

Ironically, Gordon conceded, the unifying power of Hebrew has been most effectively preserved in those areas of the Jewish world least open to Western civilization. In the West, the commitment to acculturation has resulted in the effective abandonment of Hebrew. As a result, Jews in Germany, France, and Italy have learned how to educate their children as Europeans but have no notion of how to rear them as Jews. This has caused a great deal of pain to the most sincere and committed Jews of these lands, but it is difficult to imagine that the loss can be redressed. In Eastern Europe, in contrast, Jews have been forced to retain their fluency and to express their creativity in the ancient tongue. For obvious reasons, they have not been able to produce in their midst great Jewish scholarship in the vernacular, on the order of the works in German by Zunz, Jost, Phillipsohn, Graetz, Frankel, Steinschneider, and the rest. But even these greats bemoan the abandonment of Hebrew and its magnificent possibilities on the part of West European Jews. Therefore, the best opportunity for effectuating a synthesis between Europeanism and Judaism lies with the Russian Jews. In the name both of European civilization as a whole and the Jewish national and spiritual heritage in particular, Russian Jews can and must devote themselves to two simultaneous, and utterly complementary, tasks: to learn to speak, think, and create in Russian while at the same time retaining and advancing the religious and literary treasures of the Hebrew language.

This was the credo that Judah Leib Gordon was to uphold, propagate, and defend for the rest of his life, in article after article, poem upon poem, countless feuilletons and endless letters, in Russian, Hebrew, German, and ultimately even in Yiddish. The essential message was never to change, though repetition would lead to clarification, maturity to refinement, and new challenges to subtle shifts of tone and emphases. But the obstacles to this hoped-for synthesis were substantial, as Gordon himself admitted in a poem called "On Mt. Zion Laid Waste"—an elegy to *Sion:* soon after printing his article, the young periodical folded.[9]

In the aftermath of this second setback to Russian-Jewish cultural interaction, in late 1862 or early 1863, Gordon composed what would become his most famous paean to enlightenment and integration, his poem "Awake, My People!" [*Hakizah 'ami*]. Given its importance in his life and work, this poem bears citation in full:

> Awake, my people! How long will you sleep?
> The night has passed, the sun shines through.
> Awake, cast your eyes hither and yon
> Recognize your time and your place.
>
> Has the march of time stood still
> From the day you left for all parts of the globe?
> Thousands of years have come and gone
> Since your freedom was lost and you wandered away.
>
> Many generations have been born and died
> Oceans and continents have intervened
> Remarkable changes have taken place
> A different world engulfs us today.

Awake, my people! How long will you sleep?
The night has passed, the sun shines through
Awake, cast your eyes hither and yon
Recognize your time and your place.

The land where we live and are born
Is it not thought to be part of Europe?
Europe, the smallest of continents
But the mightiest of all in wisdom and knowledge.

This land of Eden is now open to you,
Its sons now call you "brothers."
How long will you dwell among them as a guest
Why do you reject their hand?

They have already removed the burden from your back
And lifted the yoke from around your neck
They have erased from their hearts hatred and folly
They stretch out their hands to you in peace.

So raise your head high, stand up straight
Look at them with loving eyes,
Open your hearts to wisdom and reason
Become an enlightened nation, speaking their tongue.

Everyone capable of learning should study
Laborers and artisans should take to a craft
The strong and the brave should be soldiers
Farmers should buy fields and ploughs.

To the treasury of the state bring your wealth
Bear your share of its riches and bounty
Be a man in the streets and a Jew at home
A brother to your countryman and a servant to your king.

Awake, my people! How long will you sleep?
The night has passed, the sun shines through,
Awake, cast your eyes hither and yon
Recognize your time and your place.[10]

For years Gordon had been striving to cast into verse his most heartfelt beliefs. Here, for the first time, he was able to find the words, the rhymes, and the melody that would perfectly capture and convey his song of enrapture and of hope. In its obvious message "Awake, My People!" contained little that had not been said hundreds of times before in Haskalah panegyrics from the time of Moses Mendelssohn on, and dozens of times beforehand in Judah Leib Gordon's own works. But in the sixth-to-last line of this poem Gordon hit upon the most striking and the most memorable phrase he ever wrote, five words that would be known by heart to hundreds of thousands, if not millions, of Jews who might never have read anything else he wrote: *"Heyeh 'adam be-z̦'etkha vi-yehudi be-'ohalekha"*—literally, "Be a man in your going out and a Jew in your tents." Hebrew readers clearly heard and marked the resonances of the biblical imperative in the penultimate chapter of Deuteronomy: "Rejoice O Zebulun in thy going out, and Issachar in thy tents."

But what exactly did Gordon mean to say in his reworking of this injunction? The line quickly became famous as the summation of the Russian Haskalah, but it has generally been taken to urge something entirely at odds with Gordon's own view of the world. The prevailing interpretation of "Be a man in the streets and a Jew at home" is a variation on the following theme:[11] Drawing on the standard Enlightenment distinction between the realms of the sacred and the secular, between the private and the public domain—a distinction perhaps first articulated in Hebrew in Hartwig Wessely's *Words of Peace and of Truth,* which differentiated between the "wisdom of man" and the "wisdom of God"—Gordon proposed a sharp contrast between man and Jew. In so doing, and in line with the general naive taxonomy of the Haskalah, Gordon advocated a bifurcation of Jewish identity that was the Jewish version, as it were, of the separation between church and state. In his famous line, Gordon called on the Jews to limit their Jewishness to the home or synagogue and to suppress it in public, in other words, to deny their nationality, become part of society around them, and relegate Judaism to the private sphere of life. In the pathological course leading from Haskalah to assimilationism to self-hatred, Gordon's dictum early on epitomized the psychic damage inflicted on modern Jews by the specious distinction between man and Jew.

This interpretation of "Be a man in the streets and a Jew at home" was first adumbrated, it seems, by the Zionist ideologue Moshe Leib Lilienblum in an important critique of Gordon that will be discussed at length later in this study.[12] Lilienblum's attack on Gordon and the Haskalah as a whole was trenchant, devastating, and vastly influential. In this respect, it also was utterly misleading in that it represented Gordon preaching something entirely at odds with his view of the world and of the Jews.

Judah Leib Gordon's cultural and linguistic ideology—as exemplified in his last work before "Awake, My People!," the Russian article "Hebrew among Russian Jews"—was an intriguing variation on the melange of Romanticism and the rationalist faith in the power of education that was characteristic of liberals in Russia and the West in his day. Gordon provided, as it were, a Judaized gloss of this worldview, which entailed, among many other things, a reworking of the old Enlightenment dichotomy between the realm of the secular and the realm of the sacred. For him, the crucial distinction was not between church and state, or between religion and nationality—such a differentiation was foreign both to Jewish self-conception and to Russian realities. Rather, the distinction called for by the new age of progress and humanity, and crucial to the future of the Jew, was between two different aspects of culture, two different but ultimately complementary facets of life. Russian Jews must at one and the same time partake of the shared culture of civilized European man—which for them meant assimilating to the local version of that genus by adopting the Russian language, Russian mores, and Russian patriotism—*and* remain vibrantly attached to the specific tradition of the Jews. That tradition could be defined neither as a religion nor as a nation, but as a "national-spiritual" whole. This national-spiritual whole, Gordon insisted, evolves throughout time in consonance with its environment. For Jews to ignore universal culture is thus not only to deprive themselves of the beneficent blessings of civilization but also to deny their own true heritage, for the natural state of the Jews, destroyed by the bigoted ravages of the Middle Ages, is one of integration with the outside world.

For Jews to cut themselves off from Jewish culture, on the other hand, is to deny the very possibility of continued creativity and to render sterile their spiritual life. The modernization of the Jews, therefore, requires their assimilation to Russian culture, their becoming loyal and equal citizens of the tsar, *and* their remaining proud, loyal, and creative Jews. Only by combining all these elements, moreover, will the Jews be true to themselves and creative contributors to civilization as a whole. "Be a man in the streets and a Jew at home," therefore, was a call not for the bifurcation of Jewish identity, but for its integration; it advocated being both a full-fledged man—a free, modern, enlightened Russian-speaking *Mensch*—and a Jew at home in the creative spirit of the Hebrew heritage.

Gordon not only preached this message but lived by it as well, attempting to turn his life and those of his loved ones into paradigms of an integrated Russian-Jewish existence. On the intellectual front, he assisted in the creation of a bilingual Russian-Jewish scholarship by publishing learned articles on "Ancient Babylonia and its Scholars" in Hebrew and on "The Meaning of Various Proper Names in the Talmud" in Russian.[13] On the more personal front, he strained his meager salary to support his three brothers while they trained for admission into Russian educated society. His youngest brother entered the gymnasium of Shavli, another moved from the Vilna rabbinical seminary to the University of Moscow to study law, and a third was enrolled in the University of Kiev.[14]

In the summer of 1862, Gordon faced an unexpected challenge to his commitment to Russification: Hayim Zelig Slonimsky, the distinguished conservative maskil, scientist, and inventor who edited the prestigious Warsaw Hebrew journal *Ha-Zefirah* (The Dawn), was appointed inspector of the state-sponsored rabbinical seminary in Zhitomir and nominated Gordon to replace him as editor. Gordon considered the offer, but turned it down, explaining that the proferred salary was not sufficient to support his household in a large city such as Warsaw and that he had intimations from the authorities that he might be promoted to a better post in the Jewish school system.[15] It is intriguing to ponder what would have happened to Gordon and his image of the future had he in fact accepted the appointment in the Polish capital. For only a few months after he turned down the position, Warsaw and the rest of the former commonwealth exploded in insurrection. The Polish Uprising of 1863 was far better organized, if weaker militarily, than its predecessor, which had accompanied Gordon's birth thirty-two years earlier. In the first six months of 1863, the rebellion spread like wildfire from Warsaw and the rest of Congress Poland to the Lithuanian, Belorussian, and Ukrainian provinces. In Lithuania alone there were over two hundred armed skirmishes between Polish partisans and Russian soldiers. After the rebellion was crushed, the Russian authorities retaliated in an intense, cruel, and efficient suppression of Polish culture and politics. In Gordon's backyard, Lithuania, repression of the Poles and their civilization was particularly crude, as the tsar's plenipotentiary set into motion a reign of terror that killed, exiled, and maimed countless people.

The effect of this crisis on the Jews was complex. The Russian authorities were unsure of how to treat the Jews in the wake of the rebellion: this time, as opposed to 1830–1831, many Jews—particularly in the Congress Kingdom—did join the fight on the side of Polish freedom. On the other hand, the vast majority of the Jews, particularly in the Lithuanian, Ukrainian, and Belorussian provinces, still viewed the Polish struggle as irrelevant to their lives and either remained aloof from the battle or in some measure supported the tsarist regime. It began to dawn on some Russian officials that the Jews could possibly be used as a conduit of Russification in the formerly Polish provinces.[16] Judah Leib Gordon was a prime candidate for collaboration in such a policy. Though born in Vilna in the heat of Polish national fervor, he harbored absolutely no sympathy for the Polish cause. In a long report from Shavli published in the *Allgemeine Zeitung des Judentums* in October 1863, for example, Gordon enthusiastically repeated his unilaterally pro-Russian position. Central to his concerns was, of course, the attitude of the respective forces to the Jews. To his German-Jewish readers, Gordon reported that the tsarist forces sent to Lithuania to quell the uprising were remarkably well disposed to the Jews. On Yom Kippur and Simḥat Torah the Jews were allowed to celebrate their holidays despite curfews and bans on public conduct, and high-placed military officials even attended synagogues and made sure that their troops behaved. At first, the Russian military command suspected the Jews of support for the Poles, but slowly, surely, the Jews' loyalty to Russia was demonstrated beyond a doubt.

However, Gordon continued, that loyalty is not entirely altruistic; it is based on a conscious calculation of self-interest as "subjects who await the amelioration of their present status and the safeguarding of their future through the peaceful development of the state as well as voluntary concessions on the part of the legitimate regime."[17] In a tone far more strident than he had evinced before, Gordon fleshed out the bases of his call to the Jews in "Awake, My People!"—to be not only men in the streets and Jews at home but also "brothers to your countrymen and servants to your king." There are rumors afloat, he reported, that the government would extend to broader segments of the Jewish population the right to settle outside of the Pale of Settlement. But such an extension was not being calculated as a result of the victory of the century-old struggle for Jewish freedom of mobility in the Russian Empire or, indeed, out of any principled opposition to the uncivilized treatment of the Jews. Rather, the government was speculating that the movement of Jewish entrepreneurs into the interior of Russia would stimulate competition in industry and commerce and hence raise the productivity of the Russians.

Gordon forcefully rejected such reasoning. Our fatherland must recognize us as true subjects and equal citizens, he argued, and must grant us rights not as a means to the improvement of others but for our own benefit and in the name of justice. Jewish history is replete with examples of Jews being used as pawns between opposing groups, and the result of such actions is always disastrous. Free mobility of the Jews in Russia must be acknowledged as an innate right and must be attained as the first fruit of emancipation. The same is true of the rumored permission of Jewish graduates of educational institutions to enter the Russian civil service; that is fine and good, Gordon asserted, but insufficient—as Leopold Zunz put it, "The time has come for the Jews in Europe to be granted justice and freedom instead of rights and freedoms [*Recht und Freiheit statt der Rechte und der Freiheiten*]."[18]

This position evoked an interesting protest from the editor of the *Allgemeine Zeitung* himself, the veteran battler for German-Jewish emancipation Ludwig Phillipsohn. In a footnote to Gordon's report, Phillipsohn cautioned his young Russian friend not to be so wary of rights gained solely for material, rather than ideological, reasons. Basing himself on the experience of German Jewry's substantial social, economic, and even political gains without full legal emancipation, Phillipsohn counseled that victories that stem from economic raison d'état are more lasting than those based on alleged liberal principles. In any event, it is the solidity and quality of the freedom rather than the condition of its attainment that is important.[19]

For Gordon—*Ostjude* through and through, despite his presumptive emulation of West European Jewish mores—patience was hard to come by and principle outweighed practicality. After this rather astonishing call for the emancipation of the Russian Jews—a demand that could not, even in the most liberal hours of Alexander II's reign, be made with equal candor in a newspaper published in Russia—he turned to the pace of the modernization of Jewish culture in Russia and displayed equal impatience. He had recently visited the liberal synagogue in Vilna, which had been founded sixteen years earlier by a handful of maskilim. Unfortunately, no progress could be reported on this score: the synagogue building was still primitive, tiny, and rather undignified. Had the progressive Jews of Vilna made so little progress since 1847 that they could not improve their synagogue or so much progress that they were no longer interested in a house of prayer? The writer I. M. Dik was on the right track when he rose in front of the congregation at the end of Yom Kippur services and announced: "Gentlemen! The synagogue board announces that next year, Rosh Hashanah services will begin at 7:00 A.M."

Behind this anecdote, Gordon warned, lay a grave danger facing Jewish Enlightenment even in Vilna: it must not succumb to "indifference with regard to everything national, and must proceed hand-in-hand with rational faith and refined worship."[20] The neglect of the progressive synagogue is a symbolic augury of disaster for the spiritual health of the enlightened Jewish community. Perhaps the situation can be improved if a sermon in the German language is introduced, to help revive the cold hearts of the worshippers bored by formulaic prayers. But even this recommendation is unlikely to have much effect on the spread of indifference to Jewish concerns on the part of Vilna's enlightened Jews. Emblematic of their indifference is that not one copy of the *Allgemeine Zeitung des Judentums* ever reaches Vilna, and it is the only Jewish newspaper in a living tongue in the entire world. The ignorance of matters Jewish is not confined to the Vilna modernists. In Grodno, a Jewish public library has been open for a year, but it contains only Russian newspapers and political tracts and not one book or periodical on Jewish concerns. The members of this library think of themselves as enlightened and progressive Jews, but are entirely ignorant of modern Jewish culture outside of their narrow confines; they have never heard of Jost's or Graetz's histories of the Jews or the other grand accomplishments of contemporary Jewish scholarship. Their only modern authorities on Judaism are a local government rabbi and supervisor of a state school who are neither willing nor able to lead their community to see that it is possible to forge a better, purer, and more attractive form of Judaism.[21]

Thus, even in 1863, at the time of the composition of "Awake, My People!," at the very apogee of his optimism over the inevitability of emancipation and reform, Gordon was assailed by the realization that the Haskalah—like so many ideologies that insist on the inevitability of progress but depend for their success on human bearers of the message—depended on a very delicate balance between the march of history and its mortal subjects. Throughout his subsequent career he would at one and the same time express complete confidence in the ideology of the Haskalah and grave misgivings about its implementation by irresponsible or ignorant louts. To chart Judah Leib Gordon's intellectual and spiritual course, it is necessary to remain alert to such rumblings without mistaking them for shifts of belief or ideological turns.

To a former pupil and close friend he confessed in private that the challenge was exhausting, if not overwhelming: Here I am, at age thirty-three, already past my prime, working without rest from dawn to dusk, running from lesson to lesson, from school to school, struggling to earn my keep, never having a moment to pause and catch my breath, to enjoy myself or my family. In the evenings I try to feed my soul, to pour out my feelings in ink, but no sooner do I begin than my eyelids shut of their own accord, and when I awake, the grind begins again. There seems to be no hope, but then I look around and am inspired: the times truly are changing. Only a short time ago a Jewish student who wanted to attend a gymnasium had to hide his uniform at school and sneak through the streets in traditional ghetto garb; only when he reached the safe halls of the gymnasium could he don his mark of civility and hide his sidelocks behind his ears and under the cap of education. But now, even in the most obscure Jewish townlets, eyes are being opened, minds are expanding, and in the light of day thousands of young Russian Jews are streaming to the gymnasia, searching for knowledge, and struggling for tolerance. Hundreds of their brothers are attending universities, becoming physicians, lawyers, pharmacists. In many towns, Jewish doctors are already at work as government physicians, healing the sick and improving the collective lot of their nation. The number of Russian Jews speaking Russian, German, or French is continuously growing, and in the highest reaches of the land there are respected Jews, publicly proud of their heritage but outwardly civilized Europeans. The challenge is formidable, the obstacles are mighty, but the future is ours.[22]

In March 1864, Gordon took an important step toward playing an even more public role in that future. In a long letter to the newly formed Society for the Promotion of Enlightenment among the Jews of Russia, he listed the various measures that he would recommend for the spread of Western education among his compatriots: concentrating on small towns rather than large cities; appealing to the government for financial support of maskilim who require aid; improving the state-sponsored Jewish schools, which are the most important medium of enlightenment, but are in a terrible disarray and ought to be reformed to follow more closely the model of the German-Jewish community schools; publishing a Russian-language periodical for the Jews that would consciously follow the lead of the journals of Leopold Zunz and Zecharias Frankel and concentrate solely on scholarship and literature and not on current affairs. In addition, he offered to make available to the society fifty copies of his books for Jewish libraries around the empire and asked that a library for Jewish girls that he had just opened in Shavli be added to the list of such institutions.[23]

Far more important than the specific recommendations contained in this letter was its establishment of a firm link between Gordon and the society, already the bulwark of the Jewish Enlightenment in the Russian Empire. Soon after offering his help to the society, he was elected a member of its relatively exclusive ranks. The newly emerging leadership of Russian Jewry, based in St. Petersburg and reflecting the political and cultural coloration of that most European of Russian cities, was slowly becoming aware of the ambitious young teacher in the provinces. Within a decade, he would be summoned to the capital to head the society itself.

Meanwhile, he was still barely eking out a living as an ill-paid, overworked teacher in a stultifying and poor town in which he had virtually no kindred spirit to commune with. His poetic work in this period testifies to the doubts and pessimism that coexisted in his mind with his trust in humanity, in the Enlightenment, and in the Russian state. Thus, only a few months after penning his letter to St. Petersburg, he sent off—to the same friend to whom he had earlier confessed his ambivalence—a copy of the first part of a new work entitled, after the euphemism for a cemetery in Job 30:23, "The House Assigned for All the Living" [*Bet mo'ed le-khol ḥai*]. This three-part elegy begins with a citation from the Russian poet V. A. Zhukovsky ("Who knows what awaits us beyond the grave?") and is clearly a reworking of Zhukovsky's own translation of Thomas Gray's "Elegy Written in a Country Churchyard."[24]

Gordon's variation on these famous meditations at a graveyard differ from their models in fundamental ways. Like Gray and Zhukovsky, Gordon reflects on the leveling nature of death, bemoans the loss of those taken away before their lives were fulfilled, and wonders how many geniuses and lovers lay silent and buried under the ground. But Gordon's musings on death entirely lack the essential theme of his predecessors—sympathy for the little, obscure man, as noble as the greatest artist or soldier laborers. Gray had sung (and Zhukovsky had reproduced in his mellifluous Russian):

> Beneath those ruggled elms, that yew-tree's shade
> Where heaves the turf in many a mould'ring heap,
> Each in his narrow cell for ever laid,
> The rude Forefathers of the hamlet sleep. . . .
>
> Let not Ambition mock their useful toil,
> Their homely joys, and destiny obscure;
> Nor Grandeur hear with a disdainful smile
> The short and simple annals of the poor.[25]

Gordon's "The House Assigned for All the Living" has none of this glorification of the lot of the simple villager. To begin with, celebrating the nobility of the simple farmer was alien to Gordon, the elitist Jewish intellectual to whom the folk—whether Russian or Jewish—was the incarnation of ignorance and superstition. The Sentimentalism of Gray and Zhukovsky was for this reason foreign to Gordon's aesthetic; his own road from Neo-Classicism to Romanticism and beyond would take a different turn. Instead of looking to the lowly workman to seek answers to the meaning of life and of death, Gordon directed his gaze to the heavens, reflecting on problems and raising doubts that are absent from (and perhaps irrelevant to) the English and Russian elegists. Thus, Gordon's musings among the tombstones ponder not the democracy of the dead but the constitution of the afterlife:

> Dreadful eternity—who can know its ways?
> It hides like the Lord, who can discern it?

Who can understand what you are, what your plan,
No beginning, no end, no length and no breadth,
No scale, no pace, no size, no measure. . . .

Awake, o awake, you who sleep down under,
Rise up from the dust of rot and ruin,
Open your mouths, move your tongues,
What lies beyond the grave and beyond?
What lies beyond the stars above? . . .
Is there a reckoning and knowledge?
Is there a bridge to the other side?[26]

This was not the first time that Gordon's poetry dealt with the meaning of death and of Providence, but it was the first time that grave ontological doubts were introduced in his verse and not satisfactorily resolved in a traditional manner. Indeed, this elegy marked a crucial shift in Gordon's poetic direction: for the next several years, theological queries and gnawing doubts about the hidden God would begin to consume Gordon's mind and to dominate his muse.

This major change of course occurred in the period of Gordon's life that is most resistant to reconstruction, due to an unfortunate documentary gap. Gordon's ample correspondence, which covers virtually every aspect of his public and private life from 1857 on, has not been preserved for the twenty months between August 1864 and April 1866. By Gordon's own testimony, however, it was precisely at this time that he wrote several of his most important new poems and contracted for the publication of a new book, *The Songs of Judah* [*Shirei Yehudah*]. In the first letter to be preserved after the hiatus, Gordon complained that he had not heard a word from the publisher. As it turned out, the man who had promised to publish the book had become involved in a serious criminal case in Vilna and had skipped town to avoid the police, Gordon's manuscript in tow. He later surfaced in Warsaw as a proofreader for a Hebrew printer and never delivered on his promise to issue *The Songs of Judah.*[27]

For the next two years, Gordon would struggle to have his new collection of poems see the light of day. He drew up a new contract with the publisher of *Ha-Karmel* in Vilna and in March 1867 delivered a copy of the manuscript to him; the book sat at the press for months without any movement. At the end of May 1867, the manuscript was approved by the government censor in Vilna. Still, the volume remained at the printer, to Gordon's mounting frustration, for a whole year and appeared only in May 1868.[28]

It is abundantly clear, therefore, that *The Songs of Judah* was completed by Gordon some time in 1865. Of the thirty-five poems included in the volume, twenty-one had either appeared in print by 1865 or were dated by Gordon himself as having been written between 1851 and 1865; none was ever attributed by Gordon to a later year.

This chronology of *The Songs of Judah* raises serious questions about one of the most common assumptions of the scholarly literature on Judah Leib Gordon as poet. Basing themselves on Gordon's own claim in the introduction to his *Collected Works,* published in 1884, that his poems could easily be divided into two periods—a youthful period of beautiful but nonuseful poems and a mature period of simply put didactic and satirical verses[29]—critics have maintained that *The Songs of Judah,* in the words of one influential Hebrew literary historian,

> stands on the border between Gordon's Romantic period and his Realistic period. . . . Gordon became a thorough Realist under the influence of the currents at play in Russia in the [18]60s and 70s. It was difficult for any sensitive man not to be influenced by the articles of Pisarev, Chernyshevsky, and Dobroliubov, by the sharply satiric stories of the Russian writers Gogol and Saltykov-Shchedrin, and by Nekrasov's poems of rebuke.[30]

In line with this evaluation, 1867—the year in which Gordon delivered the manuscript of *The Songs of Judah* to its ultimate publisher—was taken to mark the crucial watershed in his development. The poems included in this volume were themselves neatly divided into two classifications: Romantic, representing Gordon's work before 1867; and Realistic, characteristic of his creative outlook thereafter. Indeed, some poems were seen as straddling both categories, including some stanzas that belonged to the earlier type of poetry and others belonging to the later. Thus, some poems written in the early 1860s—most notably "Awake, My People!" "The Way of My People," and the elegies on *Sion* and *Razsvet*—supposedly belonged to Gordon's Realistic period, while works written later, including the bulk of the new poems in the volume, allegedly adhered to the earlier period.

This taxonomy of *The Songs of Judah* obviously cannot be reconciled with Gordon's own dating of his works. But the problem is not simply a pedantic quibble over precisely when the new book was written; the chronological confusion is the least of the problems inherent in this evaluation of *The Songs of Judah.* More substantive is the notion that there was a sea change in Gordon's poetics that occurred either with or immediately after the completion of this book, and that this transformation can be explained as a movement from Romanticism to Realism; that Gordon was a Romantic until some point and then became a Realist under the influence of the Russian "nihilist" critics. There is ample and incontrovertible evidence, however, from Gordon's own pen that this particular "sensitive man" living in Russia in the 1860s and 1870s was not only not influenced by the aesthetic theories of the Russian Realist critics Pisarev, Chernyshevsky, and Dobroliubov, but was fervently opposed to them.

The first piece of evidence is the first poem in *The Songs of Judah* itself. This is a new fable entitled "The Nightingale and the Wasp," submitted, as Gordon says, "in place of an introduction." This fable begins with the wasp complaining that the nightingale's songs serve no useful purpose either to contemporaries or to those who will follow and moreover sin against the spirit of the time, for

> Now is the time to do only things useful!
> Every enlightened being
> Must labor to this end.
> If you claim to be enlightened
> You must hearken to this truth
> Abandon your songs
> Toil like an ant
> Spin webs like a spider

> Build like a beaver
> Spread honey and wax like a bee.[31]

But the nightingale refuses to heed this call. Perhaps you're right, he concedes to the wasp, but I won't change my tune, for to do so would be to traduce my very nature. This is what God created me to do; indeed, this is why He implanted in me His spirit and His mission. Far from adopting the wasp's call for utility in song, "I shall continue to sing the way I have always sung."[32]

This fable can only be understood as a direct response to the charges leveled by the Russian nihilist critics and their Jewish apostles against what they termed non-useful literature. There is no need for speculation on this point: precisely at the time that Gordon was putting the final touches on *The Songs of Judah* and composing this fable, the Hebrew writer Avraham Uri Kovner published the first of a series of rather simpleminded rehashings in Hebrew of the aesthetic theories of the Russian nihilist critics. Kovner was, to say the least, a deeply troubled Vilna Jew who ended his life as a famous cause célèbre: after absconding with the funds of a St. Petersburg bank for which he worked, he was the object of a Europe-wide manhunt that resulted in his eventual capture and subsequent exile to Siberia, where he converted to Russian Orthodoxy in order to marry a peasant girl with whom he had fallen in love.[33] But in the 1860s he was simply the first maskil to attempt to apply the extreme positivist critique of aesthetics to Hebrew literature. Judah Leib Gordon was, of course, keenly aware of Kovner's works and the vituperative controversy they evoked. In the summer of 1866 (in the second letter after the gap in his correspondence), Gordon reported to a friend that he had read Kovner's first collection of essays, *Ḥeker davar* [Reflections], and concluded that "the critic ought to be criticized."[34] What upset Gordon was not especially Kovner's specific claims about the difference between lyrical and realistic poetry, or the notion that "the first criterion for a true poet must be that his poetry contain at all times new ideas, concealed in pleasant scenes. The jewel of a poem is its idea; the form is merely inlaid gold, adding to its lustre and worth."[35] To Gordon, the crucial failing of Kovner's approach was its assumption that Hebrew literature of all time could be subjected to the critical canons of contemporary Russia or Germany, forgetting that each nation and each language has its own spirit and that the Hebrew tongue is as different from its European counterparts as East is from West. Kovner simply cannot condemn all the Hebrew writers from the days of the Talmud through the Middle Ages to the Enlightenment, since they do not conform with his flawed sense of good literature. Given his lack of appreciation for the mutable social context of literature, Kovner cannot evaluate the question of the utility of Hebrew writers through the ages:

> He has forgotten how much indeed they were useful, for without the scholars and writers through the ages we would have ceased to exist and the name of Israel would have disappeared from the world. But these are great issues which cannot be discussed [in a letter.][36]

This was not to imply that Hebrew literature must not be subjected to severe criticism that separates the rubbish from the good, but only that Kovner is not the man to do the job.

Gordon repeated this line of reasoning in a letter he wrote to Kovner after the publication of both *The Songs of Judah* and Kovner's second collection of essays, *A Wreath of Flowers*. Kovner's basic error was to ignore the fact that every poet is the product of his environment and his national culture, and thus one cannot apply the same criteria to every literary or intellectual creation. Moreover, it is nonsensical to ask, as Kovner and his Russian mentors do, that poets, as well as theologians, philosophers, and philologists, be compared to scientists and subordinated to the supremacy of the natural sciences. It is correct to demand that a poet write good poetry, a historian good history, and a linguist good linguistics; but "do not attack a poet for not writing statistics."[37]

On the other hand, Gordon expressed complete agreement with Kovner's arguments against the "impractical direction of modern Hebrew literature" and in favor of the notion that "science and literature must go hand-in-hand with life." These thoughts were contained in one of Kovner's essays that had, at the same time, lavished praise on Gordon's most recent work as the best exemplars of contemporary Hebrew literature. Gordon agreed with these statements by Kovner not only because they praised his work but also because they reflected his basic aesthetic stance. Gordon resolutely repudiated not the very notion of "realism" in art, but the specific, and to him vulgar, positivist version of realism as utterly subordinate to social utility.

Thus, it would be misleading to conclude—as has an influential recent critical reappraisal of Gordon—that his attack on Kovner, either in his letters or in his introduction to *The Songs of Judah,* betokened a thoroughgoing commitment to the purely emotional or lyrical qualities of poetry and a consequent denigration of the pragmatic or didactic effect of a poem as, at best, of secondary or marginal importance.[38] To the contrary, in his letters, critical essays, and indeed in his poetry itself, Gordon repeatedly stressed his vision of the indivisibility of the aesthetic, mimetic, and social aspects of poetry. What was offensive about the new criticism was its untempered reductionist rendering of realism, its presumption of universal canons of the true and the beautiful in the name of science. In "The Wasp and the Nightingale" Gordon forcefully rebuffed this reductionism, pledging to continue to sing the way he had always sung—seeking the harmonious intertwining of form, Hebraic national spirit, and the ideas of the Haskalah.

This aesthetic creed Gordon held firmly both before and after *The Songs of Judah.* Although he did of course abandon the dreaded narrative overkill of his early works in favor of a lighter style and more contemporary subject matter, he did not flit between the categories of "Romanticism" or "Realism" either during or after the completion of this volume. Rather, in his view of poetry and its place in culture he held true, at all times, to the theory of literature that was most commonly held among Westernized (and Westernizing) intellectuals in the Russia of his day—a view that cannot easily be pigeonholed as either Romantic or Realistic. As one contemporary opponent of this point of view noted, there was one literary theorist whose authority held sway throughout the Russian Empire, including its provincial centers, in the late 1850s and early 1860s:

> The name of [Vissarion] Belinsky is known to every thinking young man, to everyone who is hungry for a breath of fresh air in the reeking bog of provincial life. There is

not a country schoolmaster who does not know—and know by heart—Belinsky's
letter to Gogol.[39]

That famous letter accused the author of *Dead Souls* of betraying Russia's trust
by preaching that the road to salvation lay in mysticism or in an obscurantist celebration of Muscovite traditions. To the contrary, Belinsky argued:

> Therefore you failed to realize that Russia sees her salvation not in mysticism or
> asceticism or pietism, but in the successes of civilization, enlightenment, and human-
> ity. What she needs is not sermons (she has heard enough of them!), but the awak-
> ening in the people of a sense of human dignity lost for so many centuries amid dirt
> and refuse; she needs rights and laws conforming not to the preaching of the church
> but to common sense and justice, and their strictest possible observance.[40]

Russia's hope, in other words, lies in education, Western civilization, and humane
culture, and specifically through writers who alone can provide their society with
"its leaders, defenders, and saviours from the darkness of Russian autocracy, orthodoxy, and nationalism."

The aesthetic stance inherent in this passionate plea has long been the subject
of keen debate among Russian intellectual and literary historians, particularly as a
result of Belinsky's posthumous induction into the pantheon of Soviet revolutionary heroes.[41] But despite the fact that Belinsky has been canonized as the originator
of the social criticism of literature, he was in fact as much an enemy of the crude
materialist and utilitarian perception of literature as he was an opponent of notions
of "art for art's sake." He argued at one and the same time that pure art is a dreamy
abstraction that has never existed anywhere, that "poetry has no purpose beyond
itself," and that denying art the right of serving public interests means debasing it.[42]
He was able to resolve these ostensibly contradictory sentiments by insisting that
good art will naturally be an expression of the spirit and the reality of its society;
thus, the social dimension of good poetry cannot be separated artificially from its
purely aesthetic attributes. Similarly, it is easy, and indeed natural and necessary,
for the poet to reconcile his art with service to his community.

As Isaiah Berlin has explained, Belinsky believed in the duty of the artist

> to tell the truth as he alone, being uniquely qualified to see and to utter, sees it and
> can say it; this is the whole duty of a writer, whether he be a thinker or an artist.
> Moreover, he believed that since man lives in society and is largely made by society,
> the truth must necessarily be largely social, and that, for this reason, all forms of
> insulation and escape from environment must, to that degree, be falsifications of the
> truth and treason to it. For him the man and the artist and the citizen are one . . .
> you are morally responsible as a man for what you do as an artist. You must always
> bear witness to the truth, which is one and indivisible, in every act and in every
> word.[43]

It is this view of the nature and function of the poet, with all its cultural and
political corollaries—and perhaps in all its naiveté—that is refracted in Judah Leib
Gordon's self-image, his art, and his incidental comments on aesthetic principles.
Inherent in this view of literature and the mission of the writer is the commitment

to one's own national spirit and national community in such a way as to accord with the march of progress and universal civilization. For Gordon, therefore, the mission of the authentic Hebrew poet was to create aesthetically pleasing works of art that at the same time, as if by definition, reflect and advance the battle for the spiritual and moral elevation of the Jews. While in Russian poetry the true and the beautiful do battle with the autocracy, the Church, and the Muscovite legacy as a whole, the struggle in Hebrew poetry is with the rabbis, the lay leaders of the Jewish community, and the God of Israel as He is manifest in history.

It is the third of these questions that dominates the new poems in *The Songs of Judah,* as Gordon amplified the themes that first arose in his reworking of Zhukovsky and Gray. As an anthology of his poetic works from 1851 to 1865, the collection, to be sure, contained poems of a large variety of genres and approaches. Included were such diverse works as "Awake, My People!," "The Way of My People," "David and Barzilai," and "Unwillingly, You Live!" Some of the newest works, in addition, merely replicated the techniques and themes of Gordon's earlier fables and epics. Thus, for example, "'Asenath, the Daughter of Potifera" written in the summer of 1865, almost exactly paralleled Gordon's *The Love of David and Michal,* written a decade earlier.[44] This new biblical epic elaborates on famous rabbinic conjectures about the relationship between Joseph and his eventual bride, 'Asenath, the daughter of an Egyptian priest. Like *The Love of David and Michal,* the true subject of "'Asenath" is love itself, and especially the romantic, quasi-erotic bond between a devoted woman and a biblical hero. The best that can be said for this poem is that it is marginally more introspective and less wordy than Gordon's previous efforts in this vein; perhaps more important to his poetic development, the biblical narrative is here more and more reduced to a bare dramatic frame, and divine intercession is no longer adduced as the motor of love. But this is far from the crisp and incisive strophes of "Awake, My People!" or "The Way of My People" or even the best of the *Fables of Judah,* not to speak of the other new poems in the collection. Part of the problem was undoubtedly Gordon's continual, and still largely unresolved, struggle to master the form of epic poetry. But there was also something deeper and more portentous at work here: Gordon's personal wrestling with the philosophical meaning of existence in general, and Jewish existence in particular, led him to direct his greatest attention and talent to poems reflecting these critical issues.

The three major new poems of the new collection did have as their focus precisely these new questions. More than that, these poems—"Between the Lions' Teeth," [*Bein shinei 'arayot*] "In the Depths of the Sea," [*Bi-mezulot yam*] and "The Woman and Her Sons," [*Ha-'ishah vi-yladeha*]—all take their cue from one well-known Talmudic passage that itself is devoted to the question of the relationship between God and the Jews. Through the explication of the historical referents of important biblical verses, the rabbis explained the meaning of the destruction of the Temple and then turned to a curious tale:

> On one occasion four hundred boys and girls were carried off for immoral purposes. They divined what they were wanted for and said to themselves, If we drown in the sea we shall attain the life of the future world. The eldest among them expounded the verse [Psalms 68:23] "The Lord said, I will bring again from Bashan, I will bring again

from the depths of the sea." I will bring again from Bashan" [means] from between the lions' teeth [*bein shinei 'aryeh*]. "I will bring again from the depths of the sea" [means] those who drown in the sea. When the girls heard this they all leaped into the sea. The boys then drew the moral for themselves, saying, If these for whom this is natural act so, shall not we, for whom it is unnatural? They also leaped into the sea. Of them the text says, "Yea for thy sake we are killed all the day long, we are counted as sheep for the slaughter." Rab Judah, however, said that this refers to the woman and her seven sons.[45]

The three major new poems in *The Songs of Judah* took their subject matter, their titles, and the order of their presentation from this discourse; their exegesis, however, is profoundly at odds with the original. The first poem, "Between the Lions' Teeth," tells the tale of the simultaneous deaths in Rome of the Jewish guerilla leader Simeon Bar Giora and his wife, Martha. The scene opens on Jerusalem besieged by the Romans, its inhabitants unable to save themselves from the assault. The narrative line is loosely adapted from Josephus; the setting and even the language are openly borrowed from Hebrew translations of the *Iliad,* Byron, and the Austrian poet Ludwig August Frankl. But by the second stanza, Judah Leib Gordon breaks through and in his unmistakable tone interjects:

> You are ruined, Israel, for they have not taught you
> To wage war with wisdom and knowledge
> Strength and rebelliousness yield nought
> In the absence of tactics and discipline.
> For centuries your teachers have led you,
> Built houses of study, but what have they taught you? . . .
> They have taught you to deny real life
> To shut yourselves behind fences within fences
> To be dead to the world, to seek pie in the sky,
> When awake, to dream and to babble in dreams. . . .
> They have taught you to turn away from Reason,
> The source of all good, the refuge from destruction,
> To labor on vain laws and confuse true faith,
> To harden your hearts away from the world
> They've taught you no real skills or wisdom
> To strengthen a nation, to civilize the land,
> You've been filled with petty laws and decrees
> Like a pond full of fish but without water.[46]

This timeless complaint is then restored to history: While Jerusalem was besieged, the sages met in counsel to plan strategy against the Romans, but all they could come up with was one more mindless regurgitation of their picayune prohibitions against intercourse with the outside world. In the hour of crisis there were brave souls who were prepared to go to battle in defense of their land, their nation, and their faith, but they were waylaid by their putative teachers. As a result, they went off utterly unprepared, to meet their inevitable demise.

After the defeat, Simeon, one of the leaders of the failed defense, and his wife part, pledging eternal devotion. The narrator cannot restrain his own emotions in observing this farewell and questions whether the "all-seeing eye" marks these

tears, whether there is any point to this travesty. Simeon is led away in chains, and
Martha is sold into the service of a Roman matron. She is taken to the capital and
later accompanies her mistress to the festivities at the Circus Maximus. Here
stream throngs of Romans eager to celebrate the latest imperial conquest in the
presence of the emperor himself. Into the center of the ring is thrust one of the
conquered Jews—none other than Simeon himself, his physical beauty withstand-
ing the marks of his shackles and torturers' zeal. At the sight of her humiliated
beloved, Martha agonizingly appeals to her God in words reminiscent of Gordon's
elegy at the graveyard:

> All-hearing ear, do you hear my plea?
> Will a redeeming hand appear? Will a miracle occur?
> Or are you hidden eternally in clouds within clouds,
> Abandoning the earth in the hands of murderers?[47]

A fierce and hungry lion is let loose in Simeon's direction. Desperately he turns
his eyes to the heavens, but catches sight of Martha dressed as a slave; his remaining spirit is sapped and he expires, to the immense approval of the crowd. In the
din of delight no one hears a sound as Martha falls to the ground at the sight of her
hero felled in the lions' teeth and dies along with him.

In later years, Judah Leib Gordon would return to this poem several times and
eventually rework it into what several critics have called the most successful
Hebrew narrative poem of the nineteenth century.[48] In the process, Gordon would
shift the tone and the plot slightly, but significantly, by focusing more attention on
the actual struggle between Simeon and the lion and drawing more effectively the
emotional travail of the lovers. Moreover, in the final redaction, written after grave
changes in Judah Leib Gordon's universe, Simeon joins Martha in challenging the
heavens, and the narrator explicitly answers their doubts by announcing that the
former God of Israel has now gone over to the other side, abandoning the Jews to
ceaseless destruction. All hope for redemption is lost.[49] In the original version, however, the theology is far less radical, for Martha's question is left unanswered: Is the
God of Israel simply a hidden God who has left the world in the hands of murderers? If so, what is Israel to do, what is the meaning of its fate?

The next "song of Judah," "In the Depths of the Sea," pursues the same questions in a new historical setting—not the destruction of A.D. 70 but that of 1492.
"In the Depths of the Sea" opens with the exiled from Zion living peacefully and
pleasantly as fully emancipated citizens of the Iberian Pensinsula. The idyll of harmonious fraternity of Muslim and Jew is destroyed, however, by the onslaught of
the evil and errant "priests of iniquity," who, in a recreation of Cain's sin, exile the
Jews from their homes. Europe turns its back on the Jewish refugees and they are
cast onto the open seas, seeking a haven wherever they can. Not only are they at
the mercy of the rulers of the lands beyond the shores, but their very lives are
dependent upon the goodwill of the sailors, who are not much better than pirates.
On one of the boats are to be found the widow of the martyred Rabbi 'Abu-
Sha'am of Tortona and their beautiful and enlightened daughter, Penina. The cap-
tain of their ship becomes enamored of Penina and threatens to drown all the refugees if she does not succumb to his advances. She promises him that when they

reach shore she will do his bidding. To her mother Penina confesses that she will kill herself first, and asks her mother:

> Please tell me, mother, why is God torturing us?
> What iniquity have we committed to merit His anger?
> Of all nations of the earth, why has He chosen us
> As the target of His fury and vengeance?[50]

The pious widow counsels her daughter against such heresy; God is just and will accept their sacrifice as He has accepted that of the other martyrs of Israel, including the rabbi of Tortona. Penina, however, is not convinced; she willingly accepts her fate but implicitly rejects her mother's theological motivation for their suicide: "I would prefer to die than to profane my virtue,/ And like Jephthah's daughter, in my death I shall save my nation!"[51] With this cry, Penina and her mother leap into the sea pledging their faith.

For Penina to cite this particular biblical precedent was to evoke a highly ironic sanction: as related in Judges 11:29-40, Jephthah the Judge made a vow that if he conquered the Ammonites, he would sacrifice to the Lord whatever would first come out of the door of his house upon his return. To his chagrin, as he approached his house, his only daughter emerged. After allowing her to spend two months with her friends bewailing her maidenhood upon the hills, he proceeded to sacrifice her; thereafter, for four days a year, the maidens of Israel would mourn her death. Clearly, this sacrifice was a meaningless act that contributed in no way to the salvation of Israel; the rabbis themselves denounced the sacrifice as a sinful and disgraceful act resulting from Jephthah's ignorance and imprudence. His punishment was dismemberment limb by limb.[52]

Penina's self-sacrifice, then, was at the very least based on a spurious notion of helping her people. The narrator, therefore, is not swept up by the piety of the suicide. Continuing his bold subversion-by-evocation of biblical precedents, he describes the women's death with phrases wrung out of Moses's song at the crossing of the Sea of Reeds and the Psalmist's celebration of the same miracle:

> The sea saw them and fled, its waters quaked
> The waves crashed and stormed
> And the two pure souls of the finest gold
> Sank like lead in the depths of the sea.[53]

No one marked or mourned their sacrifice; the dawn once more lit up the face of the earth, which silently continued its course, not shedding a tear.

If such sacrifice itself is suspect, if the effect on the world is nil, if God is hidden from man, then what possible meaning can martyrdom have? Gordon's answer to this query seems to lie in the story cited in the Talmudic prooftext by Rabbi Judah—that of the woman and her sons, the subject of the third, and last, poem on the theme of martyrdom and destruction in *The Songs of Judah*.

"The Woman and Her Sons"[54] is far less ambitious than either "Between the Lion's Teeth" or "In the Depths of the Sea." Its dramatis personae, however, are some of the most central characters in Jewish martyrology, the woman (frequently

named Hannah) and her seven sons who willingly submit to death rather than profane the faith under the command of the wicked Antiochus IV. In his narrative
line, Gordon did not stray too far from the classical sources of this tale, which he
himself cited as The Second Book of Maccabees and the Talmudic tractate of
divorce.[55] Only in two significant ways did Gordon's variation depart from the traditional versions. First, in Gordon's poem the story ends with the mother and her
youngest son together committing suicide by jumping off a roof. By this invention,
at once the horror is heightened for the reader and is rendered parallel to the simultaneous deaths of Penina and her mother, and even to Simeon and Martha. Perhaps more significant, however, is the difference between the self-proclaimed moral
of Gordon's poem and that of the Apocrypha and the Aggadah. In the Second Book
of Maccabees the narrator ends the story by proclaiming: "Let then this be enough
about eating of idolatrous sacrifices and inhuman tortures"; in the Talmud, the
rabbis follow the description of the lone suicide of the mother with "A voice thereupon came forth from heaven saying, 'A joyful mother of children.'"[56] The lesson
of the tale, quite obviously, was that the self-sacrifice of the martyrs was part of a
divine plan in which God would ultimately wreak vengeance on evil and redeem
His children. By contrast, Gordon's "The Woman and Her Sons" ends with the
following peroration:

> And the snake from the stock of an asp quaked
> And poured forth venom and dismay:
> The strength of a tyrant is vain, his power nought
> He cannot imprison a man's soul.
> All of your cruelty and might
> Could not subdue the woman and her children.[57]

As was his wont and special talent, Gordon's point was made through his dextrous manipulation of biblical imagery and language: "the snake from the stock of
an asp" [nahash mi-shoresh zef‘a] is an inversion of a phrase used only once in the
Bible, in Isaiah 14:29, where the prophet warns Philistia not to rejoice that "the
staff of him that beat you is broken. For from the stock of a snake there sprouts an
asp, a flying seraph branches out it"—in the end, God will redeem the Jews. Here,
once more, the biblical message is subverted by the medium of its evocation: the
snake is no longer a metaphor for the divinely inspired rejuvenation of Israel, but,
like the serpent in Eden, it is the incarnation of evil. Observing this archetypical
case of Jewish martyrdom, the serpent recoils in anger and despair, for it realizes
the vanity of power, the lesson that might cannot in fact vanquish the right.

For Gordon, to rely on divine intercession is to court disaster and self-decep-
tion, for God does not emerge from the clouds. To rely on those who claim to
represent His teachings is equally ill-advised, for "they have destroyed you, they
have taught you to go against life." The only possible moral of this classic story,
then, is the indestructible freedom and dignity of the human being in the face of
oppression and evil. Faced with the formidable challenge before them, the only
appropriate response for the Jews of Russia is to reform themselves to be free and
dignified human beings while remaining vibrant and authentic Jews.

In the end, then, The Songs of Judah must be seen as one coherent text, reflecting not a schizophrenic straddling of opposing worldviews but the salient political and aesthetic ideology that Judah Leib Gordon developed in the course of the first half of the 1860s, from "The Way of My People" and "Awake, My People!" to "Between the Lions' Teeth" and "The Woman and Her Sons" and the many prose pieces along the way. Consistent at once with the mainstream of Westernizing Russian thought and culture in his day, and the traditions of the pan-European Jewish Enlightenment movement, Gordon was slowly finding his true voice, both as poet and as publicist. Still mired in the bogs of provincial Lithuania, he was emerging as a bright young star in the constellation of Russian-Jewish life.

In *The Songs of Judah,* Gordon's transmutation of scriptural precedent in the name of a new ideology was often implicit, accessible only to those able or willing to decode subtle shades of texture and allusion. As Gordon gained more confidence, on the one hand, and became the object of public controversy, on the other, his heterodox identification of the redemption of the Jews with the goals of the Enlightenment would become explicit and the cultural history of Russian Jewry would be permanently transformed.

5

Religious Reform I:
The Battle Is Pitched
1865–1868

Only a few months after the completion of *The Songs of Judah,* Gordon received word of his longed-for transfer to a new position and a new town. This time the authorities were not only transferring him to a new school but also rewarding him with a promotion to a more prestigious and lucrative post—principal of the government Jewish school in Tel'shi, Lithuania.

Roughly the same size as Shavli, Tel'shi (Telz in Yiddish, Telšiai in Lithuanian) lies along the hilly banks of Lake Mastis some 75 kilometers west of the Baltic Sea and 100 kilometers southwest of Riga. Founded in the sixteenth century, Tel'shi grew under the auspices of influential Lithuanian magnates into an important local trading center and seat of the regional dietine. Thirty years before the Russian annexation of 1795, Tel'shi's impressive Baroque church was built, and a secondary school founded by the Franciscans claimed three hundred pupils at the beginning of the nineteenth century. This academy was shut down by the tsarist authorities after the 1831 Polish Uprising; in the wake of the 1863 rebellion, the seventeenth-century Franciscan friary was seized by the government and transformed into a prison. In 1847, the population of Tel'shi was approximately six thousand, including 2,248 Jews; by 1864, the Jewish population was reported to be 4,204.[1]

Gordon arrived in Tel'shi in late 1865 and was not exactly impressed with his new home. Despite its large Jewish community and proximity to the enlightened city of Riga, Tel'shi was still a rather bleak outpost of emasculated colonial gentry and traditional Jewish petty merchants unfriendly to the bearers or notions of Enlightenment. (A decade later, a famous yeshivah would be established in the town, based on the principles of the growing *musar* movement, but even the mixed blessing of such formidable competition was not available to Gordon during his sojourn there.) As principal of the Jewish school he received a larger salary than he had ever had before, but he was far from satisfied with the prospect of raising his family in this forlorn place. Four months after his arrival he complained to a friend:

> I still haven't dared to inhale the stale air or drink the water. The local chroniclers maintain that in the heyday of papal rule, sinners and heretics from all Catholic lands were exiled here to expiate their sins, and to this day there is still a street called "Siberia." I say that Satan once flew into this valley on the wave of a tempest, carrying a sack of ruins on his back. He cut a hole in his pack, and out fell heaps of decrepit huts mired in sand, and he called this place Tel'shi.[2]

The new schoolmaster did not try to endear himself very much to the local Jews. A fortnight after his arrival, he published a report in the Hebrew journal *Ha-Karmel* that criticized the way in which the Tel'shi Jewish communal leaders carried out one of their most sensitive assignments, the drafting of Jews into the Russian army. A new levy had just been announced, Gordon explained, and it was to be administered under new rules set forth in the previous year. The tsar, "whose every effort and wish is to improve the status of his servants and to alleviate as much as possible their duties to the state," had issued a gracious law allowing Jewish communities lacking sufficient potential recruits to meet their conscription duties by buying deferments. This, Gordon advised his readers, was a wonderful concession, but he hoped that the Jews of Tel'shi and other communities would not take undue advantage of the tsar's mercy and uniformly buy their way out of military service. Such a policy would merely lead to a reenactment of the horrors of the age of Nicholas I, when the kahal leaders exploited both the laws and their charges. If the Jews should try to avoid discharging their civil duties with honor, they will invariably pay the price: if no Jews report in person to the draft committee in Tel'shi and similar communities, soon the facts will appear in print. This will undoubtedly lead to an outcry that the Jews are cowardly draft dodgers, and the deferment concession will be repealed. Exactly that happened when the government permitted Jewish communities to buy replacement recruits from among the non-Jews; so many kahals rushed to find willing non-Jews in ways legal and illegal that the loophole was rescinded. Rather than spending the community's money on buying draft deferments, the sums could better be spent on feeding the local Jewish poor, including sixty families left to starve by the floods of the past winter. And rather than allowing poverty to flourish, the rabbis and lay leaders should fund poor, local Jewish artisans to take advantage of the beneficent decrees of the tsar that allow such people to move to the interior of Russia, where they have previously been forbidden. Such a move would benefit both the migrants and those left behind, and the government, impressed with the Jews' willingness to help themselves, would continue to issue such progressive decrees.[3]

There is no record of the response of the local Jewish leaders to Gordon's advice, and it is unlikely that his patriotic pleadings had any impact on their intended audience. But Gordon's musings on Jewish military service and its historic horrors did have one unanticipated but significant result: they inspired him to add to the growing genre of what might be called "Cantonist literature"—poems and stories describing the fate of the Jewish children in the army of the late Emperor Nicholas I. Gordon's contribution was in an utterly new medium for

him—the Yiddish language. A poem entitled (in the then-prevalent artificially Germanized literary version of Yiddish) *Der mutter abshied fun ihr kind im yahr 1845
vos me hot obgegebn far a rekrut* ["The Mother's Farewell to Her Child who Was
Recruited in 1845"] thus marked his fourth, and final, literary debut. This first of
twenty-odd Yiddish poems composed by Gordon during his lifetime was published
in *Kol Mevasser* (The Voice of the Herald), the Yiddish supplement to *Ha-Meliz,*
which began to appear in late 1862.[4] Meant to be sung to the tune of a popular
Russian lullaby, this poem obliquely refers to the miscarriages of justice that per-
vaded the Cantonist system. Its main key, though, is of despondent hope rather
than social criticism, for here the aggrieved mother prays that her son remain a Jew
while serving the tsar loyally—in many ways the leitmotif of Gordon's ideology.
One snippet will convey the tone and thrust of the piece:

> Be well, my dear child,
> I shall never see you again;
> Go whither the wind takes you
> What God wills shall obtain. . . .
>
> I carried you and bore you
> Fed you at my breasts,
> Raised you all these years
> With no pleasure and no rest.
>
> I was able to send you to ḥeder
> The Talmud you did rate
> I hoped to sew you wedding clothes
> And now this horrid fate. . . .
>
> Be not afraid, my dear son,
> Serve the emperor true;
> In all dangers, in all frights,
> Be brave through and through. . . .
>
> Go quickly, go on ahead,
> Wherever they're sending you to,
> Give me your hand and swear to me
> That you'll remain a Jew.[5]

Gordon, or course, was neither the first nor the last maskil to despise Yiddish
and yet to write in it. The strategy of using Yiddish to reach the masses despite its
allegedly despicable characteristics was one of the earliest discoveries of the Galician Haskalah at the beginning of the nineteenth century, and already found expression in Russia in the 1840s. But the untold story of Judah Leib Gordon's Yiddish
writings differs in many ways from the standard version of the encounter between
ideology and creativity in Yiddish letters. In sharp contrast to the later, and more
famous, cases of Shalom Ya'akov Abramovich (Mendele Mokher Sefarim) and
Shalom Rabinovich (Sholem Aleichem), as well as dozens of lesser writers who
used Yiddish as a didactic tool but soon fell in love with its richness and dexterity,
Gordon never felt at ease creating in this, his mother tongue. As a result, his Yiddish verses, with one or two exceptions, do not in the least measure up to the standard of his Hebrew poems. Gordon's Yiddish is often humorous and inventive,

but it utterly lacks the virtuosity and finely honed sheen of his Hebrew. Ironically, when Gordon's characters speak Hebrew, they seem far more natural and more convincing than when they speak Yiddish. This may be easy to explain: Gordon's tendency to long-windedness and to superficial satire was tamed in his Hebrew works by his tight control over the precision of his diction, motivated by his boundless love for the language, for the words themselves. In Yiddish, his disrespect for the language itself gave vent to his own weaknesses; in turn, the lack of complexity and discipline of his language rendered the poems less compelling, and ultimately far less successful, than their Hebrew parallels.[6]

To be sure, Gordon gave little thought to the quality of his Yiddish verses, regarding them as mere trifles unworthy of serious consideration or aesthetic deliberation. Far more important to him was the search for the most successful articulation of the ideology that cast Yiddish aside. To his delight, three weeks after the appearance of "The Mother's Farewell," "Awake, My People!" was published for the first time, as the lead piece of *Ha-Karmel* for April 6, 1866.[7] The eleven passionate stanzas filled three-quarters of the front page of the journal; the rest of the page was a short report, reprinted from a circular of the Ministry of Interior, explaining that Jewish soldiers who have completed their service in the Russian army and have mastered a trade could now enjoy the right of free residence throughout the empire. How perfect the confluence between poetry and law!

For anyone deaf to the rhythms of his song of liberation, six weeks later, in the same journal, Gordon provided a prose gloss—a manifesto in simple sentences ringing out the sins of the Jews and their road to salvation. Gordon chose as title of this trumpet call "House of Jacob, Come Let Us Walk" [*Bet Ya'akov lekhu ve-nelkha*]. As his readers well knew, this was an obvious evocation of Isaiah 2:5, "House of Jacob, Come let us walk by the light of the Lord." But this was not simply a citation of a stirring biblical imperative for its hortatory value alone. In Isaiah, this invocation followed immediately upon one of the central texts of the liberation theology of biblical Judaism, the prophet's vision of the nations of the earth streaming to the Mount of the Lord's House to accept His word, as swords are beaten into plowshares and spears into pruning hooks, and nation not take up sword against nation nor know war anymore. This promise of the majestic end of all time, moreover, itself flowed directly from the ruthless castigation of Israel as insolent child who has rebelled against its parent, as the faithful city became a harlot, offering up specious religiosity instead of piety and morality: "What need have I of all your sacrifices?" asks the Lord through His prophet. "I am sated with the burnt offering of rams. . . . Your new moons and fixed seasons fill me with loathing, they are become a burden to Me, I cannot endure them." But all is not lost; on the contrary, all can be redressed and salvation assured if the Jews change: "Wash yourselves clean, put your evil doings away from My sight, cease to do evil, learn to do good."

In alluding to this vision, Gordon was not merely straining for symbolism; he was consciously and deliberately appropriating Isaiah's charge as the prooftext for a new vision of redemption. Following the order of Isaiah's first two chapters, Gordon first castigated the Jews for forgetting their heritage. The prophet of yore had proclaimed: "O House of Jacob, Come let us walk by the light of the Lord. For you have forsaken [*natashta*] [the ways of] your people, O House of Jacob! For they are full of practices from the East . . . they abound in customs of the aliens." Retaining the crucial verb but transforming its object, Gordon proclaimed:

> O House of Jacob, Come let us walk! For you, my people, the House of Jacob in the lands of the north, have forsaken [*natashta*] walking in the spirit of the age and giving with full heart that which is demanded of you by the time in which you live, as your fathers and their forefathers did.[8]

To Gordon's mind, as previously explained, the integration of the Jews and world culture was the grand heritage of the Jewish people through the ages. But Russian Jews, Gordon here maintained, had forsaken their fathers' ways and isolated themselves from the rest of humanity, forgetting how to trust others, how to communicate with non-Jews, how to absorb all wisdom necessary to an appreciation of God and His world. This is not the fault of the Jews, but of the ages and agents of persecution and superstition that attacked Jews and locked them up in dark ghettos away from the light of the sun. But these evil times and evil men have been vanquished and have disappeared. A new age has dawned that has torn down the edifice of ignorance and bias and has invited the Jews wholeheartedly to return and enjoy the bounty of Reason and goodwill. All the nations turn to the Jews with this new love and tolerance; in Russia, too,

> there prevails this spirit of God, the spirit of grace and mercy emanating from the depths of the heart of our king, His Majesty, to the hearts of all his advisers and ministers, to help us and lift us from our misery. But you! Why are you anxious, why do you stand aloof to be accused of iniquity? Arise and go forth O House of Jacob, Come let us walk in the light of the world [*be-'or 'olam*]![9]

To walk in the light of the world, Gordon forthrightly advised his readers, they can no longer remain stubbornly attached to Asiatic customs and manners unsuitable to Europeans. Even the rest of Asia and Africa is hearkening to the new spirit and allowing Europe into its midst: the Great Wall of China has been pierced, the kings of Japan and Abyssinia send envoys to Europe to learn its ways. Any book of history will demonstrate that many nations have believed in God and trusted in Him, but they have not on the basis of this faith ignored the rest of the world and relied solely on miraculous help from the Almighty; they have taken their fate into their own hands.

Thus, the theological stance implicit in *The Songs of Judah* now became explicit. Study the natural sciences, Gordon pleaded wtih his readers, and you will see that God runs the world by means of invisible powers and fixed, eternal laws that never change or depart from a set order. If farmers refuse to plant their seeds and cry out to the Lord for help, He will not hearken to their call. The laws of economics decree that all men devote themselves to labor as best they can, to learning a craft or trade so that they can fulfill their responsibility both to their families and their societies and not rely on beggary or thievery. Too many Jews in Russia have neglected this requirement and thus have placed their children in mortal danger. They must also cease allowing their communities to be run like ships without captains, and instead introduce order and honesty, philanthropy and mercy, and advise their artisans to take advantage of the opening up of the interior of Russia. Finally, the Jews of Russia must abandon the degrading tongue in which they now babble and learn to speak Russian as their natural tongue, just as the Jews of Germany, France, England, America, and the rest of the world naturally speak the language of the lands in which they live. It is incumbent upon Russian Jews to speak Russian "when you stay at home and when you are away, when you lie down and when you get up."[10] The obvious allusion to the "Hear, O Israel" prayer was in no way lighthearted; the point could not have been made more clearly or emphatically.

Continuing wildly to mix his metaphors while paraphrasing dissonant snippets of the liturgy, Gordon concluded:

> Vast is the labor in the vineyard of the House of Israel, to cleanse it from the mire into which it has sunk over thousands of years of ignominy and gloom, but it is not for our generation alone to complete the task, for in every generation and generation we must stand and weed the thorns from the vineyard, and thus there slowly will draw nigh the time of our redemption, for just like the sun glimmering on mountaintops, so too the liberation of Israel is gradual and slow. But the light of Israel and its holiness will come to our aid to abandon the dark and walk in the light of the Lord.[11]

Stripped of its high-flow flourishes, this homily is remarkable, for it explicitly extends the ideology of "Awake, My People!" in an astonishing new direction, already implicit in "Between the Lions' Teeth," "In the Depths of the Sea," and "The Woman and Her Sons." This appears to be one of the earliest attempts of an East European Jewish intellectual to sift the traditional idea of redemption from its supernatural context and to argue that the Jews can bring about their own salvation through their own actions, through their own economic, cultural, and religious reforms. To be sure, the specific content of these reforms had long been the staple of Haskalah ideology. But now there was an unequivocal identification of that transformation with the ultimate liberation of the Jews. This was not, it must be stressed, simply an attempt to secularize the process and meaning of redemption: Gordon did not omit the words "in the light of the Lord" from his battle cry (as would, not incidentally, barely a generation later, the first group of Russian Jews calling for emigration to Palestine under the banner of the very same words.)[12] On the contrary, Gordon insisted that "walking in the light of the world" is, in fact, following "the light of the Lord," for the two are synonymous and lead inexorably to the salvation of the Jews.

What were the implications of this radical identification between God's will and Western European mores, between Isaiah's prophecy and the promises of the Enlightenment? Was Judah Leib Gordon cognizant of similar trains of thought, similar arguments and challenges to traditional Jewish faith being articulated in Western Europe at the same time? Did Gordon believe, for example, that the essential belief in a miraculous messianic advent was superseded by the new age of progress and of tolerance? In "House of Jacob, Come Let Us Walk," Gordon did not spell out any answers to these crucial questions. But in this remarkable manifesto, he forthrightly served notice that he was pondering such profound problems, not merely mouthing over and over the cliches of the Hebrew Enlightenment.

It is impossible to gauge how this manifesto was received by its intended audience, whether its subtle shift from standard Haskalah panegyric to a new and more threatening level of discourse was marked by the readers of *Ha-Karmel*. Certainly, the defenders of the traditional interpretation of Isaiah did not yet seize upon Gordon's arrogation of the myth of redemption and denounce him as a heretic. Very soon, however, Gordon would take the crucial next step from clarion call to attack, and the Kulturkampf of Russian Jewry would escalate into guerilla warfare.

The first impetus to the escalation of the warfare was an utterly insignificant event. On Saturday night, June 25, 1866, two bandits approached an inn on the outskirts of the town of Tel'shi. Convinced that the innkeeper and his wife were hoarding gold—that was obvious for, like almost all innkeepers in rural Lithuania, they were Jewish and therefore rich—the thieves broke into the hostel and mortally wounded its inhabitants, father, mother, son, and daughter. In their frenzy, they missed a four-year-old child hiding in its bed. To their chagrin, they found that the mountain of lucre they had expected totaled, in fact, forty-two kopecks. Apprehended by the local police, the murderers at first denied their crime, but soon succumbed to the incontestable evidence of the authorities and confessed their guilt. They were, in fact, inveterate degenerates: in custody, one of them admitted that several years earlier he had killed his own father.

Three days after the event, Judah Leib Gordon reported this tale in all its gory detail to the Vilna Hebrew newspaper *Ha-Karmel*.[13] Barely seventy-hours later, he dashed off a second, more detailed follow-up report: in the wake of this sad and senseless loss of human life, a different kind of sadness has gripped the reporter, a spiritual sorrow over the foolishness that rules the hearts and minds of the Jews of Tel'shi and exposes them to ridicule and scorn among their neighbors. After the murdered innkeeper and his family were buried, a Jewish baker in town lit his oven as he did every day, but heard strange noises emerging from the fire, sounds akin to the moans and groans of a suffering human being. Fearful that within his oven there had lodged some reincarnated souls, he sought the advice of his spiritual mentors. The local rabbi laughed off the baker's fears as silly superstition, but the local religious teacher disagreed with his senior colleague and corroborated the baker's worst fears: indeed, it stood to reason that the souls of the recently, and so cruelly, departed inkeeper and his family had transmigrated into the kindling wood in the baker's oven. The branches, ruled the teacher, may therefore not be used to bake any bread and their ashes must be transported to the Jewish cemetery and be given a decent burial.

(Before continuing with the story, Gordon could not contain himself from injecting an editorial comment; obviously, had these foolish people eyes in their heads, they could see that there was, of course, a natural explanation for the mysterious sounds—either the wood was wet and crackled and hissed as it was kindled, as often happens, or there was some draft in the oven itself.)

In the event, however, the baker heeded the teacher. He took care to burn the wood without letting it contaminate any bread and scrupulously collected the ashes and deposited them in the graves of the victims. The news of this affair spread like wildfire to the rest of the town, and many non-Jews laughed in delight at the ignorance and backwardness of the Jews in their midst. To make matters worse, the teacher and his ruling were staunchly defended by a growing number of ignorant followers. The inspector of the local government Jewish school (who was none other than Judah Leib Gordon himself) stepped in, to defend the honor of the faith. Summoning the teacher to a public meeting, the schoolmaster warned the culprit that the laws of the empire forbade a person who spreads such nonsense and foolishness to teach children. The teacher, certain that the doctrine of metempsychosis was as sacred and valid a part of Judaism as anything else, erupted in fury at his accuser: "You so-called enlighteners! With all your labors you will never succeed in changing one jot or tittle or ancient custom of our holy faith." Gordon was shocked at this insolence, but even more chagrined that such

> vile and foolish wickedness could enter our pure faith. Is this not a desecration of God's name and a disgrace to our faith? Therefore we have seen fit publicly to name the teacher—Zvi Benyazov—so that he will be scorned and humiliated by all readers of this paper.[14]

With this report, Judah Leib Gordon crossed a crucial threshold in his strategy for enlightening the Jews. Up to this time, he had expressed his dedication to the ideology of the Haskalah in sundry genres and forms, and had even dared to insinuate that the reform of the Jews in the spirit of the Enlightenment was tantamount to their redemption. But now Gordon took two new and, for him, unprecedented steps. First, he acted publicly in a dramatic and forceful manner as an agent of the Russian government in defense of the Haskalah. Second, in his writings, accessible to all readers of Hebrew, he began clearly and forcefully to argue that traditional Judaism in Russia was rife with arrant superstitions and absurd beliefs that threaten not only the honor of the Jews but, more importantly, the sanctity and purity of their faith. This evil must be extirpated and its main promulgators, the ostensible religious leaders of the Jews, must be exposed in all their ignominy. The battle for the religious reform of Judaism in Russia had begun.

Gordon was dedicated to fighting his war on several fronts. He continued to write and to publish articles exposing such cases of gross superstition and to spread what he considered the truth by teaching more and more children the ways of Europe and the Hebrew tongue. But his prime vehicle was neither reportage nor pedagogy but poetry. And so, beginning with the very same issue of *Ha-Karmel* that carried his report about the Tel'shi transmigration, Gordon began to publish poems that squarely set forth his belief in the necessity of religious reform.

After completing the manuscript of *The Songs of Judah* and awaiting its publication, Gordon returned to one of his favorite poetic genres, the fable. Several weeks before the critical report from Tel'shi, he had published in *Ha-Karmel* the first of a new series of poems that he would later entitle "These Too Are the Fables of Judah: Small Fables for Big Children." The first new fable, entitled "The Deer and the Rabbit," like the bulk of its predecessors and some of Gordon's later fables, merely mocked human foibles in transparent animal parodies.[15] But the majority of the new adult fables picked up the minor strain that could be detected between the lines of *The Fables of Judah* and manifestly satirized the leaders, mores, and values of traditional Judaism in Russia. Thus, the poem that was published alongside the attack on Jewish superstitions in Tel'shi, "The Pillar of Fire and the Pillar of Cloud," directly extended the presumption of biblical grounding for the platform of the Haskalah.

Here it was not Isaiah's mantle as prophet of redemption that was evoked, but the central constituent event in Jewish history—the exodus itself, under the stewardship of the supreme prophet, Moses. As related in Exodus 13, when Pharaoh let the children of Israel go, God did not lead them along the straightest road to the land of milk and honey, but led them roundabout, by way of the wilderness at the Sea of Reeds. "The Lord went before them in a pillar of cloud by day, to guide them along the way, and in a pillar of fire by night, to give them light, that they might travel day and night. The pillar of cloud by day and the pillar of fire by night did not depart from before the people."

In the classic exegetical mode, Gordon began where the Bible left off, examining the effect these pillars had on the desert ecosystem. In his version, the light emanating from the divine fire rouses from their slumber all the fauna of the wilderness—the foxes, hyenas, jackals, and bats. They are furious that the darkness in which they thrive has been lifted, and set upon those whose path is lit by God. Their colleagues the snakes, serpents, and the hordes of scorpions begin to bite those who disturbed their peace, and kill many who dared get in their way. But God, the Creator of light, does not succumb to this challenge to His illumination:

> He said: Let there be light unto Jeshurun forever,
> Despite these snakes who dwell in the dark.
> "Go forth," he ordered his prophet, "complete your path,
> The pillar of your fire will shed on your people
> Light for ever and ever.
> The children of darkness who attack you,
> The enemies of light mired in bloom,
> They will get their darkness and their desire:
> The pillar of cloud will settle upon them
> Dashing their hopes and their attacks
> Smothering them until they expire,
> Their name and memory covered with darkness."
>
> This is the law for the children of Israel through the ages.[16]

Gordon's fabulistic technique had gone a good distance since the original *Fables of Judah*. Not only is the language of "The Pillar of Fire and the Pillar of Cloud" at once richer and simpler than the earlier fables, but its satiric thrust is sharpened by the boldness—if not hubris—of the subject matter. Gordon's attempt to merge politics and poetry here begins to betray a curious inner dynamic: the fiercer the thrust, the more vituperative the satire, the better the poem.

On the heels of this evocation of Moses's enlightened—and enlightening—stewardship of the children of Israel came another poem, based overtly on the famous biblical fable of Jotham, son of Jerubaal (Judges 9:7–15). Jotham's tale relates the decision of the trees to anoint a king over themselves; the good trees—olive, fig, and vine—decline the offer; only the thornbush accepts. Gordon's modern variation on the theme was written in uncharacteristically light and amusing rhyming couplets, with a quick pace and thin plot. A Jewish community in need of a new leader approaches each segment of society seeking a volunteer for the important post. First, a fancy, well-connected son of a rabbinical clan declines the position as beneath his dignity. Next, a member of the merchant elite spurns the offer, since it offers no profit and requires working with the unwashed; a pious recluse refuses to deal with the sinful masses; a teacher explains that he knows nothing but the Talmud and therefore can't deal with the real world; a maskil huffs and puffs, insulted by the suggestion that he abandon his research into the reign of Og, the king of Bashan, to be a communal worker. Finally, the search devolves upon a simple cobbler, who agrees to lead the flock, leaving aside all his tools save his leather whips.[17]

This fable, far more explicit that Gordon's previous poem on the same theme (his 1859 version of "The Mice in Council"), is important for more than its stylistic innovations, for it emphasizes in poetry—the highest rung on Gordon's aesthetic and ideological hierarchy—the unity of his critique of East European Jewish life. In order to lead the Jews to a new, enlightened life and culture based on the precepts of the Enlightenment and the authentic faith of Israel, Gordon subjected all facets of Russian-Jewish society (including the self-righteous enlighteners) to critical and satirical treatment. To his mind, the reform of the Jews could not be divided into neat compartments—politics, religion, sociology, aesthetics. All the issues were interrelated, and more: laxity on one front would inevitably lead to defeat in the battle as a whole. Ultimately, this insistence on the indivisible nature of the reform of the Jews would propel him into a devastating and irreparable breach with most of his fellow maskilim.

Meanwhile, Gordon's belief in the comprehensiveness of the battle over Jewish minds was manifest in another direction: the education of women. In the autumn of 1866, he founded in Tel'shi a school modeled on the girls' academy he had run in Shavli. In a fascinating speech delivered in Russian at the opening ceremony of the school, Gordon set forth the purpose of the institution and its place in the hoped-for cultural revolution of Russian Jewry. It is true, he confessed, that the masses of Jews shun progressive education and use every possible means to evade the state-sponsored Jewish schools. But this aversion to enlightenment, based on a centuries-old, if utterly misguided, notion of proper learning, affects only boys. Nothing inhibits Jews from educating their daughters in the modern spirit. Therefore, the new school will be able to transform the Tel'shi Jewish maidens into cultivated, educated women—primarily by teaching them in the Russian language and by requiring that conversation in the school at all times be conducted in that tongue alone.

There is something strange and unnatural, Gordon continued, in the culture of Tel'shi's Jews. Some have learned German, others French, but not one can express him- or herself adequately in "our native tongue" [*na otechestvennom nashem iazyke*]. Part of the reason for this strange phenomenon undoubtedly lies in the proximity of the Prussian frontier, and hence the utility and attractiveness of German. But this Germanization is outrageous: Do the Prussians living near the Russian border learn Russian? No, they are too proud of their patrimony and their patrie. "Where is our patriotism? Where our love to our homeland?" But the true cause of this propensity to German can be found elsewhere, in the fact that the jargon spoken by the Jews is nothing more than "a slovenly, degenerate German that must, for our own good, die out among us. Think of it, what an anomaly! Russian Jews speak German. Shouldn't they, as Jews, speak Hebrew [as *evrei* speak *po-evreiski*] or as Russians, speak Russian?"[18]

The first option, clearly, is unthinkable. Hebrew died out as a spoken tongue millennia ago and is utterly unsuitable to modern life. The solution, then, is obvious—Russian Jews must learn to speak Russian, just as Jews throughout history have spoken the vernacular of the countries in which they lived and Western European Jews speak the language of their compatriots. Only the Jews of the Slavic lands have remained mired in an ugly foreign dialect that distorts all aspects of life but is nonetheless deemed sacred. All efforts must be bent on eradicating this anomaly. Reflecting the new direction—and the new boldness—in his thought, Gordon concluded that "Russification will not prevent us from remaining Jews by religion, just as Jewishness will in no way hinder us from becoming Russians."[19]

This phrasing of the goal of Jewish cultural enlightenment in Russia evidenced a crucial movement in Gordon's intellectual development: his inching closer than perhaps even he was conscious to a formulation of Jewish identity similar to that espoused by the Western European reformers of Judaism. While continuing to criticize the derogation of Hebrew in German Jewry, Gordon could no longer be satisfied with the simple claim that Russification will not prevent the Russian Jews from remaining Jews. He felt it necessary to add: Jews by religion. For Gordon, the "national-spiritual" whole that was Jewishness was indivisible; to redeem the Jews, then, both facets of their identity—the national and the religious—had to be addressed and reformed.

Gordon's active struggle with the spiritual component of the reform of the Jews was not, to be sure, a solo quest undertaken for idiosyncratic reasons. On the contrary, it was precisely at this time that the battle between the Russian maskilim and the traditionalists was beginning to heat up in public. More often than not, the cause of the public fracas was the ostensible religious laxity or innovations of the enlighteners themselves. Often, of course, the alleged heterodoxy was not active but ideational. As more and more Hebrew newspapers and books appeared espousing the multiplicity of interests and approaches to tradition of the growing number of dissident Jews, tension between the two camps in Jewish society began to flare into open squabbles, which in turn were reported in the Hebrew press and even in local Russian newspapers.

Thus, for example, in the spring of 1867, *Ha-Karmel* reported the following tale: the moderate maskil Moshe Aharon Shatzkes recently came to Grodno to sell his newly published work *Ha-Mafteah* [The Key]—an analysis of the Aggadah that claimed that Talmudic legends that obviously contradicted reason and logic were not meant to be taken literally but were merely ethical allegories. The Grodno maskilim welcomed Shatzkes cordially, but the traditionalists exploded in fury at his visit. Claiming that his book contained the worst sort of heresy, they proclaimed that it had been excommunicated by scores of rabbis and must be ripped to shreds and burnt. After in fact burning the book, they proceeded to the prayerhouse, where they hung notices on the door condemning Shatzkes in the strongest terms of abuse.[20]

In a letter to Shatzkes written soon after this incident, Judah Leib Gordon expressed sympathy but little surprise. In Tel'shi Gordon had attempted to sell Shatzkes's book, but there were no takers. The local Jews are all vulgar boors, Gordon reported, though divisible into several categories: learned boors, pious boors, enlightened boors, and plain, ordinary boors. The book burning in Kovno is simply in keeping with this boorishness. Who among us has not felt the brunt of the obtuse obscurantists among whom we dwell? Moreover, we are not the first and won't be the last to suffer from the perpetual ignorance of the Jews, decried by the prophets themselves. Our people's refusal to see the truth is endemic and eternal; those committed to combatting it must be prepared to suffer abuse and even physical attack or they ought not even to take up the fight. Indeed, Gordon admitted, he was steeling himself to suffer such consequences in his own life, for after eight years of avoiding public controversy,

> in the coming days of Passover, I am off to Vilna to publish one of my works in Hebrew, and I know in advance that the fury of the fanatics will fall upon me, for I have revealed just the tip of the iceberg that they strive with all their might to conceal. But I fear not their ire, I shall not shy away from affronts, and may God help me.[21]

This prediction would indeed soon come true—but not as a result of the appearance of *The Songs of Judah,* which Gordon delivered a fortnight later, in late March 1867, to the publisher of *Ha-Karmel* in Vilna. As noted above, to Gordon's mounting fury, the manuscript sat at the printer for over a year and was published only in May 1868.[22]

Before this anthology appeared in print, Gordon returned to poetry to try to express his new thoughts in successful verse form. The most important result of this attempt was "Through the Shaft of a Litter Bethar Was Destroyed" ['*Ashaka de-rispak hariv Betar*], a poem completed in the spring of 1867, though not published for several years.[23] Here, Gordon returned to the Talmudic discussion that had served as the inspiration for the major pieces in *The Songs of Judah*—the rabbis' deliberations on the causes of the tragedies that befell the Jews. One tradition had it, they explained, that the last stronghold of the revolt of Bar Kokhba in A.D. 135 was besieged by the Romans because of the following curious episode: One day the shaft of the litter of the emperor's daughter broke, and her servants lopped some branches off a cedar tree that the Jews had planted for religious purposes. Angered at the desecration of their traditions, the Jews fell upon the imperial aides and attacked them. When the emperor heard that the Jews were rebelling, he marched against them.[24] In this reading, the beginning of the end of Jewish glory and power was thus caused by an insignificant, virtually meaningless accident.

Gordon's versified commentary on this text at once continued and extended the new accusatory and reformatory direction of his work since *The Songs of Judah.* For the first time in a narrative poem, as opposed to a fable, Gordon chose the present for his setting and the oppressive life of East European Jews as his subject. As in "Between the Lions' Teeth," the beginning of the poem moves directly from an evocation of time and place to a condemnation of the causes of the sad plight of the Jews. Now it is Passover eve in a town in the Pale of Settlement; the Jews are called upon to begin their ancient rites, to celebrate their liberation from slavery unto freedom. But the narrator interjects:

> Do we not lose ground year after year?
> Are we not still bound in chains
> In bonds of lies, vanity, and deceit?

> Strangers no longer persecute us—our oppressors are among us!
> Our hands are not tied but our souls are enchained!
> Therefore we eat the bread of affliction every day of the year
> And in our slavery we are doomed; yet we read:
> "This is the bread of affliction eaten by our fathers,
> This year we are slaves, next year we shall be free!"[25]

The story is short and simple. Elifelet, a poor wagoneer, sits down at the seder table to tell his children of the exodus from oppression. Suddenly, a shout from the kitchen: his wife, Sarah, discovers that two grains of barley—forbidden on Passover—have fallen into the soup. Panic ensues. Sarah wants to rush to the rabbi for advice, but her husband objects, refusing to condemn the fruits of his hard labor and to leave his children hungry. He orders Sarah to serve the food, which she does, though she herself refuses to eat the offensive gruel, and the festive spirit is reduced to gloom. The next morning, to her alarm, Sarah discovers one more grain of barley, and while Elifelet is at his prayers she steals off to the rabbi to ask for his opinion. The rabbi, of course, lives up to Elifelet's expectations and orders Sarah to destroy all her food and her utensils; she is not even allowed to sell her wares to non-Jews, for no profit from the forbidden can be permitted. Sarah is aghast: What will she tell her husband, who will beat her? How will she feed her children? The rabbi calls for his sexton to help sort out the problem. The narrator again interjects: What do you think, reader, that the rabbi ordered that these poor creatures be given victuals and new utensils, at the expense of the community? God forbid! He ordered that Elifelet be put in prison, in order to protect his wife. Later, Elifelet—who according to biblical law deserves excommunication for his sin—is punished only with a monetary fine. Upon his release he fortifies himself with drink and beats his wife. Their life is never peaceful again, and finally he divorces her, sending her away from her home and children, condemning her to the life of a wandering beggar. On the Ninth of Av, in the women's synagogue, during the lamentations bemoaning the destruction of the Temple, she hears the verse "Through the litter of a shaft Bethar was destroyed," and recalls her woes, lifting her voice to the heavens and weeping: "Lord, God of my father, two grains of barley wrecked my home and my joy."[26]

As always, it is Gordon's dextrous use of language, and particularly his bold manipulation of biblical allusions, that most arrest his readers and make his point. To describe Elifelet's beating of his wife—a shocking travesty of Jewish norms, to say the least—Gordon wrote: "Elifelet remembered [*pakad 'et*] Sarah as he had promised, and Elifelet did for Sarah as he had spoken." Every reader heard in these lines a mocking inversion of the opening words of Genesis 21: "The Lord remembered Sarah as He had promised, and the Lord did for Sarah as He had spoken." This act of remembering Sarah, moreover, resulted not in the realization of God's promise to Abraham of the eternity of the covenant between the Jewish people and God, but in the destruction of a blameless, pious Jewish woman. Just as the Temple was destroyed and Jewish honor lost over a trifle, so too has the substitute for the Temple, the Jewish home, been devastated over an insignificant accident, deemed crucial by a heartless legalist.

For Gordon, the theological and social lessons are inseparable: God does not intervene or determine human history, and to believe that He does is to mock His own words. The world is set on its own course, and often insignificant events assume global importance. Faced with such a universe, we should at least not exacerbate our plight through obduracy and obscurantism. Gordon here provided another hint of his emerging strategy for the religious reform of the Jews. It is not the biblical commandments or even *halakhah* as a whole that are at fault for the misery of the Jews, but the corruption and perversion of mean-spirited and close-minded rabbis who distort the laws by not attempting to enforce them with kindness and charity. The destruction of Sarah's life was not caused by the rules and regulations of Passover, but by a blindly rigid interpretation of these rules on the part of a venal rabbi. The Jews will remain slaves so long as they do not comprehend this lesson and act upon it.

This frontal attack on the rabbis was conveyed in lesser poems published in *Ha-Karmel* in the spring and summer of 1867. Now, at long last, the targets of Gordon's ire began to take note of his thrusts and to respond in kind. Their fury was not simply (or as yet) expressed in polemics on the pages of obscure Hebrew periodicals; the traditionalists invoked a far more serious means of dealing with malcontents, one that had well served the leadership of Jewish communities in Eastern Europe in previous controversies—denunciation to the authorities. Letters were written to the Tel'shi school director, the curator of the educational district, the governor, even the governor-general, denouncing Gordon as a subversive heretic leading his students to sin and vice. The charges and countercharges went back and forth for over six weeks, but nothing came of the matter.[27]

In retrospect, it is apparent that this minor incident reflected important changes that had occurred in the balance of power of Jewish society in Russia. As a result both of internal processes within the Jewish community and the alliance between the Russian authorities and the maskilim, in effect since the early 1840s, the disciplinary might of the rabbinate and the Jewish communal leadership had been so debilitated in the previous decades as to be virtually nonexistent.[28] For the rabbis and their lay supporters to counter the opposition to them from within the Jewish community, a new offensive strategy had to be deliberated, one that in large measure used the tools of the modernists to subvert their claims. In addition, the traditionalists had to find some way to convince the Russian government that there was a clear and present link between the intellectual heresy and religious laxity of men like Gordon and their political behavior—in other words, that the bearers of the Haskalah were in fact preaching rebelliousness and sedition to the Jews.

These arguments were not yet twinned by Gordon's opponents. On the one hand, the transformation of traditional Judaism in Russia into an Orthodox Judaism, consciously and vociferously fighting the heterodox on their own turf and evincing sophisticated new political tactics in the battle for the faith, had only recently taken on a serious cast. On the other hand, Judah Leib Gordon was not yet well enough known to be the object of a major attack by the power brokers of traditional Judaism in Russia. Soon, however, both Gordon's fame and the evolution of a self-conscious Orthodoxy in Russia would spread, and the two processes would be joined, with significant consequences for both sides.

At the time, however, Gordon was only buoyed by the ire he was inciting in the rabbis. Of what use is a social critic who is ignored by his enemies? he asked a close friend; with tongue lodged firmly in cheek, he continued: "Gordon desired nothing but to live in peace in Tel'shi, but the fury of the fanatics was unleashed against him."[29] He then proceeded to make his own alliances aimed at advancing his notoriety and promoting his message. Most significantly, Gordon began to cultivate a relationship with Alexander Zederbaum, the editor of the important Hebrew journal *Ha-Meliz* and its Yiddish supplement *Kol Mevasser.* Zederbaum was, *mutatis mutandis,* the Lord Beaverbrook of Russian-Jewish journalism. Born in Zamość in 1804, Zederbaum spent his adult years first in Odessa and then in St. Petersburg, where he founded, funded, edited, and more often than not led into ruin a host of journals and newspapers in Hebrew, Yiddish, and Russian. Although he and Gordon agreed on almost all the political, cultural, and religious issues of the day, there were sharp generational, cultural, and psychological differences between the two that rendered their cooperation most difficult. Zederbaum combined the attributes of a typical Polish-Jewish petty entrepreneur with those of the old school of East European maskilim who never quite lost their Yiddish accents in any foreign tongue. Ready to cut corners in both the financial and the ideological aspects of his life, he was eager to uplift his audience in the spirit of the Haskalah but never dared to offend his readers, both out of fear of losing business and because of his essentially sentimental attachment to traditional Judaism. Always ponderous, prolix, and ungrammatical in his prose, he was utterly devoid of both a sense of humor and organizational skills, in print as well as in the flesh.[30]

Gordon, in sharp contrast, was in many ways the stereotypical Lithuanian Jew, albeit in a modernized cast: scrupulously honest, teetotaling, and intolerant of human foibles, disdainful of sentimentality and folksiness in any guise. A consummate elitist, he spoke perfect Russian and German and delighted in precise diction and the minutiae of Hebrew grammar. Imbued with a caustic sarcasm that expressed itself not only in his satiricial writings but in his human relations as well, he was capable of great warmth and loyalty to friends, family, and nation, but never was willing to compromise on either ideological or personal matters.

The collaboration between these two men, of vital importance for the cultural history of Russian Jewry, was thus a terrible mismatch from the very beginning. Even at this embryonic stage, the correspondence between the two was charged with much tension.[31] But Zederbaum was desperately looking for new talent, and Gordon was equally eager to find new sponsors and mouthpieces, and they agreed to work together on two projects—the publication of some of Gordon's Yiddish satires in *Kol Mevasser* and of his short stories in pamphlet form, as supplements to *Ha-Meliz.*[32]

The fruits of this agreement reflected the heightened antirabbinical thrust of Gordon's pen at this time. Of his Yiddish satirical verses, perhaps the most successful was "The Communal Turkey," a poem that outraged the rabbis and their supporters even further, especially since it was accessible to far greater numbers of readers than its Hebrew predecessors. "The Communal Turkey" was in fact far wordier and more obvious than Gordon's Hebrew fables; as noted above, as a result of his disrespect for the Yiddish language and disdain for its readers, the parody of Gordon's Yiddish verses was not very subtle and the diction imprecise. But "The Communal Turkey" nonetheless made its point succinctly and wittily. The town of Pipkevitz had some extra money in its coffers, since there was no recruitment levy to fulfill, no government school to support, no government rabbi to employ. The communal leaders therefore decided to use their budget surplus to buy a turkey, to feed until Passover. The turkey did nothing all year but strut about and stuff its face at the community's expense, but the kahal leaders were nonetheless delighted with their new acquisition. Although they couldn't understand the various noises uttered by the turkey, they believed that he was holy, related to famous and righteous fowl of previous generations. Soon, quite naturally, the town turkey married off his daughter to a talented rooster who was renowned for his piety. Afterward, the whole turkey family lived off the largesse of the community and depleted its resources, but the kahal leaders continued to groom the fat turkey and his offspring. Finally, Passover came and the ritual slaughterer did his duty. The whole town erupted in hysterical mourning, assuaged only when the strutting rooster was appointed to be the official town turkey in his late father-in-law's place.

The moral of this obvious antirabbinic tale is baldly announced at the end:

> Not in Pipkevitz alone, to be sure,
> In other towns the same plague runs wild.
> In the winter, they groom a turkey for Passover
> And in summer, a rooster for *kapores.*
> And let anyone ever awaken to the ruse
> And dare ask the leaders to explain
> Why we are so sinful
> To require a big fat turkey
> Or of what use is the rooster with his screaming?
> Then the enquirer himself will be cooked.[33]

The other fruit of Gordon's first collaboration with Zederbaum was more representative of its author's intellectual and political cast of mind, though perhaps no more successful artistically. This was the novella *The End of Happiness Is Sadness,* a no-holds-barred attack on Hasidism as the primary evil afflicting Jewish society in Eastern Europe.[34] Intended as a complement to Gordon's first short story, "Two Days and a Night at an Inn," written seven years earlier, *The End of Happiness Is Sadness* was even more wooden and artificial than its predecessor and five times as long. Based on an actual confrontation between the enlightened and Hasidic Jews of the city of Pinsk several years earlier, in which members of the wealthy Luria family, which Gordon had befriended during his stay in Pinsk in the early 1850s, were involved, the story covered some 120 pages divided into twenty-three chapters (and almost as many subplots).

The core of the plot is simple and straightforward, alternating between scenes of Hasidic depravity and idealized Haskalah bliss. The large Jewish population of a good-size town in Russia is dominated by a corrupt, ignorant, and immensely popular Hasidic rebbe. The outrages committed by the local Hasidim in the name of their master consist not merely in the intellectual, spiritual, and liturgical distortion of Judaism but also in their immoral activities and criminal behavior, including theft, fraud, physical assault, and even capital offenses. Fortunately, there are some virtuous people in town, who see through the Hasidim's drunken revelries and antinomian deceptions: Yokheved, the liquor-tax-farmer, a granddaughter of

the Gaon of Vilna and an enlightened and generous woman; Albert, the Jewish
doctor and archetypical maskilic do-gooder; Sarah, a young, French-speaking
widow, in love with Dr. Albert; her brother Abraham, the only Jewish student at
the local gymnasium, forced to hide this accomplishment by wearing Hasidic garb
in the streets; and the various Russian officials—schoolmaster, policeman, mayor,
and the like—who sympathize and fraternize with the enlightened Jews. The conflict between the two camps erupts after Sarah's older brother, Mordecai, a dedicated Hasid, brings his wife and newborn son to the rebbe's court for the circumcision, as ordered by his master but against doctor's orders. When the baby dies,
Mordecai loses his faith and joins forces with his sister and her allies in unmasking
the crimes and degeneracy of the Hasidim, resulting ultimately in the expulsion of
the rebbe from the town and the retribution of all his evil acts. Now that justice
has triumphed, Mordecai allows true love to blossom as well, and Sarah and Albert
wed and move into the former mansion of the rebbe. In this holy place, spiritual
elevation now takes the form not of chicanery and mystical hocus-pocus, but of
Sarah's piano playing and delightful singing, while Albert removes from the book-
cases nonsensical kabbalistic books and replaces them with the works of Lessing,
Humboldt, and prominent German medical authorities.

This meager and stereotypical tale is not well served by the length and the repet-
itiveness of Gordon's endless mockeries of Hasidic discourse or by his preposterously exaggerated lionization of the humanity and philo-Semitism of the provincial
Russian bureaucracy. Indeed, the story's black-and-white portrait of the evils of
traditional Jewish society versus the unblemished nobility of the enlightened Jews
and their Russian friends has occasioned much controversy and discomfort among
Hebrew critics, from the moment of its first publication to the present.[35] But what
is most significant about *The End of Happiness Is Sadness* from the point of view
of Gordon's biography is precisely the fact that its verbosity and artistic failings
reveal its author's ideological and spiritual stance in all their naked candor, without
the compression and dexterity of his poems or his journalistic pieces.

It is in the description of one of the heroines of this story, Yokheved—not incidentally, the mother of Moses both in this novella and of course in the Bible—that
Gordon's voice is heard in its most heartfelt and plaintive key:

> She loved her brethren the Jews with all her heart and all her soul, but not with that
> foolish love that seeks to hide all sins. Her love for her people did not lead her to
> corruption, did not blind her from seeing their faults, did not shame her into silence
> or misrepresentation, for she knew that there is no nation or state or family or tribe
> that does not include some individuals who are defective or sinful. She never once
> believed that "all Jews are princes," or that "all Jews, even the most ignorant among
> them, are full of good deeds as a pomegranate is full of seeds." With patent hatred
> she battled idleness, laziness, the rabbinate, superstition, perverse behavior, and
> aided and defended all those who loved work and honesty. She did not seek to protect
> from his due punishment any Jew who committed an offense, for she knew that one
> sinner causes much harm, and that evil must be redressed. But at the same time she
> extended herself boundlessly and ceaselessly to defend the innocent and the
> oppressed, to protect them from persecutors or injustice. Therefore, all who knew her
> respected and admired her as a superior human being.[36]

Behind Gordon's hatred of the rabbis and trust in the tsar, it must be understood, lay this image of the sublime mission of the enlightened Jew, at once a proud and dedicated son of his people and a severe critic of their flaws. At no time did Gordon fool himself into thinking that this would be an easy or popular mission; he recognized at an early stage the dangers of sentimentalism and even chauvinism on the one hand and self-hatred on the other. Yet he was convinced that the moderate path between defensiveness and self-denial was open to those sturdy enough to blaze the trail. This faith would guide and sustain him through the frenzied battle with the rabbis that had only just begun, a war that would continue for the rest of his days, involving alliances and disputes that could not yet be imagined.

6

Religious Reform II:
The Battle Is Joined
1868–1871

Judah Leib Gordon's first public altercation with the rabbis did little to change his life. He remained secure in his position in Tel'shi, which yielded him quite a respectable salary—substantial enough, in fact, to lead him to reject an offer of a post in Vilna that paid much less. Gordon still regarded Tel'shi as an intellectual and cultural backwater and yearned to move to a larger city. But he was content to remain where he was, so long as he was able to support his family in a decent and enlightened manner. The major problem facing him in this regard was the education of his two growing daughters. In repeated letters to friends and correspondents across the length and breadth of Russia, Gordon sought recommendations for a governess for his girls. He was seeking a woman, Jewish or Gentile, Russian or German, who spoke perfect Russian and could instruct his girls in French, German, music, and etiquette. When these letters did not turn up a suitable candidate, he traveled to Riga and Mitau to locate an appropriate teacher to mold his daughters into perfectly educated European ladies.[1]

Satisfied, for the time being, with his material life, Gordon was delighted with the recognition he received from another, unexpected quarter: the governor's council appointed him, along with two Jewish merchants and a doctor, to serve on a special commission to apportion relief to the Jews of Tel'shi during a disastrous famine. Gordon proudly reported on the work of this committee to various Hebrew newspapers, as indicative of the beneficial results that automatically accrue from the close and civilized cooperation between enlightened Jews and the Russian authorities.[2]

To cap these triumphs, Gordon was beginning to see some progress in his literary career as well. At long last, *The Songs of Judah* appeared in print in Vilna, and the first reviews were uniformly positive.[3] At the same time, his story "Two Days and a Night at an Inn" was published in Odessa by Alexander Zederbaum, who also opened the columns of *Ha-Meliz* to Gordon. Gordon began regularly to contribute poems and short stories to this periodical, which he would later fashion in his own image.

These pieces for the most part continued the antirabbinic thrust of his work in the last year or two. The most significant poem of this period, "And You Shall Rejoice in Your Festivals," repeated the essential moral of "Through the Shaft of a Litter" in a less melodramatic and more humorous vein; a short story, "Fear at Night," reworked the anti-Hasidic theme of *The End of Happiness Is Sadness* into a more tightly wrought and entertaining tale.[4] In an open letter responding to a friendly review of *The Songs of Judah,* which agreed with its author that unless Judaism in Eastern Europe were reformed the young generation of Jews would be lost, Gordon summarized the point of all his new poems, stories, articles, and letters:

> The words which rushed forth from the depths of my heart convinced you, too, to speak out against the evils committed by the rabbis. But my brother! On whom do we waste our words and our breath? He who speaks to rabbis is like one who talks to trees and stones. . . . Our rabbis lie hiding in rooms within rooms, crying "Non possumus," while the wild ones among us carry on like Garibaldi's forces, rejecting everything and destroying all institutions. Who knows where it will all end? Only God knows! And who bears the blame for this breach that is widening ominously in the House of Israel? May God see and judge.[5]

This was the first clear articulation of a concern that Gordon would bear for the rest of his life—that the moderate path of reform was being subverted not only by the traditionalists on the right but also by extremists on the left of the Jewish community. At this stage, however, Gordon was stirred into action not by Jewish radicalism but by a far older and more troublesome form of Jewish self-denial, the revenge of an apostate. There now appeared the first book written by Jacob Brafman, the most infamous Russian convert from Judaism in the nineteenth century. Brafman was a poorly educated Belorussian Jew who escaped military conscription in 1858 by converting to Russian Orthodoxy. After an unsuccessful attempt at running a photography studio, he hit upon the strategy devised by many previous and subsequent apostates from Judaism: making a mark for himself by attacking his erstwhile coreligionists on the basis of alleged inside information. In 1860, Brafman was appointed a teacher of Hebrew in the Minsk (Russian Orthodox) Seminary as well as a missionary to the Jews; several years later, he began publishing articles in reactionary Russian periodicals charging that the Jewish communal and supracommunal organizations in Russia and abroad were in fact cells of a worldwide Jewish conspiracy aimed at subverting the European powers and reconstituting a Talmudic state. These articles, first issued in booklet form under the title *Jewish Communities,* later formed the basis of Brafman's most famous work, *The Book of the Kahal* [*Kniga kagala*], a classic of anti-Semitic literature.[6]

One of Brafman's favorite arguments was that traditional Judaism, although dangerous to the Russian state and offensive to the Russian Church, was preferable to the new-fangled versions of Judaism that were being promoted in Russia by the Society for the Promotion of Enlightenment among the Jews of Russia and in the rest of the world by the Alliance Israélite Universelle. These organizations and their concomitant new expressions of Jewish identity were merely masquerading as bearers of European culture; in fact, they were preparing the way for the Jews to take

over the world in the name of Talmudic separatism. Their attempts at reforging
Jewry and Judaism in accord with modern principles of education and Western
mores were but the latest link in the continuous and unyielding international Jewish conspiracy, whose pedigree stretches back to ancient times. The most effective
way to combat this ominous threat to Christendom and the tsar, Brafman counseled, was to shut down the schools and institutions run by the so-called Jewish
modernists and to outlaw all manifestations of Jewish separatism in Russia.[7]

Judah Leib Gordon and the other protagonists of Jewish Enlightenment in Russia took Brafman's attacks very seriously, especially since he seemed to have the
ear of influential conservative statesmen and newspaper editors. The columns of
all the periodicals catering to Russian Jewry were filled with denunciations of Brafman's charges, on both historical and sociological grounds. Gordon's anonymous
response (which, incidentally, has never before been attributed to him in the scholarly literature, though he himself testified clearly to his authorship of the piece)
appeared in *Den'* (The Day), the newly founded organ of the Odessa branch of the
Society for the Promotion of Enlightenment among the Jews of Russia.[8]

Gordon began his rebuttal by confronting head-on the grave challenge presented by Brafman to the enlightened Jewish enterprise: how should critics of the
established Jewish leadership and traditional Jewish mores respond to attacks on
that leadership and those mores by forces antagonistic to the Jewish community as
a whole? This was the first time that Judah Leib Gordon was squarely faced with
this classic dilemma of modern Jewish politics. To deny the truth of many of Brafman's specific criticisms of Jewish life in Russia would be to play into the hands of
the obscurantists; to join forces with Brafman and his friends, or even to appear to
do so, would not only be impolitic, but immoral as well.

Gordon decided on a combative approach, clearly identifying his opponent as
someone well known for his animosity to the Jews and, more specifically, as a renegade Jew who delighted in wreaking revenge on his former coreligionists. Since
Brafman's whole case was based on a manipulation of traditional Jewish texts, particularly the Talmud, ostensibly to prove the existence of an ancient and international Jewish brotherhood dedicated to taking over the world, Gordon went for the
jugular. He demonstrated swiftly and confidently that Brafman was utterly and
astonishingly incompetent in Hebrew and Aramaic, and therefore that his invocation of Talmudic sources was pure nonsense, devoid of any factual grounding.

Gordon conceded, however, that like all big lies, Brafman's calumnies did contain a germ of truth, overwhelmed by inaccurate generalization. The way in which
the Jewish communities in Russia were run was reprehensible and, often, oppressive. Many of the Jewish communal institutions denounced by Brafman, such as
the burial societies that often exercised enormous control over the Jews, were in
fact repressive vestiges of medieval Rabbinism that ought to be reformed or demol-
ished. But Brafman's attacks on the other philanthropic and educational societies
were both ill-informed and motivated by sheer perversity, as were his ludicrous
assertions that the Society for the Promotion of Enlightenment among the Jews of
Russia or the Alliance Israélite Universelle were somehow dedicated to establishing
Talmudic hegemony over the world. Quite to the contrary, these new Jewish organizations were committed to healing the ills of Jewish society by invoking the only
appropriate medicine, internal reform, based primarily on educational and cultural

advance. Unfortunately, contrary to Brafman's claims, there was absolutely no coordination between the progressive forces in the Jewish community in Russia and around the world. There ought to be such coordination, since both the problems and the solutions were the same in Eastern Europe and in the realm of the Alliance. But if such cooperation were to be effectuated, Gordon concluded, it must be based on a positive program of reform, informed by solid intellectual and historical research, and not by the specious and hateful lies of Brafman and his friends.

This article is of substantial importance in the reconstruction of Judah Leib Gordon's intellectual and political development, for reasons that have little or nothing to do with the primary target of its attack. For in this obscure vehicle Gordon adduced three arguments that would soon dominate his own platform for the rehabilitation of Jewish life and culture in Russia. First, Gordon here (much more clearly than in his earlier poetic defense of *Razsvet*) stood fast against the notion that solidarity with the Jewish people in the face of external attack required the public muting of the critique of Jewish society that was the basis of his, and the other modernists', political and cultural creed. This dilemma had confounded Jewish public discourse in Russia since the earliest years of the Haskalah and had become more problematic with the establishment of Jewish periodicials in the Russian language, laying bare internal Jewish debates to audiences that included non-Jews. Gordon always insisted that the natural tendency to close ranks in the face of external enmity was a cowardly and intellectually dishonest surrender to one's enemies that would ultimately rebound against the interests of the Jews. The true test of this principle would not come in opposition to Jacob Brafman and other anti-Jewish polemicists and politicians, although Gordon would be drawn into debates with them several more times in the next decades. More critically, and painfully, his position would be called into question in the internal Jewish debates of the 1880s, when Gordon refused to allow actual violence against the Jews to determine his views of their path to salvation.[9]

The second critical point made by Gordon in this article was his rather surprising defense of the honesty and sensitivity of the Talmudic sages, a position that was coupled with an attack on Talmudism in contemporary Jewish society. Using the stock arguments of his trade, Brafman had accused the Pharisees of being the leaders of a secret Jewish society that forced the Jews of ancient Judea to conform to a repressive system of rules and regulations, which they resisted at every turn. Gordon countered that the Pharisees, far from oppressing the masses of the Jews, were in fact popular leaders who at once represented the best interests of their nation and raised its spiritual and intellectual level by means of clearly enunciated religious and educational reforms. Thus:

They opened the hearts of the nation to moral prerogatives: learning, religiosity, rejection of asceticism, and especially to the strict observance of the laws and customs of their forebears—qualities which always, and still, inspire confidence in the Jewish people. The Pharisees taught that spiritual life is superior to secular life, religion higher than politics. This idea was accepted wholeheartedly by the Jewish people; strengthening and growing in a difficult period, it finally was absorbed into their flesh and blood after the loss of their independence, when political life and civil prowess became for them merely abstract principles.[10]

For Gordon, a crucial distinction was, once more, in order. In their time and place, he argued, the Talmudic sages valiantly led their flock in a direction deemed necessary by the vagaries of history, thereby revolutionizing Judaism as it existed at the time. Their success at reformulating a cult based on Temple and homeland into a portable spiritual universe advocating high moral principles as well as a keen sense of national patrimony and honor was an act of supreme wisdom and profound sensitivity to the needs of their people and the dictates of reason. His quarrel, Gordon insisted, was not with the Pharisees, or with the laws and customs they developed in the Talmud. Rather, he would elaborate, his fight was with those who canonized the Talmud in a way that contravened the very spirit of flexibility and responsiveness to outside stimuli that was the hallmark of the Talmudic rabbis themselves. To honor the Talmud as one of the primary building blocks of Jewish culture and spirituality was, in Gordon's mind, in no way inconsistent with an all-out attack on Talmudism as it was practised in nineteenth-century Russia. On this basis, Gordon would consistently rally to the defense of the Talmud in the face of attacks by both anti-Jewish publicists and radical Jewish Reformers in the West. Unlike many of the latter, Gordon did not base his call for a religious reform of Judaism on a return to the Bible in the search for the purest expression of Hebraic spirituality. To Gordon, the centrality of the Talmud in the religious and national development of the Jewish people was axiomatic.[11]

The third, and final, crucial point made in this article regarded the question of whether there was an appropriate model for the solution of the plight of the Jews of Russia. The two main illnesses plaguing Russian Jewry, Gordon asserted, were "religious fanaticism and civil isolation"; both of these evils could only be addressed by one remedy, internal reform conditioned on a thoroughgoing reeducation of the Jews. Such a sensitive and moderate inculcation of modernity would evoke in the Jews of Russia "the spirit of dissatisfaction with Talmudic oppression, which will then impel the rabbis themselves to concessions and reform. The example of the German Jews is not far off."[12] For Gordon, more so than for any other Russian-Jewish *intelligent* of his day, German Jewry would remain a beacon of inspiration and hope in the perplexing maze of the search for a modern Jewish identity. While he would always find fault with the most radical Reformers in the West, at the same time he continued to see himself as but an Eastern representative of the struggle for Jewish modernism led by intellectuals and rabbis in Berlin, Leipzig, Breslau, and Vienna. Eagerly he consumed the scholarly works of the *Wissenschaft des Judentums* movement in Germany, the publications of the Institut für Förderung der israelitischen Literatur, and the volumes of *He-Ḥaluẓ* (The Pioneer), a Vienna-based Hebrew journal dedicated to religious reform.[13] In the coming years, when the image of German-Jewish reformers from Moses Mendelssohn to Abraham Geiger would be tarnished in the eyes of many Russian-Jewish intellectuals, Gordon would consistently rally to their defense, proclaiming the profundity and importance of their scholarly and religious accomplishments, as well as the unity of the battle for Jewish modernization throughout Europe.

Precisely at the time that Gordon published this important article in *Den'*, the Hebrew press in Russia was newly aflame with debates on all of these controversial questions. The cause of this intense, and often scurrilous, journalistic melee was twofold. From Germany, news came of the religious revolution culminating in German Jewry at this very time. The Reform tendency was now clearly consolidating itself as an articulate and attractive movement, battling for the hearts and minds of German Jews: at a conference in Cassel and a synod in Leipzig, Reform rabbis buoyantly proclaimed their abandoment of many of the essential doctrines and practices of traditional Judaism.[14] The Hebrew press in the East exploded in seemingly endless reports and discussions of these deliberations. At the same time, the local battle over religious reform was reaching an unprecedented pitch, primarily over a series of articles written by a young Lithuanian demimaskil named Moshe Leib Lilienblum, who would soon play an enormously influential role in the political and cultural life of Russian Jewry and in the private universe of Judah Leib Gordon.

As related in his fascinating autobiography, *Sins of My Youth,* Lilienblum took the typical path to enlightenment of an East European Talmud prodigy gone bad.[15] Born in 1843 in Keidany, Kovno province, he was celebrated as a young child for his precosity in Talmudic studies; engaged at the age of thirteen and married three years later to a girl from the town of Vilkomir, he moved to his wife's hometown to study in the local yeshivah and take up the stipend offered by his in-laws. Gradually, he began to delve into works deemed unsuitable by his elders and betters in Vilkomir, and to question the infallibility of traditional Judaism as it was practised in Lithuania. With no access to real-life maskilim, foreign languages, or financial resources, young Lilienblum struggled viscerally with the conflicting drains on his emotions. Quickly burdened with a family, he attempted to make a living first by running a yeshivah of his own and then by giving private lessons, but he rarely earned enough to feed his wife and children. At the same time, he risked whatever measly income he had by opening in Vilkomir a library and reading circle dedicated to disseminating the works of the Haskalah, and by publicizing his heterodoxy by sending articles to *Ha-Karmel* and *Ha-Maggid,* thus further alienating his employers, neighbors, and in-laws. Scorned as a heretic unfit to teach Jewish children, he attempted to earn his keep by opening a store, in which he and his wife worked punishingly long hours; but to no avail. Nor could he fulfill his dream of moving to a larger town and studying medicine or engineering—beyond his lack of funds, he could not be admitted to any secular school, since he lacked any formal education or knowledge of German or Russian.

Despite his rather desperate personal plight, Lilienblum continued to write articles for the Hebrew press at home and abroad, believing that he had the answers to the cultural and religious morass facing Russian Jewry as a whole. In the spring and summer of 1868, he published in *Ha-Meliz* an eight-part essay entitled "The Ways of the Talmud" [*'Orhot ha-talmud*],[16] which attempted to respond to the attacks on the Talmud by Jewish and non-Jewish critics and to propose guidelines for a moderate religious reform of Judaism in Russia. While clearly reflecting a mildly untraditional point of view in its analysis of the composition and historicity of the Talmud and calling for the rabbis to convene an assembly to legislate new rules and practices for Russian Jews, the tone of "The Ways of the Talmud" was mild, conciliatory, virtually unassuming. It refrained from attacking any rabbinical figures or urging any substantive liturgical, ritual, or doctrinal innovations, and could be interpreted as but one more call for rabbis to rule leniently within the parameters of traditional halakhic jurisprudence.

Lilienblum, however, thought that in these articles he had shaken the universe to its foundations, and he eagerly awaited the mad flurry of responses and accusations that he was certain would descend from the rabbis and their opponents. To his shock and distress, no one seemed to care, no one seemed even to have noticed. The editorial offices of *Ha-Meliz* received only two letters in response to his piece, neither one written by a public figure.

Lilienblum was devastated; he had sacrificed his life and the welfare of his family on the altar of enlightenment, and all his work had been for nought. To cap his frustration and anger, he lost another tutoring job because of his heterodoxy (but not in response to the appearance of the article) and his two sons were taken ill with a seemingly serious malady. He therefore decided to strike out against the conspiracy of silence by writing a second article that would really stir up the world—"Additions to 'The Ways of the Talmud,'" [*Nosafot le-'orhot ha-talmud*], which appeared in five installments in *Ha-Meliz* in the winter and spring of 1869.[17] Now the tone was strident, furious, accusatory; the target not the opponents of the Talmud but the entire edifice of Rabbinic Judaism. The very essence of the original Talmudic process, Lilienblum now maintained, was the continuous reform of Judaism to comply with changes of time and circumstances. But the canonization and sanctification of the Talmud traduced the true spirit of the Talmud: "The medieval commentators distorted the ways of the Talmud and its methodology" by treating the Talmud as the sages treated the Bible, resulting in a petrification of Judaism. Perhaps the worst culprit in this millennium-long crime was the code of law of Rabbi Joseph Caro, which had conquered the Jewish world in the sixteenth century: "the *Shulhan 'Arukh* was not written in the spirit of the Talmud, and requires sweeping criticism and revision."[18] This revamping must be carried out by rabbis, but their capacity to do so is questionable, since their silence in the face of Lilienblum's first article testified to their deep-seated obscurantism and inability either to defend the faith against attacks by extremists or to provide any sort of rational leadership to Russian Jews in their hour of need. To recoup their ignominy, the rabbis must hearken to one call:

> We call on you in the name of the truth, in the name of the Talmud, and in the name of the giants of our people mentioned above, to convene at once in the company of enlightened and learned scholars, noble of heart and sensitive to the times, to give us a purified and reformed *Shulhan 'Arukh,* free of all senseless legal fictions and spurious superstitions.[19]

In addition to issuing a new code of laws, the major rabbinical figures of Russian Jewry—named in a list at the end of the article—must go back and read Lilienblum's "The Ways of the Talmud" and other pleas for religious reform, in order to make certain that our greatest authors can no longer say (in the words of Judah Leib Gordon), "He who speaks to rabbis is like one who talks to trees and stones." The hour of judgment has arrived, Lilienblum concluded, and the rabbis must recognize that the Lord who gave the Torah to Israel has also created the new times and circumstances that demand a response from them.

Much of Lilienblum's argument in this article was a recasting of the analysis of Rabbinic Judaism put forward by Galician and German-Jewish thinkers in the previous decades—especially by the chief authors of the Viennese journal *He-Ḥaluẓ*.[20] What was original to Lilienblum was at once the naiveté and the passion of the argumentation, the sincere belief that in response to one article by a suspect twenty-six-year-old *melamed,* the entire rabbinic establishment in Russia would shrivel and collapse. In sharp contrast to Judah Leib Gordon, at first his closest comrade-in-arms and then his most bitter enemy, Lilienblum combined keen intellectual acuity with an overarching lack of sophistication and enrootedness in non-Jewish culture and modes of thought, compounded by a fundamental emotional instability. Throughout his long career as polemicist and politician, Lilienblum would exuberantly latch on to a succession of novel causes or ideologies, which he imbued with unfulfillable expectations that inevitably rendered him frustrated and alone, even if part of the struggle was actually successful.[21]

In a curious way, Lilienblum's then current goal was partially met, although, to be sure, the rabbis did not convene an assembly to produce a new *Shulḥan ʿArukh,* neither could they ignore Lilienblum this time. The rabbis named in the last paragraph of his article were outraged not only by the personal attack on their integrity but also by his thrust at the jugular vein of traditional Judaism—unprecedented in Russia, whatever its pedigree in the West. Never before had such a clear-cut call for a religious reform been expressed in Hebrew within the frontiers of the Russian Empire. As one of the leading spokesmen of the traditionalist camp later explained, the strategy of the rabbis of the day had heretofore been to ignore the catcalls and insults that appeared in the Hebrew press, as the medium of the newspaper itself was deemed unfit for consumption by the pious, and all the more so for rabbinical responses. But now things had gone too far, and the offence had to be answered in kind. Therefore, one of the leading rabbinical figures in Russian Jewry, Rabbi Israel Lipkin of Salant, commissioned a response to Lilienblum's distortions of the Talmud and the work of the sages through the ages. Even more significant, several other prominent rabbis of Russian Jewry wrote direct answers to Lilienblum's attacks, which they had published on the pages of the journal *Ha-Levanon* (The Lebanon), published in Paris. In fact, now the Russian rabbinical authorities decided to make that journal, which had recently moved to the French capital from Jerusalem, into the major organ of the traditionalist rabbinate in Russia.[22]

This appropriation of a Hebrew newspaper as a central tool in the defense of the faith was a crucial milestone in the transformation of traditional Judaism in Russia into an Orthodox Judaism. Soon thereafter, another tool of modern society was co-opted by the traditionalists, with the organization in Kovna and Vilna of two overtly political societies aimed at countering the Haskalah through propaganda and lobbying activities.[23] Both of these processes gained momentum as the rebuttals to Lilienblum themselves became the object of public attack—this time by the more famous, and the more self-controlled, doyen of anti-Rabbinism in Russia, Judah Leib Gordon.

Gordon had been in contact with Lilienblum for over a year, although the two had never met. After reading "The Ways of Talmud," Gordon asked a mutual friend to contact the young author and give him a copy of the recently published *The Songs of Judah.* This gift inspired Lilienblum to begin to correspond with his idol Gordon—a correspondence that lasted until 1889, albeit with several interruptions caused by severe ideological and personal friction between the two men.[24]

Gordon was outraged not only by the tone and substance of the Orthodox attacks against Lilienblum but also by the measures taken against him by the community of Vilkomir. Lilienblum was shunned in the streets and the prayer houses and pelted with stones and abuse; the businesses of his father-in-law and wife were boycotted, his children taunted on their way to school. More substantively, the community leaders banded together and resolved to rid themselves of this troublemaker, first by offering to pay him to leave town, and then, when he refused this offer, by denouncing him to the governor-general in Vilna as a heretic and subversive. As had happened several years before with Gordon himself, nothing came of this denunciation, due to the general protection given by the Russian government to the bearers of the Haskalah. But, unlike Gordon, Lilienblum had no independent means of employment or support and was thus left in a terribly precarious financial predicament. Gordon offered to secure a position for the destitute young reformer in the government school in Tel'shi, and sent him ten rubles from the fund to aid the famine in that town. This offer was bettered by the maskilim of Kovno, who banded together to support Lilienblum, first finding him pupils in that city and then helping him travel to Odessa, to find some sustenance in the stronghold of Jewish modernism.[25]

Gordon's most important response to Lilienblum's plight came in writing. A fortnight after the appearance of his Russian-language attack on Brafman, Gordon published in *Ha-Meliz,* under the pseudonym "Daniel Bagar," a vituperative satire entitled "To the Credit of the Rabbis."[26] The point of this short piece was ostensibly to counter those maskilim who had recently defamed the rabbis as useless parasites on the Jewish community. This calumny, pretended the author, could easily be refuted by elaborating the many heroic actions performed by rabbis in recent times: enforcing unusually strict prohibitions in regard to food despite the raging famine; banishing the renowned heretic of Vilkomir from his town; disqualifying a writ of divorce after a remarriage had taken place and a child was born. One passage will convey the tone and substance of this satire:

> Just before last Passover, when famine was raging in our city and both prices and the lack of food were rising, we were trying with all our might to stem the tide and provide matsah, potatoes, and other holiday necessities for the town poor. . . . At this time of great suffering and adversity, our great local rabbi did not stand aside but came to our assistance—with a new ruling requiring all bakers to cover their wooden rollers with metal casings. True, in order to do so, the bakers had to raise the price of the matsah, and then they had to raise the price once more when they discovered that the cold and damp metal caused the dough to stick to the rollers, and thus much dough was wasted. But how beneficial this ruling was to our nation, and to the poor masses in our midst. . . . Are there to be found in other nations such examples of self-sacrifice and dedication, such delights to God and to man? And you still say that our rabbis do nothing for the benefit of the Jews?[27]

Through Gordon's supple pen, the attack on the rabbis was made at once sharper and more accessible to those not attuned to the subtleties of halakhic history. By the use of irony and humor, Gordon drove home the point that the suffering of the Jews, both material and spiritual, was directly caused by the obscurantism and isolation of their putative leaders.

The message was not lost on the targets of the sarcasm. Within a month, an article appeared on the front page of *Ha-Levanon* entitled "To the Credit of the Rabbis: A Response to Daniel Bagar."[28] The venom of the parry rivaled that of the original thrust. The cowardly author who hides behind the pseudonym Daniel Bagar, revealed the Orthodox author, is none other than Judah Leib Gordon, the well-known liar and evil heretic who dares to besmirch the honor and misrepresent the deeds of the greats of our generation. Following the lead of Abraham Geiger and the other founders of a new religion that has nothing to do with Judaism, Gordon spouts outrageous libels and insults that reveal him in all his ignominy as a disciple of the Spanish Inquisition, aiming his arrows at the heart of Judaism and the Jewish people. Like his friend Lilienblum, Gordon distorts the actions and wondrous works of our great rabbis and flaunts his utter ignorance of the Talmud and Scriptures. In his degenerate poetry, he plainly reveals his hatred for the Jewish people and their holy teachers throughout the millennia, and exhibits his true aim—sexual licentiousness and the destruction of all norms, the abandonment of all that is respected and sacred. Let such evildoers rejoice in their evil and delude themselves in their dreamworld, the world of the fantasies of Islam; we, the bearers of God's true word, will look down upon their carcasses from the world of righteousness and rejoice that God has separated us from the sinners, by granting us His Torah of truth.

It took several months for the issue of *Ha-Levanon* containing this article to reach Tel'shi from Paris, but before Gordon actually saw the piece he had heard about it in great detail from friends. One correspondent reported to him that the signature that appeared at the end of the article, Moshe David Wolfsohn of Vilna, born in Shavli, was a pseudonym for none other than the rabbi of Shavli himself, Zekhariah Joseph Stern. This supposition seemed logical, since Rabbi Stern had been the most vociferous respondent to Lilienblum's articles on the pages of *Ha-Levanon* and, besides, the numerical equivalent of the letters of his name was the same as that of the pseudonymous author.[29] In fact, this was not true. The attack on Gordon was written by Jacob Halevi Lifshiz, one of the organizers of the Kovno circle of antimaskilic activists, who would later play a major role in the religious and political battlefield of Russian Jewry but was at the time simply an ambitious young teacher out to make his name while defending the faith.[30] Gordon, not fully convinced that Rabbi Stern had written the answer to Daniel Bagar, would never learn the true identity of his vilifier, but would nonetheless several years later choose Rabbi Stern—who in fact was a rather moderate and enlightened traditional scholar—as the model for the cruel and despicable rabbi in "The Tip of the Yud," perhaps Gordon's most famous and influential poem.[31]

Meanwhile, Gordon determined that it was beneath his dignity to respond to the attack on him in print. This did not mean that he was withdrawing from the struggle, he reassured his friends; on the contrary, he was now even more convinced than ever that an all-out war had to be fought with the rabbis. If he resorted to satire and sarcasm, it was only because his tears had dried up over the plight of his people, which was worsening day by day; the fault lay with the supposed spiritual shepherds of the people, who were standing idly by and only exacerbating the crisis. In a letter to one of his defenders he articulated in the clearest terms yet the basic articles of his creed: "the material improvement of our nation is intertwined with its religious reform—of this I have absolutely no doubt. . . . The economic, moral, temporal, and spiritual plights of the Jews cry out in unison: Reform me!"[32]

Perhaps all the legal fictions and stringent restrictions and prohibitions were necessary and even helpful when the Jews were persecuted and oppressed, but now, "when there is no possibility that the nations of the world will return to their former foolishness, just as the sun cannot change its course," it is time to abandon all of these fictions and restrictions and to institute "a moderate reform, guided by the Torah and pure faith, along with reason and the needs of the hour."[33]

In this same letter, Gordon confided that although he had no intention of responding to the attack against him, he was considering suing Ha-Levanon itself, for contravening international norms of etiquette by revealing his real name, when he had used a pseudonym and had not libeled anyone. To another correspondent he went further, asking for help in convincing the government authorities to ban the import of Ha-Levanon into Russia, as a journal detrimental to the cause of progress and enlightenment. Soon, after considering the matter further, he decided to abandon the legal route and to return to the literary front, composing a satirical response to the attack against him, in which he ostensibly begged for forgiveness and pledged to repent for his sins. He sent this piece, along with his unpublished poem "Through the Shaft of a Litter" to Ha-Meliz in Odessa, but to his shock, Alexander Zederbaum refused to publish either the poem or the tongue-in-cheek apology.[34] This was the first serious breach between the two men, and the first sign to Gordon that the editor was unreliable, incompetent, and, worse, unwilling to risk his readership by taking up such crucial, if controversial, issues as the fight against the rabbis.

While Gordon and Zederbaum were squabbling about what ought to appear in Ha-Meliz, the Vilna Orthodox society for defense of the faith published a brochure that repeated the charges that Gordon and Lilienblum were not only the Russian avant-garde of Abraham Geiger and his flock of heretics but were also sexual deviants who desired nothing but unbridled license and immorality. In addition, the brochure took a radically new step, making explicit the hitherto implicit claim that would soon become a standard, and very effective, part of the arsenal of militant Orthodox Judaism in Russia: it charged Gordon and Lilienblum not only with disobedience to the laws and authorities of Judaism but also with disloyalty to the Russian state and the Russian tsar.[35]

Gordon's ire now peaked; he could not stand by and allow such an argument to be made in public. He therefore decided to abandon wit for frontal attack and composed a long and detailed call for religious reform, which he himself termed his "confession de foi."[36] If Zederbaum did not have the courage to publish this article in his paper, Gordon would have it printed as a separate booklet. But Zederbaum's mercurial editorial line did not intervene this time, and Gordon's "Wisdom for the Errant of Spirit" [Binah le-to'ei ruah] appeared in nine installments in Ha-Meliz from July to October 1870, under the citation of Isaiah 3:12: "O my people! Your leaders are misleaders, they have confused the course of your paths."[37]

The argument begins with a paean to the new age of open debate in Russia. The proliferation of the press and the institution of a modern court system has effected a radical change in the nature of public discourse. No longer could anyone hide in a corner, bribe judges, vilify his opponents without exposure in the light of day.

The reigning authority was now simply the truth, logically and publicly presented. The rabbis, Gordon maintained, are paralyzed by this new situation, since they are used to having their way in private, through deceit and corruption, and are unable to make their case in a civilized public arena. It is useless to debate such primitives; clearly their brains have been diseased by the base *pilpul* in which they engage, to the exclusion of any rational or logical thought. They have been damaged by their addiction to a literalist reading of the *'aggadot* and *midrashim*—a reading that not only distorts the profundity and wisdom of the Talmudic teachings but also has blinded the rabbis to the difference between fact and fiction. They therefore are unable to disprove the charges brought against them by the maskilim and must resort to vile lies and filthy innuendo, all expressed in laughably ungrammatical prose.

When the rabbis charge the enlighteners with disloyalty to the state and insubordination to the government, however, they only reveal their own true nature:

> Those who say in a sycophantic voice: "We are loyal subjects and abide by the laws of the king," are in fact hiding in their caves and concealing their acts from the light of day. They have no contact with the world around them and do not obey the laws of the king. On the contrary, they try with all their might to evade those laws: they conceal their numbers from the tax rolls, conscript recruits illegally, levy taxes and fines not approved by the government, deal in contraband and smuggling, and distance themselves as best they can from the country and language in whose midst they live and from any practical or theoretical knowledge known to Europe as a whole. They stubbornly cling to their bastard singsong tongue unknown to our forefathers, and hence act like those devoid of writing or civilized culture. They teach their children to call their neighbors—whom the Torah has designated as friends—"goy" and "goya," "shiksa" and "shegets," terms of vile opprobrium. . . . These then are the true traitors, disloyal to the state which is attempting to improve the lot of our nation.[38]

In the Russia of 1870, these were truly fighting words. Gordon had never before publicly corroborated the most common and most extreme criticisms of the Jews leveled by the reactionary Russian press and public opinion. He now charged that not only were the poverty and the ignorance of the Jews caused by their presumed religious leaders, but their collective criminality as well. The entire blame for the degradation of the Jews rested solely and squarely on the shoulders of the rabbis. If nothing else, in this retort Gordon consciously and deliberately burned all bridges of reconciliation between the two camps of Russian Jewry.

With no strategic advantage to preserve, Gordon laid out in all of its details his vision of a new religious order for the Jews of Russia that would solve all their problems—moral, spiritual, even material. The rabbis, he explained, have distorted the true religion of Israel by reducing it to absurd customs such as sidelocks, peculiar hairstyles, rags granted the status of holy garb. What must be done is to bring religion into harmony with knowledge, to reconcile the laws of the Torah with the demands of the new age, to improve the situation of Jews by abandoning customs forced upon them by their erstwhile servitude and decrepitude. Such improvement, or acts of harmonization, are not only dictated by necessity or enlightened reasoning, as Russian maskilim have argued from the beginning of the nineteenth century. More than that: at the heart of Gordon's thesis lay a new concept of the essence and history of Judaism that he—and Lilienblum as well—had learned from *Wissenschaft* scholars and modernist rabbis in the West: reforms were dictated by the true inner dynamics of Judaism itself, which had evolved historically to conform to changes in time and circumstances. Reformulating the main historical argument of "Additions to 'The Ways of the Talmud'" in clearer, less hysterical, and more forceful language, Gordon continued:

> Several times our religion has cast off its old form and taken on a new one, without changing its character. Since this is an extremely important point, let us elaborate: If our rabbis were not blind, if they could hear and understand, if their necks were not pinned by an iron rod that prevented their heads from nodding, they would have to hear and see and acknowledge in public an absolute truth that cannot be doubted and should not be feared: that the religion of Israel as it obtains today is the reformed religion of Moses. These reforms began in antiquity, from the days of Ezra, who is explicitly said to have instituted reforms, and they have continued ceaselessly in every generation and in every place, so long as the Jews had courageous and intelligent leaders who understood in their entirety the spirit and purpose of the lawgiver.[39]

The sages of the Talmudic period, as well, recognized the meaning and demands of true religion and brought about reforms that were in consonance with the needs of the time, the changing conceptions of faith in general, and the evolving character and circumstances of the Jewish people. In the course of the centuries, then, the original Mosaic faith was transformed into the reformed faith of Israel. This process at times required and approbated the clear abrogation of scriptural commandments and prohibitions as well as the adoption of obvious innovations that had no biblical authority. But all of these reforms were nonetheless accepted by the entirety of the Jewish people as wholly legitimate and authoritative.

The implications of this thesis of the essential evolutionary character of Judaism were straightforward: the Torah tolerates reforms that are in accord with the dictates of changed times and circumstances; indeed, only by means of such reforms has Judaism survived; any conception of Judaism as a static body of commandments that cannot be altered is both dangerous and not in accord with the true meaning of religion or the will of God. The Russian rabbis' brand of Judaism is thus a petrified distortion not only of the practices of the authentic faith of Israel, but also of its eternal religious verities as well.

Two examples, Gordon maintained, will prove the point. The Torah and the sages repeatedly insisted on physical and bodily cleanliness as requisites to health and godliness. But what have the post-Talmudic rabbis done to this teaching and this goal? They have added a host of mystical ceremonies and incantations that over time have entirely overwhelmed the original intent of the laws of washing. Now, any Jew who cares for his bodily hygiene is regarded at best as an idler and more likely as a heretic. The second case in point is perhaps even more revealing. All of the previous summer there were terrible floods in Russia that ruined the crops and led to much famine. The Jews, quite logically, prayed incessantly to the Lord to stop the rains. Suddenly, on Shemini ʿAẓeret, they changed their tune and pleaded with God—of all things!—for rain:

> At that moment, undoubtedly, the Lord Himself sat back, smiled, and said: "Fools! You seek to harm yourselves. For your own sake, I'll not accept your prayers today."

The rabbis, of course, would counter, "We're praying for rain in the Land of Israel, not here." Ask them: Why? Five million Jews throughout the Diaspora are praying for rain for 80,000 inhabitants of the Land of Israel who till no fields or vineyards, who do no physical work and live off the charity of their brethren in Exile. Wouldn't it be smarter for them to pray for us when we need water? Or are we praying for the Arabs and the Bedouin?[40]

The rabbis, moreover, have not only deliberately damaged the Jews' national psyche and religious integrity, but they have also persistently refused to ameliorate the plight, to accept the remedies offered by the enlightened Jews and the Russian government since the dawn of the modern, tolerant era. This was not only reprehensible but inevitably counterproductive. What have the rabbis wrought, for example, by boycotting the government-sponsored school system and rabbinical seminaries? They could have cooperated with the authorities and taken the upper hand in leading the Jews to a moderate rapprochement with reality. Instead, their adamant refusal to participate in any such scheme has led to the proliferation of Jewish students in the regular Russian gymnasia and universities in which no semblance of Judaism is preserved, and thus to the radicalization of a significant portion of Russian-Jewish youth. They are, then, at fault if there appear among Russian-Jewish youth extremists who deny everything held holy not only by the rabbis, but by the enlighteners as well—"those who are ashamed to call themselves Jews and term themselves nihilists."[41] True enlighteners have nothing to do with such specious and extreme ideologies and are honestly moved by love of their nation and its faith; they have dedicated their whole being to the amelioration of the lot of the Jews. By identifying all change with heresy, the rabbis have confused truth and error and have condemned themselves to be the losers in the new, irreversible march of history. For it is no longer a matter of choice; progress and reform are the verdict of history. The tide of change cannot be stemmed. We are in a new world, and this new world demands a new kind of Judaism, which will inexorably lead to a new and better chapter in the history of the Jews.

Parting company with his friend Lilienblum and the other local maskilim, Gordon openly elaborated on the allusion to the German model for the reform of Russian Jews that he had made a year earlier in his Russian-language attack on Brafman. Frustrated attacks upon the Reformers in Germany and America are pointless, he counseled. Abraham Geiger and his colleagues may well have made serious errors, but they have not been forcing their followers to pursue radical change. Instead, the reverse has occurred. The masses of Jews in Gemany have recognized the inevitable and have demanded that their leaders lead them. Geiger's reforms and the deliberations of the synods, therefore, are not radical pronouncements meant to waylay the Jews, but a positive reaction to the abandonment of Judaism on the part of the young. For this reason, the German Reform movement must be lauded, not decried. Its leaders have not been motivated by charlatanism, ignorance, or the desire to become Gentiles, as the East European rabbis (and most of the maskilim) charge. On the contrary, the German Reformers are motivated by intelligent, serious, and sincere religiosity and devotion to the Lord. In many ways they have gone overboard by neglecting to instill in the hearts of their followers a proper reverence for the traditions and culture of the Jews, but on the whole they have done a praiseworthy job of salvaging the holy from the profane, of constructing a new kind of Judaism that will survive and flourish in the modern world.[42]

This logic, previously unheard of among East European maskilim, led Gordon to confront one of the most controversial issues in the debate between modernizers and traditionalists in the nineteenth century, and one of the cardinal doctrines of Judaism in any generation, the messianic idea. Even in the relatively liberal years of Alexander II's reign, open discussion of this crucial divide between Judaism and Christianity was a sensitive matter in Russia, and the government censor excised the installment of "Wisdom for the Errant of Spirit," in which Gordon's views on this subject appeared. Gordon sent the censored material to Peretz Smolenskin, the editor of a new Hebrew journal, *Ha-Shahar* (The Dawn), in Vienna, who published it there.[43] This text is long, but given the subsequent importance of its subject matter both in Russian-Jewish politics and in Gordon's life, it must be cited at length:

A belief that is not based on reason and knowledge is worse and more detrimental to faith than is utter heresy. [In Russia, the Jews] recall every day the belief in the coming of the messiah; the Reformers in the [West] have abrogated this dogma. But in truth, both the German Jews who publicly despair of redemption and you who wait for a miraculous messianic advent equally deny this fundamental precept of our faith. For you must finally recognize that miracles will no longer occur, and therefore all of your actions, your way of life, testify that your ceaseless repetition of "I shall await him every day" is but a meaningless cliche, which you yourselves do not truly believe. You are not prepared to receive him; you are not preparing your children for him!

If the Son of David were to appear today, the [German] Reformers would be able to repent at once, to say, "We have sinned. May we be servants of our Lord." And he would forgive them and find among them worthwhile men, needed for all his tasks. But what would he find among you, what use would you be to him? With your hair-splitting hermeneutics and contrivances and nonsensical exegeses? Could he find among you men equal to his task of renewing our days as of yore? Will he find men among you capable of serving as ministers of the Crown, court treasurers, military strategists, diplomats, engineers, surveyors, builders of markets and roads and bridges, linguists suitable to be ambassadors, translators, scribes in foreign tongues, doctors, pharmacists, artisans, inventors, farmers? You will be small-time rabbis!

And what will you do if Jewish law will change in accord with the dictum that the commandments will be rescinded in the messianic age? Perhaps you will persist in the ways you run our communities today and attempt to apply the same rules to the agencies of government, and will try to propagate your views on the problems of the world, the rest of the nations, the other faiths? Perhaps you'll restore the biblical death penalties for the most trivial derivation of offences on the Sabbath or every jot and tittle adduced by medieval commentators?

If you would do so, you should come to the Land of Israel today, all the nations around it would fall upon you and drive you from the land, for it is impossible for civilized society to bear such an offence, and especially in a land at the hub of the world! A Jerusalem built by your kind will be a burden on all of mankind.

Therefore, your daily hope in redemption and your way of life and education contradict one another blatantly and absolutely. If we want to preserve for ourselves and for our children this belief, which is at the heart of the Jewish faith, we must reinterpret it in a manner acceptable to reason and logic: that if God desires us, there is hope for the future, for us as well as other nations which have not been lost in history. But can this hope be fulfilled solely in accord with nature? Perhaps it can, if we are prepared and worthy of it; if we change our system of education from top to bottom and make use of the great talents which God has given us for matters of greater value than esoteric Talmudic quibbles—for knowledge of substance. If we banish from our hearts all hatred of other faiths, and inculcate in our children the cardinal principle of the Torah: Love your neighbor as yourself. If we abandon the stammerer's tongue which we have inherited to our disgrace from the recent past; if we train our sons not suited to spiritual concerns to be craftsmen and laborers, farmers and workers; if we teach our merchants to be honest and fair, to treat the property of their customers, Jew or Gentile, in an honest fashion; if we reform our communities along honest lines so that they could be run openly, according to the laws of the land, and not rely on bribing officials to cover malfeasances.

If we do all this, then there is still hope that the day will come when the nations of the earth, roused by God in the spirit of Cyrus, will say: Verily, this nation is intelligent and wise, talented in many ways, loves work and hates idleness, is tolerant of other faiths and peoples—it is a nation we must respect and compensate justly for all the trials and tribulations we have subjected it to for thousands of years.

Perhaps then, when God will cause justice to triumph, the day will come which we all await, when the Jews will awake, and the rest of the world will see that we will bring no harm to civilization and no longer be obstacles to knowledge and wisdom; but that, on the contrary, we will be of great use to the whole of mankind by living free and normal lives guided by our talents and natural inclinations. We will be free to draw from the depths of our being the many treasures that the God of our fathers has planted in us, the stores of wisdom that can enrich all of mankind. Only with acts of goodness can we win the hearts of men; only in acts of righteousness will Zion and her captives be redeemed.[44]

Such an interpretation of the messianic idea, Gordon continued, was recently articulated by the writer David Gordon, in an article in *Ha-Maggid* that was of great merit but evoked only the vile opprobrium of *Ha-Levanon.* Undoubtedly, the obscurantists will pounce on this expression of support for David Gordon to fortify their denunciation of Judah Leib Gordon as a traitor to the government, but be that as it may.

This entire passage must be carefully parsed, both because of its importance to an understanding of Gordon's designs for the reform of Judaism and due to its misperception in the scholarly literature on Gordon and his times.[45] In the intense ideological battle that raged in the Jewish world from the early 1880s on over the question of the proposed return of the Jews to the land of Israel and the establishment there of an independent Jewish homeland, an attempt was made by polemicists and scholars to cull through documents and debates of previous eras in the search for support for the emigration of the Jews to Palestine. In this effort, much energy was expended on locating and identifying Zionists *avant la lettre,* or "precursors of Zionism." As has happened more often than not in analogous pursuits of progenitors of controversial ideologies, the complexity of the historian's dilemma in positing a causal link between autonomous phenomena has at times been muted, if not effaced, and sentiments that seemed to serve the position being celebrated were torn out of their original context and misrepresented.

In this passage of "Wisdom for the Errant of Spirit," Judah Leib Gordon made overt the subtle message of his 1866 article "House of Jacob, Come Let Us Walk." Sifting the traditional idea of messianism from its supernatural context, he argued that the Jews can bring about their own redemption through their own actions, through their own economic, cultural, and religious reform—in other words, that the staples of Haskalah ideology through the decades were unequivocally identified with the messianic advent. Now, for the first time, Gordon added that a necessary and glorious consequence of the self-reform of the Jews would be the return of the Jews to their ancient home and the reestablishment of Jewish political independence in the Land of Israel. He had high praise, in this connection, for the recent article by David Gordon, the assistant editor of *Ha-Maggid,* which criticized the traditional interpretation of the messianic age as reliant on miraculous intervention by God and called for Jewish colonization in Palestine as a positive step in the hastening of the redemption of the Jews.[46]

For Judah Leib Gordon, the ultimate return of the Jewish people to the Land of Israel was a consistent and central component of his vision of the future, and he therefore at all times supported the new efforts at Jewish colonization in the Holy Land that began in the late 1860s. However, it is absolutely crucial to understand that Gordon's sincere hope for the return of the Jews to Palestine was conditioned, in this piece and thereafter, on their *prior* religious, social, and cultural Europeanization. If that Westernization did not precede any emigration, he clearly warned in the excised chapter, the inevitable result would be an obscurantist theocratic regime in the Land of Israel. Moreover, his belief in the return to Zion was not predicated on the alpha and omega of later Zionist thought, the belief that Jewish emancipation in the Diaspora was an illusory goal, since European civilization, as if by definition, was inevitably antagonistic to the Jews. Quite to the contrary, Gordon believed that once Jews around the world—like the Jews of Germany—had joined the march of Western civilization and enlightenment, the messianic age would arrive, for the "end of the days" was in fact synonymous with the harmonious coexistence of the Jews and the Gentiles in a world free of hatred and intolerance, a world governed solely by righteousness and rationalism. In that world, the enlightened nations would inevitably permit the Jews finally to vent their vast creative genius to the benefit of mankind as a whole, and to return to their historic home, there to inculcate the lessons and culture of the West.

Gordon's recasting of the messianic doctrine in the service of the Haskalah was undoubtedly an important step in the effort of East European Jewish intellectuals to invoke for their emerging new strategies for redemption the most profound and evocative chords in Jewish consciousness, while at the same time subverting traditional Judaism, its politics, and its culture. This process would soon culminate in the quasi-messianic posture of both the Zionists and the Jewish socialists. However, when these later formulations were in fact expressed, Gordon vociferously rejected them as deleterious to the future of the Jews—although, for reasons already explained, he would always be sympathetic to the call for the colonization of Jews in Palestine. To the unrelieved chagrin of Moshe Leib Lilienblum and many others, however, Gordon would hold true to his conception of the necessity and primacy of the Jews' Europeanization, even after the outbreak of the pogroms in Russia and the emergence of racial anti-Semitism in the West.[47]

Indeed, if "Wisdom for the Errant of Spirit" is to be located in its proper intellectual and historical context, it ought to be understood not only or even especially as a precursor of later political ideologies, but as a fascinating East European resonation of the program of the moderate wing of the Reform tendency in Western

European Jewry, especially the stream in Jewish spiritual and intellectual life based at the Breslau Jewish Theological Seminary and personified by Zecharias Frankel. This approach was based on a conception of Judaism as a continuously evolving religious tradition and called for moderate reforms guided by the spirit of "Positive Historical Judaism."[48] Like Frankel and his colleagues, Gordon hesitated to produce a clear catechism of Judaism or to define precisely which rituals or practices ought to be modified or dropped. He, too, insisted that the Talmud "have a vote but not a veto" in the adumbration of a modern variety of Judaism, that reforms of Judaism had to flow at one and the same time from the Jewish masses and from their leaders, in accord with the demands of the Zeitgeist. At all times, Judaism had to be viewed as a pluralistic tradition, allowing for differing and even opposing interpretations of laws and customs, recognizing the sanctity and inviolability of the individual religious conscience. For Gordon as well as the moderate Reformers in Germany, in this evolving amalgam of modern Judaism the Hebrew language and the return to Zion would always command signal heights, but they would be complemented by adoption of the vernacular in daily life and the fight for civil rights and liberal politics in the Diaspora.[49]

This parallel between Judah Leib Gordon's views and those of the Breslau school would be made several years later by Gordon himself, in his call that Russian-Jewish students be sent to the Breslau seminary to learn there how to lead the masses of Jews in Eastern Europe to a moderate rapprochement between Judaism and modernity.[50] But in 1870, Gordon did not reflect further on possible Western models for this ideas, obsessed as he was with the battle with the traditional forces in Russia itself.

As may well have been predicted, "Wisdom for the Errant of Spriit" only upped the ante of antagonism between Gordon and Orthodox spokesmen. Attacks and counterattacks continued in the pages of *Ha-Meliz, Ha-Maggid,* and *Ha-Levanon,* dominating their pages as they did the lives of Gordon and his opponents. It was only in summer of 1871 that both sides realized that nothing new was being said, and that neither party was emerging victorious in the deluge of impassioned articles and long-winded ad hominem denunciations. The Kulturkampf of Russian Jewry seemed to be mired in a stalemate that would last a decade, until dramatic new external events and internal strifes charged both sides with new vitality.

In the meanwhile, Judah Leib Gordon wavered between great pride in the role he played in leading the fight for religious reform among the Jews of Russia and bouts of depression and pessimism. He was certain that the enlighteners had scored great successes, at least on the literary front, and that the tide of change could now not be resisted. On the other hand, the low level of the debate, the name-calling, and even the embarrassingly amateurish proofreading and printing of his articles evoked much anger and despair and brought to the surface his deep-seated frustration at being stranded in a small town where there was no one who shared his interests and views. Again, he began to explore the possibilities of moving to a larger city, especially Kovno or Vilna. He was on poorer terms than ever with the local Jewish community and felt he had to get away; he was still concerned about the education of his children, in particular his younger daughter, whom he had sent to the Russian gymnasium in Riga but now had to find some other place for her to study. Most important, he yearned to live in a more cosmopolitan community where he could find people who thought as he did, who were possessed by the same dreams and the same fears.[51]

As usual, Gordon turned to poetry to express his most heartfelt hopes and emotions. To one correspondent he confided that he had begun to work, but had not made much progress, on a major new poem to be called "The Tip of the (Hebrew Letter) Yud," [*Kozo shel yud*] which would tell of the plight of an innocent Jewish woman ruined by a heartless rabbi. The new Hebrew journal founded by Peretz Smolenskin in Vienna eagerly solicited Gordon's literary wares, and he was thrilled to see published in this journal his poems "Through the Shaft of a Litter" and "You Shall Rejoice in Your Festival." In addition, he sent to *Ha-Shahar* a compendium of twenty-two verses grouped under the heading "These Too Are the Fables of Judah"—mostly not very original variations on the antirabbinic theme his poetry had focused on for the last few years.

But by far the most impressive and important poem written by Gordon at this time was submitted as an introduction to this series. Entitled "For Whom Do I Toil?" [*Le-mi 'ani 'amel*], it read:

> The muse of poetry still steals away to me
> My heart still murmurs, my right hand
> Writes poems in a language long forgotten.
> What is my fate, my hope, my aim
> And for whom do I toil in the prime of my life
> Depriving myself of comfort and of joy? . . .
>
> My brothers, the enlightened, acquired knowledge
> But loosened their bonds to their people's tongue
> And scorned the aged mother and her crutch:
> "Abandon the language whose hour has passed
> Abandon its literature, so awkward and bland,
> Leave her for the language of the land."
>
> Daughters of Zion! Perhaps you
> Will turn your hearts to my plaintive cry?
> God has planted in you the spirit of mercy
> As well as grace, taste, and warmth—
> But alas! you've been raised as captives
> "He who teaches his daughter Torah teaches her folly!"
>
> And our sons? The generation to come?
> From childhood they take leave of us,
> For them above all my heart bleeds.
> They go forward, year after year,
> Who knows how far, who knows how wide?
> Perhaps whither there is no return.
>
> For whom, then, do I toil, I mere mortal,
> For the handful remaining lovers of Hebrew
> Who have not yet mocked her and scorned? . . .
> Yes, to you I sacrifice my soul and my tears
> I weep on your shoulders and share my pain
> I grasp you and embrace you again and again

O who can foresee the future, who can say
Am I not the last of Zion's poets
And you, the last readers?[52]

This brooding and poignant—if ultimately self-serving—*cri de coeur* quickly became one of Gordon's most famous poems; ironically, despite its last line, it would be known by heart by generations of readers reared in Hebrew. But this poem, too, has often been misrepresented in the popular and scholarly literature, miscast as a confession by Gordon of his loss of faith in the principles of the Hebrew Enlightenment.[53] Gordon had far from lost his faith. Quite to the contrary, at this time he was as secure in his belief in the invincible march of progress and enlightenment as he ever was or would be. "For Whom Do I Toil?" was not a confession of failure or despair, but the most successful of Gordon's periodic ponderings on the meaning of his life, on the frustration he felt as a lonely campaigner for a moderate reform of the life and culture of the Jews of Russia, caught between the Orthodox on the one hand and the "nihilists" on the other.

He, more than anyone else, knew what dangers and obstacles lurked in his path, but Judah Leib Gordon was far from abandoning his hopes for a bright new future. But even he did not yet imagine that within a few short months his wildest dreams would be surpassed, as he was called to move from the dreaded provincialism of small-town Lithuania to the most glittering, sophisticated, and European city in Russia, the capital itself.

7

St. Petersburg:
Culture and Politics
1872–1877

One of the many myths that cloud the perception of Jewish civilization in Eastern Europe is the notion that barely any Jews legally resided in the grand capital of the Russian Empire before the fall of the tsars. It is not only that the history of the Jewish community of St. Petersburg remains to be written—that is true of all the major Jewish centers in Russia and Poland; but the story of the intriguing Jewish community that lived and thrived in the shadow of the Winter Palace can serve as a uniquely tantalizing metaphor for the radical transformations that overwhelmed Russian Jewry in the nineteenth century.

Here was a city that had an enormous impact on Jewish history but which, unlike Vilna or Warsaw, had no Jewish presence before the nineteenth century and, in sharp contrast to Odessa, developed its character entirely independent of Jews or their culture. For the first century and a half of its existence, from the beginning of the eighteenth century to the late 1850s, St. Petersburg was all but closed to Jews. Then slowly, suspiciously, uncertainly, first a tiny number of Jews were received into its midst, and then more and more until, at the end of the Old Regime, St. Petersburg Jewry was one of the largest and most important in the empire.

This growth was almost completely regulated and determined from the palace—much like the development of the city as a whole. For unlike any of the other great capitals of Europe, St. Petersburg was founded as an act of will by a single monarch, Peter the Great, and assumed the character of its creator: rigorously rational, secular, tilted patently to the West, away from Moscow, the Church, the supposed Russian soul. St. Petersburg acquired its classic shape and style in the late eighteenth century, the age of Enlightenment, of unbridled optimism in the possibilities of progress and the uncharted vistas of mankind. Its deliberate and self-conscious modernism, its grandiose, almost absurdly broad boulevards and luxuriant architecture, its elaborate canals obscuring murky swamps, its eerie light that casts a golden glow on pastel palaces—all these would lead Dostoyevski to call St. Petersburg "the most abstract and premeditated city in the world." Here, everyone was uprooted and lived side by side, cut off from homes, roots, contexts: nobles and prostitutes, wealthy parvenus and beggars, students and stockbrokers, and, most of all, tens of thousands of that most modern of all creatures, bureaucrats.[1]

How foreign this picture is to the prevalent image of East European Jewish life, characterized by "shtetl" existence, in which the rhythms of the Jewish calendar were preserved as naturally as the changing of the seasons. However, from the 1820s to the 1930s, the small market town gradually ceased to define the locus of Jewish life in Eastern Europe, as Jews moved from villages and small towns to bigger towns and even larger cities, and finally to a handful of metropolises. This migration led vast numbers of Jews away from the time-honored centers of Jewish settlement in Lithuania, Belorussia, and the western Ukraine to new areas in the east, south, and north of the Russian Empire, where Jewish life invariably took on a substantially new cast.

The cause of this internal migration—like that of the great emigration overseas—can be pinpointed rather easily: not, as popular imagination has it, in violence and attack, but rather in the startling biological explosion of East European Jews in the nineteenth century. For the Jews of Russia and Poland were among the most explosive populations in this time, spurting from approximately 1.6 million in 1820 to over 4 million sixty years later. Feeding the enormous number of new mouths was bound to be a formidable problem for the Jews of Eastern Europe, even disregarding their dismal political status; faced with substantial legal, social, and economic restrictions, the dilemma soon came to be virtually insuperable. The best strategy to cope with this dilemma was one shared with dozens of other overpopulated groups in Europe—migration to areas where opportunity was supposed to abound. That meant, for one subset of Russian Jews, to seek their fortunes across the seas; the great emigration of East European Jews to America began, in fact if not in public memory, in the 1870s, when some thirty thousand Jews left Russia for the land of the free and the home of the brave.[2]

But for the majority of Russian Jews this solution was too radical; indeed, even in later years the fact is that most Russian Jews opted not to leave Russia even when they could. Far less disruptive, more popular, and longer lived was another sort of migration—to the cities of Russia proper.

The attractiveness of large cities to immigrants from the provinces is, of course, a classic phenomenon of all European societies in the nineteenth century, cutting across all lines of culture, language, class, and religion; more suprisingly, perhaps the metropolis's drawing power occurred as much in times of prosperity as in periods of recession. Sharing in this experience, the Jewish centers of the Russian Empire grew steadily through the century: Grodno's Jewish community trebled, Vilna's increased in size 10 times, and Minsk's 16 times; in cities with less of a Jewish past, such as Ekaterinoslav and Kiev, the increase was 215 and 245 times, respectively; and in the open port city of Odessa, the terminus of the substantial southeastern stream of Jewish migrants, the number of Jews increased in size 620 times over the course of the nineteenth century.[3]

But one of the most dramatic changes of all occurred in the capital of the empire. Here, as in Moscow and other cities outside the Pale of Settlement, Jews were not permitted to reside at all until the late 1850s and early 1860s, with very few exceptions. Thus, in 1802, almost a century after St. Petersburg was founded, its official register included the names of only 10 Jews legally resident in the city.

Twenty-five years later, the number had increased to the paltry figure of 230 Jews tolerated only on a temporary basis. The situation changed with the accession to the throne of Alexander II. The Liberator Tsar allowed wealthy Jews and those pursuing professional or vocational training to live outside the Pale and in the major cities of the realm. In 1860, the number of Jews in St. Petersburg was about 700; within a decade, the community doubled in size, bolstered by an estimated 4,000–5,000 Jews who lived in the capital extralegally, dodging and bribing the police at every turn. The hopeful years of the 1870s saw an impressive rise of the legal Jewish population of St. Petersburg to nearly 17,000—matched, undoubtedly, by an equal number of illegals. In the years after 1881, the numbers would tumble quickly as the police acquired more force and the Jews less influence, but in the latter years of the century the Jewish population began to grow once more, at a slower pace, until the onset of World War I brought to Petrograd (as the capital was now called, in a feeble stroke of Russification) a huge number of Jewish refugees deported from the war zone. Through revolutions and civil war, the Jewish population of Peter's city continued to grow in geometric progression. When the dust settled, and Petrograd was transmuted into Leningrad, there were some 85,000 Jews in its midst, a population that skyrocketed to some 250,000 on the eve of World War II.[4]

But it is not simply, or even especially, the demographic dynamic that is most captivating about this city's Jewish history. Rather, it is the specific nature of the Jewish community that emerged in the capital of all the Russias that may serve to epitomize the complex and paradoxical relationship between Jews and modernity that lies at the heart of modern Jewish history in Eastern Europe and the West. On the one hand, the Jews—or at least those Jews who had broken with their traditional way of life—were correctly identified by the bearers of power and the brokers of change as potentially potent allies of all that was new, exciting, and path-breaking; on the other hand, the very same Jews were resented, maligned, and feared precisely because they personified the break with tradition, the past, the known. In the Russian context, this meant above all that Jewish entrepreneurs, skilled in money transactions and frustrated by the lack of investment potential in the traditional world of the Pale, were perfect partners in the adventurous schemes to modernize Russia's economy and infrastructure. The first Jews to be invited to live in St. Petersburg in the late 1850s and early 1860s, then, were a handful of wealthy Jews who had accumulated vast reserves of capital primarily in the liquor industry in the Pale and were anxious to branch out into new, more lucrative ventures. Topping this list was the Gunzburg family, headed first by Joseph Yozel (Yevsel), who founded the important bank carrying his name in St. Petersburg in 1859, and then by his son Horace, ennobled as a baron in 1871 by the archduke of Hesse-Darmstadt.[5] Along with the Barons Gunzburg there settled in St. Petersburg lesser but still substantially wealthy and influential merchants and investors such as the Varshavskiis, Poliakovs, and Rosenthals. These men were at one and the same time the stalwart pillars of the new and proud Jewish community in St. Petersburg— and hence the de facto political leaders of Russian Jewry as a whole—and active participants in the creation of the modern Russian banking system, the railroads, and the industrial plant. It would be easy to exaggerate the role of these Jews in the building of modern Russia, just as many writers have greatly overstated the role of other Jews in the creation of Western capitalism. In both cases, the Jews were important players in the drama, but not its only protagonists, directors, or managers.[6]

But the Gunzburgs, the Varshavskiis, the Poliakovs, the Rosenthals gave the Jewish community of St. Petersburg its basic bent, which might be described as unilaterally haut bourgeois. The nucleus of St. Petersburg Jewry was composed of the wealthy great families around whom orbited a steadily growing retinue of assistants, agents, secretaries, nephews, and freeloaders. Virtually all of these Jews, from the barons down to the servants, joined in the seemingly ineluctable process of Russification that marked the St. Petersburg Jewish community from the very beginning. In the capital Jews spoke, wrote, did business, and made love in Russian; they sent their children almost exclusively to Russian gymnasia, commercial schools, and universities. Their Jewishness remained potent and heartfelt, but it was increasingly expressed in the Russian tongue. Even the small group of traditional Jews who moved to St. Petersburg—and later would prove to be Judah Leib Gordon's nemesis—were substantially Russified and adept at maneuvering in the corridors of power in ways far more sophisticated than the old-fashioned Jewish lobbyists in the Pale.

All of this was typical, to be sure, of the process of Jewish embourgeoisement throughout Europe and the New World. Similar processes were at play not only in Berlin, London, Paris, Rome, Vienna, and New York but in Warsaw, Cracow, Odessa, Bucharest, Budapest, and Prague as well. And like their upper-middle-class cousins elsewhere, the Jews of St. Petersburg rushed headlong into the liberal professions and into cultural roles at which they were peculiarly adept. Thus, Jews in the Russian capital became doctors, lawyers, pharmacists, journalists, and publishers in numbers far out of proportion to the size of their community. In Russia, as in Germany, Jews could not aspire to the highest ranks of the military or civil service or the academe, and so the many Jews in St. Petersburg—as in Berlin— who set their sights on such positions converted to Christianity to attain them. But by far most Jews hesitated before such a step and remained in the middle rung of the professional and intellectual hierarchies even during the most liberal of periods. Only in the arts least susceptible to national exclusivity—painting, sculpture, and, perhaps most of all, music—could Jews reach the pinnacle of St. Petersburg society. Many other Jews concentrated on specifically Jewish cultural endeavors, gradually establishing St. Petersburg as the capital of Jewish creativity in the Russian language. Here flourished a plethora of periodicals, newspapers, cultural and commercial societies, communal and philanthropic organizations that were unparalleled in the rest of the empire. The only competition was, of course, Odessa, but the two cities were poles apart in all respects, including their Jewish characteristics: the Jews of the southern port shared in (or perhaps exacerbated) the rakish, seedy, at times even demimonde attributes of this great international seaport in which Russian seemed to be spoken with a Sicilian twinge; the Jews of the capital cultivated the northern dignity of their hometown, a Russified Hanseatic trading center, with manners and mores to match and unbridled political power to boot. Soon, even the major Hebrew periodicals of Russian Jewry moved from Odessa to St. Petersburg, to be close to the center of government, commerce, and culture.

By the early 1870s, then, Jewish life in the Russian capital had acquired its distinctive cast. In the first place, the Jews of St. Petersburg never congregated in any quarter or section of town, and hence there never was anything akin to a Jewish neighborhood. Jews lived in all parts of the capital and were not confined or concentrated in any particular area. Even their communal institutions were not centered on any one locale but were scattered throughout the several islands that made up the city. This unusual pattern of residential and institutional integration was doubtless a function of the strange, random mix of populations characteristic of St. Petersburg as a whole.

But the demographic integration of the Jews of St. Petersburg hinted at a far deeper and more complex kind of integration, a psychological and ideological sense of belonging, unrequited by formal emancipation. The Jews of St. Petersburg believed themselves to be at one and the same time loyal subjects of the emperor and dedicated Jews, exemplars of a Russian-Jewish symbiosis that would one day devolve upon the entire Jewish population of the empire.

To broadcast this cultural ideal, the leaders of St. Petersburg Jewry, headed as always by the Gunzburgs, founded in December 1863 the Society for the Promotion of Enlightenment among the Jews of Russia.[7] In the first years of its existence, the society had modest success in spreading modern educational and cultural ideals to the Pale, publishing textbooks and curricula for use in the government-sponsored Jewish schools, and locating and subsidizing bright young students who needed financial help on their road from ḥeder and yeshivah to gymnasium, university, and service to their people. But the bankers and industrialists and railroad magnates who funded the society could hardly take time from their more pressing commitments to run educational and cultural programs with any degree of efficiency, and they were hardly able to keep in touch with the intellectual and literary tempests of the Pale. As a result, the Society for the Promotion of Enlightenment was a listless, virtually dormant organization, unable to carry out the imperatives of its generous sponsors. At the same time, the leading Jews of the capital, and particularly the elder Baron Gunzburg, realized that the growing Jewish community could no longer be managed as a private domain and required some coherent administrative hand to run the daily affairs of the philanthropic agencies, the synagogue, and the cemetery in a manner suitable to the style of the capital. The current unpaid and unofficial secretary of the community refused to take on the new job and salary, and was hired instead as a manager in a business concern run by one of his patrons.[8]

In the autumn of 1871, therefore, the baron and the other half dozen patrons of Jewish St. Petersburg decided to search for a suitable person to fill both of their organizational lacunae: a joint position as secretary of the St. Petersburg Jewish community and secretary of the Society for the Promotion of Enlightenment among the Jews of Russia. On October 24, 1871, they offered the post to none other than Judah Leib Gordon.

Gordon was by now frantically determined to quit Tel'shi for a larger, more enlightened town. For a short while, he was tempted by the possibility of a post in Odessa, but that was blocked by the always fractious inner politics of that tempestuous Jewish community. It is difficult to imagine what Judah Leib Gordon's subsequent life and career would have been like had he in fact moved to Odessa, so out of consonance was he with the spirit of that town and its Jewish ethos.

St. Petersburg, on the other hand, was breathtakingly suitable to Gordon's self-image, ambitions, and cultural politics. Was this not precisely the place where the charged imperatives of "Awake, My People!" had most graphically been brought to life? Was not the Society for the Promotion of Enlightenment exactly the sort of vehicle Gordon dreamed of to lead the charge of Jewish modernism in Russia? Here, at last, Gordon would have the chance to live not only in a big city but in the most European and cosmopolitan enclave in all Russia. If any more incentive were needed, in St. Petersburg there lived the one family member to whom Gordon was closest, his brother Abraham, a respected and successful attorney with powerful connections in the government.

True to his character, however, Judah Leib Gordon did not rush to accept the offer from St. Petersburg before carefully negotiating its terms and considering the potential effects on his family. The discussions with the St. Petersburg magnates went on for several months, during which Gordon was never quite sure whether they would end in success. Finally, a trial contract was agreed upon. He would take up the job for three months, at a modest salary below his real income in Tel'shi. If both sides were satisfied with the results, a new contract would be negotiated, with more generous terms.[9]

Depositing his family in Riga for the duration of the trial period, Gordon arrived in St. Petersburg in June 1872. His frame of mind upon leaving the provinces, he hoped for good, was hinted at as usual in a Hebrew poem deposited in his drawer. "On My Departure from Tel'shi" took up the other side of the coin of "For Whom Do I Toil?," lamenting not the abandonment of Hebrew for the fleshpots of assimilation on the part of the young, but the frustration of the self-sacrificing modernist who dedicated his life to the improvement of the traditional Jews of small-town Lithuania. Playing on the coincidence of his seven-year tenure in Tel'shi with the biblical parameters for the liberation of slaves, the poet mourned the seemingly fruitless efforts he had expended in Tel'shi: grooming and educating recalcitrant children, cultivating in them notions of civility and self-awareness, helping to feed the starving, and resisting obscurantist oppressors. All his efforts, however, yielded not gratitude and praise but denunciation and venom. But, the poet concludes, his work was not in vain:

> Six years, then, I served my brethren,
> Now I leave penniless, but not without gain,
> I did not waste my strength on nothingness,
> For I shall reap my reward from the generations to come.[10]

If "On My Departure from Tel'shi" revealed Gordon's private emotions upon his move to St. Petersburg, his ideological stance and public aspirations were most explicitly summarized in a long survey of contemporary Hebrew literature published in a new Russian-language journal called *Evreiskaia biblioteka* [Jewish Library] before he left Tel'shi.[11] In this article, Gordon analyzed in great detail a large number of important Hebrew books that had recently appeared in Russia and abroad, singling out for special praise Zecharias Frankel's *Introduction to the Jerusalem Talmud* as the model of sensitive historical research, and for searing criticism Eliezer Zweifel's *Peace on Israel,* which attempted to portray Hasidism from

a sympathetic but still enlightened point of view. But it was in his prefatory observations about the nature of Jewish life and culture that Gordon set forth the principles that would guide his work in the Russian capital.

He began with a rather innocuous citation from Leopold Zunz: "The Jewish
people may in truth be called the people of the book." Gordon enthusiastically
seconded this cliche, noting that "the Jewish people has twice lost its territory, its
political independence, but it did not cease to exist; but take away its books, and it
will disappear."[12] For Gordon, Jewish history is synonymous with the history of its
literature. That literature can be divided into three periods: the biblical age, in
which Jewish creativity encompassed all areas of human knowledge; the medieval
or Talmudic age, during which external oppression led to internal stultification and
the neglect of worldly wisdom;[13] and the modern era, beginning with Moses Mendelssohn, in which the Jewish creative genius was once more exposed to universal
culture and civilization. Naturally, the medium of this exposure was the German
tongue, which the Jews learned assiduously and completely, while not abandoning
their Hebraic literary and spiritual heritage. This marvelous combination led German Jewry to remarkable heights of wisdom and knowledge, but the creative genius
of German-Jewish culture was compromised by its progressive abandoment of the
Hebrew language and Hebrew literature. This unfortunate development resulted in
massive ignorance among German Jews, and more: it led to the decline of German-
Jewish scholarship and German-Jewish religious life, phenomena noted and
bemoaned by the best leaders of German Jewry itself. The torch was passed, therefore, to Russian Jewry, where knowledge of Hebrew and Jewish culture is still
intense, but where the further development of a modern Jewish culture, a modern
Jewish science, a modern Jewish literature is seriously threatened by several obstacles. The most substantial battle is the "cruelest and most tiresome, the battle with
fanaticism."[14] Repeating here his call for a thoroughgoing religious reform of the
Jews, he argued once more—but for the first time in the Russian language—that
the Russian rabbis' obscurantist antimodern extremism might prove more destructive than their German counterparts' reformist extremism. The mighty potential
for a creative synthesis between Jewish culture and modernity is threatened by the
rabbis, but it has a good chance to succeed if the modernists do not despair too
soon and if the whole venture is not subverted by the absence of well-run cultural
institutions in Russian Jewry.

Equally destructive, Gordon continued, was the recent tendency on the part of
the enlightened youth of Russian Jewry to relegate the Hebrew language and
Hebrew literature to the trash bin of history, the decision of Russian-Jewish students to divorce themselves from the classics of the Jewish tradition in the belief
that "Moses, David, and Isaiah must yield to Homer, Sophocles, and Virgil."[15]
There are even new-style rabbis and teachers in Russia, Gordon lamented, who
know no Hebrew and are ignorant of Jewish literature. Touching upon the subject
matter of "For Whom Do I Toil?" but avoiding its self-righteous tones, Gordon
fleshed out his linguistic ideology:

> We hope that we will not be accused of [abandoning] hope in a rapid and complete
> Russification of our co-religionists, or in not understanding the importance of the
> creation of a Jewish culture in our native tongue [na otechestvennom iazyke]. Pre-

cisely in the interest of such a Russification, which we believe in ardently, and of the creation of such a culture, for which we have worked so hard, we must denounce the views of our extremists in regard to the Hebrew language and Hebrew literature as rash and erroneous.[16]

The value of Hebrew, he pointed out, was best articulated in an article he had written a decade earlier in the journal *Sion,* but to no avail. The utility and importance of Hebrew may be argued from an ideal or abstract point of view, regarding the vital force preserved in the Hebrew language for those who master it. It may be argued that Hebrew is the only link that unites contemporary Jews to their long history and to Jews in all parts of the world. But the most fundamental argument in favor of Hebrew is on the practical or material level. First, it will take at least two generations, and possible a century, before the Russification of the Jews is complete; and until then the only means to enlightenment for Russian Jews will remain Hebrew. But even after that long process of acculturation is realized—"in that blessed time, when we will speak and think in Russian, even then knowledge of the Hebrew language will not lose its practical importance, as the key to the treasure-house of Jewish wisdom and culture."[17] Jews active in all endeavors, in all the professions, as well as in literature and scholarship, must retain a keen and intimate knowledge of Hebrew. This is not a call for making Hebrew into a spoken tongue, counseled the most important Hebrew poet of the day:

> In the first place, that pious hope in the resurrection of the Hebrew language can for the most part only be heard out of the mouths of the most fervent dreamers; secondly, the expression "to raise the Hebrew tongue" means, in that figurative Oriental language, only to assist in the proper teaching of the language and the development of Hebrew literature, . . . the preservation of the Hebrew language in the school and in literature.[18]

Opposition to that noble and essential task, Gordon repeated, was shared by the two extremes of Russian Jews, the Orthodox and the nihilists; the moderate progressive forces must join together to lead the way to a revitalized Judaism and Jewish culture, historically sound and sensitive to the demands of the time and the spirit of the future.

It is with this commitment that Judah Leib Gordon thrust himself with all his energy into his two new jobs in the capital. Within a very short time he proved his mettle to the leaders of St. Petersburg Jewry, and particularly to the Barons Gunzburg, who took a quick liking to Gordon and served as his benefactors and protectors for years to come. He soon became indispensable to both the Society for the Promotion of Enlightenment and the Jewish community of the capital, and his temporary contract was replaced with a permanent agreement promising him the substantial sum of eighteen hundred rubles per annum.[19]

One of Gordon's first duties as secretary of the Jewish community of St. Petersburg was the orchestration of the reception tendered by the Jews of the capital to Sir Moses Montefiore, upon the English dignitary's visit to St. Petersburg and audience with the tsar in July 1872. Several Jewish communities in Russia had asked Montefiore to visit Russia to mark the two hundredth birthday of Peter the Great, and Sir Moses agreed to do so, despite his advanced age. Gordon was thrilled to have a private audience with the famous Jewish nobleman, to whom he delivered a new poem and copies of all his books. He was more than gratified to hear Montefiore praise the advance of the Jews of Russia since his first visit there in 1846, and to single out for special attention the cultivated state of the Jews of the capital who "dress like any gentlemen in England, France, or Germany; their schools are well attended, and they are foremost in every honorable enterprise destined to promote the prosperity of their community, and the country at large."[20]

But the thrust of Gordon's job had nothing to do with greeting foreign dignitaries. For the most part, his work for the community centered around planning for and negotiating a restructuring of the basic institutions of Jewish life in the capital—a new synagogue, cemetery, burial society, rules of procedure. Most of Gordon's time, however, was devoted to his duties at the society, which consisted in large measure in the allocation of the roughly thirteen thousand rubles budgeted annually by the society for grants to Jewish authors, students, and educational institutions throughout the Pale. Gordon's responsibility was single-handedly to wade through the hundreds of applications, manuscripts, and petitions that reached his office every year and to decide which merited a subsidy in the furtherance of "Enlightenment" among the Jews of Russia. From the published minutes of the society, it is clear that he was formally allowed to make decisions in the name of the society without consulting with his superiors, although, to be sure, his actions were subject to the approval of the governors of the society.[21]

Two of Gordon's pet projects, which stemmed directly from his personal ideological preoccupations, occasioned some opposition and even public controversy. The first was his backing of a recommendation that the society aid Jewish female medical students in the Russian capital. In 1872, the St. Petersburg College of Physicians and Surgeons began to offer special "Women's Medical Courses," attracting 4 Jewish women the first year and larger numbers in every successive term. By the end of the decade, 169 Jewish women had been graduated from these courses, over a fifth of the total number of alumnae. Many of these women could not afford to pay their own tuition, and application was made to the society for assistance. While at first the governors of the society were reluctant to support this endeavor, under pressure from Gordon and others they relented, and the society contributed generously to funds established to help women medical students regardless of their religious affiliation.[22]

Gordon's second, and even more controversial, move was to convince the society to subsidize Russian Jews studying for the rabbinate at the Jewish Theological Seminary in Breslau. The director of that seminary, Zecharias Frankel, had written to St. Petersburg complaining that only a few Russian students attended his academy and expressing his desire that more be enabled to do so. Gordon enthusiastically took up this cause, as it accorded perfectly with his own religious and cultural predilections, as discussed above. Moreover, there were persistent rumors that the Russian authorities were considering closing down the government-sponsored rabbinical seminaries in Vilna and Zhitomir, and Gordon argued that the society should step into the breach and actively promote and subsidize the training of Russian rabbis in the Breslau seminary. That, he argued, would not only enable the major Jewish communities of the empire to employ at their heads truly well-educated rabbis, as opposed to the generally unsatisfactory products of Vilna and Zhitomir, but would also be an enormous boost to Jewish *Wissenschaft* in Russia. Local Judaic scholarship, he patiently explained to his board members, was demonstrably weak but absolutely vital to the benefit of the Jewish community as a whole. True knowledge about the history, literature, and faith of the Jews would undoubtedly rebound to their political benefit, as had happened in the West.[23]

This open insistence that the solution to the spiritual and cultural plight of Russian Jews be found in the Breslau version of "Positive Historical Judaism" was strongly opposed by several members of the society who believed that it would be wrong to train Russian rabbis in the German language and the "German spirit." (Included among the opposition to Gordon was none other than Dr. Leon Pinsker of Odessa, who would later challenge Gordon for being too dedicated to Russian culture and liberal politics.) Gordon, as usual, had his way, and the society went on annually to award grants to at least one Russian student studying at the Breslau seminary.

This move soon led to a minor public scandal. The formerly liberal, but now increasingly conservative, Russian newspaper *Golos* published a scathing editorial denouncing the society for supporting Russian students at German schools: Were not German institutions of higher learning the breeding ground for most of the revolutionaries who were causing so much damage to Russia? Why should the society, whose primary purpose ostensibly was to spread knowledge of the Russian language to the Jews, support students outside Russia? In addition, fulminated. A. A. Kraevskii, the editor of *Golos* and an honorary member of the society, why was the society, supposedly dedicated to Russifying the Jews, publishing works in the Hebrew language? Clearly, something was rotten in the administrative cadres of the society.[24]

Gordon attempted to answer these charges in a long letter to *Golos* itself, but the newspaper refused to print his rebuttal. Incensed, he considered suing Kraevskii on the grounds of slander, but was convinced that it was better to answer the attack in print. In a short response in the St. Petersburg *Stock Market News,* and then at greater length in *Evreiskaia biblioteka,* Gordon took on Kraevskii's charges, following a tack analogous to that he had taken in answering Jacob Brafman's similar accusations several years earlier. The editor of *Golos,* Gordon alleged, had for some mysterious reason abandoned the ideas of equity and justice that he previously had espoused, and was now thrown into an irrational frenzy every time the word "Jew" appeared in print. This animosity resulted in gross perversions of the truth and confusion of principles—most important, in a distortion of the goals of the Society for the Promotion of Enlightenment. *Golos* and others had supposed that the Russification of the Jews and their enlightenment were synonymous, but that was not the case. On the contrary, a clear distinction had to be drawn between the two processes. No one is opposed to the Jews' adoption of the Russian tongue in the fullest and most complete manner; indeed, that process has begun to such an extent that it is today virtually impossible to find a Russian-Jewish youth who has not started to study the vernacular. But what is crucial to understand is that linguistic acculturation is not coterminous with the inner transformation of the Jews, their abandoment of degrading superstitions and outdated mores that cannot be synthesized with modernity. There are many Jews, Gordon confessed, who speak perfect Russian but maintain all the habits, observances, and beliefs of traditional Judaism; what therefore must be done is to ensure not ony that the Jews speak, read, and think in Russian, but also that their inner life is modernized in the process. In sum, the guiding principle of the Society for the Promotion of Enlightenment among the Jews of Russia, revealed its secretary, is: "Enlightenment leads the Jews directly to the Russian language, but Russification alone does not guarantee their enlightenment."[25] For this reason, stipends to Russian Jews studying in Breslau or in other foreign academies are more than justified, for they are wise investments in the future of Russian Jewry as a thriving, creative enterprise. For the same reason, works in Hebrew that promote the goals of the society are salutary and indispensible.

This altercation between Gordon and *Golos* was a fascinating adumbration of two processes that would emerge with full force a short time later. The proponents of Jewish Enlightenment in Russia would have to come to terms not only with the segment of the Russified Jewish population disinterested in matters Jewish or in Hebrew culture, but also with the emergence of a possibly more substantial number of Jews who had realized the advantages of learning the Russian language but had not internalized the cultural dictates or reformatory goals of the Haskalah. Gordon and his colleagues were slowly awakening to the complex reality that the objects of their educational and cultural mission could be receptive to external modifications of their speech and dress while retaining many, if not most, of the religious, social, and psychological attributes of traditional Judaism. At the very least, it was becoming even clearer to Judah Leib Gordon that the inner reform of the Jews could not be separated from, and indeed had to precede, their external amelioration.

On another front, Gordon and his patrons in the St. Petersburg Jewish plutocracy had to come to grips with the embryonic appearance of a new phenomenon that would threaten their campaign for the extension of Jewish political rights in Russia. The accusations made by the editor of *Golos,* a former supporter of Jewish legal advance, were grounded in and symptomatic of two parallel lines of anti-Jewish invective that were only beginning to be heard in the 1870s but would gain tragic momentum in the next decades. On the one hand, the Jews were charged with fomenting and leading the revolutionary movement, based in student organizations at Western universities, that aimed at destroying the Russian state in the name of nihilism and cultural radicalism. At the same time, the Jews were condemned for insisting upon their own cultural separatism, despite their ostensible Russification. In other words, Kraevskii and many other former supporters of the Jews were beginning to argue that the original liberal goal of integrating the Jews into the Russian polity had been subverted by the Jews themselves, thus demonstrating the error of the naive original integrationist intention.

In 1873, these dual threats to the cultural and emancipatory politics of the Haskalah were not yet joined in a coherent ideological or political platform or ratified by significant external events. Judah Leib Gordon and his co-believers, therefore, could still rest assured that they were on the path to a successful revivification of the Jews and Jewish culture in Russia, with the active support of the Russian government and enlightened public opinion. To validate this belief Gordon, for one, had only to look to three significant events in his own life. First, in October 1873 the government awarded him the title of "Honorary Citizen," the highest legal status accessible to a non-noble in tsarist Russia, affording him the right of permanent residence in the capital and throughout the empire and significant financial benefits as well.[26] In other words, by the standards of the Russian autocracy, Judah Leib Gordon was now effectively an emancipated citizen of the Russian state, and he had attained this emancipation by dint not of wealth or formal academic degrees but of his cultural service to the Jews and the Crown. He was now de jure as well as de facto "a man in the streets and a Jew at home" in the sense that he envisioned the goal for all of Russian Jews. Second, Gordon personally witnessed the defeat of the forces of reaction in the Russian realm. His old enemy, Jacob Brafman, now a government censor of Hebrew books, attempted to outlaw the publication of Gordon's short stories, claiming that they were defamatory to Christianity, but was overruled by one of the most prominent Orientalists in Russia, Professor K. A. Kasovich of the University of St. Petersburg. Kasovich, a renowned expert on Sanskrit and Hebrew, had personally reviewed Gordon's work and deemed it praiseworthy and worthy of publication. Moreover, he had translated one of the stories into Russian and arranged to meet Gordon in person. Finally, equally gratifying to Gordon was the fact that *The End of Happiness Is Sadness* sold out almost its entire run of twenty-five hundred copies as soon as it hit the stands, and a second printing of "Two Nights and a Day at an Inn" was issued in Warsaw in an even larger edition.[27]

For the first time in his life, Gordon was now earning substantial royalties from his writings, which combined with his respectable salary to afford him a style of living consistent with his new-found legal status and social prominence. He was now veritably a St. Petersburg gentleman, meeting with important personages in the Russian administration, debating with editors of prominent Russian publications, and corresponding with foreign dignitaries such as Adolphe Crémieux.[28] His work for the Society for the Promotion of Enlightenment and the community was time-consuming and often rife with frustration, but on the whole he was thoroughly pleased with himself and his life in St. Petersburg.

This self-satisfaction, not surprisingly, was not terribly stimulating to his poetic muse. In his spare moments he would return sporadically to the long poem he had started in Tel'shi on the plight of the Jewish woman, but free time was at a minimum and was soon taken over by two large translation projects that demanded a good deal of attention. First, the society decided to undertake the first Russian translation of the Pentateuch specifically addressed to Jews and conforming with Jewish exegetical traditions. Even in the Russia of Alexander II, translating the Bible into the vernacular was a very sensitive matter, and Gordon, charged with supervision of the venture, had to proceed with great caution and tact. He also undertook to translate the Book of Exodus himself, and to edit the other four books as well. The resulting Russian-Hebrew bilingual edition passed the censor's approval in late 1874 and was published in Vilna in early 1875; its preface, written by Gordon, declared that it was meant to respond to the spreading use of the Russian language in "home, school and synagogual services" and strictly followed traditional Jewish interpretations of the Scriptures.[29] This important landmark in the advance of a Jewish culture in the Russian language was very well received by its intended audience, selling four thousand copies in its first year.[30]

While Gordon was absorbed in the Bible project, he was also entrusted by the society with the supervision of another massive translation venture—that of a collection of excerpts from the Talmud and other Rabbinic sources meant to serve as an introduction to the ethical and religious teachings of Judaism. The original idea for the collection had been put forward by Professor Daniel Chwolson a decade earlier, and the material had been selected by two conservative Vilna maskilim, Sh. Y. Fin and H. L. Katzenellenbogen. Now the texts, which ran to three large tomes, had to be translated into Russian—a formidable challenge that entangled Gordon in a myriad of personal, ideological, and financial complications he did not relish. More satisfying was the scholarly work he undertook on the project, the compilation of annotations and bibliographical guides to modern Rabbinic scholarship.

This Rabbinic compendium was meant, from the start, for two different audiences. It was quite blatantly an attempt to counter the negative image of the Talmud and Rabbinic Judaism purveyed to Russian public opinion by Brafman and others; at the same time, the volume was meant to be used as a basic textbook in Judaism for Jews who had no access to the Hebrew and Aramaic original texts, and in courses in Jewish religion at Russian-language Jewish schools. After negotiations and much divisiveness among the collaborators in the project, the first volume of *The Worldview of the Talmudists* [*Mirovozzrenie talmudistov*] appeared in St. Petersburg in 1874, followed by volumes two and three in 1876.[31]

The publication of this work involved Gordon in yet another taxing public battle with Jacob Brafman. Since moving to St. Petersburg Gordon had had several unpleasant encounters with the author of *The Book of the Kahal.* The most recent had occurred in February 1874. In his capacity as secretary to the Jewish community, Gordon had compiled a special prayer service for the dedication of the new Jewish cemetery in the capital. Brafman, as censor of Hebrew books, refused to allow the service to be printed, since it contained a memorial prayer for the souls of non-Jews that he deemed hypocritical. Gordon met with Brafman to appeal this decision, and was successful, but he was shocked at the offer the censor advanced: if the Barons Gunzburg were disposed to be generous to him, he would use all his connections in the government and the press to advance the idea that the only solution to the plight of the Jews in Russia was their immediate dispersal throughout the entire empire—in other words, the abolition of the Pale of Settlement; if rebuffed by the barons, he would continue and intensify his attacks against the Jews. Gordon advised Brafman that the Gunzburgs would never agree to this sort of blackmail, but agreed to relay the offer to them. As he had predicted, nothing ever came of the matter.[32]

However, when the last volumes of *The Worldview of the Talmudists* appeared in print, Brafman lashed out in a long, negative review in *Golos,* entitled "The Jewish Jesuits." The compilation put out by the "Brotherhood for the Spread of Enlightenment among the Jews of Russia," as he called the society in consonance with his general charge that Jewish fraternal and communal organizations were conspiring to take over the world, deliberately misrepresents its purposes as well as the authorities it cites and the general tenor of Judaism. Masquerading as a textbook aimed at Jews, it is in fact meant to fool naive Christians into believing that Jewish teachings are the opposite of what they truly are. Thus, rather than promoting tolerance among faiths and loyalty to Gentile authorities, as the volumes under review maintain, Judaism actually mandates hatred and exploitation of the non-Jew, avoidance of secular courts, and a separatist political stance based on the hope of the restoration of a Jewish kingdom in Palestine. This goal is financed and orchestrated by the worldwide Jewish conspiracy, of which every Jewish community and organization is a part. The only difference between the traditional Jews and the modernists is the means by which they hope to achieve their final victory over the nations of the earth: the Talmudists await miraculous intervention on the part of the Almighty in the person of the Messiah, while the so-called enlighteners argue that the return to Zion and the subjugation of the Gentiles must come about by natural means, and especially through education. The best proof of the latter stance, Brafman maintained, was an article written by none other than the secretary of the notorious Brotherhood of Enlightenment himself, Mr. Gordon. In the Viennese journal *Ha-Shaḥar,* Brafman revealed to his readers, Gordon had published a manifesto that called on Russian Jews to train themselves as soldiers, engineers, physicians, and the like, to prepare themselves for the ultimate battle with the Gentiles and the restitution of Jewish political independence in Palestine. Obviously, Brafman continued, the very words uttered on this subject by the secretary of the Society for the Promotion of Enlightenment prove that "whatever gloss a Jew puts on [the messianic] doctrine, he can in no way ever consider himself a permanent citizen of the country in which he lives, but merely an exile awaiting the blast of the trumpet heralding liberation from that yoke and the renewal of the Jewish monarchy."[33]

This basic alienation from the Russian government and the Russian people is disguised by the utterly dishonest *The Worldview of the Talmudists,* and by the brotherhood, which paid for its compilation as well as the distribution of secretive books and brochures in Hebrew dedicated to its disloyal purposes. All this demonstrates once more that the goal of integrating the Jews into Russian society is merely a dangerous and duplicitous charade, an effort on the part of Russian Jewry, armed with enormous financial resources, to weaken and ultimately to destroy Russia, as the avant-garde of a worldwide movement whose basic credo is "one for all and all for one."[34]

Gordon and the society could not let this attack pass in silence. Two months after its appearance, Gordon responded on the pages of *Golos* with a lengthy article originally entitled "Literary Buffoonery," but changed to "The Worldview of the Talmudists" at the insistence of the editor.[35] Gordon's retort was very similar to his first polemic with Brafman almost a decade earlier. Everyone is familiar with Brafman's animosity to the Jews and his consistent and seemingly deliberate misrepresentation of Judaic teachings and texts. No amount of public display of his massive errors and lies seems to dissuade Mr. Brafman from continuing to repeat his phony claims and to cite his mistranslated texts. The work that elicited his calumnies this time is a truly innocent work, a straightforward attempt to present in the Russian tongue a succinct handbook to the ethical and moral teachings of Jewish sages through the ages. Such a work in the Russian language is aimed primarily at the growing population of "moderate-conservative" Russian Jews who "seek their salvation in a prudent combination of the national-Jewish with the universal."[36] They want to raise their children both in the Russian language and in the Jewish faith and national heritage, and recognize that works such as *The Worldview of the Talmudists* are necessary and useful. In addition, it might very well be that some traditional rabbis are beginning to recognize the utility of introducing the

Russian language into their classrooms, and they, too, will find the ethics textbook and the Pentateuch translation sponsored by the society helpful tools in the dissemination of Russian literacy among their charges. In addition, many non-Jews will learn a good deal about their Jewish neighbors from this work, and it is recommended to them as well. Clearly, enemies of the Jews such as Brafman oppose all these goals and seek to discredit the veracity and honesty of the compendium. In so doing, as usual he merely demonstrates his astonishing ignorance of the Hebrew language and the Talmud and his inability even to copy texts without grievous mistakes and outrageous miscitations. There is no denying the fact that the Talmud and Rabbinic literature contain much material that cannot be accepted as valid in the modern world, or that some of the medieval Jewish philosophers cited in the collection may have expressed some sentiments foreign to nineteenth-century notions of religious pluralism. But the goal of *The Worldview of the Talmudists* and the other publications of the Society for the Promotion of Enlightenment is precisely to instruct the Jews in differentiating between the relevant and irrelevant aspects of their spiritual legacy, to direct them to the treasure houses of true religious wisdom contained in the Talmud, the Midrash, and later Rabbinic literature. Any fair-minded and enlightened reader will learn from this work and others like it that those aspects of traditional Judaism that are offensive to humanitarian sensibilities and unacceptable in the modern world were in all cases simply the result of the persecutions to which the Jews were subjected through the millennia. To restore Judaism and the Jews to their rich and noble heritage is possible in the modern world, even if Brafman and his ilk oppose this very effort, for a reformed and purified Judaism is more destructive of their nefarious intentions than is traditional Judaism as practiced in the Pale. Therefore, scoundrels like Brafman must attack works such as *The Worldview of the Talmudists* and distort the words of the great teachers of the Jewish people through the ages.

Touching on the personal affront contained in Brafman's piece, Gordon proposed that while ancient authors cannot rise to their own defense against their vicious manipulation, living authors can do so, even though it is distasteful even to appear to grant credence to lies by responding to them with a statement of one's own belief. Thus, Gordon confessed, he is compelled to refute Brafman's ingenious attempts to fool his readers into thinking that everywhere Jews are huddling together planning an imminent advance on the Holy Land and a coronation of a Davidic successor on his throne, that even in St. Petersburg there exists an organization dedicated to assisting Jews in preparation for their political restoration. In support of this preposterous fantasy, Brafman cites a purported epistle to the Jews written by the secretary of the society. The words that Brafman reproduces from the pages of *Ha-Shaḥar* were indeed penned by their author, Gordon explained, but they must be understood in their proper context, as a snippet from a long monograph attacking the rabbis and calling for religious reform in Russian Jewry.

The article cited by Brafman, therefore, was in no way a manifesto to the Jews actually to plan an active return to the Holy Land, but was a polemical device aimed at refuting the superannuated messianic belief of the traditional rabbis:

> The existence among the Jews of an article of faith in the coming of the Messiah,
> deemed by Brafman for greater effect as a *political* doctrine, is hardly news to anyone,

and can scarcely be claimed as a discovery by him. Who does not know that the Jews still await their redemption? But how do right-thinking Jews regard that belief? Do they hope for their redemption by means of the universal recognition of their human rights, or do they really portray the messianic era in the forms alleged by Mr. Brafman? An answer to this question is superfluous.[37]

Even Brafman knows that the Reform Jews in Germany have dispensed with the messianic faith; but even in its traditional form, the Jewish belief in the restitution of the Jerusalem monarchy can frighten only sick imaginations or serve as the subject of cunning rogues; people with healthy minds or serious dispositions look at this matter differently. When, for example, at the beginning of the nineteenth century, Polish patriots began to be hounded by the police for singing their national hymns and prayers, they protested that the Jews were allowed to bemoan the destruction of Jerusalem and to pray every day for its reconstruction; they were advised that when they would find themselves in the same situation as the Jews, they too would be permitted such prayers and sentiments.

Thus, Gordon concluded,

> We do not regard Mr. Brafman as naive enough to believe in a danger facing the Ottoman Empire on the part of the Jews. Meanwhile, his alarmist article is written in such a serious tone that it cannot be taken seriously and cannot alarm any right-thinking person.[38]

Debates over such matters are merely diversionary tactics employed by Brafman to lead his readers astray, to confuse their understanding of the situation of Russian Jews and to confound the workings of the society and all intelligent men and women who realize that only through education and enlightenment can the Jews be redeemed.

This response scarcely convinced Brafman, who dashed off to *Golos* yet another scabrous attack on Gordon, the society, and the whole notion of enlightening the benighted Jews.[39] More important than the immediate effect of this debate, however, is its further revelation of Judah Leib Gordon's views on a subject that in the mid-1870s, was at best marginal to the overall concerns of the Jewish intelligentsia in Russia, but would soon overwhelm all other issues. As Gordon explained, in no way had he seriously advocated that the time had come for the Jews of Russia to partake in or lead their ultimate redemption in Palestine. Quite to the contrary, he insisted that it was utterly impossible for the Jews to be liberated in any sense of the word until they had reformed themselves in line with the dictates of the Haskalah. Only after the Jews were transformed, only after the Jews of Russia had been elevated to the level of the German Jews, without replicating their unfortunate errors, could the liberation of the Jews ensue. That liberation was synonymous with the nations of the earth granting the Jews all their human rights, including the right to return to Zion, for that return, according to Gordon, was a necessary part of the eventual redemption of the Jews, which would result not from miraculous intervention on the part of God but from the actions of the Jews themselves. Until such time, however, the notion that a return to Palestine was imminent was simply silly, and the idea that the Ottoman Empire need fear the Society for the Promotion of

Enlightenment among the Jews of Russia or the Alliance Israélite Universelle was utterly preposterous.

The public pronouncement on the question of the return of the Jews to Zion reinforced sentiments that Gordon had expressed only a few months earlier in a private letter to a friend. Hearing that the Anglo-Jewish community was organizing support for Jewish colonization in Palestine as a way to honor Sir Moses Montefiore, Gordon confessed that in his fondest fantasies he had always dreamed of the Land of Israel and the return of the Jews to their homeland, and thus was excited by the news hailing from London, which undoubtedly would elicit the ire of the Orthodox. The establishment of Jewish colonies in Palestine was not only a fitting tribute to Montefiore but also was an important stepping-stone to the ultimate redemption of the Jewish people as a whole. If his dream could be realized before his death, he would become another man: he would doff his European cloak and drape himself in a haircoat and wander over the hills and dales of Judea proclaiming the advent of redemption. In reality, however, he doubted that this could ever come to pass, given the fact that the Jewish community of Palestine was nothing more than a nest of useless parasites, the arch-personifications of the evils of traditional Judaism. The efforts of the modern colonists, therefore, were laudable in theory but compromised in practice:

> To reach this end, however, we must start from a different source, we must purify the Land and exile from its midst all the Jews currently living there, so that not a trace of them remains; we must sweep out with a new broom all the vile spiderwebs that these myriapods have spun, and bring a fresh spirit to the Land, whose air now reeks with the stench of the study-houses, their filth and ignorance. If all this is not done, all our labors will be in vain and our efforts will yield nought.[40]

In its original rhetorical context, this call for the expulsion of the traditional Jewish population of Palestine—what came to be known as the Old Yishuv—as a prerequisite to any new Jewish settlement may well have sounded less vitriolic than it does today. But time and time again, in private and in public, Gordon would repeat his basic contention that any colonization by Jews of the Land of Israel that is not preceded by a thoroughgoing religious reform was doomed to fail (just as any Russification of the Jews not preceded by internal reform was insufficient and dangerous). As the agitation over emigration to Zion became more and more pressing in the coming years, both the "Palestinophiles" and their opponents tried to enlist Gordon in their causes, but to no avail. Even half a century after his death, an unsuccessful attempt was made to attribute to him an anonymous German pamphlet, published in 1877, calling for a Jewish state in Palestine under British aegis— a position that in no way he could have endorsed.[41] Convinced as he was in the absolute truth of his basic proposition, Gordon would never stray from the belief that the enlightenment of the Jews must precede their physical, political, or even psychological liberation. This conviction would set Gordon in direct opposition to some of his closest friends and would occasion enormous controversy in Russian-Jewish public life. But Gordon would not be moved.

The battle with Brafman took a much less onerous psychic toll on Gordon than the inner Jewish fights that would presently ensue, but in its aftermath Gordon still felt rather debilitated, both physically and emotionally. Especially egregious was the fact that the fracas had come at a time when he was overworked with his latest duty for the Jewish community of St. Petersburg—working up statutes by which the communal agencies could be run along efficient, modern lines. By the summer of 1876 Gordon was utterly exhausted, and his doctors advised him to take the most common remedy of the age, a cure at one of the German spas. Gordon had never stepped foot on foreign soil before and enthusiastically accepted his physicians' recommendation, setting forth for the famous baths at Marienbad. On the way, he spent three days in Berlin, a visit he described with great panache some years later in a marvelous memoir entitled "One Hour of Pleasure."[42] In this piece, he recalled only half-sarcastically that he was not very impressed with the normal tourist attractions of the Prussian capital: the emperor's residence paled in comparison with the Winter Palace; the government buildings fell far short of the grandeur and sweep of their counterparts along the Neva. But what most interested the visitor from the north was not these sites but the landmarks of the birthplace of modern Judaism. He wanted to extract from the Berlin Jewish community lessons that could help his work at home. He therefore called on the headquarters of Jewish Berlin, visited the various synagogues and temples representing the new-fangled versions of Judaism he had only read about beforehand, and tracked down the tomb of his hero, Moses Mendlessohn, in the Berlin Jewish cemetery. These visits merely depressed him, however, and provided him with no model easily exportable to the Russian capital. On the one hand, he was much impressed with the way in which the Jewish community of Berlin was run, but realized that its elaborate and well-oiled machine was predicated on the compulsory tax that the government permitted the Jewish community to impose on its members. The Russian authorities, to be sure, would never adopt such a system. On the other hand, he was frankly put off by the temple services he sampled, as indicative of an enfeebled Judaism striving desperately for some coherence, but in a way thankfully not transportable to Russia.

Only in one Berlin locale did Gordon eventually find the satisfaction that he sought, in the home of the greatest living Jewish scholar, the founder of the *Wissenschaft des Judentums*, Leopold Zunz. Not that the encounter with Zunz occurred without initial difficulties. As Gordon humorously described the event, one Saturday afternoon he decided to call upon the famous scholar and located his home. At the front door he was greeted by a rather somber and intimidating woman (who turned out to be Zunz's niece) who would not allow the stranger inside the house. Gordon all but barged through the door and found himself face to face with a wizened old man. Realizing that he could just as easily be mistaken for a thief, Gordon calmed down and asked in polite tones if Dr. Zunz was at home. To his surprise, the tiny ancient introduced himself as Leopold Zunz and asked who, pray tell, was the visitor? Gordon replied that he was a Hebrew writer from the East, here to pay his respects to the great scholar; now that he had laid eyes on the object of his search, he could leave in peace. Zunz invited him to sit down and asked his name. After being informed that his Russian guest was Judah Leib Gordon, the old man rubbed his forehead, as if trying to summon up lost memories. "Yes, yes, I know the name," Zunz replied. "You are a writer; give me a moment to recollect what you have written." Gordon helped his host out with the titles of his books,

but thought to himself that had he been a medieval Hebrew poet, Zunz undoubtedly would have known all of his poems by heart; since he was a modern, though,
the world's greatest expert on Hebrew poetry could not remember one of his lines.[43]

This is the basis for what has become undoubtedly the best-known anecdote
about Judah Leib Gordon, the only story about him to be enshrined in the pantheon of Jewish humor. The point of the oft-retold story—which often ends with
Zunz asking the Hebrew poet, "When did you live?"—is ostensibly to demonstrate
the radically divergent paths of Jewish history on either side of the Oder River: on
the one hand, the East European Jew, nationalist, Hebraist, vital, if a bit uncouth
and more than a little brash; on the other hand, the all-too-sober, indeed virtually
desiccated German-Jewish professor, pedantic, unimaginative, antiquarian. The
only problem with this reading of the meeting between Gordon and Zunz is that it
is subverted by Gordon himself in the rest of the story, which is never cited. After
Gordon started to list his books for Zunz, the old scholar interrupted him:

> Of course, of course, I remember now; thank you for helping to prod my memory.
> Here is proof that I know exactly who you are and what you have written: you are
> the one who took issue not long ago with Moritz Sch[teinschneider] for making use
> of your work without your permission. And you regularly submit reports to the *All-
> gemeine Zeitung des Judentums,* do you not?[44]

Gordon was more than pleased that Zunz now recalled exactly who he was, but
was made uncomfortable by the older man's obvious embarrassment at his temporary inability to place his guest's name. After this shaky beginning, however, the
rest of the afternoon went very smoothly, with Gordon meeting the famous Professor Lazarus of Berlin University and his wife and having an entertaining and
gratifying discussion of several matters, including the rude behavior of East European Jewish migrants to Berlin. Gordon half-seriously tried to defend the behavior
of the refugees from the East, claiming that he, too, had behaved roughly when
coming to Zunz's door. Indeed, in response to this behavior the old professor had
looked fearfully at the visitor's hands, as if expecting to see a weapon in them. To
the shared laughter of the assembled company, Gordon learned what actually had
happened: Zunz and his niece Bertha were simply afraid that here was yet another
young writer trying to peddle his wares, and that is why they checked to see if he
came with empty hands.

In the end, the true lesson that Gordon extracted from his afternoon with Zunz
was very far from the moral of the famous anecdote—that German Jewry was irrelevant and inappropriate as a model for Russian Jewry. Rather, as Gordon himself
reflected in yet another part of the story never cited:

> My intention is not to criticize [the accomplishments of the German Reformers] but
> only to say that they do not provide me with the complete satisfaction that I seek. . . .
> In Russia our reformers must model ourselves on our German predecessors, but not
> follow them blindly, for their reforms are themselves in need of reform.[45]

With this conclusion firmly fixed in his mind, Gordon continued on to Marienbad, where he spent the rest of the summer. Here, away from the burdens of the
society, the St. Petersburg community, and his family, he not only regained his

strength but returned with a clear mind to the major poetic project he had begun in Tel'shi and had pursued with more vigor in the last several months. For the rest of the summer in Marienbad, he worked doggedly to complete what he—and hosts of later readers—would come to regard as his best poem, the mock epic "The Tip of the Yud" [*Kozo shel yud*].[46]

The opening lines of this passionate threnody on the plight of the Jewish woman sung out its stark but bold moral:

> Jewish woman, who knows your life?
> You come in the darkness and never see the light,
> Your woes and your joys, your hopes and desires,
> Are born within you and die unfulfilled;
> Daughters of other peoples and tribes
> Enjoy some pleasure and comfort in this life
> But the fate of the Jewess is eternal servitude.[47]

The next ten stanzas expand on the depth of this degradation in lines clear and precise and melodiously scanned, despite their bitter thrust. Though graced with intelligence and taste, the Jewish woman is deliberately kept from learning, the rabbis ruling that "teaching a girl Torah is like teaching her folly," that her voice and hair incite lechery, that she must be restrained like an enemy at bay. She is not taught Hebrew, but that is all to the good, for the doors of the synagogue are locked in her face and inside, every day, the prayer "Blessed be the Lord who has not made a woman" is intoned. She is held to be no better than a slave, an instrument for birthing and milking. No sooner does she come of age than she is sold to the highest bidder, enchained to a man not worthy of her or capable of sustaining her or even himself. When he fails, as he must, he simply abandons her to rot, as he absconds in search of another senseless dream.

This brazen beginning was deliberately poised to shock the reader and focus his attention. As usual, to twist his knife deeper into the wound, Gordon invoked and inverted sacred biblical images. For example, to make his point that women are married off without consideration of their feelings and that true love itself is condemned by the culture, he cited the famous biblical phrase "Should our sister be treated like a whore?"—the words used by the sons of Jacob to justify their slaughter of the rapists of their sister Dinah.[48]

The prolegomenon concluded, the sad but simple story unfolds. Bat-shuʿa is a wise and virtuous Jewish beauty engaged at the age of fifteen to Hillel, an unkempt Talmud whiz sent off to the Volozhin yeshivah. Two years later they marry, to the envy of the town's maidens but to the bride's secret despair. As the groom's foot smashes the glass in remembrance of the razing of the Temple, the narrator, privy to the new bride's woes, interjects: "For thousands of years we recall the destruction of a city/ But to the destruction of the people we harden our hearts."[49] The couple immediately have children, but when Hillel's subsidy from his father-in-law runs out, he is incapable of supporting his family, being entirely ignorant of anything but the sacred folios. He decides to seek his fortune abroad, where gold is said to pave the streets. Left with no support, Bat-shuʿa sells off her jewels and opens a small store in order to feed her children. From dawn to dusk, year in, year out, she toils to earn her keep, since Hillel is heard from no more. Mocked as a presumptive 'agunah—a grass widow who can marry no more—she cries herself to sleep every night. But her tears will soon be stilled, the narrator assures her and his readers, for

> The cries of the destitute are not whistles in the breeze,
> There is an all-hearing ear and imminent salvation.
> If men of evil heart, folly and deceit
> Fill the earth with perversity and pain,
> God's eye shields His creatures and His mercy His works,
> He will bring justice and charity to the oppressed.
> Be strong, then, Bat-shu'a, have hope, pure soul,
> For the Lord has preceded your affliction with its cure.[50]

The sensitive reader of Gordon's previous epics might well have marked these words as ominous, for other heroines of his verse—Martha in "Between the Lions' Teeth" and Penina of "In the Depths of the Sea"—had invoked the same belief in an "all-hearing ear" to tragic results.

The deus ex machina soon arrives on the scene, in the person of Fabi, an enlightened Jew working as a supervisor on the railway lines now penetrating the Pale (and, not incidentally, causing Bat-shu'a's father, a keeper of a post-station, to lose his income and die in poverty). Fabi, the perfect symbol of the modern age, discovers Bat-shu'a's plight and secretly falls in love with her. Apprised that Hillel may be living in Liverpool, he contacts a friend in that city who tracks down the recalcitrant husband and extracts from him a promise that he will send his wife a proper bill of divorce in exchange for a substantial payoff. Without letting on to Bat-shu'a that her liberty is in the offing, Fabi dispatches the requisite fee to Liverpool, and Hillel keeps his word, sending his wife a divorce decree before setting off on an ocean voyage to America. Back home, Fabi exuberantly reveals his scheme and his emotions to his beloved, who responds in kind, falling into his arms.

As the entranced lovers await the arrival of the messenger from Liverpool, they read of the sinking of the ship bearing Hillel; saddened, they nonetheless keep on dreaming of their new life in St. Petersburg, amid luxury and comfort. Finally, the writ of divorce arrives at the rabbi's house, and all rejoice to hear that soon Bat-shu'a will be free. But that was not to be, for now the narrator recants his previous words of pious hope:

> What is man's hope, to what avail
> If he is assailed by the floods of evil? . . .
> Though God's eye and His mercy shield his creations
> And this earth was formed with wisdom and charity,
> Alas, evil men full of folly and deceit
> Overwhelm His mercy and fill His world with pain.
> O, woe to you, Bat-shu'a, you soul so pure,
> The doctors of iniquity have preceded the cure with an affliction.[51]

The tragic, if avertible and nonsensical, denouement crashes forth. When the local rabbi examines the bill of divorce, he discovers that Hillel's name is spelled without the letter yud. His assistants assure him that this is the correct rendering of the name, but he insists that a grievous error has been made and that the writ of divorce is therefore null and void. Since Hillel is dead and cannot correct the scribal error, his wife can never marry another man. Bat-shuʿa hears of her fate and faints dead away. For months she lies sick, and her business disintegrates. When she recovers, she cannot carry on her trade. Fabi, ever the noble gentleman, offers to support her even though they can never marry, but she refuses, claiming that God obviously willed this to be, and she cannot accept charity from a stranger. The narrator turns to God and complains: You know the suffering of all your creatures, why do you keep silent and hide your face? In Your name, the priests of folly light fires that consume innocent souls; in Your name, they destroy lives because of a "tip of the yud!"[52]

Rebuffed and alone, Fabi goes off, never to be heard from again, and Bat-shuʿa is soon forgotten. When the train line is completed, amid the crowd of poor Jewish women hawking food to the travelers can be found a bent old hag, grey before her time, clutching two young children to her breast. This, of course, is poor Bat-shuʿa, who refuses to blame her God for her misfortune—it is the "tip of a yud" that felled her.

Published in Vienna only a few months after it was completed, "The Tip of the Yud" elicited storms of controversy and of praise from the moment of its appearance. For the next century, virtually without cease, critics of countless points of view have debated and analyzed this poem, with much of the fuss centering on questions of accuracy. Did Jewish law indeed require the voiding of the divorce? Was the rabbi a believable figure? Was his supposed model, Zekhariah Joseph Stern of Shavli, such an obscurantist or, in fact, a more lenient jurist? Could such a thing ever have happened? Would a married Jewish woman kiss her suitor before her divorce? In sum, in both his accusations and his characterizations, was Judah Leib Gordon being fair and accurate?[53]

Only a very small number of critics have pointed out the irrelevance of these questions to Gordon's purposes in writing "The Tip of the Yud." The poem was a satire, not a legal brief.[54] As befits the satirist, Gordon quite consciously exaggerated both the positive and the negative characters in his tale and took substantial liberties with the "truth," as his critics would later reconstruct it. Whether or not the rabbi ought in real life to have nullified the divorce clearly had no bearing on Gordon's depiction of the climactic event, which in its very language was meant to lampoon reality, not to replicate it. Thus, in a caustic but highly amusing rhymed couplet, Gordon described the outrageous rabbi holding fast to his position like an *ʿez shosul*—the Psalmist's "tree planted besides streams of water," the simile to the godly man—crying out, *"Ha-get posul"* ("the divorce is invalid!").[55] As the poet well knew, no reader of this couplet imbued with a sense of humor could restrain a smile at such a rhyming apposition, and therefore the point would be made regardless of the reader's ideological stance.

In "The Tip of the Yud" Gordon strove not to depict a typical, or even likely, scene in Russian-Jewish life, but to satirize the treatment of women in traditional Jewish society in order to kill three birds with one stone: to write a great poem, to demonstrate once more what he took to be the ignorance and obscurantism of the Russian rabbis, and, for the first time in verse, to argue for the emancipation of the Jewish woman. The latter cause was dear to his heart, as had been apparent for some time. Both in Shavli and in Tel'shi he had founded schools for Jewish girls and worked strenuously for their success; in order to secure a governess for his own daughters, to ensure their proper education, he combed through Russia and expended substantial sums; at the society he argued for support of female students. To the Hebrew poetess Miriam Markel-Mazessohn (to whom he would dedicate "The Tip of the Yud") he revealed his firm belief that the essential equality of men and women is obvious and clear-cut: "in the human body there is a difference in gender, but men and women share the same spirit."[56] Soon thereafter, he gleefully welcomed the news that the U.S. Congress had declared that the difference between the sexes did not affect the brain or intelligence—hadn't he himself written the same?[57] Interestingly, to the poetess, Gordon confessed that he did not really believe in the claims he had made in the opening lines of "The Tip of the Yud." Truly insidious notions about women had never been accepted among the Jews, as opposed to other groups; Jewish women had never been treated as poorly as others, never placed in harems and isolated from the real world. But whatever his private, rational thoughts on the subject, Gordon believed that satire was the most effective medium for cultural or political change. Write serious articles and treatises that call for reforms in Jewish life, he wrote to one of his publishers, and you will be ignored. But

> how mighty is the power of satire, which causes those asleep to awake, the mute to speak out, and mountains to move. . . . Satirize your enemies, poke fun at them and their flesh, and they will suddenly arise and lunge at you en masse. I have seen this myself; I am speaking here from experience.[58]

Judah Leib Gordon believed that "The Tip of the Yud" was his most successful poem, both in its aesthetic and linguistic accomplishments and in its ability to stir his opponents as well as his sympathizers to consider the plight of the Jewish woman. While the artistic merit of the poem can, of course, be disputed, there is no denying the fact that "The Tip of the Yud" did more than any other work of literature in any tongue to force the question of the treatment of women to the forefront of the debate over the transformation of Jewish society in the modern age.

Vilna in 1830. Lithograph by Karol Raczynski
(Columbia University Library)

אהבת

דוד ומיכל

מ א'ת

יהודה ליב גארדאׁן

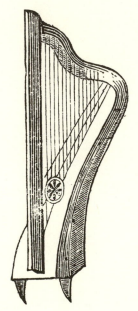

מַחֲדָפִיתֹ וּמַהֿנָּעַמְתְּ אַהֲבָה בַּתַּעֲנוּגִים ׃
(שיר ז' ז')

ווׁילנָׁא ·

שְׁנַת תרי"ז לפ"ק

Cover of Gordon's first book, *The Love of David and Michal* (1857)
(Columbia University Library)

L'AMOUR

DE DAVID ET MICAL,

POÈME ROMANTIQUE DE L'ECRITURE SAINTE

par

LEON GORDON

maître de la Religion à l'école hebraique
à Ponives.

Que tu es belle, et que tu es agréable,
A m o u r délicieuse!
Cant. de Cant. VII. 7.

WILNA

—

MDCCCLVII

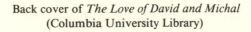

Back cover of *The Love of David and Michal*
(Columbia University Library)

СТИХОТВОРЕНІЯ

Л. О. ГОРДОНА

ВЪ ЧЕТЫРЕХЪ ЧАСТЯХЪ.

Изданіе кружка любителей древне-еврейскаго языка
въ С.-Петербургѣ.

ЧАСТЬ I:

ЛИРИЧЕСКІЯ СТИХОТВОРЕНІЯ.

С.-ПЕТЕРБУРГЪ.
Типо-Литографія Г. Пинеса и Ис. Цедербаума. Невскій пр., д. № 1.
1884.

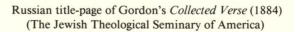

Russian title-page of Gordon's *Collected Verse* (1884)
(The Jewish Theological Seminary of America)

Judah Leib Gordon. Photograph in his *Collected Verse* (1884)
(Jewish Theological Seminary of America)

№ 1
ששית
סך כל . שורה מהורעות
10 קא"פ

ג' אייר תרכ"ז
שנה
מחירו לשנה – 14 רו"כ
עם פאריכא 50 ק'

הכרמל

מכתב עתי לבני ישראל

עם נוספות בלשון רוססיא

יוצא לאור מדי שבוע בשבוע

הָקִיצָה עַמִּי ·

הָקִיצָה עַמִּי ! עַד מָתַי תִּישָׁנָה ?
הֵן גַּז הַלַּיְל, הַשֶּׁמֶשׁ הֵאִירָה ;
הָקִיצָה, שָׂא עֵינֶךָ אָנָה וָאָנָה
וּזְמַנְךָ וּמְקוֹמְךָ אָנָא הַכִּירָה .

הֲכִי עָמַד הַזְּמַן וּכְנָפָיו רָפוּ
מִיּוֹם אֶל כַּנְפֵי הָאָרֶץ יָצָאתָ
אוֹ שָׁנִים אֲלָפִים לֹא תַמּוּ סָפוּ
מִיּוֹם תַּם חֻפְשְׁךָ וּבָאָרֶץ נֹד בָּאתָ ?

מֵאָז עַד עַתָּה דּוֹרוֹת רַבִּים סָפוּ
יָמִים וַאֲרָצוֹת מֵשָּׁם יַפְרִידוּנוּ
וַחֲלִיפוֹת סָאֱלִיפוֹת בָּאוּ חָלָפוּ
אַף קוֹרוֹת אֲחֵרוֹת עַתָּה עֹדֶנוּ

* * *

הָקִיצָה עַמִּי ! עַד מָתַי תִּישָׁנָה ?
הֵן גַּז הַלַּיְל, הַשֶּׁמֶשׁ הֵאִירָה ;
הָקִיצָה, שָׂא עֵינֶךָ אָנָה וָאָנָה
וּזְמַנְךָ וּמְקוֹמְךָ אָנָא הַכִּירָה .

הָאָרֶץ בָּהּ עַתָּה נֵחָיֶה נּוֹּלֵד
לְגֵלִילוֹת אֵירוֹפָּה הֲלֹא נֶחֱשָׁבָה —
אֲרוּכָה הַקְּטַנָּה מֵחֶלְקֵן חָדָל
וּבְחִקְרֵי הָחָכְמָה מִפָּכֵן נִשְׁעָנָה .

אֶרֶץ עֵדֶן זֹאת הֵן לָךְ תִּפָּתַח
בָּנֶיהָ אֶחֱזוּ לָךְ יִקְרְאוּן עַתָּה
עַד מָתַי תִּהְיֶה קִרְבָּה כְּאוֹרֵחַ
לָמָּה מִנֶּגֶד לָהֶם תֵּלֵךְ אָחֹתָה ?

וּכְבָר גַּם יָמִים שַׁקְדוּ כְּפָעֲל
אֶגְעַל צַוָּארְךָ יֵלֵךְ יָדִימוּ
מֵלִבָּם יִחָיוּ שִׂנְאַת שָׁוְא וָהֶבֶל
יִתְּנוּ לָךְ יָד, קַךְ שָׁלוֹם יָשִׂימוּ .

הֲרִימָה נָא רֹאשְׁךָ, הַיְשֵׁר גַּבֶּךָ
וּבְעֵינֵי אַהֲבָה אֵלֵימוֹ הַשְׁגִּיחָה
וּתְנָה לַחָכְמָה וָדַעַת לִבֶּךָ
וֶהְיֵה עַם בִּינוֹת וּבִלְשׁוֹנָם שִׂיחָה .

כָּל בַּעֲלֵי בִינָה בָּךְ חָכְמָה יִלְמֹדוּ
פּוֹעֲלִים וְאָמָנִים כָּל מַעֲשֶׂה חֹרֶשֶׁת
אַמִּיצֵי הַלֵּב בַּצָּבָא יַעֲבֹדוּ
אִכָּרִים יִקְנוּ שָׂדוֹת וּמַחֲרֶשֶׁת .

אֶל אוֹצַר הַמְּדִינָה הָבָא חֵילֶךָ
וּבְנִכְסֵיהָ קַח חֵלֶק וָזֵכֶר
הֱיֵה אָדָם בְּצֵאתֶךָ וִיהוּדִי בְּאָהֳלֶךָ
אָח לִבְּגֵי אַרְצֶךָ וּלְמַלְכְּךָ עֶבֶד .

* * *

הָקִיצָה עַמִּי ! עַד מָתַי תִּישָׁנָה ?
הֵן גַּז הַלַּיְל, הַשֶּׁמֶשׁ הֵאִירָה ;
הָקִיצָה, שָׂא עֵינֶךָ אָנָה וָאָנָה ,
וּזְמַנְךָ וּמְקוֹמְךָ אָנָא הַכִּירָה .

יהודה ליב גארדאן

על דבר בעלי המלאכות היהודים מן הסלדאטים שכלו ימי עבודתם בצבא

בצירקולאר של שר פנים המדינה (מיניסטער וונוטרעניך דיעל)
מיום 21 יאנואר שנה זו 1866 בבאור דברי
פקודת הקר"ה מיום 28 יוני שנת 1865 אשר יצאה , לתת
לבעלי מלאבות היהודים הישים לדור בפנים ארץ רוססיא ,
נאמרו הדברים האלה :

א) היהודים אשר עבדו עבודת הצבא , ויודעים לעשות
במלאבה , יש להם הזכות הנתונה לכל היהודים בפקודה
הגזברת .

ב) ובדבר תעירורות הראויות להיות בידם להעיד עליהם כי הם
בעלי מלאכות , הנה היה זה יהיו להם האפסאמ שהם
מקבלים בעת צאתם מן העבודה בצבא , ששם מפורש
שם המלאבה שעתעסק בה הכאלדאט בימי עבותו בצבא ,
לתעודה ובתב ראיה (דאקמענט) הנגרשים בסעיף השני
בפקודת הקר"ה . (ארעפט וויעסטאניק נומר 59)

First Publication of "Awake My People!" *Ha-Karmel* April 6, 1866
(The Jewish Theological Seminary of America)

Gordon's home, 1886, Ul. Voznezenskii, corner Bol'shaia Sadovaia
(as photographed by author in 1984)

Office of Ha-Meliẓ, 1886 Bol'shaia Sadovaia 62, St. Petersburg
(as photographed by author in 1984)

View of St. Petersburg from Office of Ha-Meliẓ, 1886
(as photographed by author in 1984)

Judah Leib Gordon
(National and University Library, Jerusalem)

8

Exile
1877–1880

While "The Tip of the Yud" was still at press, Judah Leib Gordon celebrated a personal triumph over the social norms castigated in the poem: his elder daughter Minna was engaged to marry the man she loved, Maxim Kaplan. A successful young lawyer employed first by the Russian Senate and then by a prominent private jurist, Maxim secured his future father-in-law's fervent favor not only because of his educational and professional accomplishments but also because he was the son of Ze'ev Kaplan, Gordon's longtime friend and fellow Hebrew litterateur and schoolmaster. When Minna and Maxim were married the next year, Gordon handed them a dowry of two thousand rubles, a testament to his secure financial situation at the time. Within a year they had a son, and Judah Leib Gordon was transformed, at the age of forty-eight, into a doting and enthusiastic grandfather.

For the first time in his adult life, he was at peace. To his brother-in-law Mikhl he rather triumphantly proclaimed that he had no real complaints, no true worries. He only hoped that his younger daughter would find as wonderful a mate as her sister had and that his son, now studying at a prestigious gymnasium, would be admitted to the university. He was working hard, but loving every minute of it. For a while, he had been concerned that the death of the senior Baron Gunzburg might jeopardize the financial stability of the Society for the Promotion of Enlightenment and the St. Petersburg Jewish community, but the young Baron Horace, now head of the family, took over his father's commitments willingly, and all was proceeding apace.[1]

Gordon complained that his duties at the society and for the community left him no time for his literary musings, but he continued to produce a good number of minor pieces, in genres both tried and new—several short stories and fables, four pseudobiblical prose poems, and Russian translations of the lamentations over the destruction of the Temple.[2] He also began a major new narrative poem, "Two Josephs Son of Simeon," which took several more years to complete.[3] In sum, his personal and professional bliss was paralleled and reinforced by a newfound literary success. "The Tip of the Yud" had confirmed his status as the most important

129

Hebrew poet of the day, and a well-heeled publisher offered to print a second volume of *The Songs of Judah,* to include all the poems written since the mid-1860s.[4]

Never one to overstate his own worth, Gordon realized that the success and fame he had garnished were rather circumscribed; that, after all, was the fate of a Hebrew poet. In an ironic fantasy penned to his friend and now in-law Ze'ev Kaplan, he jokingly wished that he could have a funeral like the one he had just attended, that of the great Russian poet Nekrasov. Here was a successful poet; his coffin was surrounded by wreaths of flowers sent by admirers from all walks of life, mourning their departed national hero. I, too, would like to be honored by my people, Gordon wrote. I always wanted to be a Nekrasov for the Jews, but my people don't listen to me and I won't leave this world to such an outpouring of emotions.[5]

This tongue-in-cheek lament has been taken seriously by a number of critics as proof that Gordon saw himself as a disciple of Nekrasov, striving to emulate the poetics and politics of the radical Russian poet. In fact, although Gordon may well have been inspired by some of Nekrasov's verses—in particular his famous paeans to the Russian peasant woman—Gordon viscerally rejected the aesthetic and political stance embraced by Nekrasov, who had become a staunch comrade of the critics Chernyshevsky and Dobroliubov. What Gordon admired about the deceased poet was, quite simply, his popularity and success.

As if to dispel any analogy between himself and the heroes of the new generation of Russian literature, increasingly lionized by the younger Hebrew readers and writers, Gordon composed a new poetic credo to commemorate the renewal, in late 1878, of Peretz Smolenskin's journal, *Ha-Shahar,* in Vienna, which had shut down for a year because of financial difficulties. Punning on the title of the journal, which meant "dawn," Gordon's "On the Rise of the Dawn" struck a caustic, if more than slightly self-righteous, autobiographical tone. In my youth, the poet began, I rose with the earliest light of day to sing sweet songs, to celebrate love and faith and hopeful dreams. But

> Suddenly I became another man,
> I can no longer sing but only mourn!
> Nightmares disturbed by my peaceful sleep—
> My people I saw face to face![6]

Confronted with the faults of his nation and the abundance of evil in the world, the poet's muse turns black and morose, able only to convey tales of woe and want. Asked to submit poems to "The Dawn," he demures with the claim that he is "not a poet but a mourner!" However, he will agree to have his verses published as testimonies of national sins and communal misdeeds, for perhaps there is still some slim hope that the diseased can be cured, that the dying will be revived. With the help of bearers of enlightenment such as *Ha-Shahar,* a new spirit will inevitably descend upon the Jews, vanquishing those who preach iniquity and raising the people as a whole to their former glory.[7]

Only a few weeks after this poem appeared in print, the harmonious balance between hope and despair that defined Judah Leib Gordon's life and worldview was shattered, never to be fully restored. The new year of 1879 had begun rather inconsequentially: the St. Petersburg Jewish community was electing a new board of governors and preparing finally to set into motion plans for the construction of a new main synagogue for the capital. Gordon was discomfited by the latter development, fearing that his work as secretary would be vastly increased, and therefore pressed the new board for a substantial increase in his salary. On a different level, the synagogue project worried him greatly, for he had distinct—and, as usual, quite idiosyncratic—ideas about what sort of building would be appropriate for what inevitably would be regarded as the central shrine of Judaism in the Russian Empire.

These ideas involved him in a minor public controversy. Eight years earlier, when the proposal for such a synagogue first had been approved by the government, the noted Russian architect V. Stasov had published an article in a Russian-Jewish journal denouncing the common notion that the Jews had no art of their own. A liberal philo-Semite, Stasov had contended that recent scholarship had established Jewish art as but another branch of Oriental aesthetics; consistent with the national genius of the Jewish people as expressed through their art and architecture, the proposed synagogue in St. Petersburg ought to be built in the Moorish style, capped with the Star of David. This was the design chosen for the central temple in Berlin and other major European cities, and ought to be employed in the Russian capital as well.[8]

The notion that St. Petersburg Jews would mark their emancipation and accomplishments with a house of worship that emphasized their "Orientalism" (and hence their ostensible foreignness) threw Judah Leib Gordon into a frenzy. Fearing that Stasov's weighty opinion would carry favor among the status-conscious patrons of the Jewish community, Gordon wrote an article rejecting the architect's conclusions as historically naive and spiritually ill-informed. It is one thing to claim that there is such a thing as Jewish art history through the millennia, and quite another to conclude that Jewish synagogual architecture at present must reflect the Oriental or Moorish style. Why choose only one example of Jewish-Gentile rapprochement as the expression of Jewish style par excellence, Gordon queried. In fact, wherever Jews lived, they engaged in the culture of their surroundings and copied the external trappings of their neighbors when building their houses of worship. What truly concerned them was inner spiritual truth and not the outward mode of expression. Therefore, the main synagogue in St. Petersburg ought to be built in a appropriately Russian style, reminiscent of Russian Orthodox cathedrals, save of course for any symbol of Christianity. At the same time, the St. Petersburg synagogue must not fall into the trap of replacing the Cross with the Star of David, as many Western European Jewish prayer houses had done, and as Stasov had advised, for that emblem has no historic integrity in Judaism and was merely a superstitious emblem used by kabbalists in their disgusting amulets and nefarious pseudospiritual machinations. A modern synagogue built by a progressive Jewish community should eschew any such spurious symbols of Judaism and should reflect the fact that the Jews in St. Petersburg practice a Western religion that is in utter harmony with the spiritual concerns of their neighbors of other faiths.[9]

This controversy had no immediate consequences, for the main St. Petersburg synagogue was in fact not built for another two decades. But Gordon's rather unpopular notions about synagogual architecture—ideas abandoned by West European Reformers already in the 1840s—did reveal the extent of his commitment to the Westernization and Russification of the Jews and his insistence, as chief functionary of official St. Petersburg Jewry, that the Jewish presence in the Russian capital conform totally to the modern spirit. This insistence led Gordon into an explosive public battle over another aspect of St. Petersburg Jewish politics, the appointment of a new rabbi for the capital. For a long while, Gordon had bristled at the fact that the spiritual head of St. Petersburg Jewry was Isaac Blazer, a traditional rabbi from the Pale. In 1875, when Gordon drew up the new statutes governing the inner affairs of the Jewish community, he had included in them a requirement that any new rabbi be a secularly educated representative of progressive Judaism in Russia. Two years later, Rabbi Blazer left St. Petersburg for Kovno and in his stead Gordon orchestrated the appointment of Rabbi Isaac Olshvanger, a moderate modernist. The large number of traditional Jews who had flocked to the capital in the past decade staunchly opposed this appointment and on their own contracted the Hasidic Rabbi Zalman Landau of Vitebsk to serve as their spiritual mentor. The problem was that Rabbi Landau had no right to live in the capital, as he fit none of the professional categories yielding the privilege of permanent resident outside the Pale. His supporters campaigned long and hard that he be formally registered as an assistant to the "Government Rabbi" of St. Petersburg, but Olshvanger already filled that post. At one point, the board of governors of the Jewish community was willing to register Landau as a second assistant to the state rabbi, but the city officials refused to permit this open charade, and Landau's legal position remained most precarious. Outraged at this rebuff, his supporters continued their campaign on his behalf and sought revenge against the one man who, they believed, stood most in their way, the powerful secretary of the Jewish community, Judah Leib Gordon.[10]

Late on Friday night, March 23, 1879, Gordon left his house to visit his colleague Adolph Landau, the editor of a Russian-Jewish journal.[11] Gordon's wife was ill, as usual, and had already gone to sleep, as had his son; his daughter was out visiting friends in the neighborhood and was due to return home shortly. On his way home in the early hours of the morning, Gordon noticed from afar that his house was totally illuminated, each window lit brightly in the dead of the night. Fearing that his wife's illness had taken a serious turn for the worse, he rushed home, passing a large carriage in front of his door. Entering the house, he found the cook in a state of alarm, screaming that the police had taken over the residence. Inside, he encountered ten officers armed to the teeth, standing guard over his wife, son and daughter, who were dressed as if they were embarking on a journey. The presiding officer, idly striking the notes of the piano, asked Gordon if he was head of the family but refused to answer any questions while his men conducted a thorough search through the Gordons' possessions, leaving nothing untouched. Outraged, Gordon insisted on knowing what was going on, who were these men, where was their warrant, what right did they had to invade his home and carry on in this manner. Certain that they had simply fallen upon the wrong house—after all, for seven years he had dealt with the highest officials in the capital and had done nothing to merit any suspicion—Gordon demanded at least that the officer reveal the name of his suspect. Surely this was simply a confusion of identities, the wrong house was being searched. After an hour of debate, Gordon heard his name pronounced by the policemen and his heart sank in dismay.

The search continued until five in the morning. The police seemed especially concerned, Gordon later recalled, with his photograph albums and correspondence, but swept up every written piece of evidence they could muster, including his daughter's letters to her classmates and his son's Greek and Latin notebooks. In the end, however, they recorded that they found nothing suspicious in this mass of material. Nonetheless, they insisted that the whole Gordon family come along with them and leave the house in the care of the servants. Convinced that the whole matter would be clarified as soon as they reached the police station, Gordon thought to take with him all the cash, important documents, and valuables he had at home, but no extra clothing or personal belongings. Hurried into the waiting carriage, the Gordons soon found themselves led not to a police station or a government office but into the notorious prison of St. Petersburg, the "Lithuanian Fortress." Gordon had once before been led through these corridors—he had been given an official tour when visiting some Jewish inmates; now he was receiving a different sort of tour of the premises.

In the main office of the prison, Gordon espied some ninety new inmates being processed in what had obviously been a busy evening for the secret police; at one point, the official in charge complained, "This is really a St. Bartholomew's Night!" As the male and female prisoners were separated and discharged to their quarters, Gordon still believed that he and his family were simply waiting to be interrogated and would be free to leave after the misunderstanding had been cleared up. Suddenly, to his utter shock, his wife and daughter were pulled away from him and led into a separate room; in a short while they returned, dressed in prison garb, and bade him farewell. Within a few minutes, he and his son were stripped of their clothes and possessions, handed prisoners' outfits, and thrown into a cell. Here they joined a nineteen-year-old university student who had just spent nine days in solitery confinement and was overjoyed to have company, despite the fact that there were now three people in a cell meant for one.

Only slowly did it dawn on Gordon that he was really in jail. This reality came alive as he convinced his son to overlook the indignity forced upon them by what passed for a toilet in the cell. As morning dawned, he was called out of the cell several times, but only to sign a variety of documents and to verify the disposition of his money and goods. The day dragged on, as did another night, with no food or sleep, as the erstwhile secretary of Jewish St. Petersburg and world-renowned poet tried to fathom what tragedy had befallen him and his family.

Lying awake in the darkness, trying not to stir so as to allow his son to sleep, Gordon mulled over and over again the possible reasons for his arrest and could find no answer. He knew that he had done nothing wrong, but only feared that his substantial Hebrew correspondence would be misrepresented by some evil official, perhaps even by Brafman himself. The next morning, as he was led to the washroom, he discovered in the corridor an employee of the Jewish community of St. Petersburg: that fellow had come to Gordon's home the night before, seeking him on some official business and had been arrested by the guards surrounding the house. Clearly, Gordon concluded, something serious was going on. Swallowing his pride, he thankfully accepted the offer of some leftover bread and milk tendered by his cellmate and advised his son to eat all that he could.

Later that afternoon, a police official appeared bearing gifts sent by Gordon's brother Abraham—oranges and other fruits, as well as money. At last, Gordon concluded, the outside world had heard of his plight, the torture could not last much longer. He only feared that his older daughter and son-in-law, who were scheduled to come to his house that evening for the Passover seder, would be arrested before the mess was resolved.

But the ordeal continued. Allowed pen and paper, he wrote a short autobiographical statement naming the influential people he knew, a note to his brother asking for cigarettes, and a letter to the Government Rabbi requesting that food be brought to the prison from the kosher restaurant in St. Petersburg, because of the impending holiday of Passover. That evening, instead of celebrating the festival of freedom at home with his family, Gordon and the other Jewish prisoners marked their servitude in the corridors of the Lithuanian Fortress. Here he was approached by a young man whom he had never met before. He introduced himself as Mark Gordon, a distant relative from Vilna. Only later would Judah Leib Gordon discover that his own imprisonment was related to the arrest of this Mark (or Max) Gordon, charged with revolutionary activities.

The next day, Gordon sighed with relief as his son and daughter were released from prison, but he still had no word about his feeble wife, kept in the other side of the jail. Settling into a daily routine of endless boredom, interrupted only by the delivery of food and the daily walk in the halls, Gordon learned that he and his family had been swept up in the arrest of some twenty-nine persons because of a mysterious case involving "the Gordons from Vilna." He resolved to steer clear of his namesakes in jail, but still had no idea why he was implicated in their alleged crimes. His hopes were buoyed by the release of one of his cellmates, but as the days passed by, and especially as Russian Orthodox Holy Week and Easter approached, Gordon lost all faith in an imminent release.

Soon, he realized that his stay might be even longer than he ever expected: on April 2, a revolutionary terrorist named Soloviev attempted to assassinate Tsar Alexander II, and the prison was filled with suspects. Gordon and his cellmates seemed to be forgotten, languishing in the mire of their lesser crimes. Scraping up shards of coal, Judah Leib Gordon began to scribble poems on the walls of his cell.

Two weeks after his arrest, Gordon was permitted his first meeting with a relative from the outside world. His son-in-law Maxim Kaplan broke into tears when he saw before him his fastidious father-in-law reduced to the state of an unkempt prisoner. Maxim informed him that he had in fact been implicated in the revolutionary activities of the Vilna Gordons, but assured him that he would have been released were it not for the assassination attempt; still, there was hope that his innocence could soon be proven. But liberation was not forthcoming. On the contrary, another three weeks passed without even one visitor, and Gordon learned from other inmates that no meetings were allowed with any of the accused. The only consolation throughout these horrifying weeks was the fact that he was finally allowed to communicate by note with his wife, who was alive and well in the women's prison down the hall.

On April 25, he was called to the warden's office and asked whether Mark or

Max Gordon of Vilna was his brother; two days later, he was allowed a visit with his son and younger daughter, but they had no encouraging news; three days later, he was at long last able to meet with his wife. Gradually, the implications of all that had passed were becoming clear. From Maxim he learned that he would be sent into internal exile in the near future, probably to Vilna. As soon as he conditioned himself to this fate, he met for the first time since his arrest with his brother Abraham, who had been in touch with the governor-general and other high officials and had learned the true nature of the decree: Judah Leib and Bella Gordon were to be exiled to the northern Russian province of Olonetsk. Abraham, ever the optimist, was certain that this order would be rescinded and that the family would be reunited in St. Petersburg within a week; his brother Judah Leib had already learned to be skeptical of such promises.

That evening, Abraham's pledge was revealed as merely wishful thinking. At 8:30 P.M., Judah Leib Gordon found himself accompanied by guards to the front door of the prison, where Bella was already waiting, frightened out of her wits. Carriages pulled up to take them away in a convoy with other prisoners, and Gordon learned that he and his wife were being sent into exile in the town of Petrozavodsk, some 150 miles to the northeast of St. Petersburg. Other inmates were being sent to Archangel, and the mysterious revolutionary Gordons were off to Moscow, en route to Siberia.

Soldiers rudely scurried back and forth, demanding signed pledges from the prisoners, now exiles, that they would not attempt to escape along the way or when they reached their destination, on pain of imprisonment in Siberia. Gordon was allowed to write a letter to his children, but not to wait for them to appear on the scene to bid farewell. In a flash, he and Bella were hurled into two separate carriages, accompanied by three guards, and were soon galloping off in the direction of their presumptive new home. Gordon implored his guard to allow him to join his sick wife in one carriage and to proceed at a slower pace. At the next stop, the first request was acceded to, and Gordon was at least able to comfort the weak and nearly hysterical Bella.

After a few hours they were loaded onto a boat to traverse the canals circumventing Lade Ladoga en route to Petrozavodsk. For a full day and a half they proceeded at an excruciatingly slow pace, and only thereafter were able to spend the night on terra firma, in a peasant's hut. For the next two days, they fought storms and rough waves on a series of small fishing boats. Pleading with their guards to slacken the pace, they learned that if they did not arrive in Petrozavodsk on time, they would be imprisoned again, rather than assigned to internal exile; scraping together the last resources of strength and determination, they shifted from one carriage to another in a frantic attempt to reach their destination. After a full five days of harrowing travel, they arrived in Petrozavodsk and were transferred to the control of the local authorities.

After a short rest, Gordon discovered that he and Bella had to travel farther, to the town of Pudozh, on the other side of Lake Onega, where they would actually spend their exile. Protesting that his wife was too sick to go any farther, Gordon was able to secure a physician to examine Bella and then to have their further travel postponed until she was well enough to proceed. In the intervening time he got to know all the local officials and was much impressed and encouraged by the civilized treatment they afforded him. He also learned that the officials themselves had no idea why he had been arrested and exiled: the order they received had merely stated that upon the direction of the governor-general of St. Petersburg, Honorary Citizen L. Gordon and his wife B. Gordon were exiled to the province of Olonetsk, for "political reasons."

While Bella recuperated, Gordon was able to cable their family in St. Petersburg, and learned from them that his daughter Nadia would soon be joining her parents in Petrozavodsk. After four days of anxious expectation, Nadia arrived, along with her parents' possessions and a maid. Nadia's arrival provided the Gordons not only with vital emotional succor but also with the first hard information about the reasons for their calamity. In St. Petersburg, Abraham Gordon and Maxim Kaplan had used their political contacts to obtain a copy of the charges against their exiled relative. With trembling hands Gordon read the following accusations:

1. You provided stipends to revolutionary students;
2. In the name of the Gunzburg firm you collected monies for revolutionary propaganda;
3. For your work in bringing to St. Petersburg the Mogilev [or Vitebsk?] rabbi you received large sums, which you used for the purposes of revolutionary propaganda;
4. You were in contact with foreign socialists;
5. It was reported that you are a brother of Max Gordon.[12]

Immediately Gordon discerned the serious difficulties he was facing. None of these charges was true, as could easily be demonstrated to objective officials: he never had any truck with revolutionary students or propaganda; he had opposed the appointment of Rabbi Landau from the first moment; he abhorred the doctrines of socialism and had never met any foreign revolutionaries; he had no brother named Max or Mark Gordon. However, Gordon realized, it would be very difficult to disprove the first allegation, as he had in fact administered the granting of large sums of money to students both in Russia and abroad, and an aggressive prosecutor could easily distort that activity into secret funding of revolutionaries. On the other hand, he reasoned, if he really were charged with revolutionary crimes, why would his sentence be so light, relatively speaking? Exile to an area so close to the capital was not a common punishment for so grave an offence. He concluded, therefore, that the true cause of the catastrophe lay in the third accusation, that somehow the Hasidic community of St. Petersburg, the supporters of Rabbi Landau, and particularly one man by the name of Rosenberg, had concocted this whole scheme as a vicious act of vengeance against Landau's major opponent and had bribed officials into adding trumped-up charges of revolutionary collaboration.

For their part, Abraham and Maxim were also convinced that the source of the whole affair lay with the Orthodox party in the capital, and this was the line of defense they were taking in their ceaseless efforts to disprove the allegations and liberate the prisoners. There was no way of knowing, however, how long that would take or whether indeed it would ever be successful. Perhaps, Gordon admitted to himself, he and his wife would spend the rest of their days in exile. He therefore arranged for the sale of all their belongings in St. Petersburg, for there was no way to secure their safety, and liquidated all their holdings, save only their beloved piano, which was sent to Maxim and Minna's for safekeeping. More painfully, he and Bella decided that there was no sense in having Nadia stay with them in Pudozh, for that was clearly no place for a teenage Jewish girl to live, perhaps permanently. She ought to return to the capital to live with her sister and look after her brother.

On May 15, 1879, Judah Leib, Bella, and Nadia Gordon left Petrozavodsk for the way station of Vytegra; here Nadia set sail to return to Petersburg and her parents boarded a ship to continue on to Pudozh. The parting was excruciating. While waiting to leave for his new home, Gordon wrote to his confidant, Ze'ev Kaplan:

> From the depths of the sea of distress you hear my voice, as I compose these words to you from the deck of the ship of pain. My pen shakes in my hand in time with the rocking of the boat and the sinking of my heart over the disaster that has befallen us. Look through your letters and search through your letters and you will see that seven years ago, when I first was called to the capital, my heart told me not to go, that some horrifying evil would await me, that I was not worthy and prepared to live in such a dangerous place. But you advised me, "Go forth, for this is why you were born." Now do you see who was right?[13]

Two days later, the Gordons arrived in Pudozh and were horrified by what they found. Smaller and far less civilized than any of the Lithuanian towns they had lived in, Pudozh was surrounded by dense forests and barren plains and had barely any houses that were not decrepit. (Even twenty years later, when the first all-Russian census was taken, Pudozh claimed only 3 stone and 261 wooden houses for its 1,469 residents.)[14] With much travail, Gordon and Bella rented the attic of the most acceptable dwelling they could find, and located a servant girl to help with the housekeeping. From the police inspector they learned that every morning they would have to sign a register to prove their presence in Pudozh; any absence, even to the outskirts of town, would be deemed an escape attempt, and the punishment would be exile to Siberia.

Apart from this daily ritual, nothing else was demanded or expected from the forty-odd offenders exiled to this forsaken outpost. Gordon learned to his surprise that many of the government officials in Pudozh had themselves been exiled there because of some malfeasance back at home, and several lived in grand style, collecting huge bribes from their fellows. There were two other Jewish prisoners in Pudozh, one smuggler and one counterfeiter, and one Jewish soldier who worked as a blacksmith; later there arrived a converted Jew who was accused of being a member of the terrorist group "Land and Liberty." With no one to befriend, Gordon spent his days and weeks struggling to fill his time by reading the newspapers in the local library and helping his wife prepare their daily fare. Living was cheap in Pudozh, although certain essentials such as vegetables and ink were unattainable and bread had to be baked from scratch by each household, since the loaves sold in the local market were filthy and unpalatable. The weather was similar to that of St. Petersburg, though a bit colder and damper; wood, however, was plentiful and cheap, and the Gordons kept warm, if utterly bored and lonely, throughout the long summer.

To divert his mind, Gordon tried to write, though his pen was constrained by the knowledge that his papers could always be subject to police search. Mostly he kept to the Russian language, on the theory that he could thus not be accused of harboring secretive scribblings. Throughout the long months he kept a detailed journal of his life and thoughts in prison and exile; at the beginning of this diary he recalled the events of 1839, when his parents' home in Vilna had been disturbed on a Friday night by police and his father taken away. That fright, however, had ended with the safe return of the head of the household, conscripted for a few hours due to his reputation as a Russian patriot. What would happen now, when that patriot's even more patriotic son was accused of antigovernment conspiracy? To prove to the outside world that he was still alive and thinking, he sent off a short article to a prestigious Russian historical journal explaining that a memoir published in its pages had confused the recently deceased Hebrew poet Ada"m Ha-Kohen Lebensohn with the founder of the Jewish Enlightenment movement in Russia, Isaac Ber Levinsohn.[15]

Although he later would attribute to the days of his exile a major new narrative poem on a most poignant theme—the imprisonment of the last king of Judah, Zedekiah—it is clear that he did not in fact write that poem while in Pudozh, though it is likely that he began to sketch out its plot and versification in his head.[16] In Hebrew he wrote two short pieces that are of substantial interest. The first is a valuable memoir of his childhood that provided more details than any other account of his early years.[17] He composed this work, he explained, since he now unfortunately had more free time than ever before to recall his past, and such recollection provided some emotional succor in the face of the uncertainty of the future. He stopped his autobiography at his sixteenth year, but would never return to memorialize the subsequent years, only sporadically jotting down isolated reminiscences. At the same time, inspired by the popular novel *Women* by the minor Russian author Meshcherskii, he wrote a little story in Hebrew entitled "A Mother's Mercy."[18] Subtitled "The Story of a Former Communal Official," this tale was cast in the form of a memoir written by the administrator of the St. Petersburg Jewish community who had witnessed a strange event in the spring of 1873. The wife of a high military aide of the tsar had revealed herself to him as a Jewess who was hiding her origins to protect her family. Her mother—the daughter of a famous Italian rabbinical family—had helped her hide her origins through the years and upon her deathbed had even agreed to be buried in the Catholic cemetery in town. But she did have one last request of her daughter, that somehow it be arranged that memorial prayers be offered for her soul in the St. Petersburg synagogue. Upon hearing this moving story, the narrator was able not only to fulfill her request but also to reunite her with her long-lost brother, who—it turned out—was a well-known Jewish merchant in the Russian capital.

This charming and succinct, if rather implausible, tale, told with much sympathy and warmth, was a good deal more successful than any of Gordon's previous short stories. Not surprisingly, it soon became the first of Gordon's works to be translated into another language, appearing first in Polish in 1880, in Russian in the following year, and in a German-language Hungarian-Jewish journal in 1882.[19]

In Pudozh in the summer of 1879, however, Gordon was far from contemplating the ultimate distribution of his new tale. There still was no news from Peters-

burg on the disposition of his case. Maxim and Abraham kept on pursuing their
connections in the hope of having the charges dropped, but no significant progress
had been made. From a newspaper Gordon learned that General von Kaufmann,
the former governor-general of Vilna province, now serving in Turkestan, was visiting St. Petersburg. In the 1860s, while serving in Lithuania, Gordon had met the
general and made a good impression on him; in 1875, during a stay in the capital,
von Kaufmann had offered to intercede for Gordon with any government officials
should he ever require any high-level support. In a plaintive letter, the desperate
exile now reminded von Kaufmann of that pledge:

> At that time, I was happy with my fate and gratefully answered that I wanted for
> nothing. But now I am burdened with a terrible sorrow: I have had the misfortune of
> being the object of an investigation by the secret police. I have not been informed of
> the reasons for that investigation, but from private sources I have learned that I was
> the victim of a false denunciation by the fanatical party of my coreligionists, who
> bore me malice because of my work for their enlightenment. My loyal and productive
> efforts in this regard were greeted with royal favor, yielding me the status of Honorary
> Citizen "for the successful spread of enlightenment among his coreligionists"; these
> efforts also won me Your Excellency's favor, but now have led me to this abyss of
> despair. . . . In this critical moment, I have decided to take up your generous offer
> and humbly request that you inform the Provisional Governor-General of St. Peters-
> burg that you know me . . . or at least knew me to be an honest toiler for the enlight-
> enment of my coreligionists, as politically loyal, and as incapable of committing those
> reprehensible acts with which I was charged by the obscurantist Jews who used the
> government as a vehicle to effect their own vile purposes.[20]

Meanwhile, Gordon was devastated by the news that his positions in St. Petersburg were no longer being kept open for him: the society had decided that it could
do without a paid secretary and the community had engaged another official in his
place. Now, even if he were set free, he would have no means of supporting himself
and his family, no way to return to his former life of ease, comfort, and prestige.
Not only had the Orthodox destroyed him, he concluded, but the so-called progressive forces had traduced him as well, fearing to express their confidence in a
colleague suspected of political crimes, even though they knew him to be innocent.
    In frequent letters, Abraham and Maxim kept promising that he would soon be
set free, but he discounted their assurances. Ze'ev Kaplan wrote a letter that reeked
of vain consolation: Gordon was merely a victim of the revolutionary turmoil facing the government of Russia at the time, and his suffering, like Kaplan's own
recent loss of his wife and daughter, will soon pass. In his journal Gordon recorded
his fury at this advice:

> Instead of raising my spirits, this letter infuriated me to no end. . . . He forgets that I
> am a victim not of the revolutionaries but of the regime, which counts me among the
> rebels. Moreover, what possible analogy can be drawn between the death of his wife
> and daughter two years ago and the harsh decree that felled me out of the blue? Man
> is born to fall sick and die, but not to be imprisoned and exiled. To be jailed and sent
> into exile is to die before one's time, to die without losing one's consciousness and
> one's sense of living. What he experienced still awaits us, but what has befallen us is
> totally unexpected and uncalled for. Finally, with the death of his wife, his children

still had him to raise them and educate them, but my poor children were deprived in one stroke of their father and mother. What will become of them if we are not freed in the near future?[21]

Weeks went by without any progress. The clouds burst forth with endless storms, and Bella fell sick time and time again, never truly regaining her strength. Finally, in mid-July, the skies cleared and a letter arrived from Minna with the news that Gordon had been exonerated and would presently be released. But the days kept dragging on, turning into weeks, with no respite and no release. Bella's health took a serious negative turn; she could barely move without writhing in pain and was at the breaking point. A visit from a doctor—himself an exile—eased her pain a bit, but aggravated Gordon's spirits: the doctor heard that Gordon's petition to be permitted to live in the larger town of Petrozavodsk had been denied because one of the police officials there heard that this Hebrew poet had written a poem called "The Tip of the Yud" that ridiculed the rabbis; this poet, reasoned the official, would undoubtedly exert a negative influence on the local Jews.

To Judah Leib Gordon, the idea that the Russian government had not only exiled one of its most loyal sons due to the pressure of the Orthodox but also was succumbing to the moral sway of the rabbis was excruciatingly painful. Now, the anxiety became intolerable: Maxim kept writing that the decree of innocence had been approved and was on the verge of being sent to Pudozh, but no message or messenger ever arrived bearing such news.

At long last, on August 15, the police inspector himself appeared at the Gordon's door bearing a telegram from Maxim: "The police chief issued his decree; immediately upon its receipt the ministry promises to inform the governor; a carriage has already been sent; you are permitted to come through St. Petersburg. See you soon."[22] The decree, therefore, was as expected: the Gordons would be freed, but forbidden to live in the capital, and probably would be sent back to Vilna. At least they could stop in St. Petersburg along the way to see the children. Gordon began to worry about how he would reconstruct his life in the city of his birth, which he had abandoned decades earlier. Pondering these thoughts, he read in *Ha-Meliz* that ten days earlier the house of Rabbi Landau had been subjected to a police search; Gordon fumed that the editor of that newspaper, Alexander Zederbaum, had angrily protested the rabbi's treatment but had not written a word about the far worse fate of his former colleague and supposed friend, Judah Leib Gordon. More intriguing though, was the fate of Rabbi Landau. Was he arrested, Gordon wondered, and, if so, for what crime? Perhaps he and the rabbi would change places, perhaps they would even meet on the road, halfway between Petersburg and Pudozh, like Byron and his nemesis.

A week later, Gordon learned the exhilarating news that his honor was to be fully restored and that he would be allowed to return to St. Petersburg. On August 26, five months and three days after his arrest, the long-awaited cable arrived from the capital: he was free! In his journal of imprisonment and exile, Gordon recorded a final entry: "Tomorrow we leave. On Friday, we see the children. Blessed be the name of the Lord!"

It is impossible precisely to reconstruct the course of events that led to Gordon's arrest and exile. Two decades later, in the brief interstice of free access to the Russian state archives, the historian Shaul Ginzburg retrieved some of the police documents relating to Gordon's case, but discovered, too, that Gordon's dossier in the St. Petersburg governor's office was one of the multitude of files burned by the raging mobs who attacked that building in February 1917.[23] On the basis of the materials he did locate, Ginzburg was able to confirm Gordon's own hypothesis that the root of the matter was a denunciation by a supporter of Rabbi Landau. A parvenu tailor named Rosenberg, for many years a thorn in the side of the official Jewish leadership of the capital, apparently had bribed a secret police official named Pursov into helping him wreak vengeance on the secretary of the Jewish community. The connection with the revolutionary circle around Max or Mark Gordon remained unclear. What seems most likely is that Pursov staked out Judah Leib Gordon's home for weeks in the hope of pinning some crime on him, but to no avail; when the twenty-three revolutionaries known by the collective name of the "Vilna Gordons" were arrested, Pursov simply added Judah Leib Gordon's name to the list and had him and his wife arrested as alleged accomplices in illegal antigovernmental activities. For months, Pursov was able to hide his nefarious scheme, but Abraham Gordon and Maxim Kaplan used their high governmental connections and the intercession of General von Kaufmann to overrule the corrupt secret policeman. In the end, it was the head of the secret police himself who overturned the conviction and permitted the Gordons to return to St. Petersburg to build their life anew.

Whether in fact the denunciation by the supporter of Rabbi Landau preceded or followed the mistaken connection between Gordon and his revolutionary namesakes cannot be ascertained for certain. But what is most important is the effect that the episode had on Judah Leib Gordon's psyche and view of the world. To the end of his days, he believed with all his soul and all his might that the greatest tragedy that had afflicted him and his family was directly the result of a false and vengeful denunciation by Orthodox Jews; moreover, his previous friends and colleagues among the St. Petersburg Jewish plutocracy did not have the courage or the honesty to stand up for him in his hour of need.

Back in St. Petersburg in the beginning of September 1879, boarding with his brother and trying to pick up the pieces of a shattered life, Gordon poured out his wrath and pain to Ze'ev Kaplan and divulged the lesson he had learned from the ordeal, paraphrasing and inverting Job's lament and the prophecy of Amos:

What happened to me is one of the most blatant signs that we are going backwards and not forwards. The Haskalah made great strides among our people in our land for a generation, and the elders saw and hid, the young men rose and stood tall. The land was filled with truth, and false beliefs laid low. Now the tide has turned: the blind creep out of their holes to lead their flocks and turn things back to where they were before. The rabbinical schools are closed because Rabbi Samuel of Mogilev asks the minister to close them; rabbinical conferences deal with nonsensical trivialities . . . and Gordon is exiled since a foolish people believes that in this way their hero Rabbi Landau will live in peace. Above us all, that beacon of enlightenment, Zederbaum and his *Ha-Meliz* follow the change of every wind, now urging us backwards and not forwards. [As the prophet counseled:] Assuredly, at such a time the prudent man keeps silent, for it is an evil time.[24]

Prudence, to be sure, was not one of Judah Leib Gordon's fortes, and through-out the autumn of 1879 he cast about in search of a way to express his new central article of faith: Russian Jews had entered into a dangerous reactionary phase, abort-ing the progress of enlightenment. As usual, he tried to translate his deepest emo-tions into Hebrew poetry and prose, but depression and anger blocked his creative impulses. To Kaplan he confessed that the trauma had shattered his spirits. He tried to hide his distress from his family, hiding in his room or taking long, point-less walks, but he was afraid they were beginning to notice his odd behavior. The best remedy would be to go abroad to seek medical treatment, as he had done three years earlier, returning refreshed and strong. Meanwhile, he nervously waited to hear about the disposition of his professional career: rumors had it that Baron Gunzburg and other St. Petersburg notables had met in Paris (where they all kept residences) and decided to reinstate him to his previous posts; even if this were true, however, he was not sure that he would want to return to the work that had caused him so much pain.[25]

A few weeks later he met with the baron in St. Petersburg and was even more pessimistic about his future. Gunzburg, horrified by the sight of the physical toll the ordeal of the last year had taken on his former employee, promised that he would take care of Gordon under any circumstances but could not assure him of his former posts, since many other leaders of St. Petersburg Jewry opposed his rein-statement. Gordon was terribly upset by this news, and especially by the fact that leading the opposition to him was Leon Rosenthal, formerly one of his warmest supporters. The rumor about town was that Rosenthal had taken up with the young daughter of the man who had replaced Gordon. The puritanical poet did not want to believe these reports, but more and more became convinced of their veracity as the only possible explanation for Rosenthal's sudden volte-face.[26]

In sporadic moments of calm, Gordon did succeed in writing several incidental pieces. To the Hebrew journal *Ha-Karmel* in Vilna he submitted a series of book reviews and a new short poem expressing outrage at the second attempt at assas-sinating the tsar. At the same time, he sent off the opening stanzas of "Two Josephs Son of Simeon" to Smolenskin in Vienna. In Russian he composed a long obituary of Ada"m Ha-Kohen Lebensohn that demonstrated, above all, that his own com-mitment to the goals of Enlightenment and liberal politics, and his loyalty to the Russian state, had not been diminished by his exile and imprisonment. The nine-teenth century, he wrote, was the most glorious in human history, and no less sig-nificant for the Jews:

This is the century of the weakening of fratricidal prejudices and enmities, the century of the aspirations of all members of the great human family for rapprochement and unity. Naturally, this rapprochement has not had identical successes in every part of the world; but progress in this direction is noticeable everywhere.[27]

The work of Lebensohn and the other Russian-Jewish enlighteners was bound to lead to success, just as the path-breaking efforts of Peter the Great had pointed the way to Russia's future as a modern, Western power.[28]

Privately, however, Gordon was beginning to have his doubts about the inev-itability of the victory of light over darkness, truth over ignorance, tolerance over iniquity. In his notebooks he worked long and hard on the new verses that were to articulate the deepest stirrings of his soul, the torturous conclusions reached in the Petersburg jail and in the hell of Pudozh. Finally, in the early months of 1880, he put the final touches on the tormented poem conceived in exile, now titled "Zedekiah in Prison."[29] The very choice of the unfortunate last king of Judah as a poetic alter ego revealed a startlingly heterodox stance. In the Bible, Zedekiah was hardly a heroic figure; on the contrary, as related in Jeremiah, II Kings, and Chronicles, he was at best a naive and weak ruler and at worst a treacherous rebel who consciously traduced the word of the Lord. Raised to the throne as a satrap of Babylonia in the year B.C. 597, Zedekiah replaced his exiled nephew as ruler over a diminished and fractious populace. While at first yielding to the advice of Jeremiah to avoid a clash with Babylonia, Zedekiah soon fell under the spell of his petty princes and false prophets and led an unsuccessful rebellion that resulted in the final sacking of Jerusalem and the burning of the Temple. He tried to flee across the Jordan but was captured at Jericho and imprisoned in Riblah, where his sons were slaughtered before his eyes, before he himself was blinded. Finally, bound in chains, he was brought in ignominy to Babylonia, where he died.[30]

Gordon's poem in Zedekiah's voice is a searing monologue in rhyming couplets, signed with a final Hebrew rhyme: "In the Lithuanian Fortress I laid its foundations/ In Pudozh I set its gates in place." This signature did more than overtly stress the identification between the poet and the imprisoned king. Borrowing biblical phrases used to describe an act committed in express disregard of divine orders—the fortification of Jericho during the reign of Ahab—it subtly trumpeted the angry, all-but-blasphemous tone of the poem as a whole.[31]

The opening lines announced the torment of the prisoner, whose only crime was to try, as nobly and honestly as he could, to lead his nation in an hour of crisis:

> Blinded and forsaken, bound in iron and pain
> Is there any man in the land as wretched as I?
> [The former] king of Jerusalem
> On foreign soil, imprisoned and in chains.[32]

Caged like a wild beast, the king laments his bitter fate and turns his ire on God in words borrowed from the prophet Habakkuk, but without their pious conclusion:

> In vain, therefore, they say there is a God
> Almighty, omnipotent, a judge on high!
> Where is His judgment? Why does He not enforce it,
> Now, when the evil devour the righteous?[33]

What crime, after all, did the king commit? According to the Bible, he knows, he stands accused, since "He did not humble himself before the prophet Jeremiah." But why fall prostate before "[t]hat faint-hearted man, that submissive soul/ Who counseled disgrace, servitude, subordination?" I refused to heed this shameful call, explained the king, but not out of stubbornness or pique—out of concern for my people, just as I previously had ordered my nobles to emancipate their slaves.[34] Even if I was wrong, why punish me so cruelly, why torture not only me but my children as well? Because I did not submit to Jeremiah, who could only counsel, while the capital city lay at stake, to obey the commandments? Is this how a mighty city ought to be defended?

Moreover, the king continues, the prophet-priest Jeremiah invented a new creed for Judah: all the nation, from young to old, from yeoman to prince, must study the Torah all day long, must become scribes and sons of prophets. Jeremiah counseled, in effect, the direct inverse of the imperatives of "Awake, My People!":

> The farmers should abandon their ploughs
> Soldiers their weapons and standards,
> Artisans and locksmiths should leave their shops.[35]

But if this were to happen, the nation would be destroyed by its surfeit of prophets and scholars, each too proud to do any manual work, even to bake its own bread. But can any nation survive like this?

The answer is obvious, but this is the strategy devised not only by Jeremiah but by all the prophets and priests who have opposed secular power in Israel since Samuel's confrontation with Saul. Indeed, the war between the spiritual and the lay rulers of the Jews has gone on forever, the imprisoned leader declares, and has led not only to his own sufferings but also to destruction and want for the nation as a whole. In the end, Zedekiah confesses, he has been beaten and humbled, his children taken away from him, his hopes dashed altogether. He is abandoned and alone, defeated by his enemies. Even God on high cannot help him now. He can only hope that in his death he may glimpse his martyred children and thus repose in eternal peace.

As if the point of the poem were not self-evident, upon its first publication Gordon added an explanatory note detailing the biblical allusions of the text and claiming that Job's suffering were as nothing compared with Zedekiah's, for in the end Job won his battle, while for the king no victory was possible. Zedekiah, Gordon explained, did not opposed Jeremiah out of spite or venom, but

> because he had a different strategy for governing the nation, and his motivation was good and his plans approved by the majority of notables and the people. The dispute between Zedekiah and Jeremiah was an ancient and eternal dispute from the beginning of all time—the dispute between the secular authorities *(weltliche Macht)* and the spiritual powers *(Geistlichkeit)* which continues to this very day in every place where the two oppose one another (as, for example, in our day in Germany there is the dispute between the government and the pope, known by the term *Kulturkampf*). This dispute occurred before Zedekiah between Saul and Samuel, and after them in the time of the Second Temple between the Sadducees and the Pharisees, and an echo of this dispute is heard even today among the Jews between the enlighteners and the Orthodox.[36]

Only a few weeks after completing this poem, in April 1880, Gordon agreed to become the editor of the most important Hebrew newspaper in Russia, *Ha-Meliz.* Little did he know that within a few months, Russian Jewry would be faced with the gravest crisis of its history, leading to the rise of many new Jeremiahs and a flight both to a new Babylon and to a new Zion. Throughout the ordeal to come, however, the lessons Gordon learned in prison and in exile would determine his response. As editor of *Ha-Meliz,* and thus a primary exponent of the Russian Haskalah, Gordon posed himself as the disciple of Zedekiah rather than of Jeremiah, defending the political emancipation of the Jews and their cultural progress against the encroachments of what he termed "reactionary" forces, whether from within or from without. In the process, Judah Leib Gordon would find himself as alone and distraught as his presumptive new hero, the dethroned and destroyed last king of the Jews.

9

Pogroms and the Crisis
of Jewish Liberalism
1880–1881

"Let us take care," warned Marc Bloch in regard to the most confounding dilemma of his craft: "in history, the fetish of a single cause is all too often only the insidious form of search for the responsible person—hence a value judgment."[1] In the history of Russian Jewry in the 1880s, Bloch's caution has more often than not been disregarded, for it seemed egregiously obvious that the cause of the great ideological and biological revolutions that overtook Russian Jews lay in one and only one phenomenon: pogroms. Both historiography and popular imagination have therefore held it to be a truism, first, that the pogroms came and therefore the Jews left; and, second, that in the wake of the pogroms the liberal optimism of the Jewish Enlightenment was unmasked as naive and self-defeating and was directly replaced by the new, and more realistic, doctrines of modern Jewish nationalism and socialism.[2]

For more than two generations, a small number of historians, demographers, and economists have argued, to little avail, that in fact neither the biological nor the ideological traumas of Russian-Jewish life in the 1880s can be ascribed to or explained by the anti-Jewish violence that erupted in the Ukraine in the spring of 1881. On the one hand, as described above, the large-scale movement of East European Jews overseas began in the 1870s as a natural, if unselfconscious, response to overpopulation unmitigated by economic expansion and a seamless extension of the massive internal migration of Russian Jews throughout the previous half-century.[3] While the pogroms did provide a dramatic boost to the emigration fever, the movement of East European Jews to lands of greater opportunity, especially America, had started long before the spring of 1881 and had already become the object of substantial public concern and debate by that time. Moreover, at the very same time as Jews emigrated from the Pale of Settlement and Congress Poland, they were joined by even greater proportions of their coreligionists from Galicia, the Polish province of the Austro-Hungarian Empire, which witnessed no pogroms and granted emancipation and civil rights to all its inhabitants, regardless of persuasion. Finally, the Jews who made their way through Brody, Hamburg, and other ports of embarkation to the New World sailed alongside a parallel stream of non-Jewish

East Europeans who followed the same chronology and analogous tidal waves to comprise only a small fraction of the millions of emigrants from other parts of the continent. Clearly, at work here was not simply a reaction to political trauma, but a broadly gauged social and economic revolution, of which the Jewish case was but one small part. What most distinguished the Russian-Jewish migrants from their Lithuanian, Greek, or Italian counterparts was, for the most part, not the reason for their departure or its timing, but the fact that in the Jewish case the emigration was from the start viewed as a permanent change of venue, not a temporary move. As a result, the Jews left not only en masse, but en famille.[4]

On the other hand, it is patently demonstrable that the ideological crisis that wrenched Jewish political consciousness in Eastern Europe from its previous moorings began well before the outbreak of the pogroms and that by no means all East European Jews rallied to the new flags of nationalism and radicalism in the aftermath of the pogroms. This is not a matter of embryonic or implicit developments that assumed final shape only in retrospective clarity or of negligible relics of displaced faiths that asserted no influence on the larger community after their superannuation. Quite to the contrary, in the 1870s the Haskalah was assailed by a variety of firm, outspoken, and influential critics espousing new and devastating alternatives to the liberal creed of enlightenment and emancipation; and the political fate of Russian Jewry for the rest of its history was as much directed by critics of the new ideologies of nationalism and socialism as by their proponents.[5]

To argue thus is not to maintain that the pogroms had no effect on the demography of Russian Jews, their ideological and political cast, or their collective mentality. Rather, it is to plead for a more cautious, modest, and depoliticized evaluation of the events of the late 1870s and early 1880s in Russian-Jewish history; a suspension, at the very least, of the axiomatic assumptions of causality. The emigration crisis and the postpogrom response of Jewish liberalism and cosmopolitanism consumed a large part of Judah Leib Gordon's intellectual energy and physical stamina for the rest of the decade, and thus will occupy a good deal of the chapters that follow. What must now be painted in very broad strokes is the assault on the political theory of the Haskalah that emerged among Russian Jews, at home and in emigration, in the middle and late 1870s.

Precisely because the points of view articulated in these years were soon thereafter thrust into the very center of Jewish political discourse in Eastern Europe, it has proven exceedingly difficult, if not impossible, for scholars to divorce hindsight from analysis in the evaluation of the intellectual crisis of Russian Jewry in the 1870s. As a result, even the best of the treatments of that crisis resort to circular or, what is worse, teleological designations of the ideologues of the day as "men thinking a generation ahead of their time," advancing ideas for which the "objective conditions" were not yet ripe.[6]

What seems to have happened was much simpler than that: in the mid-1870s, large numbers of Russian-Jewish *intelligenty* began to lose faith in the liberal, emancipationist politics of the Haskalah not in the wake of physical attack against the Jews, but in response to the new theories of nationalism and socialism then gripping the minds and hearts of many intellectuals throughout Europe, and particularly the young. The first, and possibly foremost, character in this drama, Peretz Smolenskin, has already appeared in these pages as a valued colleague, friend, and editor of Judah Leib Gordon. In the course of the 1870s, Smolenskin published in his own journal, *Ha-Shaḥar,* a series of vastly controversial, if incontrovertibly verbose, essays on the nature of Jewish national, cultural, and religious identity that broke ranks not only with Gordon but also with the entire heritage of the Jewish Enlightenment. Overtly influenced by the rise of national consciousness among the minority groups of the Austro-Hungarian Empire in whose capital he lived, Smolenskin struggled to apply the emerging concepts of modern nationalism to the Jewish condition. In this effort, he began with a vociferous condemnation of the denationalized ideology of radical Reform Judaism in Germany and proceeded to identify Moses Mendelssohn as the originator of the notion that the Jews constitute a religion and not a nation. Mendelssohn's misrepresentation of the essential nature of Jewishness, Smolenskin held, rendered fundamentally flawed the entire ideological edifice of the Haskalah to the late nineteenth century in that it strove for the reform of Judaism at the expense of Jewish national pride and unity. To replace the political creed of the Jewish Enlightenment, Smolenskin outlined a rather inchoate, if oft repeated, new ideology of modern Jewish nationalism based on the definition of the Jews as a "spiritual nation." While normal nations are dependent upon a territory and a state structure, the Jews, he argued, have a constitution in the Torah, a national tongue in Hebrew, a shared history, and an unblemished love for one another that only requires channeling in the proper direction. To preserve and advance their unity, the Jews must place "national sentiment" at the center of their identity and work together to forge a revived Jewish national spirit.[7]

Smolenskin's essays unleashed a torrent of debate in Russian Jewry, stirring a host of reactions, arguments, and defenses. Not the least of the participants in these discussions was a Lithuanian Jew who, under the pen name Eliezer Ben Yehudah, in 1879 submitted to *Ha-Shaḥar* two pieces that called for the establishment in Palestine of a Hebrew-speaking Jewish state. Claiming the status of a disappointed disciple of Smolenskin, Ben Yehudah maintained that the Jews' national identity could only be preserved if they became a normal nation, living in their historical home as the majority population, speaking their revivified ancient tongue. Indeed, on the basis of this ideology Ben Yehudah had left Russia in 1878 bound for Palestine, stopping in Europe along the way to gain professional skills to support himself in the Land of Israel. He finally arrived in Jaffa in late 1881 and there quickly became famous as the head of the first modern Hebrew-speaking family and an influential educator and publicist.[8]

Ben Yehudah's idiosyncratic notions were broadcast and supported by David Gordon, the curious editor of *Ha-Maggid,* the conservative Hebrew Enlightenment newspaper published in Lyck, East Prussia. At least since the late 1860s, David Gordon had been an outspoken advocate of the various schemes to return the Jews to the Land of Israel launched by a strange mixture of rabbis, offbeat politicians and adventurers, Christian millenarians, and Moses Hess.[9] It is difficult to characterize David Gordon as an early critic of the political theory of the Haskalah, since he was ambivalent, or at least ambiguous, on the central question of whether the establishment of a Jewish commonwealth in Palestine should supplant the emancipation and enlightenment of the Jews in the Diaspora. In addition, his conscious attempt to retain an audience and a readership among the traditional Jews of Eastern Europe placed him at best on the outer edge of the Enlightenment move-ment. But as the political world of East European Jewry was transformed in the early 1880s, his position would in fact attain much popularity, despite his own rela-tive anonymity.[10]

The Palestine-centered notions of both David Gordon and Eliezer Ben Yehu-dah were adamantly rejected by Peretz Smolenskin as utopian dreams and erro-neous glosses on the essential nature of Jewish nationalism. Equally unpalatable to Smolenskin was the previous dream that Ben Yehudah had embraced—social rev-olution. From the early 1870s on, the jumble of radical postures and socialist prin-ciples that would later be lumped together under the vague epithet of Russian populism began to attract the attention and allegiance of substantial numbers of young Russian Jews. Some of these men and women ceased to regard themselves as Jews or were utterly indifferent to the fate of their erstwhile community, believ-ing that they were simply members of the new, revolutionary avant-garde.[11] Others, such as Aron Liberman, Morris Vinchevsky, and Judah Leib Levin, attempted in various ways to bring socialism to the Jewish street (to use a later cliche); some even attempted to forge a new radical Jewish identity, based on a blend of socialist politics and Smolenskin's ideas of Jewish nationalism. In St. Petersburg itself, a group of Russified young Jews espousing a vague admixture of "Jewish populism" and standard Haskalah hopes began to issue a new journal, entitled *Razsvet*—the Russian equivalent of *Ha-Shahar*—urging solidarity with the Jewish masses on the part of intellectuals.[12]

In the same vein, in the early and middle 1870s another one of Judah Leib Gordon's protégés, Moshe Leib Lilienblum, began to portray himself as a "demi-nihilist." Concluding that his pleas for religious reform would not be realized in the near future, Lilienblum underwent another one of his periodic psychic crises and proclaimed that he had lost faith in the very ideas of religious reform that he and Gordon had recently adumbrated. In a series of articles, he criticized the aes-thetics of the Haskalah in a Judaized, and rather jejune, co-optation of the radical Russian critics that was close to the earlier arguments of Avraham Uri Kovner, and then went on to extend this argumentation to the political sphere, adopting a stance of opposition to the Russian government and sympathy with the Russian revolutionaries. Later, after yet another drastic turnabout, Lilienblum would sub-stantially overstate his radicalism of the 1870s by denouncing it as that of a cos-mopolitan socialist utterly disinterested in the fate of the Jews. At the time, how-ever, Lilienblum's socialism consisted in the main in a belief in manual labor and agricultural colonization as the panacea for Russian Jews; in other words, out of the panoply of Haskalah prescriptions for the ills of the Jews, he singled out the one stance that was most in tune with the dictates of revolutionary fashion and set it as the sine qua non of Jewish self-reform.[13]

These examples should suffice to point to the wide spectrum of critiques of the politics and ideology of the Haskalah that emerged in the 1870s among Russian Jews at home or abroad. To the stalwart adherents of the Haskalah such as Judah Leib Gordon, these ideological rumblings and ramblings did not cause much worry. After all, as Gordon himself had written, the tide of progress, enlightenment, and liberation could not be stemmed, just as the earth could not change the course of its orbit. Though far from sympathetic with Smolenskin's anti-Mendelssohnianism or Lilienblum's putative radicalism, Gordon not only maintained warm relations with both men but also went out of his way to secure them financial and moral support. His sincere faith in the inevitability of emancipation and Jewish self-rejuvenation allowed him to display great tolerance in regard to younger colleagues who were struggling to forge new ideas, however immature, in the Hebrew language. In due course, however, Gordon's persistent belief in the efficacy and justice of the liberal creed would lead him to break personally and ideologically with Smolenskin, Lilienblum, and other former friends and to become one of the most vocal and public critics of both the new type of Jewish nationalism and Jewish collaboration in the revolutionary movement.

The latter cause elicited his alarm and ire before the former. Indeed, the very first articles that Gordon wrote upon assuming the editorship of *Ha-Meliz* in the early spring of 1880 were dedicated in large measure to refuting the charges that the revolutionary movement in Russia was orchestrated and manned primarily by Jews. These allegations—soon, of course, to become a mainstay of political debate throughout Eastern Europe, and remain so to this day—were first broadcast by influential public spokesmen in Russia in the late 1870s as a result of the spread of revolutionary terrorism throughout the empire. The tiny number of Jews in the terrorist ranks were seen by many conservative Russians as simply the natural heirs of the anti-Christ, now disguised in modern garb: who else, after all, would plot to assassinate the holy tsar? As the influential Professor N. Vasil'ev of St. Petersburg University put it in the widely read newspaper *Novoe Vremia* in 1880: "The dirty Jews, from time immemorial representatives of the revolutionary spirit, now stand at the head of the Russian nihilists."[14]

Judah Leib Gordon attempted to counter the identification of the Jews with the radical antitsarist forces in a series of pieces he wrote for the April 1, 1880, number of *Ha-Meliz,* the first issued under his supervision. Reviewing for his readers the events that had occurred during the previous five months, when *Ha-Meliz* was not published due to a complicated legal suit, Gordon took pains to point out that the two recent unsuccessful attempts against the life of the tsar were committed by dastardly terrorists who must be denounced by all lovers of freedom and human dignity. Alexander II had not only emancipated the serfs of the empire, introduced a praiseworthy Western-style legal system, brought railroads and economic progress to the land, and created organs of local self-government that promised a greater degree of cooperation between society and the state; he had also substantially liberated the Jews of Russia from their previous shackles, by laying open for them the riches of the Russian interior, the Russian school system, and Russian culture. All the Jews of the empire, no matter their religious cast, look upon Alexander II with love, loyalty, and respect as their master and king and condemn without hesitation the attacks upon his sacred life. The notion that Jews were responsible for these attacks is spurious and utterly without foundation; history will show that the tiny number of Jews implicated in revolutionary violence had no connection with their people and its beliefs; indeed, the one Jew actively involved in the assassination attempts had long before hand converted to Russian Orthodoxy and most likely kissed the Cross before he died. This, however, is the fate of the Jews through the ages, that they are all held accountable for the evil acts of any individual from their midst. The appropriate response, therefore, is for the Jews of Russia as a group to redouble their efforts to be at once faithful servants of the Lord and loyal subjects of the tsar, to work ever more diligently to instill in their children love both of the God of Israel and His ways and of the emperor of all the Russias and his laws. They must not despair of enlightenment and the promise of emancipation, despite the despicable acts of the wild terrorists or the attacks of Jew-haters in the press. The latter are not to be greeted with surprise, for Russian Jews are, after all, no better than their brethren in Germany, who are without question Europeans in the fullest meaning of that word, but still are the object of reactionaries' ire and attack. These enemies now masquerade under the new-fangled name of "anti-Semites," adopting a pseudoscientific pose that will not succeed in masking their identity as merely contemporary versions of the ancient Jew-haters seeking to plunder and destroy the Jews. There is nothing new under the sun of anti-Jewish sentiments, Gordon argued time and time again. These anti-Semites, like their numberless predecessors through the centuries, are piloted by Christian clergymen of a variety of stripes advancing age-old religious prejudices against the Jews, in collusion with reactionary politicians resisting the advance of progress and liberty. The new appellation of "anti-Semitism" will not protect its adherents from their inevitable defeat by the forces of justice and enlightenment. In England and France, where political, intellectual, and religious liberty flourish side by side, the Jews live in peace and freedom, in harmony with their neighbors and their God, at the same time as they are committed to aiding their coreligionists in all parts of the world. The recent death of Adolphe Crémieux deprived France of a marvelous statesman and the Jewish people of a great leader; but Crémieux's memory should best be honored by commemorating him as a model to emulate, a man who served his country in its highest posts, furthering the cause of human dignity and freedom around the globe, and giving of his best years, resources, and influence to educate the Jews in the spirit of modernity and progress. In his life, Crémieux was the best proof that, under the twin guideposts of emancipation and enlightenment, a Jew can be loyal both to his country and to the hope for the redemption of his people. The success of this dream, however, is tied inexorably to the spread of the notions enshrined at the very heart of the French republic: under the reign of liberty, equality, and fraternity, the Jews and Judaism everywhere will be free to be redeemed.[15]

This basic message was repeated by Gordon in the dozens of articles he wrote for *Ha-Meliz* throughout the spring, summer, and autumn of 1880. From the start, for each week's issue, Gordon churned out on the average at least one editorial, one summary of world news, one survey of Jewish affairs around the globe, several book reviews, and, more often than not, a short story or feuilleton. It was especially the last genre that gave most leeway to his spirit and his pen, allowing him to comment widely and humorously on events of the day in the voice of a feuilletonist separate from that of the editor.[16] But in whichever persona he assumed, Gordon relentlessly focused on what he considered to be the three main issues of the day: the rise of anti-Semitism in Germany (which he followed relentlessly, indeed almost obsessively, in his column of Jewish news around the world), the calumny of Jewish dominance in the revolutionary movement, and the rise of reaction in Russian-Jewish society.

The last two phenomena, Gordon repeatedly warned, were joined in a most unfortunate manner. In response to the fear of the spread of revolutionary sentiment among Jewish youth, a part of the enlightened minority of Russian Jews was beginning to question the wisdom of the acquisition of secular education and thus the entire Haskalah ideology. They were more and more coming under the influence of Orthodox rabbis who never ceased to proclaim the notion that the rush of Jewish students into the gymnasia and universities had resulted in the rise of socialism and support for antigovernment terrorism among Russian-Jewish students. This argument, Gordon insisted, was both ill-founded and played into the hands of the anti-Jewish forces in Russia who sought to overturn the accomplishments of the previous half-century. The identification of Haskalah with revolutionary activism confuses cause and effect, Gordon argued. What caused the flight of a tiny number of Russian Jews into revolutionary cells was not the success of the reform of Jewish society in Russia, but its painfully slow pace. Most at fault for this, of course were the retrograde forces within the Jewish community that had always opposed the spread of secular education, the appointment of modern rabbis, the rehauling of the communal system, and the restructuring of the Jewish economy. The traditionalists were now merely exploiting a delicate situation for their own nefarious purposes. Indeed, their colleagues in Germany were employing exactly the same strategy in the battle against anti-Semitism, alleging that the rise of anti-Jewish politics resulted from the entry of the Jews into the German educational, economic, and cultural world and their parallel abandonment of the traditional practices of Judaism. Whether at home or abroad, these arguments must be battled on every front and in every way; a retreat back into the ghetto will not cause either anti-Semitism or socialism to disappear. What is required (as the title of one of his best-written editorials had it) is that the Jews move "forward, not backward": that they rededicate themselves to rearing a new generation of Jews in a harmonious synthesis between Russian (or German) patriotism and Jewish honor, based on a conservative approach to the reform of Judaism paralleled by respect for individual liberty and the individual religious conscience. Recent events have only proven once more that the enlightenment of the Jews and their emancipation are intertwined, with the latter inevitably resulting from the former.[17]

By the end of 1880, Gordon had written more than 140 pieces for *Ha-Meliz*, most making the same points over and over again. Only one new issue began to vie for space in his columns, news summaries, and feuilletons: the fate of the new Jewish settlement in Palestine. At first, Gordon's reports on the growth of the Jewish colonies in the Land of Israel were optimistic and laudatory. Particularly praiseworthy were the efforts of the Alliance Israélite Universelle to build a new kind of Jewish community in the ancient Jewish land, based on modern cultural and educational premises; it was to be hoped that the Alliance could succeed in Palestine as it had in other parts of Asia and in North Africa.[18] By the summer of 1880, however, news was reaching the St. Petersburg offices of *Ha-Meliz* of attacks on the new settlers in Palestine on the part of the traditionalist Jewish community, the Old Yishuv. Even the Orthodox organizer Yeḥiel Mikhl Pines—one of Gordon's old antagonists in the debate on religious reform, but of a decidedly modernist bent—was denounced and abused by the Jerusalem rabbis and their supporters, who were concerned that the time-honored methods of allocating Jewish philanthropy from abroad were threatened by the new arrivals. This news from Jerusalem served only to vent Judah Leib Gordon's deepest fears about the incipient movement to resettle Jews in the Land of Israel, fears expressed in his controversial letter on messianism published in *Ha-Shahar* in 1870 and repeated in private correspondence in the interim. If Jewish settlement in Palestine were not preceded by the religious, cultural, and economic modernization of the Jews, he had argued, it would be doomed to failure, for the rabbis would take over. They might hide their true colors for a while, pretending to make peace with the modernists, but ultimately they would emerge and prevail and replicate in the Holy Land the religious and communal institutions of the Pale of Settlement.[18] In column after column Gordon denounced and ridiculed the actions of the Jerusalem rabbinate in regard to the new colonists and warned that unless immediate action were taken, the entire dream of a new Jewish society in Palestine would be fatally compromised.[19]

Throughout the spring, summer, and fall of 1880, then, Judah Leib Gordon filled the pages of *Ha-Meliz* with countless articles and feuilletons on the various crises of the day—terrorism in Russia, colonization in Palestine, reaction among the Jews, anti-Semitism in Germany. Despite the dire tone of his pen, however, Gordon was in very good spirits as the fateful year of 1881 approached. His personal affairs were finally improving, the trauma of Pudozh receding into memory. His younger daughter, Nadia, was engaged to be married to a Jewish medical student in St. Petersburg; he was making a decent living at *Ha-Meliz,* working at his own pace and on his own schedule. He was able to supplement his income by accepting an offer to become the literary critic of a new Russian-Jewish monthly to be called *Voskhod* (another synonym for "dawn") and by becoming Hebrew tutor to Baron Gunzburg's sons. The latter job was hardly stimulating, but it paid well and allowed him to frequent the baron's home, thus remaining close to the center of power in Russian Jewry.[20]

It was to the political and financial powerhouses of Russian Jewry that Gordon addressed the most salient of his editorials in *Ha-Meliz* and critical pieces in *Voskhod* at the top of the new year of 1881. A few months earlier, the leading St. Petersburg Jewish philanthropists had generously assisted in the creation of a new organization to aid Russian Jews, the Society for Manual and Agricultural Work among the Jews, known by its Russian acronym as the ORT *(Obshchestvo raspostraneniia truda sredi evreev).* Bucking the fashions of the hour, which had penetrated even to the highest reaches of Russian Jewry, Gordon insisted that the cultural models that the Jews must strive to adopt were not necessarily those of the simple peasant or artisan. While the work of the ORT aimed at improving the material lot of the Jews was laudable, Gordon reflected, the trendy rush to emphasize manual labor as the sole, or most important, solution to the woes of Russian Jews was very troubling:

> Let us bless the [ORT] and pray that God will grant it success—but we worry about the spiritual state of the future Jewish agriculturists. We fear that Jewish farmers will follow the example of their counterparts around the world, burying their spiritual life in the soil, drowning their creativity in mud. [Tilling the soil] devours all the energies and time of its servants, their wives, and their children, from morning till night, from the start of the year to its end, from infancy to the grave—leaving no time to plough one's spirit or one's heart, no time to study works of science or sacred texts. This is an inescapable result of the life of the farmer—as witnessed by the fact that in our vernacular the very word "peasant" means an ignoramus or a boor.[21]

Thus, the Jewish leaders ought to support the work of the ORT but must not lose sight of their greater task, the expansion of the cultural improvement of Russian Jews through such agencies as the Society for the Promotion of Enlightenment. The spiritual and physical amelioration of the Jews must go hand in hand; as the famous Talmudic line had it, "Without flour there is no Torah; without Torah there is no flour."

Further, Gordon insisted, the nexus between the intellectual and physical salvation of the Jews demanded much more than mere philanthropy. The trials and disappointments of the previous year demonstrated anew that the most vital desideratum for Russian Jewry was an articulate and combative *Wissenschaft des Judentums* in the Russian language: a locally trained and supported scholarly community able to proclaim to all, in sophisticated academic language, the truth about Judaism and the Jews. All Western Jewries learned early on in their histories that the decline of traditional religion resulting from the assault of science rendered naive religious faith inadequate as the basis for Jewish survival in the new world. What was required was that the ancient faith be buttressed by scholarly authority and intellectual justification. Such a "Science of Judaism" need not produce only one type of Jewish religious or ideological sensibility; on the contrary, in the West both the conservatives and the modernists have been able to yield divergent interpretations and philosophies from the same scholarly principles and procedures. All parties to this new type of intellectual enterprise agree, however, that it is essential to the rebirth of the Jews. But Russian Jewry has not joined in this essential explosion of creativity; after twenty-five years of Russification and modern education, there is no Russian analogue to *jüdische Wissenschaft* in Germany to speak of. "How many S. I. Rapoports, how many Naḥman Krochmals, how many Zunz's, how many Zecharias Frankels have arisen in our midst?" Gordon asked.[22] Russian Jews are forced to rely exclusively on German-Jewish authorities who, deliberately or not, ignore the reality and the history of the largest, and most Jewishly informed, community in the world, that of the Russian Empire. Russian Jews need their own Science of Judaism not only to pilot the religious reform essential and appropriate to their internal development, but also, in this crucial hour of political unrest, to combat the calumnies against them spread by their enemies and swallowed whole by the uninformed and the gullible.

Gordon's own experiences testified time and time again to the potent power of truth. When he was organizing the construction of the new Jewish cemetery in St. Petersburg, he revealed in an article in *Voskhod* on the early history of the capital's Jewish community, he had to deal with a highly placed Russian bureaucrat who was antagonistic to the Jews, on the basis of prejudices gleaned in his youth in the Ukraine. After attending the dedication services of the cemetery, which were conducted in Russian and Hebrew and in a dignified manner, the official found to his amazement that he was much impressed with the religious tolerance and intellectual sophistication of the Jews. As a result of this experience, he became an ardent philo-Semite. This transformation, Gordon was certain, could be replicated and generalized into a modus vivendi between the Russians and the Jews:

The Russian people are en masse akin to a good-natured, trusting child who listens to what his elders say. Their way of thinking is utterly dependent upon directions given to them from above. Erect a synagogue on Nevsky Prospect [the fashionable main street of St. Petersburg] and the common Russian, passing by, will raise his cap and cross himself; in other words, he would say to himself, this is truly a sacred place. But hide it [on the wrong side of the tracks] and he will not only regard the exiled synagogue as something foul, but deduce that it is pleasing both to God and to the tsar to beat the daylights out of the dirty Jews.[23]

Only a few weeks after Gordon penned these words, he was forced to appraise their implications in a new light. On March 1, 1881, Tsar Alexander II was assassinated around the corner from the Nevsky Prospect. Among the co-conspirators arrested in his murder was Hesia Helfman, a Jewish woman who had provided the headquarters for the actual assassins. This fact did not go unnoticed in the terrifying days and weeks that followed the assassination and the assumption of the throne by the crown prince, now Alexander III. Not surprisingly, the new emperor concluded that his father's murder had resulted directly from his liberal policies, the weakness exhibited by the authorities in the face of enemies at home and abroad. Indeed, on the very day that he was killed, Alexander II was about to sign into law the recommendation of his minister of the interior that elected commissions be convoked in St. Petersburg to advise the government on issues such as provincial government, the status of the peasants, the national economy. The new tsar denounced these plans as a blueprint for a constitution and blamed their author and his colleagues for the reformist defeatism that had left open the door to terror and revolution. Russia would now be governed properly, with strength and fortitude.

The news of the assassination reached Gordon and Zederbaum after they had already set in type the issue of *Ha-Meliz* dated March 3, 1881. There was time only to change the first page, to carry, like all other legal newspapers of the realm, a black-edged announcement from the court of the death of Alexander II. In an ironic coincidence that must have caused Gordon and his colleagues much embarrassment, immediately following the funeral announcement they had printed a piece by Gordon entitled "A Stupid King." This, to be sure, had nothing whatever to do with present events, but was a lighthearted spoof in honor of the recently celebrated Purim holiday.[24]

Gordon's real response to the events of March 1 appeared as the lead editorial of the next issue of *Ha-Meliz,* under the more appropriate heading "The King Is Dead, Long Live the King!"[25] Here, once more, Gordon rehearsed the many wonders that Alexander II had wrought in Russia for all his subjects, including the Jews. Gordon's paean to the dead emperor held no real revelations, either factual or ideological, but neither was it merely obsequious lip service, as later nationalist readers would assume. Rather, the eulogy was a deeply felt expression of pain and grief at the murder of a ruler who had for a quarter-century embodied the promise and the glory of the new age of progress and tolerance, who had indeed brought Russia closer to Europe. Equally heartfelt was Gordon's revulsion in the face of the terror that had felled the tsar—compounded, to be sure, by fear and horror that the charge of Jewish centrality in the revolutionary movement would only be furthered by Hesia Helfman's prominent role in the bloody proceedings. Pained both by the events themselves and by their probable consequences, Gordon called upon his readers publicly to demonstrate their loyalty to the new emperor and to Russia, to pledge in all honesty that they were willing to bear any sacrifice to work for the furtherance of their country's riches and power. But mere prayers and oaths of fealty would not suffice as testimonials to the dead king, Gordon concluded. Those truly committed to the fate of the Jews in Russia in these trying times, and those truly worried about the future, when the many will undoubtedly be blamed for the few, must see to it that they no longer live the way they have in the past—the rabbis within the safe four ells of Jewish law, the Hasidim and their opponents in their century-old squabbles, the maskilim in their self-assured aloofness, the rich alienated from the poor. If all the Jews work together to prove that they are loyal and dedicated servants of the new tsar, ready to improve themselves and thus contribute to Russia as a whole, then inevitably their enemies will be silenced and the Jews will be recognized as loyal and useful citizens of the realm.

Clearly, while the assassination of Alexander II saddened and frightened Judah Leib Gordon, it did not jolt him from his secure faith in the liberal emancipationist politics of the Haskalah. Indeed, that faith was so firm that in his column on Jewish affairs around the world he cited, with obvious satisfaction and agreement, a recent editorial written in *Ha-Maggid* by his namesake David Gordon that inveighed against the mass emigration of East European Jews to the West. "Our heart grieves," David Gordon had written in mid-February,

> at this sad spectacle: every year, thousands upon thousands of young Jews from the Slavic lands come to foreign lands seeking a purpose in their lives. They abandon their homelands which displeased them, and seek a new country. But this they will only seek, and never find.
>
> We will speak only in brief. We see Jewish lads leaving Russia and traveling to Germany, and from there to France, England, America, and all parts of the globe. In all of these places they seek to establish a new life, but what awaits them is merely misery and hunger, physical and moral sickness. Where are you going, you wretched people? Why do you leave your homes?[26]

Judah Leib Gordon did not yet comment further upon this fundamental issue, which had obviously been confounding East European Jewish politics well before the assassination of the tsar and the outbreak of the pogroms. The appropriate response to the assassination of Alexander II, both Gordons still agreed, was for Russian Jews to remain where they were and to work for the betterment of their own lot and that of their nation.

This stance, of course, was shared by the political leadership of Russian Jewry, headed by Baron Horace Gunzburg, and it was the baron himself who approached Judah Leib Gordon to compose the official response of the Russian-Jewish community to the murder of the tsar. Slightly amused by this request—he had, after all, been removed from his position as head of the St. Petersburg Jewish community on the suspicion of support for the revolutionary terrorists!—Gordon responded in characteristic fashion, with an idiosyncratic and inventive application of a biblical citation: on the wreath of flowers sent by the Jewish community to the tsar's funeral Gordon ordered to be inscribed the first half of Lamentations 4:20: "The breath of our life, the Lord's appointed, was captured in their traps." Not only was the sentiment appropriate (for the verse continues: "He in whose shade we had thought to live among the nations") but also the first letters of each word of the Hebrew original—*ruah 'apeinu meshiah 'adonai nilkad be-shehitotam*—spelled out none other than Romanov, the family name of the Russian dynasty.[27]

When Gordon was called to the baron's home to discuss composing a letter of condolence to the imperial family, he was informed by the dignitaries there assembled that there were plans afoot to celebrate his twenty-fifth literary anniversary with a grand public evening and a luxurious new edition of his collected works. Since *The Love of David and Michal* had first appeared in October 1856, the celebration of his silver jubilee as Hebrew poet would take place with a great flourish in October 1881. Although at first he responded to this news with an appropriate amount of false modesty and self-denigration, in private he confessed to his intimates that he was in fact thrilled and touched by these plans. Immediately, he began to work on collecting his writings for the anniversary edition. In large measure, then, Gordon's fears and pain caused by the political upsets at home and in Germany were largely offset by his personal triumphs. There was, after all, still hope for the future, for the longed-for synthesis of Russian patriotism and Jewish renewal.

And yet, it does appear that the assassination of Alexander II and the assumption of power by his son did in some measure shake Gordon's ideological resolve. He did not, to be sure, abandon hope in the enlightenment and emancipation of the Jews through the techniques long prescribed by the Haskalah, but he did begin publicly, if obliquely, to question whether indeed that goal was the policy of the Russian government. The first chinks in Gordon's loyalist armor are discernible in a literary column he wrote for *Voskhod* in early April 1881. In a review of a new Russian-Hebrew dictionary, Gordon examined the progress of the Russification of the Jews over the past half-century. The aspiration on the part of Jews to master the Russian language, he reported, progresses at a quick pace: everywhere—among children, in the schools, in family life, at public meetings, in the business world—Russian is more and more overtaking Yiddish as the preferred medium of discourse for Jews. Under favorable conditions, in the course of one or two generations the disgraceful Germanic jargon will be displaced and forgotten. "But external circumstances, it must be admitted, have not always favored this commendable internal development. In this regard no blame can be placed on the Jews, who have acquired Russian culture and stand, as it were, between a rock and a hard place."[28] The blame, rather, must be placed firmly and squarely at the feet of the Russian government itself:

> The necessity of the Russification of the Jews first became apparent in the aftermath of the [1863] Polish Uprising, when the realization emerged that the millions of Jews who were terror-stricken by the uprising constitute a power which ought not be overlooked. When it became clear that the Russian element in these areas must be strengthened, among other measures taken was the decision to attempt to Russify the Jews. But from the start, it is apparent, there was no clear realization of what this Russification meant. Some zealous administrators dreamed of an immediate and complete *fusion* [of the Jews and the Russians]. This, to be sure, would be the quickest and most radical method. . . . But it soon became apparent that such a fusion was more difficult to accomplish than clearing the woods of bands of rebels, and it was decided to settle, instead, on cultural integration based on education. But even in this

regard there was an unwillingness to comprehend that such a regeneration of an entire people cannot be accomplished with the wave of one hand, the expression of platonic desires or of sympathetic motives.[29]

Not only was there a lack of essential understanding of the meaning and dynamics of Jewish cultural change, Gordon explained, but the government moved actively to obstruct the accomplishment of its own policy. Just as it decided to Russify the Jews, for example, it forbade the hiring of Christian domestic servants by Jews and the publication in Russian of Jewish prayer books, catechisms, and the Scriptures themselves. Obviously at play here was the fear held by the Synod— and, implicitly, the conservative forces within the Russian administration allied with the Synod—that in addition to Jews learning Russian, Russians would learn about Judaism. Given these unfavorable external circumstances, the results achieved by Jews in Russifying themselves is nothing short of miraculous.

In early April 1881, then, on the heels of the assumption of power by a tsar clearly dedicated to reversing the liberal policies of the previous reign, for the first time in either his public utterances or his preserved private communications, Judah Leib Gordon began to question the commitment of the Russian state to the enlightenment, and hence to the emancipation, of the Jews. Little did Gordon suspect that by the time his words would hit the press, events would propel the doubts he raised to the very center of Jewish politics in Russia and the world.

In the weeks following the assassination of Alexander II, the notion that the Jews were responsible for the murder of the tsar was transmuted into rumors that, on account of their revolutionary perfidy, Jews could be attacked with impunity during the approaching Easter holiday, the time of greatest theological tension between Christian and Jew. On April 15, 1881, the fourth day of Easter week according to the Orthodox calendar, an anti-Jewish riot broke out in the Ukrainian city of Elizavetgrad, a flourishing commercial center with a population of forty-three thousand, including approximately ten thousand Jews. A later offical government investigation detailed what happened:

During the night from the 15th to the 16th of April, an attack was made upon Jewish houses, primarily upon liquor stores, on the outskirts of town, on which occasion one Jew was killed. About seven o'clock in the morning, on April 16, the excesses were renewed, spreading with extraordinary violence all over the city. Clerks, saloon and hotel waiters, artisans, drivers, flunkeys, day laborers in the employ of the Government, and soldiers on furlough—all of these joined the movement. The city presented an extraordinary sight: streets covered with feathers and obstructed with broken furniture which had been thrown out of the residences; houses with broken doors and windows; a raging mob, running about yelling and whistling in all directions and continuing its work of destruction without let or hindrance, and as a finishing touch to this picture, complete indifference displayed by the local non-Jewish inhabitants to the havoc wrought before their eyes. The troops which had been summoned to restore order were without definite instructions, and at each attack of the mob on another house, would wait for orders of the military or police authorities, without knowing what to do. As a result of this attitude of the military, the turbulent mob, which was demolishing the houses and stores of the Jews before the eyes of the troops, without being checked by them, was bound to arrive at the conclusion that the excesses in which it indulged were not an illegal undertaking but rather a work which had the approval of the government. Toward evening the disorders increased in intensity, owing to the arrival of a large number of peasants from the adjacent villages, who were anxious to secure part of the Jewish loot. There was no one to check these crowds; the troops and police were helpless. They had all lost heart, and were convinced that it was impossible to suppress the disorders with the means at hand. At eight o'clock at night a rain came down accompanied by a cold wind which helped in large measure to disperse the crowd. At eleven o'clock fresh troops arrived on the spot. On the morning of April 17 a new battalion of infantry came, and from that day public order was no longer violated in [Elizavetgrad].[30]

From Elizavetgrad, however, the riots spread to neighboring towns and villages, especially those on rail lines leading out of the city—apparently, after completing their looting and destruction, some of the rioters simply hopped on the first train out and continued their activities at the next stop. Although in at least one town, Aleksandriia, the riot was nipped in the bud by the military, within a week looting and violence against Jews had erupted in thirty-three locations in the Elizavetgrad region. After a few days of calm, a new wave of attacks spread like wildfire through more and more towns throughout the length and breadth of the Ukraine, including the capital city of Kiev, in which there lived a large (and mostly extralegal) Jewish population. The violence continued unabated for a fortnight, reaching Odessa on May 3 and lasting there for four days.[31]

Almost immediately after the first riot, news of the unprecedented attacks gripped Russian Jewry by its collective throat; almost simultaneously, Jews in Germany, France, England, and the United States were riveted with alarm, fear, and outrage at the tidings from Russia. For the first time, the Russian word for massacre, *pogrom,* entered the lexicon of the Western world. From the very outset, Jews in Russia and abroad all joined in the perception shared by the rioters that the government had instigated the pogroms or at the very least had approved of them.

A century after the events, the assumption of government complicity in these attacks appears highly problematic. Recent scholarship has argued quite persuasively that the pogroms were not planned, either by the government or by any conspiratorial group, but were spontaneous eruptions on the part of displaced workers reacting to the deeply embedded pathology of the Russian social fabric. Rather than approving of the pogroms, the central government in St. Petersburg actively disapproved of the violence and dislocation, fearing that they were the further work of revolutionary terrorists aiming at destabilizing the always delicate balance that obtained in the countryside, especially in the fractious Ukraine.[32]

Although this revisionist version of events is compelling, the exact constellation of cause and effect that surrounded the pogroms, and the role of the government in either fomenting or countering them, cannot be established with any degree of certainty at this stage of access to archival data. But whatever the ultimate reconstruction of events will establish, the critical historical datum is that in the aftermath of the pogroms, the perception arose that the government had inspired, directed, and approved of the anti-Jewish violence, and that this assumption has been maintained as fact for decades thereafter.

Judah Leib Gordon's first recorded reaction to the shocking news from the Ukraine was a letter he wrote to Ze'ev Kaplan on May 2, 1881, in the midst of the second wave of pogroms. Invoking Jeremiah's description of the plunderers of Zion, and speaking in his own metaphoric voice, Gordon wrote:

> The "destroyers at noonday" who rose against the Jews in Elizavetgrad and Kiev and their environs have despoiled me as well. The plan of the local maskilim in regard to my collected works and my creations will apparently not be realized, and I agree with them: is this the time for us to stroll in gardens and gather roses—at a time when prickly thorns destroy our homes, our tents assailed by thistles? Is this the time to rejoice in song when scores of Jewish homes are destroyed and multitudes of families are left without shelter and food?. . . . Who could have predicted that such horrors and devastation could happen in our days! Even in St. Petersburg there are fears that the mobs would rise against Jews. This was supposed to have happened yesterday, but nothing came of it. It seems that [the government] was prepared for such an eventuality, for Baranov, the mayor, sent one of the police chiefs and three of his men to guard Baron Gunzburg and his bank. The baron refused the guard, claiming that he did not merit any more protection than the rest of the Jews in the capital. And even though there is truly no reason to fear such outbreaks in our city, which has so many high government officials and is thus filled to the brim with police and soldiers, and where the Jews live dispersed throughout the city and not concentrated in any one area, as in the provincial towns—still, the news from afar depresses us to no end, overwhelms all our joys, and fills us with a heavy heart. You are lucky to live [in Riga] where disgusting things like this cannot occur.[33]

Judah Leib Gordon's initial response to the pogroms, then, was a combination of shock, horror, and concern, but not—at least as yet— an occasion for ideological reversal. The news was too fresh, the fear too imminent to evoke philosophical cogitation. Similarly, Gordon's political comrades and colleagues did not abandon their perception of the world and adopt a new political stance. Retroactively, after it was obvious that the April and May pogroms had merely been the first tidal waves heralding a hurricane of violence, the response of the St. Petersburg elite and the maskilim was denounced as indicative of a deeply etched paralysis resulting from a stultified political ideology. But at the time, it was not only impossible to know what would happen in the coming months; it was also the accepted consensus among both the Jews and the government officials that the pogroms were led and planned by revolutionary terrorists further attempting to destabilize the regime.

This, indeed, was the analysis conveyed to Baron Gunzburg by Grand Duke Vladimir, the tsar's brother, in a meeting between the two on May 4. The government had ascertained that the pogroms "are not to be exclusively traced to the resentment against the Jews, but are rather due to the endeavor to disturb the peace in general."[34] A similar statement was made public two days later by the newly appointed minister of the interior, N. P. Ignatiev, who denounced the pogroms as the work of

> ill-minded agitators who fan the evil passions of the popular masses and without being aware of it, act in accordance with the designs of the anarchists. Such violation of the public order must not only be put down vigorously, but must also be carefully

forestalled, for it is the first duty of the Government to safeguard the population against all violence and savage mob rule.[35]

Convinced that the Russian regime was committed to a policy of suppressing the pogroms and punishing their perpetrators, Gunzburg and the other notables embarked only on a modest philanthropic effort to aid the victims.

This strategy, however, was far from satisfactory to the younger, more radical and nationalist elements in St. Petersburg Jewry, especially to those associated with the "Jewish populist" paper *Razsvet*. In line with their own well-established political premises and organizational style, in the name of a fictitious society to aid the Jews they invited all of the leaders of the St. Petersburg community to attend an emergency meeting at the home of Baron Gunzburg and sent him a letter informing him that the meeting would take place and that he was expected to chair it and to call for an immediate audience with the tsar. For reasons that remain unclear, Gunzburg acceded to these demands and convened the assembly, which did indeed decide to seek an audience with the emperor.[36]

That audience took place at the palace at Gatchina on May 11. In addition to Baron Gunzburg, the head of the delegation, present were the banker A. I. Zack, the scholar M. G. Berlin, and the prominent attorneys A. Ia. Passover and E. B. Bank. Baron Gunzburg assured Alexander III of the Jews' gratitude for the protection given them by the army and police, and added, "One more imperial word, and the disturbances will disappear." Alexander responded that all Russian subjects were equal before him, and that it was clear that "in the criminal disorders in the south of Russia the Jews merely serve as a pretext, and that it is the work of the anarchists."[37]

This reassuring statement by the tsar was immediately published in the press, thus granting the highest degree of censure to the perpetrators of the pogroms. But what was not published in the public domain were the tsar's additional comments to the Jewish leaders, that although he was certain that the pogroms were carried out by revolutionary terrorists, the Jews were partially at fault for their victimization in that they exploited the peasantry through money lending and tavern keeping and were known to evade the draft in large numbers. The Jewish delegates respectfully pointed out that the economic behavior of the Jews was a direct consequence of their restriction to the Pale of Settlement, and that Russian merchants, as well, were renowned for avoiding military service. The tsar responded that the Jews should submit to him a detailed memorandum on all these subjects, and adjourned the audience.[38]

How Baron Gunzburg and his colleagues felt upon the conclusion of this meeting cannot be established, as none of the participants left any extant memoirs or correspondence on the subject. It is reasonable to assume, however, that they were decidedly relieved by Alexander's statement; although he did, to be sure, seem in part to be blaming the Jews for their own suffering, he forcefully and clearly condemned the pogroms and appeared willing to hear the Jews' pleading of their case.

Although Judah Leib Gordon was not present at the audience with the tsar, it is likely that he was cognizant of what had taken place there and joined in the optimistic reading of its consequences. His first public statement on the pogroms,

therefore, published in *Ha-Meliz* on May 19, was a plea for caution and circum-
spection in public, and especially foreign, reports about the pogroms:

> All the Jewish newspapers that reach us from abroad are filled with news of the vio-
> lence and attacks launched against the Jews in our southern regions. Being distant
> from the actual occurrences, and receiving their information secondhand, they are
> plagued with exaggerations and false reports. Thus, it has been reported that in Eli-
> zavetgrad 500 Jewish families were killed, and similar things that never happened.
> Now, it is not unusual that in the midst of chaos and riots there should spread
> through the world such horrific and exaggerated claims, either out of ignorance or of
> malice, on the part of people given to overstatement. But in this case there is no need
> for exaggeration and overstatement: the horrors that afflicted us are terrible enough.
> Moreover, the greater the exaggeration, the worse the effect, for the result is to raise
> doubts in the minds of the reader even about accurate reports and things that truly
> did happen. Therefore, we say to our brethren who publish newspapers in Germany:
> Watch your words, understand what is involved.[39]

Clearly, Gordon knew that as a result of the pogroms—and, undoubtedly, the
government's response to them—Russian Jews faced a new and critical political
crisis, which had to be addressed in the most responsible and cautious terms. Neither he nor the political leaders of the Jewish community believed in sidestepping
the issue, in understating the devastation, in appeasing the forces of evil. On the
other hand, they did believe that to react too quickly, too emotionally, too radically, was to risk exacerbating the problem. The correct response, therefore, was to
be vigilant, patient, and to carry on as best as they could until the situation sorted
itself out.

In this vein, directly after his warning to foreign journalists about exaggerating
the effects of the pogroms, Gordon returned to one of his major themes and topics,
the religious reform of the Jews. He reported on a controversy in Galicia regarding
the licensing of rabbis, and on the progress of Hebrew Union College, the Reform
rabbinical seminary in Cincinnati, expressing the hope that its teachers, "who are
known to us as Reformers, will be able to accomplish their goals properly and be
moderate in their reforms, in order that the teaching of the Lord will be secure in
their students, and His spirit will dwell among them."[40]

Nevertheless, it was difficult to keep one's mind off the horrors and devastation.
Gordon was especially concerned about his brother-in-law Mikhl, who lived in the
afflicted area. Gordon contacted several mutual friends to try to ascertain how
Mikhl was faring, and finally, at the end of May, received a letter from him full of
gloom and foreboding. Mikhl reported that he himself had not been caught in a
pogrom, but that he had lost a lot of money as a result of the destruction of the
businesses of his customers in Kiev and Elizavetgrad. More important, though, he
confessed, he had lived through the greatest trauma of his life:

> The rumors heard from among the masses, the landlords, the peasants living in town
> caused me endless fear all day and every day. My fright was not without cause, for
> all were posed to attack and to loot, to devour the wealth of the Jews and the labor
> of their hands. For three days and nights we did not change our clothes and did not
> allow ourselves to sleep, and were kept busy with burials—burying boxes and cases

of clothes and bedware, leaving ourselves with only one cloak, one set of clothing and linens. On the third of May, we saw peasants gathering together from all directions, each one carrying in his or her hand an empty sack, to be filled with loot and plunder. Knowing we were done for, we shook with fear and despair—until, suddenly, we saw arriving in town on the railroad an army of cavalry, led by Lord Abaza, the minister of finance, the lord of our town. When the peasants saw the soldiers, they realized that they could not carry out their intentions, and dispersed in disappointment. We were saved.[41]

Nonetheless, Mikhl concluded, he and his neighbors were still living in fear of another attack and in a general atmosphere of apprehension not felt by the Jews in Eastern Europe since the Chmielnicki uprising of 1648.

Judah Leib Gordon responded only in brief to his brother-in-law's lament, expressing relief that he had not been injured by the riots, which, in Jeremiah's words, caused "our hearts within us to be broken, all our bones to shake."[42] At the same time, though, Gordon began publicly to express the thought that jeremiads were not sufficient responses to the pogroms. Rather, it was necessary for the Jews to think through the tragedy and to grapple with its consequences.

In his Jewish news column in *Ha-Meliz*, Gordon began to present his own, quite idiosyncratic view of what had happened, reminding his readers that the physical attacks on the Jews of the Ukraine were cut from the same cloth as the verbal assaults on the Jews of Germany by the anti-Semites. Both were directed by the enemies not only of the Jews but also of progress and civilization as a whole. In the Russian case, the attackers were radical opponents of the government, revolutionaries aimed at destablizing the Crown and society who had merely chosen the Jews as useful targets; in Germany, the goal was the same, although it was directed not by anarchists but by reactionaries. In both conditions, however, the lesson was clear: the government must reemphasize its commitment to the goals of equity and progress, or the consequences would be disastrous for the whole country. Therefore, the impetus for stopping the pogroms must come from one and only one source, the government, which alone has the power and the moral suasion to control the riots. This is not only practical politics, Gordon argued, but the dictate of history as well: in Copenhagen in 1851, a crowd had planned to attack the Jews, but the king himself—a relative of Alexander III—had personally intervened to declare that he recognized no legal distinction between Christian and Jew, and the mobs were quieted.[43]

In other words, in his earliest responses to the pogroms Gordon argued quite forcefully that the pogroms were but a symptom and a symbol of the overall struggle for human freedom that defined the modern age. The opponents of liberty recognized no boundaries and merely donned different garb in different contexts. The fate of the Jews was inextricably bound to the fight against the forces of evil and destruction; this lesson ought to be learned not only by the Jews themselves but by the governments of Europe as well.

Gordon's point, however, was not taken up by most of his friends and colleagues, especially not by those who espoused the mélange of nationalist and populist sentiments that had become popular among Russian-Jewish youth in the 1870s. In one of the most famous—and most revealing—testaments of the bearers

of this mentality to the pogroms, Lilienblum confessed in a famous diary entry for
May 7, 1881:

> I am glad I have suffered. The rioters approached the house I am staying in [in
> Odessa]. The women shrieked and wailed, hugging the children to their breasts, and
> didn't know where to turn. The men stood by dumbfounded. We all imagined that
> in a few moments it would all be over with us. . . . But, thank God, they were fright-
> ened away by the soldiers and we were not harmed. I am glad I have suffered. At least
> once in my life I have had the opportunity of feeling what my ancestors felt every
> day of their lives. Their lives were one long terror, so why should I experience nothing
> of that fright which they felt all their lives? I am their son, their sufferings are dear to
> me, and I am exalted by their glory.[44]

This tone was taken up by the majority of correspondents and contributors to
Ha-Meliz, which as usual did not take a firm stand on the pogroms, since there was
a substantial diversity of opinion among its writers and because Zederbaum did
not want to alienate any readers. Zederbaum's own editorials in the late spring and
early summer of 1881 demonstrated the rather shell-shocked chaos of conflicting
positions circulating among Russian-Jewish intellectuals at the time, without any
attempt at synthesis or cohesion. In virtually the same breath he expressed unmitigated rage at the attackers, called on the Russian government to emancipate the
Jews, demanded that the Jews themselves rationalize their economic, social, and
religious life so as not to incite further pogroms, and concluded that if emigration
were to ensue from this debacle, the Jews should be directed not to America but to
Palestine, where the Great Powers, including Russia, would in due course "establish a Jewish state, as they have done for Greece, Rumania, Serbia, and Bulgaria."[45]
This Jewish state in the Holy Land would be greeted with enthusiasm by the Russian government, since the Russian Jews who would move to Palestine would forever remain true to the Russian crown and thus help advance Russian interests in
the Near East at the expense of Turkey.

More typical, and less muddled, was the reaction to the crisis articulated in the
lead piece in *Ha-Meliz* on June 9, 1881, written by Judah Leib Levin, the young
Hebrew poet who had been a central figure in the nascent Jewish socialist circles
until this time. Now, in response to the pogroms and to the assumption that it was
anarchists and revolutionaries who had launched the pogroms, Levin argued that
it was obvious that Jews should no longer rely on others to help them, but should
rally to their own aid. Ideological differences within the Jewish community should
be overlooked in this hour of need, since it is abundantly clear that the rest of the
world cannot be relied upon to save the Jews. What is required, above all else, is
Jewish unity and Jewish self-help. This call for unity, however, was quite overtly
an attack on the Jewish leadership circles in St. Petersburg, now deemed to be out
of touch with the masses, their aspirations, and their suffering. You have abandoned the poor, miserable, and destitute, Levin railed: you have spurned your
brethren, refusing even to hire them in your factories and shops, to share their joys
and pain. More important, it was you, the Jewish rich, who were in fact to blame
for the pogroms themselves. The peasants and the workers cannot be held responsible for their outrageous actions, since they were only unconsciously following the
"social laws that are in force today," organizing life around lust for private prop-

erty. The Russian government is partially to blame, to be sure, since in depriving the Jews of equal rights it implicitly gave sanction to attacks against them. But the greatest onus for the suffering of the Jews must be placed on the shoulders of their own ostensible leaders:

> You should know that it is because of you that this storm has been unleashed against the desperate Jews—you were stings in the eyes of the country and thorns in its side, and because of your sins there lie rotting now tens of thousands of your brethren, against whom their oppressors vented their spleen. You set the alien fire within the hearts of our enemies and foes, a fire which is raging now throughout the borders of Israel.[46]

The only solution, then, is for the elite to rejoin the masses. Invoking Jeremiah, Levin cried to the barons, bankers, and railroad magnates: "Return, o return, you who stumble on the mountains of shadow, return to your brethren in the provinces and become one nation, working together in faith, harmony, and peace."[47]

As can well be imagined, Judah Leib Gordon would have none of this populist-nationalist pleading. He would not share in Levin's class analysis of the pogroms or in his identification with the masses and celebration of their collective fate. Nor would he assume, with Lilienblum, vicarious glory in the suffering of the Jewish masses. Rather, to the shock of many of his readers and most of his friends, he insisted on pointing out that the Russian army did, in fact, intervene to stop the pogroms; that, more broadly, there were forces in the world at large that were on the side of the Jews. Thus, immediately following Levin's piece in *Ha-Meliz* of June 9, 1881, Gordon published his first editorial entirely devoted to the appropriate reaction to the pogroms, an article entitled "After the Fury." Throughout Europe, he noted, Jews have arisen to help the victims of the Ukrainian pogroms, and they have been joined in this effort by many virtuous non-Jews who were deeply ashamed of the actions of their coreligionists and were trying to redress the damage and rid themselves of the stigma of the attacks. As usual, the lead was taken by the Alliance Israélite Universelle, joined by many famous non-Jewish writers, politicians, scholars, and scientists. In Paris, for example, a massive gala protest was held on June 2, amassing a fund of eighty thousand francs. But the amount of relief monies raised was not all that important:

> More impressive than the material aid rendered on that day was the moral lesson vouchsafed by that assembly, the clear sign given to all the nations by the elite of the most enlightened land in Europe, in contrast to the villainy and abomination committed by the wild creatures and ignorant masses of other countries who fall upon the Jews and attack them, beat them, and rob them for no reason.[48]

He then reproduced a protest letter signed by French and German scholars and dignitaries in response to the pogroms, and concluded: "This is a sign to us of how deeply the evil we have suffered has affected these important and dignified men, and how much sympathy they have for us!"[49] The Jews, once more, are not alone: They are joined and supported by the best representatives of European society, the bearers of true European civilization and human dignity.

A fortnight after Gordon completed these lines, he—and all other Russian

Jews—were taken by surprise by an official act of a European power moved by the suffering of the Jews. The government of Spain offered to accept sixty thousand Jewish immigrants from Russia and Germany. This offer came, to say the least, as a total surprise: Spain, after all, had banned Jewish residence on its soil since 1492 and was notorious in Jewish popular culture, especially in Eastern Europe, as the embodiment of Christian persecution of the Jews. Gordon's swift and negative reaction to the Spanish announcement would be emblematic of his later approach to the overall question of emigration, which would soon overwhelm all other problems in Russian-Jewish politics.[50] Even if the sixty thousand Jews were to flee Russia and Germany for Spain, he asked, what would happen to the millions of other Jews left behind? Indeed, what would happen to the emigrants themselves, coming into a culture and a society that was so fundamentally alien to them and their way of life? How will all the tailors, shopkeepers, and peddlers who were attacked in Kiev and Elizavetgrad find succor in a place like Spain? How will they adapt to Spanish life? Who will be their leaders, their teachers? The same questions cannot be asked, he granted, about those Jews migrating to America. There they could find ample numbers of their brethren already established, eager and willing to offer aid and support. While English, too, is a foreign tongue difficult for Russian Jews to learn, the use of German is widespread in America, and the Jews could use that language as a means of transition until they are acculturated.

More important than the absence of an established Jewish community or the linguistic hurdle, however, was the nature of the Spanish political, social, and religious order. Spain, he explained to his readers, is ruled by a military junta that can at any time issue a "pronunciamento" contradicting its previous policy. This military clique rules in league with Catholic priests and Jesuits, in a political system that does not recognize the separation between church and state. Therefore, the notion that Spain could serve as a haven for Jewish migrants is preposterous by definition: this is not the road to Jewish salvation but merely building castles in the sky (the Hebrew cliché is "castles in Spain"). The Spanish government has delivered to the Jews only a moral victory, proof that societies that now persecute the Jews will one day regret their actions and plead for the return of the Jews.

Here was the crux of Gordon's attitude towards emigration: on the one hand, concern that the departure of a small percentage of Russia's Jews would not solve the fundamental problems that beset their society as a whole; equally fundamental, on the other hand, an insistence that if Jews do indeed abandon Russia, they be directed to societies that partake of liberal values and hence advance the possibility of Jewish religious and cultural self-regeneration.

This position would soon be the object of vituperative debate and denunciation, but on the day on which it was first aired, June 30, 1881, the attention of Russian-Jewish politics was directed elsewhere, at the new wave of pogroms that was raging through the southern habitations of the empire. On that day, a pogrom broke out in the town of Pereiaslav, in the province of Poltava. Here had gathered a large of number of Jews fleeing Kiev and its anti-Jewish outbreaks, to the displeasure of the local peasant and Cossack populations, who decided to use this opportunity to attack both the new arrivals and the local Jews. Following the pattern of the previous spring, from Pereiaslav the pogroms moved, again mostly along railroad lines, to nine villages in the surrounding region and then to the nearby townlet of

Borispol, where the synagogue was razed, the Torah scrolls desecrated, and Jewish property worth some one hundred thousand rubles destroyed. The rioters dispersed only after five of them were killed by a Cossack regiment sent in to enforce law and order. The same drama unfolded a week later in the neighboring city of Nezhin, where nine rioters were killed by army fire. Nonetheless, the riots continued to spread, from Nezhin to thirteen of its satellite towns and villages, and then to other major cities, small towns, and villages in the Chernigov and Poltava provinces. Finally, the frenzy of looting and pillaging ground to a halt on August 16. Since the first outbreak at Elizavetgrad in mid-April, over one hundred Jewish communities had been the targets of pogroms.[51]

Confronted with this new outburst, Judah Leib Gordon could not simply continue to believe that the attacks would cease due to governmental intervention; some other solution had to be found. And so, while the fires were still raging in the south, Gordon wrote his most detailed and revealing response to the pogroms, a lead editorial in *Ha-Meliz* entitled "Comfort Ye, Comfort Ye, My People!" This obvious invocation of Isaiah 40:1 was occasioned not only by the subject matter but also by an evocative coincidence in timing: the piece was published on Tuesday, July 28, which corresponded to the fourteenth day of 'Av according to the Hebrew calendar—in other words, three days after "Shabbat Naḥamu," the Sabbath of Consolation, when the Prophetic portion read in the synagogue is precisely this passage of Isaiah, meant to console the people of Israel after the commemoration of the destruction of the Temple on the Ninth of 'Av.

But Gordon's words of consolation are curiously posed. He begins in a tone utterly unexpected and easy to misread: a patronizing précis of the "heady vision put forward to you, readers, in the last three issues of *Ha-Meliz*: The traitors commit treachery, the plunderers plunder."[52] In a long and breathless litany, Gordon restated the nationalist-populist position articulated in the editorials of the last three weeks, written by Zederbaum. The wicked attackers have let loose their orgy of violence and plunder, rendering the government incapable, for all its good intentions, of adequate response and control. The tsar, it is true, has spoken out and acted against these outrages, but he is defenseless in the face of the mob's deeply entrenched enmity against the Jews. What good will it do the Jews if the criminals are punished? Their losses cannot be restored. And then the government runs salt into our wounds by blaming us for our own suffering. We realize that we are left defenseless from without and disunited from within, split into various castes and sects that care not for one another, guided by rulers who are paralyzed and ineffectual. We must unite together and assuage our inner rifts, for in union alone can we find redress to our pain and the strength to stand together against future woes. In the wake of suffering, then, there comes consolation: after the three weeks of assault that preceded (in accord with the traditional calendar) the Ninth of 'Av, we return to our houses of worship and together read the words of our God proclaimed through His prophet: "Comfort ye, comfort ye, my people!"

"Comfort ye, comfort ye, my people!" Gordon burst out, shifting his tone radically and speaking in his own voice. The prophet Isaiah, who saw his people oppressed and crushed, pillaged and sacked—exactly as we have just seen occur—did not merely console Israel but rebuked it for its sins and malfeasances, which contributed to its sufferings. In Isaiah's day, too the chief cause of the Jews' disaster was their internal division into two warring halves: the poor and defenseless, unable to help themselves or to contribute to their society at large; and the rich and powerful, inured to their brethren and their pain. Like Isaiah, we must awake and identify the contributing factors to our disaster. Our enemies spout forth venomous accusations regarding our many faults and defects, their words laced with hatred and lies. But

> when we are among ourselves, we must seriously and honestly judge whether all the accusations against us are false, whether there is not contained in them some shade of the truth. How will we help ourselves if we console ourselves and deny all the charges—can we "gouge out men's eyes?" [Numbers 16:14] That will not work; instead, we must acknowledge what is true: if we are guilty of any faults we must seek counsel and rid ourselves of them, to exorcise the evil from within us.[53]

The first accusation against the Jews is that they live off the labor of others, eschewing hard labor and agriculture. This must be acknowledged as true, although it is clearly not the fault of the Jews but of their oppressors through the ages. But it is not enough to point to historical explanations: it must be admitted that even when offered the opportunity to work the land or to learn crafts, Russian Jews spurn the opportunity and stick to their previous trades Their dismal schools continue to churn out untrained wretches who are a burden to their surroundings; and the culture as a whole continues to prefer Talmud students to honest craftsmen. How long can the complaint be maintained that all this is not the Jews' fault, that this is what fate has decreed? Even when a government does attempt to provide them with land for colonization, or with the right to live as craftsmen and artisans anywhere they choose, have the Jews availed themselves of these possibilities? They complain that they cannot afford to do so, that they lack the funds to undertake such radical efforts to change their way of life. But they do not lack the funds to maintain all the synagogues, prayer houses, bathhouses, rabbis, cantors, slaughterers, communal officials? Do they lack money only to establish craft schools? If they can find money to buy Jews out of the military, why can money not be found to subvent agricultural colonization and craft schools? What if each community were to decide that of every thousand boys, only one hundred would go on to a yeshivah, and of those only ten would become rabbis—would that not be enough? Would it really be so terrible if a little bit of learning and casuistry would be sacrificed to the benefit of the nation as a whole? Would it really be harmful if the rabbis and teachers instructed the children to be honest businessmen, equally concerned about money of the non-Jew and the Jew?

The wealthy Jewish leadership stand accused, as well, for their blatant display of riches and luxuries—charges that are well-founded and have been the object of self-criticism from Isaiah's time on, and moreover were pointed to by great scholars as the cause of the Jews' expulsion from the Iberian Peninsula. But the rabbis and preachers, who explode in a frenzy over any minor ritual offence, never involve their authority to combat these sins, for they simply do not know Jewish history, nor are they able to understand what is happening around them, to distinguish between actual and imaginary evil.

In sum, it is clear that a prisoner cannot free himself from jail, and that the Jews who have suffered cannot be aided unless others come to their defense. But who would not mock a prisoner who cannot feel his own fetters, who clenches his fists and refuses to be released when others come to liberate him? This has happened to the Jews of Russia: those who were prepared to help them have been demeaned and rejected, and any aid has been effected only in the face of much opposition. And now the Jews who were attacked and despoiled in the Ukraine rely on their brethren in the capital to lobby for them, to seek mercy and aid. It is good that the government has decided to declare the areas affected by the pogroms as being in the state of war, so that extraordinary measures can be taken to prevent the further outbreak of violence. But that is not enough:

> To exorcise this evil from our midst and to eradicate our neighbors' hatred of us, we must not rely only on others but on ourselves as well. From abroad there arrive well-intentioned messengers [representatives of the Alliance Israélite Universelle] who tell us to leave the country that rejects us and to go to other lands. Go to America and live there, go to Spain which opens its doors to you to resettle there as before, or go to the land of our forefathers and tend your flocks there as you did in days of yore. These counselors who live comfortably in their secure homes forget that it is far easier to advise others to leave than to do so oneself. . . . And let us assume that sixty thousand or even one hundred thousand leave from among us, what are they in comparison with the three million Jews living in Russia? If the others do not reform their mode of life, their educational system, their way of earning a living, within a generation those who emigrated will simply be replaced by equal numbers of people living in the same misery and want. In the end, our country is Russia, where over half of world Jewry lives; Russia, which will not expel the Jews as was done in the past by various nations among whom there lived smaller numbers of Jews. And even if some of us do flee to other places of refuge, the vast majority will remain in this great and generous land, and there is no hope for them if they do not set themselves to unraveling that tangled knot called "the Jewish Question" by our enemies, to blaze a new path and to remove all obstacles in their way, to remove deceit from their hearts and build a new educational system, a new mode of life and earning a living. The message of the prophet who consoles us to the ravaged daughter of Zion should never be forgotten: "You shall be established through righteousness./ You shall be safe from oppression,/ And shall have no fear/ From ruin, and it shall not come near you."[54]

This remarkable homily enunciated a response to the pogroms that would not only remain Gordon's guiding faith in the years to come, but would also set him off sharply from both the emerging nationalist and populist camps and the Russian-Jewish establishment of St. Petersburg. In the face of grievous attacks against the Jews, Gordon maintained the message of redemption he had first articulated fifteen years earlier in his "House of Jacob, Come Let Us Walk."[55] Once more, the proof-text is Isaiah's prophecy, with its finely meshed alternation between self-criticism and hope, consolation and rebuke, appropriated in a new prophecy of redemption synonymous with the vision of the Enlightenment. Once again, the sins of the Jews are equated with their retention of their insulated educational and economic systems, whose supersession is dictated by God himself. To Gordon's mind, the pogroms in the Ukraine and anti-Semitic stirrings in Germany—always linked together and equated as different manifestations of one phenomenon—required no recasting of theory, no rethinking of first principles, no reexamination of the workings of God and His relation to Israel. God's will—that is, the unstoppable universal movement toward equality and liberty—is not compromised by the actions of retrograde forces, either in the shape of ignorant mobs, as in the Russian Empire, or of cabals of priests and politicians, as in the West. In the face of iniquity and enmity, the Jews cannot and must not abandon the only road to salvation, the path of Western civilization and progress.

It is this stubborn retention of faith in the promises of Western liberalism that set Gordon sharply apart from the emerging nationalist and populist camps—not, as might appear to later readers, the rather heartless attack on the sins of the attacked. This bitter self-scrutiny (or self-mortification, perhaps) was hardly unique to Gordon; on the contrary, as seen in Levin's piece above, the castigation of the Jews' social and economic abnormality and mistreatment of one another and the peasants around them was shared by all modern Jewish political sensibilities and movements in Eastern Europe from the early nineteenth century on, transferred from the Haskalah to Zionism and Jewish socialism, with varying emphases and diagnoses. Gordon's tone, to be sure, was rather more caustic than others', caused by his relentless refusal to lionize the Jewish masses, popular culture, or popular suffering. But what separated Judah Leib Gordon from many of the other Jewish intellectuals of his day, and most of the other Hebrew and Yiddish writers and publicists, was his insistence that the pogroms did not establish as certain that the Jews must reject the outside world because it had attacked them, that the pogroms did not prove that the Enlightenment was dead.

Once more, the clearest contrast emerges from a comparison between Gordon's response and that of Moshe Leib Lilienblum. While Gordon in St. Petersburg was penning his defense of Western liberalism and European civilization, Lilienblum in Odessa was arguing that the only solution to the Jewish plight was emigration to Palestine. In his diary Lilienblum recorded his final and complete abandonment of the Haskalah, symbolized by his decision to discontinue his studies at the gynmasium, in favor of working for his new cause:

> When I became convinced that it was not a lack of high culture that was the cause of our tragedy—for aliens we are and aliens we shall remain even if we become full to the brim with culture; when my eyes were opened by the new ideal, and my spirit rose to a new task, in which, if all goes well, lies our eternal salvation—all the old ideals left me in a flash.[56]

Regardless of his ideas on the migration of Jews either to Palestine or to America, Gordon could not join the growing coalition in Russian-Jewish intellectual circles that saw emigration as the only solution to the Jewish plight. Gordon's problems with that coalition were threefold. First, he could not join any group premised on the rejection of the politics and principles of the Haskalah; second (a corollary of the first), he maintained that equal attention had to be given to the fate of the majority of Jews who would under any circumstances remain in Russia; third, he could not brook any coalition with the rabbis, some of whom were becoming active and influential in the emigrationist camp.

But Gordon, it must be stressed, was not opposed to emigration per se, and this set him apart from the Jewish establishment in St. Petersburg. At the end of August 1881, Baron Gunzburg and the railroad magnate Samuel Poliakov convened in the capital the first of a series of conferences of representatives of Jewish communities throughout Russia, aimed at planning strategy in the wake of the pogroms. From the beginning, these conferences adopted a unilaterally negative approach to emigration, as contradicting the goal of Jewish emancipation in Russia. Gunzburg, Poliakov, and others intoned the standard emancipationist argument against emigration, both before and after their time: if the Jewish leadership would support, organize, and fund the departure of Jews from Russia—even if this were legal—would not this aid and comfort the anti-Semites who argued that the Jews were irrevocably alien to Russia and never could be granted equal rights?[57] Gordon implicitly rejected this analysis, arguing that the emigration of the Jews, at least to America, did not in the least deny the possibility, or the necessity, for the legal, social, and cultural amelioration of the Jews in Russia. To Gordon, as already explained, the United States shone brightly as the clearest embodiment of the liberal enlightenment creed. As he wrote in *Ha-Meliz* in mid-August: "As much as hatred of the Jews grows in various European lands, so does love of them spread among the nations living alongside the Jews in America; and the Jews, too, live in love, fraternity, and harmony with their neighbors, with no malice or competition.[58]

In Baton Rouge, Louisiana, he reported with glee, Baptists pray in synagogues, and the Jews don't mind in the least—to which he concluded, shifting from the Psalmist to Isaiah: "How good and how pleasant it is that brothers dwell together! Who more than they fulfill the words of the Prophet: 'For My house will be called a house of prayer for all peoples.'"[59]

It would be difficult to concoct a more evocative expression of continued faith in the marriage of religious reform and political liberalism as the solution to the plight of the Jews than this paean to ecumenicism in Baton Rouge, penned in St. Petersburg in the summer of 1881. Yet, as usual, Judah Leib Gordon's deepest and most eloquent articulation of his soul emerged not in his journalism or even in his private correspondence, but in his artistic creations—not, as yet, in poetry, but in prose. In five installments appearing in *Ha-Meliz* between September 1 and September 29, 1881, Gordon published a new short story entitled "The Dry Bones" [*Ha-'azamot ha-yeveishot*].[60] No extrinsic explication is necessary to discern Gordon's intent in usurping Ezekiel's most famous and most startling image; the beginning of Gordon's story provides its own gloss, indeed its own extended metaphor and moral. At the summit of a steep hill stands a thickly sprouted oak. In the spring, the oak blossomed, providing a wonderful resting place for passing birds and a pleasing shade for itinerant travelers. But the spring turned into summer, and summer into fall; the leaves were shaken off by cruel winds, dispersing the former bearers of glory down soaked ravines and muddy ditches. No longer could the oak provide solace for the weary, only stark dreariness and cold emptiness. The oak stood among its fallen leaves, its boughs stretched to the heavens, crying: Who will renew my shriveled shoots, who will restore my glory laid bare?

"Like the days of this tree are the days of our people," explained Gordon's narrator. The Jews, too, have seen their youth sapped and decrepitude set in. They too, by divine grace, stood in days of yore at the magnificent summit of mountains and towered above the hills. The nations of the world followed their light and truth, finding stability and salvation in the Jews' faithfulness and strength. But then an evil wind blew into a fury, attacking the Jews and stripping them of their finery, casting their glories upon muddy waters, to the ends of the earth: "Is there hope for its future, that it will bud again at the scent of water [Job 14:9]? Can these bones live again? Lord God, only You know!"[61]

Then unfolds a tale rather typical of Gordon's convoluted and forced short stories. In the office of Alexei Ignatievich (formerly Ezekiel, the son of Neta), a Jewish communal notary in a small Lithuanian town, one day in 1871 there appears a Russian naval officer seeking information and assistance in the purchase of real estate on behalf of a Jewish family in a nearby town. Intrigued by this request, Alexei Ignatievich befriends the visitor and discovers that he is a former Jewish Cantonist who was abducted from a nearby town at the age of twelve due to the evil machinations of a wealthy relative. Forced into the Russian Orthodox faith, the young sailor traveled throughout the world, rose through the ranks to become an officer, and married the daughter of a wealthy landowner. Twenty-three years after his separation from his family, he returns to Lithuania on a visit and sets about to help his widowed mother and impoverished siblings. Rebuffed by his brother, who refuses to have anything to do with an apostate, the officer, with the aid of the enlightened Alexei Ignatieviech, turns his attention to the plight of another former Cantonist (who had somehow managed to return both to his hometown and to Judaism) who now seeks to become a teacher in the state-sponsored school for Jewish children but encounters opposition from the local educational inspector, suspicious of a renegade Russian Orthodox. By the end of the story the subplots all converge: the prospective teacher turns out to be not only an intimate childhood friend of the naval officer, abducted at the same time, but also the fiancé of his niece. The officer is thus able to dispense his philanthropy to his family and beloved friend all at once. His niece and new nephew have a child, whom they name after their beneficent uncle, and all live happily ever after.

Though neither Gordon's narrative technique nor his capacity for characterization had improved much since his earlier, equally awkward stories, "The Dry Bones" did mark a substantial departure from its predecessors in its depiction of Russian-Jewish society and, especially, its relations with the government. First and possibly most important, the tragedy of the conscription of Jewish children into the army of Nicholas I was here depicted by Gordon not solely as the result of the corruption of the Jewish communal leaders, as in his earlier Yiddish poem on the Cantonist trauma.[62] Rather, the Cantonist debacle was caused by the collusion of corrupt Jewish leaders and dishonest government officials, eager to convert Jewish children in ways clearly contrary to both Russian civil and canon law. Through not very subtle allusions, Gordon was able to make the point that both sorts of corruption still obtained after the death of Nicholas I; while the continuity of Jewish communal disarray and dishonesty was overtly described, the shortsightedness, obscurantism, and anti-Semitism of some Russian bureaucrats was established more obliquely, in the person of the stupid, bumbling school inspector who attempts to block the appointment of the enlightened Jewish teacher. Similarly, on the one hand, Gordon alluded to the pervasive smuggling activity engaged in by

Jews on the Russian-Prussian frontier and, on the other, to the deeply entrenched dishonesty, bribery, and criminality of the Russian military. Thus, while in the end the bearers of enlightenment prevail both in the Russian administration and among the Jews, there is a far more nuanced depiction of government officials than in any previous work by Gordon, reflecting the new mood revealed in his reportage after the assumption of power by Alexander III. But this recognition of reactionary and anti-Jewish forces within the tsarist regime did not overwhelm the essential core of Gordon's faith, or the message of this tale. On the contrary, and in dramatic opposition to the sentiments filling Russian-Jewish newspapers in the summer and fall of 1881, "The Dry Bones" insisted that the hoped-for synthesis of Russian humanism and Jewish reform could, and indeed would, triumph. In the hands of other Hebrew, Yiddish, and Russian-Jewish poets and authors, the Cantonist episode served as the most egregious example of the pathology of Jewish life under the tsars—governmental persecution, forced baptism of little children, internal Jewish corruption and divisiveness. Indeed, in the years after 1881, the Cantonist experience would provide much grist for the mill of class-based political parties and movements in Russian Jewry. But to Judah Leib Gordon, even in late 1881, the moral of the story was radically different: the lost Jewish children were the "dry bones" in a new version of Ezekiel's vision of redemption. In the prophet's day, the "whole house of Israel," reduced to dry bones by devastation wreaked by internal corruption and external cruelty, cried, "Our bones are dried up, our hope is gone, we are doomed." But God promised: I am going to open your graves and lift you up out of the graves, O My people, and bring you to the land of Israel. . . . I will put My breath into you and you shall live again." The Russian Jews, Gordon was convinced, were similarly afflicted and assailed; but in their case, as the narrator of his story concluded, "The dry bones rose up to new life, the spirit of the new age came and breathed life into the slain, revivifying them and lifting them to their feet."[63]

The lesson is obvious, more poignant at this time than ever before: Whether in the days of Nicholas I or of Alexander III, the forces of reaction and evil in Russian society will join together with the forces of reaction and evil in Jewish society; although beset by failed leaders and cruel soldiers, priests, and bureaucrats, the Russian Jews have no need for despair, no need to cry, "Our hope is gone, we are doomed." They can, and will, find their salvation in the "spirit of the new age," the only contemporary refraction of "God's breath"—the spirit of enlightenment, religious tolerance, and political pluralism.

It is impossible to know how many of Gordon's readers, in September 1881 or later, were comforted by this tale of hope or joined in retaining this vision of redemption. But what is certain is that as the months progressed, as 1881 passed into 1882 and new and more vicious pogroms appeared, fewer and fewer Russian Jews could find solace and faith in the mentality and ideology expressed by Judah Leib Gordon. In the ensuing months, not only did Gordon himself become the object of intense public controversy and attack but also, and perhaps more insidious, he too began to doubt his dreams and beliefs and to hover ever more painfully on the precipice of despair.

10

The Battle Over Zion
1881–1883

On the evening of October 29, 1881, fifty prominent members of the St. Petersburg Jewish community gathered together at the capital's kosher restaurant to celebrate a literary anniversary: twenty-five years had passed since the publication of Judah Leib Gordon's first book, *The Love of David and Michal.* To honor Gordon as the Jewish national poet, Adolph Landau, the editor of the Russian-Jewish journal *Voskhod,* had organized the festive event—the first of its kind in Russian-Jewish history—which was attended by all the Jewish newspaper editors in town and other literary gentlemen, as well as physicians, lawyers, merchants, and teachers. Landau greeted the honored guest with a printed Hebrew address embossed in silver and signed by all the assembled, and with a silver goblet and gold pen, both inscribed in Hebrew with the name "Judah Leib Gordon" and the date of the anniversary. One Jewish poet, the young Shimon Frug, read a Russian poem in honor of Gordon, and another, Joshua Steinberg, recited his translation into Russian of "For Whom Do I Toil?" A Hebrew citation by Baron Horace Gunzburg praising the poet was declaimed, as was a Hebrew verse written by the St. Petersburg rabbi, I. V. Olshvanger, and a Hebrew salutation penned by twenty-three Jewish students at the St. Petersburg Railroad Engineering Academy. Laudatory telegrams were read from admirers in Moscow, Vilna, Grodno, Kovno, Ekaterinoslav, and Samara, and from David Gordon in Lyck, Prussia. It was announced that in order to subsidize the publication of Gordon's collected verse, a special fund was being established, to which the guests present that evening had already contributed the first nine hundred rubles; a larger sum was expected from the Gunzburgs and the other magnates who had not yet returned from Paris for the St. Petersburg season.[1]

After a host of toasts, Judah Leib Gordon rose to respond. Speaking in Russian, he explained that what was being celebrated that evening was not his individual accomplishments but Hebrew poetry as a whole; indeed, the true honoree of the evening was the Hebrew language itself, the one true guarantor of Jewish culture and Jewish pride. He then proceeded to read two new poems that expressed that thought as well as gratitude that in the face of adversity Russian Jewry was uniting as one, proud of its cultural richness. In Hebrew, Gordon read a poem entitled "Old and Young, We Will Go," based on Moses's challenge to Pharaoh: "We will all go, young and old." Gordon's version ended:

> The storm bursts forth, the wind whirls by
> The choppy waters rise up high,
> Do not fear, Jacob, do not despair
> Thousands will not yield to death!
> From the tempest God's voice booms forth:
> "Young and old, we will march as one!"
>
> We will cling to our Lord, not abandon his faith,
> Not forget his sacred tongue.
> We have seen evil, but will see good once more,
> We will live again in this land as we did before;
> If the Lord has decreed that we regain our strength
> Young and old, we will march as one.[2]

Recognizing that many of the guests assembled to honor him could not understand Hebrew, Gordon continued with a Yiddish poem called "The Hebraist," a humorous, ostensibly self-deprecating autobiographical lament about the sad fate of a nice Jewish boy who decided to waste his life by becoming a Hebrew poet. Recalling the lugubrious tones of his famous cri de coeur, just recited in a Russian translation, the poet confessed that he had considered abandoning his muse, giving up the fight in the face of apathy and betrayal. However, seeing the celebration offered to the Hebraist and to Hebrew poetry that evening, his faith was restored. There are, it appears after all, people in this world who care about Hebrew and recognize that without it the Jews are doomed:

> So, dear friends, let us once more
> Raise our cups on high
> Let us drink to the health
> Of our holy tongue,
> To the health of its friends
> Let them all live well!
> To the health of all those who tonight
> Provided us with such fine fare!
> Now I regret that once upon a time
> I regretted that I became a Hebraist![3]

It is not clear if those who heard this pathetic drinking song realized that its teetotaling author was in fact lacing into his audience with venom masked in irony and linguistic condescension. For, as Gordon later complained to several intimate friends, of the fifty guests present, only six or so knew Hebrew well enough to read his poetry, and most could not even sign their names in the ancient script on the scroll of honor presented to him. Indeed, probably a good number of those present had never even heard of Judah Leib Gordon the poet, and some of those who had were responsible for condemning him to prison and exile two years earlier. Don't worry that you weren't invited to this grand affair, he consoled a young friend after the event: my family wasn't even invited! I hope that your literary talent will not linger without acclaim for twenty-five years and only then have the fast broken with a kosher feast. All this fuss was simply an artificial way for the Russified Jewish intelligentsia of the capital to be able to say to the so-called true, native Russians: you may have Pushkin, Turgenev, Saltykov-Shchedrin, and Dostoyevski, but we have our own authors and even one who, though less talented than Dostoyevski and condemned to a lesser prison and place of exile, is appreciated and celebrated before he dies, not only afterward, as is your custom. This whole celebration was just for show, Gordon concluded; now that my immortality is assured, I only have to worry about making a living in the here-and-now![4]

This sarcastic account was tinged, of course, with a good dose of false modesty. But behind the facade, Gordon was in fact deeply ambivalent about the changes he was witnessing in Russian-Jewish society in the wake of the pogroms. On the one hand, he could only be pleased with the fact that a large number of Jewish *intelligenty* were "returning to their people" as a response to the catastrophes of the previous months. Those previously dedicated to the total assimilation of the Jews were shocked to see just how profoundly problematic and unrealistic that goal was. Those attracted to revolutionary cults now recoiled in horror from the acts of the masses, whom they had hitherto lionized as the exemplars of progress. It was not that any truly new ideas were being forged in response to this disillusionment. Rather, more and more Russian Jews were coming to accept the various analyses put forward in the 1870s by the early nationalists and nationally committed populists and previously maintained by only a tiny minority of the Russian-Jewish intelligentsia. This reaction, Judah Leib Gordon believed, was only to be expected as typical of Jewish responses to catastrophe throughout history. As he explained in his literary chronicle in the October 1881 issue of *Voskhod,* Jews respond to physical attack in ways very different from other nations. Most peoples respond to catastrophe with intellectual stagnation, finding relief in taverns and pubs, drowning their sorrows in self-obliterating, artificial stimulation. But Jews act differently: attacks and persecution merely intensify their moral and spiritual power, causing them to delve ever deeper and deeper into their literary and religious treasures. In the face of adversity, Jews find succor by closing ranks and studying their ancient texts. So it is, too, "in the aftermath of the acts of the newest Pharaohs—the pogroms, robberies, massacres, profaning of the sacred, desecrations of synagogues, and blasphemous defiling of the Scrolls of Law."[5]

At the same time, Gordon was profoundly skeptical not so much of the sincerity of the newfound Jewish nationalists and populists or their ideological mentors, but of the profundity and practicality of their politics. Since he had not previously believed either in the "fusion" of the Jews with the Russians or in the sanctity and purity of the masses—any masses, Jewish or Gentile—he felt that he had nothing from which to recoil. As he wrote to M. M. Dolitsky, a young Hebrew poet who had published an article proclaiming the migration of the Jews to Palestine as the panacea to the Jewish problem, Gordon still believed in the goal of "having the language of Jerusalem in our mouths, and the thoughts of Europe in our hearts."[6]

It was, of course, precisely the abandonment of Europe in favor of Palestine, in both the literal and metaphoric senses, that began to be argued by a mounting chorus of Jewish intellectuals in Russia, to Gordon's deepening discomfort. Joining David Gordon and Eliezer Ben Yehudah, who had been proclaiming this ideal for years, were a motley crew of intellectuals including previous opponents of the Palestinian colonization such as Peretz Smolenskin and Moshe Leib Lilienblum. The latter gradually emerged as the most influential spokesman for the cause, now harnessing his substantial polemical skills and populist fervor to the "Palestinophilic" banner. The old Haskalah goal of integrating the Jews into European society, Lilienblum argued in an influential article in *Razsvet,* was fundamentally flawed, as society was now moving in an entirely different direction: the age of equal rights and religious tolerance was over, superseded by the age of nationalism. The Jew was now despised not because he believed in a different creed but because he was an "alien," a member of a different biological and cultural entity. The struggle for improving the material, moral, and legal condition of the Jews was therefore not only out of step with history and thus doomed to failure, but also counterproductive: the more the Jew became enlightened, economically successful, and culturally integrated, the more he was hated by those who deemed him of essentially different ilk. The only solution, therefore, was for the Jews to set up their own society based on their own brand of nationalism. They must abandon, massively and completely, not only Europe but also every society in which they constitute an alien minority, and return to their historic homeland as a nation in their own right. For Jews to close their eyes to this reality was to court disaster, for this was not a matter of choice but of historic necessity.[7]

Gordon accepted neither this diagnosis nor its prognosis. European civilization was still the font of justice and wisdom, he argued, and the Palestinian venture had to be judged in this light. As he repeated once more in a letter to Dolitsky:

> I do not hope for redemption and the restoration of Israel's glory in the land of our fathers at this time. . . . may this thing not come about, for it would lead only to a bitter end for the Jews themselves. As long as the rabbis rule, and the religion which they have forced upon us is in effect as they have decreed, the Jews will not be able to establish a state for themselves. Who will sit at its head? Rabbi Joshua Leib Diskin [a prominent rabbi of the Old Yishuv in Jerusalem], his wife, and their like? Woe to us if people like that grab hold of an earthly realm, if they get to sit on David's throne and rule his kingdom, with the *Shulḥan ʿArukh* as it obtains today . . . becoming our constitution, with the reinstitution of the biblical forms of capital punishment, flogging, excommunication, and bans. Even today, the rabbis rule over their communities from on high, casting us down ever lower and lower. . . . What will happen if Reb Lipele becomes the police superintendent and Reb Ḥatskele the gendarme—who will save us from such mighty divinities? Let us not lie to ourselves: our religion as it has been fashioned by the rabbis in recent years is, in its essence, opposed to culture and civilization. What future should we have to endure?[8]

I, too, Gordon confessed, dreamed such dreams in my day—look at the piece I published in *Ha-Shaḥar,* volume two, and the trouble I got into because of it in 1876, when Brafman attacked me in *Golos* for ostensibly calling for a messianic kingdom. I have suffered the pains of a Jew, I know in my bones and in my heart what exile means! But all those who proclaim that the only solution to the problems of the Jews is a Jewish state in Palestine look at this question only from the practical standpoint and deliberately ignore its religious dimension, for they know that it is impossible to move the rabbis to legislate the necessary reforms, to raise our religion to the level of reason. "And may God spare us from having a government run by such heavenly gatekeepers, for then our religion will become a burden and stumbling block for us, and a rebuilt Jerusalem will be a cup of poison for all the peoples and especially for the Jews."[9]

He requested that his correspondent not disclose these thoughts in public, for the time was not right to attempt to rid Israel of the dross that had accumulated over the ages of darkness. But if God lifts the Jews from their anger and pain, Gordon concluded, it will be the duty of every intelligent person to see to it that the Jewish religion and educational system are reformed so that on the basis of a purified faith, amenable to civilization, the Jews will be able to strive for the realization of the ancient dream of Israel—and not before then.

Here, for the first time in the aftermath of the pogroms, did Gordon explicitly reaffirm his long-lived, profoundly held, and increasingly lonely credo that the redemption of the Jewish people through the establishment of a Jewish state in Palestine must follow upon a thoroughgoing modernization of Judaism. This view he first articulated in 1870 and repeated throughout the 1870s and 1880s and, as shall become apparent, to the end of his life in 1892. Gordon did not change his opinions on this matter as a result of his bitter experiences with the rabbis, as some apologetic critics have argued. Rather, his own personal suffering merely intensified his hatred of the rabbis and deepened the objections to the colonization in Palestine that he had raised in his very first public utterance on the subject on the pages of *Ha-Shaḥar* in 1870 and repeated through the years in private correspondence and public commentary. Indeed, on the day before the outbreak of the first pogrom on April 15, 1881, he wrote one of his most caustic pieces on the dangers of a rabbinic theocracy resulting from the new Palestinian colonization, a feuilleton that unfavorably compared Rabbi Diskin's wife (one of Gordon's favorite targets over the years) with Rahab the harlot in the story of Joshua's emissaries to Jericho. At least Rahab sheltered the men, Gordon observed, while Mrs. Diskin denounced and abused the latter-day emissaries.[10]

In sum, Gordon's views on the subject did not change in response to either personal or communal suffering. From the start he believed that the return of the Jews to their historic home was a vital component of their national redemption and that of the world as a whole. But that return, he insisted, had to be conditioned on the *prior* religious reform of the Jews.

This position was no less idiosyncratic in 1881 than it had been a decade earlier, but it became more and more controversial as the political situation of the Jews in the Russian Empire continued to deteriorate. On Christmas Day, only a fortnight after Gordon wrote the letter to Dolitsky cited above, a vicious pogrom broke out in Warsaw—the first pogrom in Poland proper and particularly outrageous to Jewish sensibilities and liberal politics, since Warsaw, of all the cities in the Russian Empire, had been the seat of perhaps the most extensive Jewish-Gentile rapprochement. Three weeks later, Minister of the Interior Ignatiev granted an audience to Dr. Isaac Orshansky, a member of the editorial board of *Razsvet* (and brother of the recently deceased historian of Russian Jewry Ilia Orshansky) in which the minister declared that "the western frontier is open to the Jews." Large numbers of Jews had already availed themselves of this option, Ignatiev acknowledged, and no obstacles were put in their way so long as the emigrants were entire families that did not include young people who had not yet served in the military. The government has forbidden emigration only to those who abandoned their elders to communal welfare and those who had not fulfilled their obligations to the state. On the question of allowing the Jews to move to the interior of the empire, the minister made it abundantly clear that he and his government would not take any measures "liable to aggravate even further the relations between the Jews and the native population." Therefore, though keeping the Pale of Settlement intact, he reported that he had instructed the Jewish Committee to inform him of places outside the Pale that were sparsely settled and therefore possibly suitable for the settlement of Jews "in accord with their wishes for self-amelioration and without harm to the native residents."[11]

Dr. Orshansky replied that the Jews who were leaving Russia were doing so only in response to the unbearable political situation of the last few months and without any political motivation, and that the Jewish intelligentsia was willing to do anything to improve the lot of the Jews in Russia and their integration with the Russian society; the government, however, must allow the Jews to organize both the internal and external migration movements. Ignatiev responded that in order to found any organization, the Jews have to obey the general laws of the empire; they should bear in mind, however, that anyone leaving Russia would forfeit his right ever to return.

These remarks by the minister of the interior contained little if anything that had not been said previously in closed meetings with the St. Petersburg Jewish elite. Baron Gunzburg and his colleagues, however, had in the previous months chosen to keep such comments secret, fearing massive panic in the Pale. In sharp contrast, the editors of *Razsvet,* imbued with their nationalist-populist ideology (and possibly hoping to scoop their competition), felt that they had an obligation to publish the interview with the minister as soon as possible. Here, after all, was the most important servitor of the tsar proclaiming that the government looked with favor on the departure of the Jews from Russia and would never consider the possibility of abolishing the Pale of Settlement. Ignatiev's interview with Orshansky was therefore published in a special edition of *Razsvet* on January 18, 1882. The expected panic ensued, first in St. Petersburg and later throughout the Pale: public meetings were called to discuss the minister's remarks, rabbis proclaimed public fasts and days of prayer. Emigration fever spread through Russian Jewry as never before.[12]

Several years after the event, in a fascinating memoir, Judah Leib Gordon recalled how he had learned of Ignatiev's statement. On the fateful day, he was at Baron Gunzburg's home tutoring his sons and encountered Baron Horace pale and visibly upset. "What do you think of all this?" the baron asked Gordon, who had no inkling of what was going on. Gunzburg explained the situation, adding that a meeting of the St. Petersburg Jewish notables had convened to discuss the crisis but had not been able to decide on any response, save pleading with the editors of *Razsvet* not to send the news of the interview to the provinces. According to Gordon's recollection, Gunzburg was flabbergasted by the events and did not know what to do. He ordered the issue of *Razsvet* containing Ignatiev's remarks brought to Gordon, who was instructed to read the interview while the baron retired to dress. When Baron Horace returned to the reception room, dressed in formal attire in anticipation of a meeting with a high official, the following conversation ensued:

> "Well, then, what do you say about this?" [the baron asked Gordon.]
>
> "You know already," I responded, "that in this regard I am a radical and disposed to the most forceful actions. . . .
>
> "What do you mean to say?"
>
> "I mean," I continued, "that for as long as I had the honor of assisting you in communal matters, I always counseled 'a low profile, gentlemen.' That, too, can be regarded as a strategy, and if it had accomplished anything, it would not have demeaned our honor in the least. However, it now appears that we have groveled and bowed enough—and, nonetheless, we are being trampled underfoot, and now apparently are being shown the door. Do you know what awaits us in this connection? If the minister permits such a statement to be published in his name, nothing will prevent him from bringing this idea to the government as a formal policy—and then we shall experience a new expulsion that is greater and more onerous than that from Spain."
>
> "What, then, do you think we should do?"
>
> "I think we oughtn't to be embarrassed any longer. We must immediately send messengers to the West who will ensure the publication there of the minister's statement."
>
> "And what will that accomplish?"
>
> "As you know, there are at this moment protest meetings in London against our persecution. Even Madame Novikov [an influential Russian journalist in London] and others close to the government express the justice of the Jews' complaints and denounce the attacks on the Russian Jews. It is therefore advisable that the clear announcement of the minister be published abroad, so that it becomes known that the stories about our horrible situation are not fabricated, but the truth, the horrifying truth. Possibly, public opinion in the West will mitigate against the evil decree befalling us."[13]

Gunzburg then hinted that Gordon should contact Wallace MacKenzie, the London *Times* correspondent in St. Petersburg, with whom Gordon had met in 1878 to discuss the publication abroad of an earlier scandal about the Russian government's policy on the Jews. Now, however, Gordon declined to seek out the correspondent for *The Times,* concluding that someone more appropriate should go about this work.[14]

This episode (whose authenticity, at least in regard to its tone and conclusions, there is no reason to doubt) speaks volumes both about the state of Jewish politics in Russia in early 1882 and about Judah Leib Gordon's own state of mind at the time. Especially as a result of Ignatiev's confounding declarations—the January 15 statement was not really translated into clear government policy, and was soon contradicted by the minister himself in a meeting with the St. Petersburg rabbi— the Jewish plutocracy headed by Baron Gunzburg found itself in an exceedingly difficult bind (and one not fairly appreciated by later populist historians). If it openly and publicly advocated mass Jewish emigration from Russia, it believed that that would obviously be interpreted as submitting to the anti-Semites' claim that the Jews were not and never could be equal citizens of Russia; moreover, even if it decided to support emigration, it could not have legally and openly organized

the movement of Jews from Russia in the face of the highly ambiguous and contradictory statements emanating from the regime (which, as is now evident, in fact
had no clear policy on the Jews). At the same time, the St. Petersburg Jewish leadership felt an enormous pressure from the provinces, and from the young Turks in
the capital itself, to do something to respond to the calamity. But there seemed no
way out of the morass save calling for more conferences and meetings. Therefore,
Gunzburg and his colleagues penned a request to Ignatiev that they formally be
allowed to convene an assembly of Jewish representatives from the Pale to discuss
the problems plaguing Russian Jewry as a whole. To Ignatiev they wrote that his
statement regarding the open western frontier had had an overwhelmingly negative
impact on the majority of Russian Jews; indeed, they confessed that they could not
"find the words to express the moral stupor which the publication of your words
induced in our deeply felt and holy sense of loyalty to the crown and to the fatherland."[15] Ignatiev granted the necessary permission to convoke the conference,
which, as might have been predicted from the outset, led to nothing but publicly
perceptible paralysis. The decline of the St. Petersburg brand of traditional Jewish
politics was thus precipitated, with more and more power, or at least moral influence, flowing to the provinces and to the young politicized leadership of the nationalist and populist bent.[16]

Despite his personal relationship with the Gunzburgs, Judah Leib Gordon was
at this point not a part of the St. Petersburg political elite and did not entirely
mourn its debilitation. But, once more, neither did he sympathize with the editors
of *Razsvet* or their soulmates in the provinces. After the Warsaw pogrom and the
Ignatiev announcement he began more and more seriously to doubt whether there
was, after all, a future for the Jews in Russia. But he continued to believe that hope,
if such there be at all, still resided in a moral and political alliance between the
Russian Jews and Western civilization. Thus, his particular brand of activist politics, rejecting the passivity of the past, demanded that the leaders of Russian Jewry
openly seek the aid of the English, French, and American governments, as well as
their public opinions; only such intervention on the part of Western powers could
prevent an expulsion of the Jews from Russia. Similarly, only the regeneration of
the Jews on the basis of Western values and mores could lead to their physical
salvation and, ultimately, to their spiritual redemption.

In consonance with this idiosyncratic approach, as the nationalist camp began
to attract more and more support in Russian-Jewish society and larger and larger
numbers of Jews began to flock to the Western frontiers, Gordon returned in print
to one of his favorite themes of the previous decade—praise for the Jewish Theological Seminary of Breslau as the model institution devoted to a moderate reform
of Judaism based on an intellectually sophisticated and spiritually sound "Science
of Judaism." The Breslau seminary, he proudly reported in his Jewish news column
in *Ha-Meliz* in early February 1882, had succeeded in attracting students from all
over the world, including Galicia and Russia, and in placing its graduates in many
rabbinical posts in Germany as well as other countries—even in Odessa and in the
government-rabbi posts in St. Petersburg and Vilna. From Breslau a new form of
Jewish identity had emerged that could serve as the appropriate solution to the
malaise of the Jews everywhere.[17]

Still, politics were never far from his mind—or from his pen. Thus, in an editorial on the occasion of Purim, Gordon laid out an extraordinarily sharp critique of the Russian government, the reactionary Russian press, and the Jewish leadership itself. The biblical Haman, he told his readers, was not nearly so bad or so dangerous as the "contemporary Hamans." In the book of Esther, the anti-Jewish minister of state had merely accused the Jews of being scattered and dispersed among the other peoples of the realm; now, the new Hamans complain that the Jews are not scattered and dispersed enough, indeed that they are united too tightly in a way that threatens all of Russia and perhaps the world. This is nonsense, of course, Gordon retorted, since the Jews are in fact devastatingly disunited and tear at each other's throats. The young people demand answers and leaders, but neither is easily provided; a variety of cults and radical solutions to the Jewish problem therefore ensue. Meanwhile, reactionary newspaper editors, in their most generous mood, now counsel that it is in the best interests of the Jews if they simply will themselves out of existence by intermarrying with the Russians. Meanwhile, Jewish society in Russia is falling apart at the seams, and no help is being provided to those who suffer. While thousands upon thousands of destitute Jews are taking action by fleeing for their lives, intellectuals sit around and debate whether emigration is an appropriate solution, rabbis call for days of fast and prayer, and the rich sit on their stores of money contemplating how best to allocate their resources.[18]

It was not Purim but the coming of Passover, the holiday of liberation, that elicited Judah Leib Gordon's most passionate prose. In a lead editorial in *Ha-Meliz* entitled "Our Redemption and Spiritual Salvation," he laid bare his deepest thoughts, which he had begged Dolitsky to keep secret only a few months earlier. This year, he asked, how could a Jew at the Passover seder reenact the liberation of his ancestors and feel himself to be a free man? The twelve months that had passed between Passover 1881 and Passover 1882 insured that the traditional four cups of wine drunk at the seder would not suffice to obliterate the memory of what "the seed of Amalek" did to the Jews in the past year, the moral as well as physical destruction that had leveled Russian Jewry. The remembrance of the exodus from Egypt is overwhelmed by the reality of the new exodus that is upon the Jews:

> Everyone admits and agrees that there is no way out of this morass save emigration— but there is a difference of opinion over which direction we should take when we leave, how we should conclude the Passover seder this year—shall we say "Next year in Jerusalem!" or "Next year in America!"?[19]

It is assumed that the Jews take easily to changing their habitations—they are, after all, the wandering Jews. But this is a false stereotype. On the contrary, the Jews are more reluctant to leave their homes than any other group. Over the past seventy-five years, three million Germans have left for America alone, and more to other parts of Europe. Indeed, large numbers of Russian peasants dissatisfied with their land allotments after their emancipation have left for America, and no one regards this emigration as anything worthy of attention; in fact, the government has only recently realized that it should even study the phenomenon. But the Jews are not so adventurous and prefer to stay where they are, mired in their muck, bearing more and more babies and raising them as their parents had reared them, not realizing that there is not enough work to go around, not enough room to breathe. The

Jews sit around and wait for someone to say "Leave!" And now, that has happened: the landlord has come and ordered his tenants to depart. They all agree to go but can't seem to decide where to move to next—Zion or New York?

It is inarguable, Gordon continued, that emigration to America is easier than emigration to Palestine. America is, after all, a civilized and cultivated country that provides immense possibilities to all its inhabitants, something obviously not true of Palestine. On the other hand, it is doubtlessly true that emigration to the Holy Land is far preferable to emigration to America, "with the clear condition, however, stipulated in advance, that this return to the Land of Israel not be a purely temporal or physical emigration, aimed solely at aiding the oppressed and persecuted to find physical shelter—in which case, America is clearly preferable to the Land of Israel."[20] Rather, the movement of Jews to Palestine must be envisioned and planned as the most crucial spiritual undertaking of them all, the true spiritual redemption of the Jews. The last several years have established that the unimaginable can occur, and not only in Russia but in enlightened countries such as Germany and Hungary. If the Jews want to survive and to flourish in the future, then they must have a smaller corner of the earth that they can call their own, where they alone can develop under the aegis of enlightenment and serve as a beacon to the nations. The choice, therefore, is very clear. If all that the Jews are seeking is a physical haven from persecution and violence, then it is far wiser to move to America. If, however, they are seriously committed to spiritual renewal and redemption, then they must organize themselves to move to the Holy Land and establish there the way of life that will make possible the liberation of the Jews. The external obstacles that stand in the path of this goal are formidable and well known. But far more obstructive, less often commented upon, are the internal barriers to redemption in the Holy Land. These internal obstacles must be confronted and addressed in utter seriousness, without fear and self-censorship, at least when writing in Hebrew and discussing things solely in the in-house press:

> All of us realize and know that the way our people has been led by its teachers and leaders in the long days of darkness and gloom is not the proper path to follow for the intelligent man seeking enlightenment. Many of the customs that the rabbis insist upon strenuously and unilaterally, many of the laws, restrictions, and prohibitions that have been imposed upon us in recent generations, our educational system, and, in general, the attitude of our masses to life as a whole and to non-Jews in particular—all these things cannot be regarded as commensurate with civilization and depart from or contradict the road to human perfection which is, after all, the only possible goal of life and point of existence for enlightened men.[21]

The supposed spiritual leaders of the Jews are uneducated in the ways of the world and modern civilization; they remain committed to a petrified way of life that resists progress and improvement and condemns their followers to a life of poverty and ignorance. What will happen if the Jews come into their own, create their own society, run their own lives? Will they restore the laws that determined Jewish life in Palestine in ancient days—the sacrificial service, the sabbatical year, all the other ordinances regulating agricultural and communal life in the Holy Land? Which rabbis will take it upon themselves to rescind these commandments? None, of course.

Rather, they will institute the same laws, the same customs, the same values they imposed on the Jews in Exile, creating an unbridgeable gulf between the Jews and the rest of mankind. Granted, perhaps, that such a gap was essential to Jewish survival among unfriendly hosts; but will the same happen when and if the Jews return to their own land? Will the spiritual and moral stupor that afflict the Jews in Exile be perpetuated in the Jewish state? Will they continue to inculcate the dangerous notion of Jewish superiority, of Jewish chosenness? Only if the Jews commit themselves in advance to reforming their morals, their values, and their culture can they expect spiritual salvation to flow from physical redemption. If not, they are doomed perpetually.

The many young Jews who have returned in spirit to their people in the wake of the pogroms have not been led to understand this fundamental lesson, and instead have been fed superficial dreams and dangerous schemes. The Exile of the Jews must be conceived of as two concentric circles: the exile among the nations is only the inner circle, contained within the greater, outer exile, which is separation from civilization as a whole. It is impossible to extricate the Jews from their physical exile before they are removed from the greater spiritual exile in which they are bound and fettered. Physical redemption can only follow spiritual salvation: just as the Jews seek financial and material aid (*ezrah* in Hebrew) for their bodies, so too they must seek out leaders able and willing to do today what Ezra of old did for the Jews returning to Palestine from Babylonia, institute far-reaching religious and communal reforms dictated by the new circumstances and the new age.

The emigration of Jews to the Land of Israel, Gordon counseled, is and must remain holy to every Jew, who must therefore do everything in his power to support it and to spread that support among all his brethren, for therein lies the beginning of the messianic era and the harbinger of redemption. But in this generation and at this time, this effort is premature. It will take two or three generations to lay the groundwork sufficiently, to institute the essential reforms. It is therefore irrelevant where the exiled go now, where they escape in order to avoid persecution. What is important is only that they not forget that ultimately they must return to the land of their forefathers if they seek eternal salvation. Until then, they must strive with all their power to reform Jewish law and Jewish life, Jewish education and Jewish politics, "in the spirit of the pure Jewish faith and in light of knowledge and wisdom available to all men today."[22] Thus reformed, the Jews will themselves know when they will be ready to return home, to reclaim their patrimony and to rejoin the family of nations, just as many of the small nations of the world have done in the recent past. Until then, he concluded,

it is preferable to direct the Jews to America or other enlightened lands, for there they will learn how to be free men, liberated from both sorts of exile. Then, when they will appreciate their people and their land, they will return to the Holy Land and fill it with cultured, intelligent, eager and well-trained people; for the gleanings of these countries are better than the vintage crop of the Jews of Lithuania or of the Hasidim of Volhynia and Galicia. And the stay of the Jews in America or other enlightened lands will be like the stay of the Israelites in the desert after their exodus from Egypt— for there they received the law of life, and removed from themselves their crushed spirits and servility and learned to be free men worthy to enter the Land.[23]

This was perhaps the most candid and revealing explication Gordon would ever publicly provide on his stance on the most vital issue of his day. While others were either denouncing emigration as a dangerous tool of counteremancipation or advocating either America or Palestine as the appropriate destination of Jewish destinies, Gordon adduced this remarkably idiosyncratic point of view, which did not find support among many other Russian-Jewish intellectuals.

But Gordon's views could not be ignored as merely the private outburst of one man; after all, he was the editor of the major Hebrew newspaper in the world and the national Jewish poet just feted for his literary accomplishments. His stance on the Palestine question therefore unleashed a tempest of controversy in Russian-Jewish intellectual society, whose anger and disarray were only intensified by the outbreak of another particularly vicious pogrom at the end of March 1882 in the Ukrainian town of Balta.

In the face of the controversy that ensued immediately after the publication of "Our Redemption and Spiritual Salvation"—and possibly in response to the Balta pogrom as well—Gordon seemed to retreat a bit from the extreme conclusions he had drawn. In an article entitled "Aid and Ezra" (once more a wordplay in Hebrew: ʿEzrah ve-ʿEzr'a), and two months later in another piece called "The Dream and Its Destruction," he explained that he had in no way meant to intimate that the Jewish colonization of Palestine be totally abandoned in favor of mass migration to America. On the contrary, he tried to explain, he was fully supportive of the move to the Holy Land of individual groups of Jewish pioneers. What he opposed, with a heavy heart, was the notion that an immediate mass movement to Palestine could solve the Jewish plight, as that plight was an intricately complex result of historical processes that required time, cogitation, and planning to undo. The rush to Zion without such consideration—without, in other words, prior religious reform and cultural modernization—would condemn the entire enterprise to failure.[24]

In his own mind, Gordon was here simply repeating the same position he had taken throughout the previous decade: practical support for the colonists alongside grave doubts about the efficacy of their efforts for the liberation of the Jewish people as a whole. But to many readers he seemed only to be waffling on this crucial issue or even contradicting himself in the face of controversy. For the remaining years of his life he would find himself condemned and attacked by both sides of the debate: the supporters of mass migration to Palestine (soon to organize themselves in the "Love of Zion" movement) would soon begin to denounce him as an opponent of their ideology; those who opposed either emigration as a whole or the Palestinian venture in particular accused him of being soft on the Zionists, and soon of a more grievous offence—of selling his soul to the highest bidder.

The first attack came from the Lovers of Zion, led in April 1882 (and for much of the time thereafter) by none other than Moshe Leib Lilienblum, Gordon's old friend and collaborator in the cause of Jewish religious reform. On the pages of *Ha-Meliz* itself, Lilienblum lashed out at Gordon in an article entitled "Do not Confuse the Issues." Lilienblum began with an outright thrust at his old mentor. Judah Leib Gordon's words are followed very closely by all who know him, he declared, but now he has erred in a very serious manner. He has confused the essential question of the return of the Jews to Palestine—the sole solution to the Jewish problem,

without which all else is lost—with a marginal issue of at best secondary importance, the question of religious reform. I, too, Lilienblum conceded, have in print
as well as in private returned to ponder the question of religious reform after many
years of regarding religion in general as superfluous to modern civilization. I now
recognize that religious reforms are necessary within the Jewish community in the
name of national unity and peace—the Orthodox must grant freedom of conscience to the freethinkers or else no unified response can be organized to the crisis
of the day. But for all the importance of the religious question, its resolution cannot
under any circumstances be regarded as a precondition for the settlement of the
Land of Israel; for that goal, which is synonymous with the question of whether the
Jews will once more be a living nation, overwhelms and renders insignificant any
other question.

Lilienblum then laid out the basic political strategy of the new Love of Zion
movement:

> Be silent, all sectarian squabbles, before the salvation of Israel! The nation as a whole
> is far dearer to all of us than the obdurate rulings of legalists or the religious con-
> science of freethinkers. In [the national struggle] there are no *mitnagdim* or Hasidim,
> no traditionalists and modernists, no orthodox or heretics, only the children of Abra-
> ham, Isaac, and Jacob! Any Jew who does not abandon his nation is a Jew in the
> fullest sense, one of the chosen people.
>
> May everyone among us understand—Hasidim, *mitnagdim,* maskilim, freethink-
> ers—that only in vain do the moralists always complain that we are not all united in
> one belief. Such a unity never existed among us and never will, just as it never
> obtained among any other nation. Only sheep can be so united, not intelligent human
> beings; there is no nation in Europe that is not divided into clericalists, conservatives,
> liberals, progressivists, radicals, orthodox, freethinkers, heretics, materialists, and the
> like. We, too, always experienced similar divisions . . . for it is said that just as men's
> faces are different so are their ideas. Therefore, there is no sense to hope that when
> we return to the land of our fathers all Jews will be of the same religious cast. May
> every individual there follow his own conscience . . . the orthodox will send their
> children to schools just like those in Lithuania and Poland, and the enlightened will
> establish European schools, and neither side will oppress the other. *Our political life
> will reconcile all problems. . . .*
>
> All individual problems, be they religious or economic, must be stilled in favor
> of the one overriding goal—the permanent salvation of the Jews! Let us unite, come
> together, gather our dispersed from Eastern Europe, and ascend to our Land in joy.
> All those on the side of the Lord and His nation must proclaim: I am for Zion![25]

For Lilienblum and his comrades, then, arguments over religious reform were not
only destructive to Jewish unity but utterly superfluous. In the future Jewish state,
religious, cultural, and economic pluralism would result naturally from the very
fact of Jewish political self-determination. In the present, what was essential was a
pluralistic banding together of disparate points of view, a broad coalition of rabbis
and freethinkers, socialists, liberals, and conservatives, all committed to the same
overarching goal of creating an autonomous Jewish polity in Palestine.

This argument and, more broadly, this political mentality were fundamentally
unacceptable to Judah Leib Gordon, but it would take some months for him to
articulate in clear and comprehensible language his rebuttal to Lilienblum's pas-

sionate and increasingly popular plea for unity and pluralism. Meanwhile, if only in an oblique manner, he attacked one of Lilienblum's fundamental assumptions, that the pogroms had in fact severed all hope for Jewish survival in the Diaspora. In the same issue of *Ha-Meliẓ* that included Lilienblum's plea for religious pluralism, Gordon delivered some unsolicited advice to the recently assembled delegates to Baron Gunzburg's latest conference of Russian-Jewish notables. The last year had undoubtedly resulted in the beginning of a new era in Russian-Jewish history, Gordon stated, but all hope is not lost that in Russia, too, a new age of justice and mercy may arise to rectify the horrors of the past. Perhaps it will after all come to pass that the Jews will once again live peacefully and joyfully in Russia. Whether that will happen or not, it is certain that the Lord will not abandon the Jews as a whole, that they will live happily and freely among the nations of the world, whether in Russia or elsewhere. They will, in the future, want to know about the history of the pogroms, facts and figures that are being lost in the heat of the moment. Therefore, the delegates assembling in Petersburg from the Jewish communities throughout the Pale should, upon their return home, collect all the information pertaining to the devastation of the last year and compile the results in a book written in clear Hebrew to instruct the generations to come. Appropriating a popular image—based on Psalm 56·9· "You keep count of my wanderings; put my tears into Your flask, into Your record"—that through the centuries the tears shed by all Jews over their fate collect in one flask that, when full, will herald the redemption, Gordon repeated what he had said many times in the past, that the major conduit of Jewish memory over the centuries is and must continue to be Hebrew literature, which "is the flask into which we pour our tears over our travails, as a sign for the generations to come."[26] In every time of woe and want, he reminded his readers, such works were compiled—for example, after the Spanish expulsion, the sufferings of the Jews were chronicled in classic works of sixteenth-century Jewish historiography such as Joseph ha-Kohen's *'Emek ha-Bakha* and Solomon Ibn Verga's *Shevet Yehudah*. Today, the modern version of these classics must be written in a modern idiom, free of legendary or fantastic elements and in clear, scholarly Hebrew. But what is most important is that such an account be prepared for future generations, that the vehicles of Jewish memory in the Hebrew language be perpetuated.[27]

This incidental recommendation reveals a good deal about Gordon's deepest perceptions of his time. In sharp contrast to the Lovers of Zion, Gordon did not truly believe that the pogroms represented any radical shift in Russian—or European—society spurred by a new form of nationalism, anti-Semitism, or other new social or ideational phenomena. The pogroms did not mark a new era in Jewish-Gentile relations and therefore did not require any rethinking of those relations. Rather, quite simply put, the events of 1881–1882—like the events in Spain in 1492 (as he had earlier described in "In The Depths of the Sea")—had resulted from a clash between the forces of good and the forces of evil in the universe, the eternal struggle between the proponents of progress and tolerance and their opponents, the forces of reaction and medievalism. The Jews, therefore, do not have to find a new strategy for their survival in the face of changing realities; on the contrary, the only possible answer had already long been evinced, the alliance between the Jews and modern European civilization.

This much Gordon had already repeated dozens of times since the outbreak of the first pogrom. However, beginning in May 1882, Gordon began—if only privately and hesitantly—to express a new sense of hopelessness and despondency, new doubts about whether indeed the salvation of the Jews under the banner of liberalism was as inevitable as he had previously believed; whether, indeed, the victory of progress, as he had previously written, was as inevitable as the rising of the sun. In late May 1882, after Baron Gunzburg's assembly had, as predicted, not rendered any innovative response to the crisis and, perhaps more important (though Gordon made no mention of this), after the government had issued its famous "May Laws," temporary orders restricting Jewish settlement in the villages of the Pale, Gordon confessed to his intimate friend Ze'ev Kaplan that he was beginning to fear that "we are a nation without solutions, with no help in our times of need."[28] While holding their grandson on his lap, he began to worry that the child was condemned to belong to a nation destined only for suffering and persecution, with no end in sight, no solution to its woes.

This was not the first time, to be sure, that Gordon harbored serious doubts about the ultimate victory of Enlightenment in the Russian-Jewish community. As has already been described, even in 1862, at the time of the composition of "Awake, My People!," his most famous and most optimistic paean to progress, he was wracked with profound doubts about the future. But in the past, the object of his hesitations had always been either the capacity for reform of the Jews themselves or, since April 1881, of the true intentions of the tsarist regime. Now, for the first time, his doubts were cast far more broadly: could it possibly be that the march of progress was not in fact invincible, and therefore that the Jews were lost? He still held fast to the notion that if there was hope, it would stem from the victory of liberalism everywhere; but could it be that, in the end, liberalism itself would be defeated by the forces of reaction, and therefore all hope would be lost?

As in the past, Gordon did not yield to his doubts and fears but, rather, continued publicly to preach his faith and to act according to its principles, while from time to time exploding in a private or poetic expression of despair. Lacking sufficient information to delve deeply into his psyche, it is impossible to know exactly what precipitated this profound change of mood or precisely how Gordon balanced the conflicting sentiments of hope and despair, belief and skepticism. While it is tempting to connect this inner turmoil, on the external level, with the promulgation of the infamous "May Laws" and, on the personal level, with his frequent complaints about a variety of ailments, including depression, headaches, and dizziness, it may be an oversimplification to posit a direct link between his ideological, psychological, and physiological travails.

What can be chronicled, on the other hand, are Gordon's actions and words in the aftermath of this radically new kind of confession of doubt. On the simplest—though not necessarily least important—plane, while worrying about his grandson's ultimate fate, he began (not entirely in keeping with the wishes of the child's parents) to instruct him in Bible and to teach him simple prayers in Russian "so that he should know that there is a God in this world."[29] In the public domain, he continued to fill the pages of *Ha-Meliz* with optimistic reports about the insistent campaign for Jewish enlightenment and Jewish civil rights in the West, alongside periodic tidbits of pessimism and gloom. In late June, for example, in his news column Gordon cited the following news about the departure of Jews from Russia.

First, the *Berliner Volkszeitung* related the story of a Gentile Kiev landlord who so loved his Jewish tenants who were fleeing Russia that he accompanied them to Hamburg and paid for all their expenses. It is too bad, Gordon commented, that the names of the Jews and the Christian were not given in this report, so that the reading public could see the truth not broadly proclaimed—that "there are among the Russians those who respect and love Jews."[30]

At the same time, Gordon had to admit, the news as a whole was not so uplifting. The editor of *Razsvet* had just reported from Constantinople that the Turkish government had indeed granted the Jews permission to settle in the lands of the sultan, but had expressly forbidden them from settling in Palestine. The situation of the Russian-Jewish emigrants to the Holy Land is miserable, despite false claims to the contrary. Moreover, there are upsetting reports that some of the pioneers in Palestine have been displaying shockingly untraditional moral and religious behavior in their new colonies, as if their only purpose in leaving Russia was to free themselves of the constraints of their families and society. Their behavior jeopardizes the entire colonization program and thus ought to be condemned. Not only is the fate of the Palestinian emigration in doubt, but the movement of Russian Jews to America has also revealed itself as highly problematic. Upon arrival in the New World, the Russian Jews find that they cannot easily practice their faith there, due to economic pressure. Indeed, one New York Yiddish newspaper has recently gone so far as to advise the Jews back home not to move to America at all, for there neither the Sabbath nor the dietary laws can be faithfully observed. What ironies abound in this world, Gordon concluded: those who rushed to leave Russia for Palestine pollute the holy soil with their acts of impurity, while those who left for America suffer because they cannot carry on their faith properly in that unholy land![31]

These comments did not mean that Gordon was now retreating back into his pro-Russian, antiemigration cocoon—as some of his opponents, and later observers, assumed. More revealing of his mood was a remarkable feuilleton published three weeks later, on the eve of the Ninth of 'Av, the commemoration of the destruction of the Temple and of Jewish sovereignty. Typical of this series of feuilletons, here Gordon assumed the persona of a semifictional alter ego, this time that of a Russian Jew who was utterly devastated by the events of the past year. Not only was this man's house attacked, his property destroyed, his labor laid waste, but his spirits were sacked as well:

> They dashed my hopes, crushed my thoughts, destroyed my dreams. . . . What am I, what is my life after my goals were laid waste, my desires disbanded, my ideals demolished without hope? . . . How many beautiful dreams and pleasant thoughts delighted me in my youth and set the world before me as the Garden of Eden? They fortified me with the strength of a rock and supported me wholeheartedly, gave me wings like an eagle to soar over the vale of tears, to glide over its traps and obstacles. But like the rainbow after a storm, my dreams faded as the years went by, until this fateful year came and washed away the last tinges of color, blotted out the last rays of light to guide me and inspire me.[32]

The dejected narrator had traversed the entire trajectory of his community's cultural history in the previous half-century. Groomed from childhood to be a rabbi, he would have grown to be a lion among the learned, discovering new and ever-inventive hermeneutic twists and legal restrictions, had he not been thrown from this course by exposure to the light of the world. He therefore became a maskil, enlightening his people and cultivating their neighbors, until those neighbors slapped him in his face, rejected his advances, condemned him as an impostor and a fake, preferred Yankl the tavern keeper, in sidelocks and caftan, to Jacob the teacher of geometry and Goethe. He then realized that he must become a religious reformer, sorting through the laws of Moses and deciding which to keep and which to excise. But this, too, did not work, so he became an attorney, a businessman, a delegate to the conference called by the St. Petersburg leaders. When all of these strategems led nowhere, he joined in the clamor for the one and only solution to his plight: Exodus! He decided to flee to America, the land of freedom and dignity, where no distinction was made between native and immigrant, Christian and Jew. Stealing the frontier and arriving in Brody, he found teeming masses of starving, poor Jews encouraged to leave their homes by foreign emissaries but not provided with sufficient food, money, or clothing to keep them alive and warm upon along the way. As an aesthete too fastidious to have engaged in any manual labor or to have received any practical training, he was repelled by all this poverty and realized that America was not for him. Since he had left Russia illegally, he could not return home. He then concluded that if America was not good enough for him and Russia would not have him back, he would turn his back on all these corrupt Gentile powers and return to the land of his fathers and forefathers. He would show the rest of the world that he could have a country of his own, that he could restore once more the glory of Zion past! Reaching this conclusion, his eyes filled with tears—this, after all, was the dream of his youth, the holy mission destined for him from the day of his birth. All minds were aflutter with the same aspirations: righteous Gentiles were interceding with the sultan, the Jews were being welcomed back home, he must join the trek, the beginning of redemption. As the sages said, "If not now, when?" He then set forth for the land of his people, overcoming unimaginable horrors, and when he finally reached the Holy Land he fell upon his face and kissed the blessed soil. At first, he felt himself walking with the Lord and His prophets, but soon realized that he had come without a farthing in his pocket, with no means of supporting himself. Not only was Turkey not permitting him to stay in his Holy Land but also, to his shock and chagrin, the Messiah had not arrived and the messianic age did not appear to be coming quite so quickly as he had thought. He saw plenty of poor people and donkeys, but the donkeys were riding on the poor, not the other way around, as was supposed to happen at the End of Days. And then:

> A cry was heard in Ramah, wailing, bitter weeping: two hundred Rachels were weeping for their children, dying of hunger in the streets; and the voice of the leaders of the flock answered: Restrain your voices from weeping, your eyes from shedding tears. At this time there is no reward for their labor—they should return to the land from which they came, and wait there until the hour of favor and time of salvation.[33]

He decided, thereupon, to heed this advice: he, along with many others, had obviously been spinning unrealizable dreams, which now were spent, along with all hope for the redemption of the Jews.

This wrenching recasting of one of Jeremiah's most sublime images—God comforting Rachel weeping over her exiled children by promising that they would return to their land—marked perhaps the pinnacle of rueful irony in all of Gordon's prose. But it would be wrong to conclude from this powerful, desperate lament that the most famous Russian maskil had now abandoned all hope and was wallowing in despair. First and most obvious, the fictional persona of this piece reflected only one facet of Judah Leib Gordon's complex personality. Another, equally potent facet was revealed immediately on the heels of the appearance of this feuilleton, in two new pieces for *Voskhod* that struck an entirely different, if equally evocative, key. The first was a new, long article on religious reform among the Jews of Russia; the second was a literary chronicle reviewing several recent books, including the Magna Carta of the Lovers of Zion movement, Leon Pinsker's *Autoemancipation*.

"Attempts at Religious Reform among the Jews" took as its ostensible subject yet another important response to the pogroms, the emergence of Christianizing sects among Russian Jewry.[34] In the course of 1881–1882 there had appeared in the Ukraine two movements—"The Biblical Brotherhood" and "New Israel"—that preached a message of hope to Russian Jews, if they but joined a new faith based on fusion with the Christian populace, either by means of a radically biblicizing, anti-Talmudic creed or an overtly Christianized form of Judaism that abolished circumcision, observed the Sabbath on Sunday, and advocated mixed marriages with Gentiles. Gordon easily and rather flippantly disposed with the quasi-theological claims of the prophets of these sects, seizing the occasion to expound at length upon his own ideas on religious reform. Although in some measure he was now restating and amplifying in Russian points he had made in his Hebrew-language polemics on the subject in the late 1860s and early 1870s, there was much that was new, and of great interest, in this updated call for a reform of Judaism in Russia.

First, and perhaps most important, Gordon significantly revised his former stance on the connection between religious reform and political rights—in other words, on the link between Jewish self-reform and emancipation. Repeating the analysis of anti-Semitism he had expressed time and time again in Hebrew, he stated now in Russian that it is absolutely incorrect to believe that the antagonism evinced against the Jewish population in Russia or anywhere else is based on religious principles and, therefore, that if the Jews reform their religious lives they will be freed of that antagonism. In Germany, the Jews have significantly reformed their cult, transformed the Talmud from the cornerstone of Judaism to the subject of arcane archeological investigation, rebuilt their temples to resemble churches, and some have even moved the Sabbath to Sunday—but this did not stop Germany from producing a new form of anti-Semitism. The same is true of Hungary, where the Jews have long been Magyarized, and of Galicia, where the Jews are Polonized, but nonetheless powerful anti-Semitic figures have emerged and even the judiciaries of these lands are tainted with extensive and degrading anti-Jewish outbursts and rulings. In sharp contrast, however, in France, where the Jews have not begun to celebrate their Sabbath on Sundays or abolished the "barbaric" practice of circumcision, and in England, where the Jews, like their Christian countrymen, are notable for their religious conservatism, no anti-Semitic parties have emerged, no pogroms have erupted. Obviously, the crucial factor determining the status of the

Jews is not the reform of their cult but "the stage of development of the local population, the presence of justice in the words and deeds of the powers-that-be. Where the moving force in the nation is not 'conscience' but 'instinct,' where the major stimulus in society is 'selfish interests,' no religious reform will help."[35]

This statement in and of itself was a major change in his understanding of the dynamics of Jewish modernization. But he went even further, arguing:

> Religious reform is essential to the Jews not in order to achieve civil rights, but for their own sake. . . . It must be undertaken not with a base purpose in mind—the attainment of earthly happiness, but in the name of the highest interest of humanity, for the revival [*voskreshenie*] and awakening to a new cultural life of the invalid-nation, covered with deep scars but also with everlasting glory.[36]

A proper reform of Judaism, therefore, must include an ethical realignment of Jewish behavior but is not coterminous with the sanctification of universal norms of morality and ethics. It is not sufficient, as the radically biblicizing Reformers have proclaimed, to reduce Judaism, or any other religion, to moral behavior and ethical precepts. The rationalist credo "my morality is my religion" undermines the very concept of positive religion and, as such, has been rejected even by the atheistic French republic as unsuitable for any national community; only the so-called *Konfessionlos* party in Germany has adopted this stance. Therefore, the crucial "radical transformation of [the Jews'] way of life, morals, obsolete customs, and beliefs" must not have as its goal the obliteration or debilitation of Jewish nationality; rather, its goal must be the ennoblement and revivification of that nationality on the basis of new, universally binding ethical constraints and political precepts. In one phrase, the reform of the Jews must proceed from the understanding of Judaism as an eternally evolving amalgam of Jewish national and spiritual creativity that eschews both "religious fanaticism and national conceit."[37]

Lapsing into his typical metaphoric mode of speech, Gordon explained that the proper religious reform of Judaism must not shatter the foundations of Judaism but seek only to repair and restore defective or damaged parts of the edifice. There is no need to condemn a structure just because it is ancient; rather, it ought to be fortified using the strongest, most modern and scientifically sound techniques that will introduce into it the most light and the best ventilation as well as beautifying its external structure. The transformation of Judaism must, in other words, be radical but not deracinating. It must proceed as a natural, logical, and dynamic development of the genius of the Jewish people and its spiritual culture, based on a careful and sensitive approach to the Talmud, the fundamental core of Judaism and of Jewish civilization through the millennia.

On the one hand, the Talmud can obviously no longer serve as the exclusive legislative codex for the Jews or the sole compendium of truth and wisdom: "To retain in this day and age the worldview of some Palestinian sage that the whole world was created for and because of the Jews, or of some Babylonian rabbi that the property of a non-Jew is *res nullus,* is as reprehensible and absurd" as to accept their medical or astronomical teachings. On the other hand, the Talmud cannot simply be cast aside as an antiquated and superannuated historical document, since it and it alone kept the Jews alive throughout the centuries and created the Jewish civilization that obtains even today, to the benefit of all of mankind. Not only has the Talmud preserved and developed the Hebrew language but, alongside its many obviously antiquated teachings and exegeses, it also contains profoundly inspiring interpretations of biblical precepts and the most authoritative record of Jewish customs, laws, and beliefs in both the biblical and postbiblical ages. Most important (as even Moshe Leib Lilienblum has recently repeated), the Talmud itself is "imbued with the spirit of reforming the Law of Moses." Therefore, no acceptable reformer of Judaism ought to boast of his "deep disdain" for the Talmud, as some of the Russian sectarians and radical German Reformers had done. On the contrary, the wise, moderate reformer ought not overtly to espouse any specific ritual reforms or modifications of practices, since such conclusions can only result from the combined efforts of modern rabbis and enlightened laymen, basing themselves on a scholarly study of the Talmud.

Now, even more clearly than before, Gordon's stance on religious reform inched very close to that of the moderate party of modernists in Germany, based at the Breslau seminary. Like Zecharias Frankel and his disciples (though obviously in a very different political and polemical context), Gordon concluded that the model reformer of Judaism must walk hand in hand with the Talmud and its internal, self-reforming dynamism and "take refuge in its authority; only on the basis of the Talmud can we refute or overrule the Talmud."[38]

In sum, in late 1882, despite all the changes that had overtaken Russian Jewry in the previous year and a half and the fits of despair that assailed him in their wake, Judah Leib Gordon continued to insist that a religious reform analogous to that undertaken by the moderate wing of liberal Judaism in Germany was essential to the rebirth of Russian Jewry. In other words, the setbacks of the previous months had not in the least vitiated the fundamental credo of the Hebrew Enlightenment: Russian Jewry could be saved, *au fond,* not through emigration to America, colonization in the Holy Land, or socialist politics but through "a revolution in the yeshivot," a cleansing and rejuvenation of Judaism itself. The ultimate success of that salvation will depend, to be sure, on the economic and political status of the Jews, but there is little or nothing that they can do in that connection. In the meanwhile, they must proceed under the assumption that if there is any hope for their future, it resides solely and completely in their spiritual and cultural regeneration.

Although implicitly responding to Lilienblum's challenge on the question of the continued relevance of religious reform to the future of Russian Jews, this article did not explicitly tie that issue to the fundamental argument raised by the Lovers of Zion—that, as a result of the rise of a new form of nationalism in Europe at large and of its corollary, a new kind of anti-Jewish animus, there was no longer any possibility for Jewish survival among the nations. It was this basic premise that Gordon turned to next, in the same issue of *Voskhod,* in his guise as "Mevakker" (Hebrew for "critic"), his pseudonym as book reviewer for the periodical. Here he scanned three timely new works. The first was A. M. Lunz's *Jerusalem,* an annual survey of the social, economic, and demographic status of Palestine. As hope in a durable compromise between Jews and Gentiles seems to be declining in various countries, Gordon wrote, this book could well serve future Jewish colonists in the Holy Land by instructing them on its terrain, society, and economy. The subject matter itself inspired in every Jewish reader "melancholic-bewitching impressions," profound feelings of solidarity and enrootedness in the soil of Palestine, untouched by the distance of time and space. But what of the feelings of hopelessness that impelled Jews to the Holy Land?

To examine this question, Gordon moved on to a second tome, whose appearance, he reflected, was also related to the recent horrors perpetrated against the Jews: Naḥum Sokolov's *Eternal Hatred of the Eternal People* [*Sin'at ʿolam le-ʿam ʿolam*], published in Hebrew in Warsaw in 1882. In this work, Sokolov (at this point far from his later Zionist views) sought to document and analyze the sources of the deeply rooted and inexhaustible hatred of the Jewish people displayed by the nations of the world. In dense prose he examined the historical record for all instances of anti-Jewish sentiments and violence and elaborated on their religious, ideological, economic, and social causes. Gordon praised the work for its comprehensiveness and accuracy but damned it for its pedantic tone and long-windedness. Most objectionable to Gordon, however, was Sokolov's overriding negativism and hopelessness. According to him, anti-Semitism was a deeply enmeshed and inescapable facet of Western civilization that would only disappear in the messianic age, when lambs will lie down with lions and nations not know hatred any more. "This is too long to wait, Mr. Sokolov," Gordon objected. More important,

> based on the very same facts presented in this work, it is possible to reach a far less pessimistic and inconsolable conclusion ... for in the relations between various nations and governments and the Jews, however obstinate and protracted their antagonism, we nonetheless note a significant movement to the better, towards reconciliation.[39]

The ideals of equality and universal civilization have spread throughout a large part of the world, inducing governments to offer Jews the opportunity to engage in more productive occupations, to benefit from universal culture, and to approach more closely the goal of rapprochement with their neighbors. The fault, Gordon repeated yet once more, lies not in the stars or in Gentile governments, but in the Jews as well that they are underlings. Why has Sokolov not addressed the other side of the coin: What had the Jews done to respond to this new age of opportunity and equity? In Russia, since the time of Alexander I, under Nicholas I and his minister of education, S. S. Uvarov—"perhaps the only Russian administrator who correctly and judiciously understood the Jewish question"[40]—and especially during the reign of the Liberator Tsar, Alexander II, the Jews steadfastly refused to take up the offer of self-improvement afforded them by beneficent regimes and in so doing have left themselves in a weak position now that the possibilities seem to have passed, perhaps for good. But the situation is not so hopeless as is claimed by Sokolov. Better times, better governments, will reappear, well before the advent of the messianic age. The crux of the question, therefore, is whether the Jews themselves will be able in the future to learn from the past not to blunder again and to set themselves ably and judiciously to the task of self-regeneration.

A similarly negative appraisal is offered, Gordon continued, by the anonymous author of a third work, a brochure recently issued in German under the title *Autoemancipation: An Appeal of a Russian Jew to his Coreligionists*. The author of this booklet (who Gordon knew to be the Odessa physician Leon Pinsker) is as pessimistic as Sokolov about the prospects for Jewish life among the nations; but he offers a concrete solution to their woes. He claims that the primary cause of the unhealthy state of the Jews must be located in their loss, during the long years of medieval persecution, of both the reality and the self-perception of Jewish nationhood. The only solution to this plight, therefore, is the removal of the Jews to a territory where they can regain both the sense of nationalism and its manifestation in reality.

Every Jewish soul, Gordon conceded, is profoundly stirred by this grand call, resounding with the sounds of the trumpet heralding the End of Days. Whether the grandiose project called for by the author of *Autoemancipation* will succeed in stirring the Jewish masses and their leaders to action is impossible to foresee, Gordon advised his readers. But, whatever its viability, the project itself is based on a profoundly misguided and unhistorical premise. The Jews did not lose their sense of nationhood as a result of medieval persecutions, but "at the very start of their via dolorosa." Only in the biblical period did the Jews have a finely honed sense of nationhood, but that was necessarily sacrificed by the Talmudic rabbis seeking a new raison d'être for Jewish life after the destruction of the Temple and Jewish political autonomy: the bearing of a religious idea. Wherever Jews perform their 613 commandments, wherever they can exercise their identity—be it in an Italian ghetto or the Russian Pale of Settlement—so long as they have their kosher slaughterer and ritual bath they are happy and at ease. Offer to return them to Palestine on the condition that they reduce the number of prohibited labors on the Sabbath from 39 to 38 and they simply won't go. The depth of the religious basis of Jewish existence is so extensive that the extremes meet in opposition to the new nationalist definitions: the old traditionalist rabbis of Russia, the "Neo-Orthodox" rabbis of Germany, and even the Reformers are all in agreement on this score.

There is an important lesson to be gleaned from this remarkable coalition of opponents to the nationalist dream, Gordon insisted: the bond between religion and nationhood is too profoundly etched in the character and culture of the Jews blithely to be wished away. Twenty years earlier he had sharply criticized the radical Reformers in the West for the dereliction of the national essence of Judaism. Now he left himself even more friendless and alone by arguing that Pinsker and the other new nationalists err in equal fashion as the Western antinationalists by deliberately ignoring the problematic but nonetheless essential religious basis of Jewishness. To claim that the Jews ought simply to be a nation like all the nations is not only hollow and shallow, Gordon warned, but ultimately self-defeating, for the religious dilemma will inevitably destroy the political utopia of the Lovers of Zion. Concluding his review of *Autoemancipation,* Gordon delivered his quintessential verdict on the subject:

> All of this demonstrates how deeply within us there resides the negation of our original nationality. Should this project [of autoemancipation] ever be realized, not of course in our lifetime, but in that of our grandchildren, its creators will be forced to come to grips with this difficulty—which will, perhaps, not be the only one facing them.[41]

Here, at long last, was Gordon's most heartfelt rebuttal to Lilienblum's charge not to confuse the issues of religious reform and national regeneration. Contrary to Lilienblum, Pinsker, and the other secularist Lovers of Zion, Gordon was profoundly convinced that the Jews were not simply a nation like all other nations who could solely by force of will construct a state that guaranteed freedom of religion. Rather, he argued repeatedly, early on in their history, in the formative period of Rabbinic Judaism, the Jews had subtly and successfully been transformed by the rabbis from citizens of a nation-state into bearers of a specific national-religious tradition whose basic tenets and practices were fundamentally irreconcilable with the essential dictates of liberalism and religious pluralism. To assume that without a prior reform of Judaism there could be a neat separation between church and state in a future Jewish polity was therefore, to Gordon's mind, to indulge in an ahistoric, dangerous, and ultimately self-defeating fantasy. For religious pluralism in the absence of religious freedom is no more than a self-obliterating mirage; it is thus not only dangerous, but self-contradictory, to expect religious pluralism from those convinced that they alone hearken to the voice of the Lord. Thus, for Gordon, only in the aftermath of a thoroughgoing transvaluation of Judaism based on the philosophical tenets and cultural norms of modern Western civilization could religious pluralism and civil liberties be guaranteed in a Jewish state. Only then could there follow the true national revival of the Jews in the Land of Israel, an essential component of their ultimate redemption and that of the world as a whole.

This message Gordon repeated time and time again throughout the last months of 1882 and first part of 1883, in editorials and feuilletons and book reviews in *Ha-Meliz* and *Voskhod*. By this time, however, his readers were confronted with a substantially new reality. The intellectual and political frenzy of Russian Jewry in the previous year and a half had all but ground to a halt. Both the Palestinian and American movements seemed to be floundering on the hard rocks of reality, with many of the migrants returning disheartened to Russia. Slowly, the news spread that the new minister of the interior, Dmitrii Tolstoy, had forcefully proclaimed that the government would not tolerate any pogroms against Jews and would move with haste to prosecute any officials who did not prevent any such violence. Moreover, Tolstoy had voiced strong opposition to the mass emigration of the Jews from Russia. In this new context, Gordon's subtle explications of his views on religious reform and even his fascinating critique of Pinsker's *Autoemancipation* were all but ignored by his friends and foes alike.

The same cannot be said, however, of two new poems that Gordon published in these months, two seemingly contradictory poems that once more thrust his name and opinions into the center of public controversy in Russian Jewry. The first poem, entitled "The Flock of the Lord" ['*Eder 'adonai*] was composed on October 2, 1882, and dedicated to "the author of *Autoemancipation*." A brutal and despondent retort to Pinsker's cry of hope, "The Flock of the Lord" begins with a rendering into verse of the central taxonomic quandary of post-eighteenth-century Jewry: What are the Jews, a nation like all others or simply a community of faith? The poet responds: Let me reveal a secret, if you but promise to keep it still: We're not a nation, not a religion, but simply a flock:

> The flock of the Lord, sacrificial lambs,
> The earth an altar stretched out before us,
> Bound to it, like festal offerings, by taut chords,
> For we were born to be sheep for burnt offerings,

All our days, from belly to grave,
Led by a leash—with the blessings of our sages.[42]

This complex, multilayered manipulation of biblical and Rabbinic idioms has often been misunderstood and must be carefully parsed. "The flock of the Lord" is a phrase that appears only once in the Bible, in Jeremiah 13:17. Here the Lord once again warns the inhabitants of Judah and Jerusalem that ruin is imminent as punishment for their overweening pride, their depravity, their failure to obey Him. They must repent and be not haughty, give honor to God before He brings darkness upon them: "For if you will not give heed/ My inmost self must weep,/ Because of your arrogance;/ My eye must stream and flow with copious tears,/ Because the flock of the Lord/ Is taken captive." Gordon shockingly transmutes the context and meaning of Jeremiah's prophecy of destruction by joining the image of the captive flock of God, the nation of Israel bound to the altar as sacrificial lamb, to a jocular gloss of a Talmudic passage. In a discussion of what an animal owned by a Jew may and may not do on the Sabbath, the rabbis list, inter alia, that a calf must not go out wearing a muzzle or a cow with a leash between its horns; but, they note parenthetically, "Rabbi Elazar ben Azariah's cow used to go about with its leash between its horns, without the blessing of our sages."[43] Gordon seizes upon this last phrase and inverts it: the Jews are bound by a leash to the sacrificial altar "with the blessing of our sages." In other words, they are perpetually bound as sheep to the altar first and foremost because their prophets and teachers condemn them to such a fate.

This typical Gordonian theme—previously articulated most forcefully, perhaps, in "Zedekiah in Prison"—is now reiterated in a caustic series of mutations of biblical images of sheep. Shifting from Jeremiah to Micah, the poet denounces the presumptive leaders of the Jews as misleaders, lambasting "Our masters, our shepherds" who devour our riches, fleece us and flay us, leave our troughs empty, lead us to the desert there to suffer all storms. There, in the wasteland, we truly become "sheep for the slaughter": hordes of wolves descend upon us from all sides and tear away at our flesh:

We cry out to the Lord but He does not answer,
We shout, but no one heeds our cry,
The desert overtakes us on all fronts,
The earth is still, the heavens shut tight.[44]

We are not yet completely lost—the hungry wolves have left some bones, the fleecers some fleece, the misleading leaders some spirit, but can we survive like this forever?

Each flock on its own, we are but lost sheep,
We cannot regroup to redeem our souls,
Each man cares for himself and labors alone,
Cares not a whit 'bout his brother's travails,
There is therefore no hope, no order, no law,
We're not a nation, not a faith, but only a flock.[45]

Two months after this poem was penned, its shocking cry of doom and despair was challenged by Pinsker himself in a personal letter to Gordon that set the tone of the rage of the Lovers of Zion at the poet for the next several years. In typical Russian epistolary style—at once fawning, condescending, and brutally honest—Pinsker accused Gordon of letting his public down, traducing his sacred mission as Hebrew poet by not taking up in verse the song of joyous rebirth of the return to Zion. I have long admired you, Pinsker wrote, and guarded your letters to my father with great respect, alongside those of the other leading lights of Hebrew literature. I am flattered that your poetic genius would be linked with my prose, but cannot hide the fact that your beautiful poem leaves me with a heavy heart:

Not a ray of hope! Is it really so? Does the entire nation really resemble a corpse? Aren't there any [living] people? Won't there be any? Is this really irrevocable death or simply a deep sleep? Has the voice needed to rouse the lethargic died out in you as well? O, if so, then why are we to remain alive? To struggle desperately for the right to be rightless, for a life worse than death? In your funeral march there is no part for the trumpet heralding the resurrection of the dead! I do not want to lose hope that you can play this instrument as well! Poet laureate, please accept my desire to add one more leaf to your garland![46]

There is no record of any direct response by Gordon to this letter. But roughly at the same time he began working on another poem that indirectly answered Pinsker's queries, in a way that would cause far more outrage among the believers in autoemancipation. This was Gordon's famous poem "My Sister Ruḥamah" ['Ahoti ruḥamah], dated 1882 but only published in March 1883 in a literary supplement to Ha-Meliz issued in honor of Purim.[47] (This supplement, it ought to be noted, also contained a scholarly article by Gordon on "The Coptic Language among the Jews" and a prose poem, in the form of the Book of Esther, celebrating Alexander II and condemning his nihilist assassins.)

The title "My Sister Ruḥamah" is drawn from the rather elliptical first two chapters of the Book of Hosea, in which the Lord both condemns the House of Israel to destruction and promises in the future to draft a new covenant with the peoples of Judah and Israel. At first, the Lord charges Hosea to marry a harlot and to name one of their sons "Not My People" and their daughter "Lo-ruḥamah," or "Not Accepted"—"For I will no longer accept the House of Israel or pardon them." Then God pledges to redeem Judah and Israel together: "O, call your brothers 'My People' and your sisters 'Lovingly Accepted [Ruḥamah].'" As is Gordon's perpetual wont, a prophetic juxtaposition of rejection and redemption is usurped to serve as the prooftext of a new and jarring view of the salvation of the Jews—this time, a redemption possible only in the land of liberal freedom, America.

To elude the tsarist censor, Gordon added after the title a pseudobiblical subtitle, "In honor of the daughter of Jacob who was raped by the son of Ḥamor." But the obvious subject of this poem was not the rape of Tamar, but that of Russian Jews in the pogroms of 1881–1882:

Why do you weep, my sister Ruḥamah,
Why so downhearted and downcast,
Your lily cheeks so shrivelled and pale?
For the plunderers have come and sullen your honor?

> If violence has struck, if the insolent have attacked,
> Do you bear any fault, my sister Ruḥamah?[48]

Ruḥamah responds with the words of another biblical rape victim, Tamar, daughter of David: "Where will I carry my shame?" But where is your shame, the poet asks? You bear no reproach for what happened, you've not lost your integrity! Rise up, hold your head high, the disgrace is not yours but that of the rapists! You've not lost your purity, dignity, or honor; only your attackers are disgraced, condemned by the whole civilized world.

Indeed, shouts the poet, "It was good for me that you were raped! [*Tov li ki unait*]"—a harsh wordplay on Psalm 119:71: "It was good for me that I was humbled [*Tov li ki uneiti*], so that I could learn Your laws." Until now, he explains, my soul has borne countless indignities and travails, I've been beaten and robbed, but I've not run away. I've hoped against all hope that things would change. But this last humiliation is too much to bear; therefore, "Arise, let us go, my sister Ruḥamah":

> Arise, let us go—since we've no loving mother's home
> To seek refuge in and peace,
> No mother, no home of hers to dwell in,
> Let us find another inn to rest in and live
> Till our father is merciful to us; there
> We shall stay and wait, my sister Ruḥamah.
>
> Arise, let us go! Where the light of freedom
> Shines on all men and brightens all souls,
> Where all creatures of God are loved the same,
> No insults are waged 'gainst one's nation or one's faith,
> There the insolent will not wrong you; there abused
> You won't be, my sister Ruḥamah ["Lovingly Accepted"].[49]

By the middle of 1883, then, Judah Leib Gordon had succeeded in expressing in verse the two seemingly contradictory but, in fact, complementary poles of his being, previously articulated only in prose. To all who would listen he broadcast that the Jews were neither a nation nor a religion but a peculiar combination of both a nation and a religion, misled by their decadent and shortsighted leaders to serve as sacrificial offerings to a Lord who shuts His eyes to human travails. If there be any hope for this lost flock—and that is far from certain—it is refuge in the shelter of freedom and pluralism, where their souls can be enlightened and their bodies flourish until they are ready to go on to their ultimate redemption in the Holy Land.

It was doubtless clear to Gordon that in departing so blatantly, and in such stirring Hebrew, from the mounting consensus of his friends and colleagues, he was bound to stir controversy in the always turbulent cultural politics of Russian Jewry. But Gordon scarcely anticipated the venom of the attack that would be mounted against him. Barely a year and a half after the festive celebration of his twenty-fifth literary anniversary, both Judah Leib Gordon's poetry and his person would be challenged and assailed and the wreath of poet laureate of Russian Jewry would be snatched rather violently from his brow.

11

Attack and Despair
1883–1888

In the fall of 1882 Judah Leib Gordon set to work on what would be the culminating literary venture of his life, a complete edition of his poetic works. The subvention of such a publication was promised the previous autumn at his twenty-fifth literary anniversary, but seemed to have been forgotten during the turbulent months that followed. Finally, the project was reactivated, a sample page was printed, and presubscriptions began to be solicited. Faced with the reality of the project, Gordon began to organize and to revise his collected works, a task that would consume most of his energies for the next year and a half.

At the same time, he continued to hold two jobs that required a good deal of his attention: he was still editor of *Ha-Meliz* and Hebrew tutor of the young Barons Gunzburg. The latter position was tolerable in that it required little time, paid well, and assured Gordon continuing access to the *grande famille* of Russian Jewry. The burden of editing *Ha-Meliz,* on the other hand, became more and more onerous, especially as the perpetual chaos engendered by its publisher, Alexander Zederbaum, was only exacerbated by his old age. By the end of 1882 Gordon decided to resign from the paper, but was persuaded to stay by the indomitable Zederbaum, who feared that the departure of his editor and prime writer would adversely affect the popularity and the profitability of his paper. Indeed, Gordon claimed that some three thousand new subscribers had been won to *Ha-Meliz* since he became editor, providing Zederbaum with an additional income of some 18,000 rubles a year. With the help of Maxim Kaplan (Gordon's son-in-law and attorney), a new contract was drawn up between the recalcitrant editor and his desperate publisher. From the beginning of December 1882, *Ha-Meliz* would be transformed from a weekly to a semiweekly; Gordon would formally, though not publicly, have full control over its contents; he would receive a salary of 225 rubles per month, as well as 5 kopecks for every line he wrote, the amount he would be empowered to pay all contributors; and he would be able to hire an assistant to take care of the menial editorial work.[1]

Not surprisingly, this arrangement did not last long. Zederbaum hired the young Hebrew writer A. Sh. Friedberg as editorial assistant but neglected to inform him that he was to work under Gordon. On the contrary, Zederbaum led Friedberg to believe that he was to be an independent force on the paper, with power equal to that of the venerable poet and publicist. The very first time that Gordon asked Friedberg to do a chore for him, the proud young provincial stormed out of the room, deeply offended at the presumed insult; for several months thereafter, the two barely managed to maintain a cordial distance. Their next clash came while preparing the Purim literary supplement. Freidberg objected to "My Sister Ruḥamah" on ideological grounds and demanded that he be allowed to counter it with an article supporting the Love of Zion movement. Gordon refused to allow such a piece to be printed, and Friedberg thereupon refused to have anything further to do with the supplement. In general, Friedberg later testified, Gordon was always lukewarm at best in regard to the proto-Zionist effort:

> He only tolerated the idea of the Yishuv, since as a Hebrew poet he couldn't ignore it altogether. . . . But his position was always clear: "If our brethren are going to return to the land of our forefathers, they ought to do so via the Atlantic Ocean, while leaving the *Shulḥan ʿArukh* behind on the shores of Europe. Let them first pass through America, the land of freedom, and then, after becoming free men, let them ascend to the Holy Land, while I remain here basking in their accomplishments."[2]

Finally, at the beginning of May, the tension at the office of *Ha-Meliz* came to a head. While Gordon was out sick, Zederbaum assigned his columns to Friedberg. Gordon regarded this affront as the last straw and promptly resigned from *Ha-Meliz*. Soon thereafter, he and Friedberg were able to sort out the misunderstanding between them by examining the contradictory documents given them by Zederbaum. But Gordon refused to rejoin *Ha-Meliz,* despite repeated entreaties and apologies by the publisher. To recuperate from the trauma, as well as his recurrent headaches and dizziness, he soon decided to leave St. Petersburg to take the cure at Marienbad.

Gordon well understood that his physical malaise was caused at least in part by the fact that he felt himself to be under increasing ideological attack. The clash with Friedberg over "My Sister Ruḥamah" was but the least important, and least public, adumbration of the fracas that was beginning to mount over his politics. The controversy had actually begun many months earlier, with Lilienblum's article entitled "Do not Confuse the Issues." That, however, was an angry assault on Gordon's ideas alone, not on his poetry or his person. Soon, criticism would extend to his creative works, his position as poet laureate of Russian Jewry, and even to his character as well.

Quite surprisingly, the first one to launch such an attack was Gordon's old friend Peretz Smolenskin, now committed to the new nationalist party. In an article written to commemorate Gordon's literary anniversary, Smolenskin began from a premise that well articulated his basic worldview.[3] If the Jews were a normal, healthy nation rather than a self-denying, self-destructive entity, they would know how properly to celebrate a cultural event so important as the twenty-fifth anniversary of *The Love of David and Michal*. They would mark this date as a national feast, the accomplishment not so much of Judah Leib Gordon, the "high priest of

Hebrew creativity," but of the Jewish people as a whole. Instead, the organizers of the Gordon commemoration failed properly to organize the celebration and even went so far as to publicize it only in the Russian language, which most readers of Gordon could not understand. More important, the honors that have been heaped upon Gordon have in large measure been inappropriate. Not because Gordon does not merit celebration—quite to the contrary—but because, in typical fashion, the highest praise lavished on a Jewish poet is to crown him with the name of a non-Jewish poet. Thus, Gordon had been hailed as the "Hebrew Nekrasov." This is ridiculous, since Gordon's importance can be measured precisely by the extent to which he fulfilled the unique mission and calling of a true Hebrew poet, which are radically different from those of poets in other tongues. Gentile poets write about love and death, nature and eternity, the flowers of spring and the leaves of autumn. But the Hebrew poet cannot concern himself with such flights of lyrical fancy; he cannot focus on the present, but must deal solely with the past. He must return in verse to the days of yore in order to bring to the fore the bygone heights of both Jewish national glory and Jewish national suffering. He cannot stop to dwell on the tranquil peace of bucolic life, for where is there tranquility in the Jewish present, where those islands of calm and peace?

In centuries past, continued Smolenskin, Hebrew poetry was entirely liturgical in nature, moored in the Scriptures, which are holy to every Jew, secular or traditional, as his national legacy. But in the last hundred years, a new breed of Jews has emerged who wished to ape the nations in whose midst they lived, to deny the uniqueness of their people. Believing in imminent liberation through emancipation, they committed themselves not to the Jewish past or even the Jewish future, but only to the Jewish present. Thus, they preferred to examine solely the evils done to the Jews from within, not the wounds inflicted from without. The Hebrew poets who shared in this delusion inevitably produced inferior, evanescent verse. Indeed, if one were to gather together all Hebrew poetry since the beginning of the age of emancipation and subject it to rigorous criticism, almost nothing could be salvaged as worthwhile and true. Only Ada"m Lebensohn, his son Micah, and his disciple Judah Leib Gordon rescued Hebrew poetry from infamy. The latter two, in peculiar, shifted Hebrew verse back to its proper course by creating works based on biblical motifs, on the trials and tribulations of the Jewish past. Most successful in this regard was Gordon himself, who in his earliest poems scaled the consummate heights of Hebrew verse. He alone in modern times rose to the level of the great Hebrew poets of medieval Spain, competing even with the divine Judah Halevi himself. If Gordon had continued to write in this vein, the Jewish people as a whole would easily have looked upon him as virtually a prophet of the Lord, the model Hebrew poet for generations to come.

Unfortunately, Gordon strayed from this path and traduced his mission as well as his genius. He soon began to regard the works of his youth as puerile and sterile and chose a new poetic path, marked by analyses of the present state of his people and exposure of their gaping wounds. This he did with unparalleled skill, creating works such as "The Tip of the Yud," which perhaps has no peer in all of world literature. But despite the beauty of their language and the profundity of their vision, these poems will prove to be utterly ephemeral works of time-bound art, inaccessible and meaningless to future generations. By miring himself so completely in the fleeting present, Gordon has established himself as a poet solely of the hour, rather than an eternal Hebrew poet, as he seemed to be at first. This transformation was perhaps understandable, for the travails of the Jews in Russia were great, and so sensitive a soul as Gordon could not overlook the suffering and ignore the pain. But Gordon fell into the most dangerous trap of his day, the lure of the Haskalah, the illusion that salvation inheres in education, self-improvement, enlightenment. As a consequence, Gordon fell under the influence of non-Jewish authors, particularly the radical Russian critic Dmitrii Pisarev and his ilk, who substituted materialism for idealism and rejected all spiritual ideals as preposterous. These false notions conquered almost all of Jewish youth in Russia and set in motion a veritable war between fathers and sons. Pisarev's ideas could not but have affected Gordon, so steeped is he in Russian language and culture. He was not completely won over to this materialist cult, but was sufficiently perverted by it to turn his poetry predominantly to its themes of criticism and rot.

Gordon's lapse is all the more blatant and tragic, Smolenskin concluded, after the devastations of the last several years. Since the pogroms, the Haskalah has been unmasked as a dangerous delusion, and the Jews have recognized where true redemption lies. Will Gordon, too, see the light, will he return to his previous ways, will he cease and desist from criticizing his own people and once more console them in their woes and sing of their glories past and future? In his marvelous "For Whom Do I Toil?" he so brilliantly exposed the self-destructiveness of the Jewish enlighteners. Will he then repent from his errant ways, return to his original self, take up once more the mission and calling of a true Hebrew poet?[4]

This criticism of Gordon was deliberately couched in rather gentle tones and in frequent, and quite genuine, expressions of sympathy and appreciation. Nonetheless, Smolenskin's critique was sharp and decisive, reflecting the ever-widening gulf between Judah Leib Gordon and the Jewish nationalist camp. Ironically, the very same charge that Smolenskin leveled against Gordon—that he had succumbed to the alien aesthetic of the Russian "nihilist" critics—would later be turned on its head by Smolenskin's comrade-in-arms, Moshe Leib Lilienblum, who would attempt to dethrone Gordon from his position as national Jewish poet by invoking the theories of the radical Russian critics.

Meanwhile, Gordon felt that he had been stabbed in the back by a good friend. To a colleague who praised his work, Gordon bitterly remarked that not everyone agreed with this assessment, that Smolenskin had decreed that Gordon's time had lapsed. Confessing that his fondest hopes were that his exposure of the stupidity and rot in Jewish life would indeed become superfluous, Gordon seethed at Smolenskin's derogation of his poetic worth.[5] He did not directly respond to Smolenskin's jab, but later countered its basic points in his last editorial in *Ha-Meliz*, a bold defense of the appropriateness of Jewish self-criticism even in times of trouble.[6]

The next round in the ideological warfare involved quite a different, and utterly unexpected, issue. The Hebrew journal *Ha-Maggid* had by this time consolidated itself as the mouthpiece of what might be called the conservative-nationalist camp in Russian Jewry. Its editor, David Gordon, espoused the return to Zion and Jewish national unity in ways deliberately aimed at capturing the minds and hearts of traditional Jews, at forging a united front of rabbis, laymen, and students dedicated to the rebirth of a Jewish national home in Palestine. To Judah Leib Gordon, of course, such a position was sheer anathema, and consequently he did not subscribe to or even read *Ha-Maggid*. In mid-May 1883, however, he heard that he had been defamed in its pages in a manner that contravened literary protocol. After seeking out the relevant issue of *Ha-Maggid,* he was stunned. He found there a piece called "A Disgrace over the Tip of a Yud" that took as its target not his ideology or even his poetry but his competence as a Hebraist and, most important, his dignity and character. The actual matter in hand was quite trivial. In his scholarly article on the Coptic language and the Jews, printed in the Purim supplement to *Ha-Meliz,* Gordon had noted in a footnote that many of the great Hebrew grammarians had erred by omitting the letter yud in one relatively rare morphological construction in biblical Hebrew. This comment, the anonymous author in *Ha-Maggid* claimed, had important ideological and moral connotations. First of all, Gordon's claim was generally wrong, and when right was well known to all experts in Hebrew grammar, a group to which the esteemed poet could never belong. More to the point, who in heaven's name was Judah Leib Gordon to defame his predecessors by claiming greater knowledge than they? This astounding hubris is merely symptomatic of a widespread moral defect in Jewish society as a whole, the derogation of one's betters, a trait seen especially among the so-called enlighteners, who pretend to authority and wisdom in all walks of life but are actually dilettantes or worse. Thus, Gordon could not be satisfied with the success of his modest verses and fables and vaingloriously sought after honors that were not due him. The barbs thrust by this disrespectful scoffer at his elders and superiors merely boomeranged against him, by demonstrating his ineptitude in Hebrew grammar and more: he who criticized the rabbis as scandalous tyrants because of a tip of one yud now defames the greatest Hebrew scholars of all ages over the tip of another yud! Does he think he can desecrate the memory of his superiors and take possession of their glory?[7]

Gordon first determined not to answer this attack, and merely expressed surprise that such insults would be permitted by David Gordon, who ought at the very least to know that only due to the influence of his namesake had his paper been allowed into Russia. After a while, however, he decided to respond to the attack and published in *Ha-Meliz* a short and rather mild letter that noted that his words had been misrepresented and that the goal of his attackers was obviously not scholarly but rather personal and ideological.[8]

Perhaps the most revealing reaction to Gordon's controversial views to emerge at this stage was neither Smolenskin's criticism nor *Ha-Maggid's* ad hominem attack, but a poem composed in response to "My Sister Ruḥamah" by a minor Hebrew polemicist and Lover of Zion named Saul Hurvitz. Entitled "My Sister Is Accused," this artless verse took off on the alleged biblical basis of Gordon's verse. Based on a Midrashic passage that maintained that Dinah had gone out looking like a prostitute and thus bore some of the responsibility for her rape, Hurvitz proceeded by analogy to list the sins that Russian Jews had committed. His point, quite obviously, was that the Jews had in large measure brought their suffering upon themselves. "You, too, are to blame, my sister the accused," he wrote. You forgot your father's ways, mimicked the daughters of the land, wore their whorish clothes and adopted their wicked habits, fomenting the envy of all, without realizing how dangerous this was in an alien land. You sought only false honor and received instead unbearable shame; you nonetheless refuse to part with your rapists, to abandon the scene of the crime, to return to your own land there to be pure and free. Don't wait for miracles and signs from the heavens to guide you as they did out of Egypt, for a miraculous redemption shall not again occur. Instead, you must return to the land of your fathers, work it with your own sweat and toil, become a nation on your national soil; only thus will you insure that you will not be raped once more.[9]

The moral of this poem was perfectly representative of the harsh criticism of Russian-Jewish society espoused by most of the "Palestinophiles" of the day, despite Smolenskin's condemnation of Jewish self-castigation. This criticism was just as brutal, if not more so, than that of Gordon and the other maskilim, and was clearly based on the very same premises. Indeed, despite their substantial differences of opinion, it was perfectly possible and natural for Gordon to work closely with his friends who had formally linked themselves with the Love of Zion movement. In fact, it was Gordon who first complimented Hurvitz on "My Sister Is Accused" and who sent the poem on to Smolenskin with a recommendation that it be published in *Ha-Shahar*.[10]

Thus, when Gordon left for Marienbad at the beginning of June 1883, he felt himself enveloped in controversy but not cut off from the mainstream of Russian-Jewish intellectual life. From St. Petersburg he traveled (along with the Barons Gunzburg) to his hometown Vilna, and then made his way to the Bohemian spa, visiting en route with friends and acquaintances. At Marienbad, he spent two long, frustrating months taking the waters, which improved neither his health nor his mood, especially after word came from St. Petersburg that the publishers of his collected poems were in financial difficulty, leaving the fate of their venture in jeopardy. In addition, he was unsure of how he would support himself after returning home, since the thought of rejoining *Ha-Meliz* and subjecting himself again to Zederbaum's whims made him even more depressed and physically weak. What most buoyed his spirits was the ongoing friendship and financial support of the Barons Gunzburg, who were also summering at Marienbad. Particularly enamored of Gordon and dependent on his intellectual wares was the young Baron David Gunzburg, later a famous, if amateur, Hebrew and Arabic scholar and the patron of the unofficial Jewish university in St. Petersburg.[11]

When he returned to Petersburg, Gordon's health improved a little and his spirits were lifted by the resumption of work on the collected poems. For the rest of 1883 and the first quarter of 1884, he spent almost all of his days and most of his nights reworking old poems and finishing new ones, supervising the printers and reading proofs, hoping against hope that the dilettantism of his backers would not be reflected in the final product. How he supported himself through these long months is not entirely clear; it appears that his only source of steady income at this time was the stipend he received from the Gunzburg family. To friends and colleagues who asked for advice about articles they had written or were planning to write for Jewish journals, Gordon repeatedly answered that he had renounced any connections with the Hebrew or Russian-Jewish periodic press and would give no counsel in their regard. To one correspondent, for example, he wrote:

> . . . for my sins, I cannot satisfy you and respond to the question you posed. I can't write anything about your book because I now do not contribute to any Jewish periodical; I have washed my hands of both *Ha-Meliz* and *Voskhod* and have no truck

with them at all. . . . In fact, all Jewish journals have become loathsome to me. . . . I have lost faith in the Jewish reading public, I have completely despaired of them. If heartless and illiterate people like Rodkinson [an itinerant editor of Hebrew and Yiddish journals] can become publishers and find readers, if evil slime like Z [ederbaum] can mislead and deceive the masses for decades on end, if etc. etc. etc. . . . then of what possible worth is it for us to spill out our guts for them? They are but a flock of ewes who fall in line behind any blind leader who appears at their head; let them go on until they fall into a snare and realize that their very lives are in danger.[12]

The only hope, Gordon concluded, lies now more than ever not in the masses but in the elite, the chosen few who would preserve and protect the Hebrew patrimony and develop it, or at least preserve it intact, for future generations.

It was in this frame of mind that Gordon put the finishing touches on his collected poems, which finally appeared in early April 1884 in four handsome volumes totaling some 740 pages.[13] This was apparently the first time in the history of Hebrew letters that the collected works of a poet were issued so grandly. Indeed, the publishers of the volumes—formally identified on both the Hebrew and the Russian frontispieces as "A Group of Lovers of the Hebrew Language in St. Petersburg"—explained in a rather peculiar foreword that the purpose of their unprecedented effort was not simply to assure that Gordon's verses would be preserved but also to redress a grievous lapse in Jewish life. "All enlightened nations," they explained, honor their sages by publishing their works and distributing them to all classes and groups in the nation: "the pauper buys his copy on plain paper for a few copper coins, and enjoys it during his free time; the middling man buys a better edition; and the rich man an even more expensive one, on fine paper, with a fancy binding, meant both for reading and for display in his library."[14] In this way, the national legacy is passed on from generation to generation, and even the young admire and respect their literary heroes. But the Jews have sadly not followed this noble custom. Though a wise people, they have never seen fit to honor their poets and thinkers in a proper fashion. Thus, worthy Hebrew authors have to scrape and borrow to issue their works, while charlatans and scurrilous scribblers are able to dominate the book trade. For many years "we, the lovers of Hebrew in the capital, recognized this plight and said: 'When will we Jews, too, be like all the nations? When will we learn to emulate the advanced nations that honor their authors not only with eulogies after their death, not only with lip service, but with deeds?'"[15] Therefore, the lovers of Hebrew in St. Petersburg decided to publish this collection of Gordon's poems, delegating the task to a seven-man committee that included Alexander Zederbaum and the other Jewish publishers and editors of the capital (of whom Gordon had recently spoken with such disdain). The publication was interrupted by the outbreak of the pogroms, but now the promised volumes— which cost the substantial sum of five thousand rubles to produce, paid for by a group of munificent philanthropists—can at long last be presented to the public. Gordon's collected works are available in a luxury edition selling for ten rubles, and in a cheaper edition for only 3 rubles; any profits will be donated to a fund to further Hebrew literature in the future.

Gordon doubtless was embarrassed by these remarks but did not record how he felt about them, only confessing to his friends and relatives that he was far from happy with the financial arrangements announced therein. His own introduction to the collected poems struck a far different key, unconcerned with the mundane concerns of book prices and public policy. "Ought I to write an introduction to my book or not?" Gordon queried. It is said that a book without an introduction is like a body without a soul, but a book of poetry is an exception to this rule, for what is poetry if not the outpourings of one's soul? If the reader is sensitive and attuned to the thoughts and feelings of the poet, then no introduction or explanation is needed; if not, no introduction will help. Indeed, poetry is like the manna eaten by the Jews in the desert, which required no seasoning and had any taste desired; or, as Plutarch put it, reading poetry is not work but an act of wisdom.[16]

Therefore, Gordon continued, he would not try to explicate his verses or "the moral and religious lessons included in them," but would leave that to each reader. He merely wanted to explain that the poems fell into two time periods, before and after his dedication to social criticism, and that they were classified into two categories, lyrical and epic. He knew that they were being published in so magnificent an edition not by reason of his own accomplishments, but rather because the time was ripe for such a celebration of Hebrew creativity. He wanted, then, to thank the Lord and the lovers of Hebrew for this honor, and hoped that his works would prove useful and enlightening to the Jewish people.

The tone of these last comments was sustained in a new and somewhat mawkish dedicatory verse placed at the front of the collection. But the careful reader could very quickly discern that the over two hundred poems included in these volumes were hardly marked by soppiness or sentimentality. Though the large majority of the poems were simply reproduced in their original form with minor lexical corrections, some of Gordon's most famous works were significantly altered in the new edition, and others—most notably "Zedekiah in Prison"—appeared here in print for the first time.

Three examples should suffice to demonstrate the thrust of both the revisions of the established works and the new poems. First, "Between the Lions' Teeth" was significantly transformed. In the original version, it will be recalled, when the heroine Martha espies her beloved Simeon facing the lion in the Roman circus, she cries out, "All-hearing ear, do you hear my plea?" and wonders whether the God of Israel is simply a hidden God who has left the world in the hands of murderers; her question is left unanswered. In the 1884 revision, Simeon joins Martha in challenging the heavens, and when he sees the lion preparing to charge at him a second time, he loses all hope and shouts: "Where is the God of Samson!"—the God who helped Samson tear asunder a roaring lion with his bare hands. The narrator intervenes to answer this question:

> Brave hero, haven't you yet learned,
> Where is your God, the God of Samson?
> Your God, the God of Samson
> Has abandoned His chosen people and their heroes
> To side with the uncircumcised Philistines, their foes,
> And you, like your nation, were not favored.
> The wrathful God who handed over His chosen flock
> To a powerful nation who neither knew Him nor served Him,
> Who allowed His Temple to burn in ruins,
> By flames lit without purpose or sense,
> He now has caused the sword to fall from your hand,
> And has left you as food for the wild beast.[17]

This addition clearly reflected the dramatic changes in Gordon's universe since he composed the poem a quarter-century earlier. In the 1860s he could believe, though always assailed by doubt, that in the face of a hidden God the only answer to the trauma of the Jews was trust in the indestructible freedom and dignity of the human being. By the mid-1880s, this faith was all but shattered. The Jews seemed clearly to be deprived of God's favor; evil was allowed to flourish unrestrained; the world seemed devoid of divine grace and marked by senseless, brutal horror. Faith in the inevitable victory of righteousness and reason was now difficult, if not impossible, to sustain.

The same point is made even more stridently in "Two Josephs Son of Simeon" [*Shenei Yosef ben Shim'on*], a poem begun in the late 1870s but not completed until late 1883 (a chronology not noted by some of Gordon's most sensitive critics).[18] The poem sounds a harsh note from its very start, when the reader is led through a long, and rather tortured, parody of a High Holy Day prayer praising the almighty, the omnipotent, and the omnipresent being, who turns out to be not the Lord on high, but the treasurer of a typical Jewish community in Eastern Europe. In nearly eight hundred more lines there unfolds a typical Gordonian plot about a corrupt communal official who sells to a despicable Jewish horse thief the internal passport of a maskilic hero, a medical student who combines scientific erudition with unbridled devotion to the Hebrew heritage and the Jewish people. When the hero, Joseph (what better name for a dashing lad who has prophetic dreams and ultimately is unjustly consigned to prison?), returns home to visit his dying mother, he is arrested for the crimes of the horse thief bearing his passport. His poor mother dies before seeing her beloved son, and as her funeral cortege passes through the streets, Joseph calls out to his bereaved father, but the two are kept apart, and the son is condemned to a life sentence of hard labor. The narrator returns at this point to the liturgical parody begun at the beginning of the work, but now with a dreadful rather than a jocular twist. On the Days of Awe, soon after the bone-chilling prayer "Who will live and who will die," and immediately preceding the inspiring hymn "And all believe," come the lines "Without an advocate before the prosecution, proclaim your law and judgment unto Jacob, and judge us in justice, O king of justice." Gordon turns this celebration of divine justice on its head: "And without an advocate before the prosecution,/ In place of justice, there prevails only evil." This is the ultimate reality: the wicked reign free, the righteous are punished; there is no justice.[19]

But it would be misleading to represent the overarching tone of the collection— or even of its new verses—as one of unmitigated *Angst*. A new poem, "Immortality of the Soul" [*Hash'arat ha-nefesh*], continues the lament of near hopelessness and personalizes it, but strives nonetheless to blunt the despair of the poet in the face of the arbitrariness of the universe. Written on Gordon's fifty-second birthday, this chilling meditation on death begins with a rather morbid paraphrase of King David's dying words celebrating God's justice—"These are the last words of the poet"—and continues:

> Fifty-two years I've lived
> And already feel old age creeping in on me,
> My strength is drained, my eyes grow dim,
> A leaden gloom enshrouds my soul.[20]

This gloom, the poet knows, is nothing but the shadow of death moving steadily closer to him. But he does not fear death, he is ready for it, certain that his mission is accomplished. He has poured out his soul to his people, he has immortalized his message in words that can never be erased. In lines frantically juxtaposing snippets of the High Holy Day liturgy and Ezekiel's vision of the resurrection of the "dry bones," the poem concludes:

> Consume my flesh and skin, bitter death, put an end to me,
> Pound me to dust, crush me to nought
> (For you are the creator and I the clay),
> My spirit lingers in my words and cannot be blotted out.
>
> My many enemies will rejoice when I die,
> They'll attack me still, cast stones on my grave,
> But I'll be comforted when someone will look
> Upon my soul poured out here and understand my thoughts.
>
> Understand my thoughts, mold them and rework them,
> Flesh and skin will again encase my soul,
> If my nation then gets even a fleck of help from me,
> I'll lie and rot in peace, and in my grave I'll rest.[21]

As Gordon later explained to a friend, these words were consciously crafted to answer his critics, to defend himself against those who might frown upon his expressions of hopelessness and despair. To mute their criticisms, he added explicatory notes to many of his poems, old and new, but was still certain that "all the judges of Israel" would pounce upon his collected verse and denounce him for a variety of sins. No fair judgment would be rendered against his work, he was certain, because only poets could truly understand him, and where were there other Hebrew poets able and willing to wade their way through four huge tomes of verse to discern their intent and worth?[22]

Nonetheless, after the collected poems were published and distributed, Gordon was in very high spirits, despite his expectation of impending controversy. For the first time in many years he was able to write new poems at an impressive clip. Clearly buoyed by his productivity, he returned to journalism, publishing in *Voskhod* a scathing attack on his successor as literary critic of that journal—a twenty-four-year-old, newly arrived from the provinces, named Simon Dubnov. Dubnov had harshly panned a work by two of Gordon's friends, and in a letter to one of these friends Gordon explained that he had personally picked Dubnov to be the literary editor of *Voskhod,* as he was a quick and able fellow who wrote Russian brilliantly and had a good future ahead of him, even though at times he was guilty of overstepping his competence and dabbling in matters about which he knew nothing.[23]

Gordon's public reproach of Dubnov appeared in the very same issue of *Voskhod* that contained a long, glowing review of *The Collected Poetry of Judah Leib Gordon* written by none other than Simon Dubnov. Subtitled "The Jewish Nekrasov," Dubnov's paean to Gordon was virtually the mirror image of Smolenskin's recent critique: Gordon's latest poems were lauded as vast improvements over his naive early works; "My Sister Ruḥamah" and "The Flock of the Lord" were celebrated as inspired reflections on the contemporary trauma of the Jews; "The Tip of the Yud" and the other satires were lionized as the apogee of Gordon's poetic genius. In sharp opposition to Smolenskin's prophecy of Gordon's increasing irrelevance, Dubnov ended his comments with the conclusion:

> This poetry has had, and undoubtedly will continue to have, enormous influence on the Jewish world, thanks especially to its mimetic character and its humane and progressive aspirations. It will be as important to Russian Jewry as the poetry of Nekrasov was for the entire Russian nation. Infused with "the reasonable, the good, the eternal," the significance of Gordon's poetry cannot be only fleeting or transient.[24]

Gordon was generally pleased by this review, though he was offended by its rather trenchant criticism of the forced pietism of *The Love of David and Michal* and the other pseudobiblical epics. If Dubnov's later testimony is to be trusted, Gordon went over the proofs of this review with the editor of *Voskhod* and personally wrote the editorial rebuttals printed at the bottom of each page.[25]

This incident reveals the extent to which Gordon was unable to tolerate any criticism of his work. In large measure, he seems not to have recognized the rather obvious fact that his poetry—so deeply didactic and charged with polemical fervor—would be judged more on the basis of its ideology than on its aesthetic or literary worth. What distinguished Dubnov's evaluation of Gordon from Smolenskin's, for example, was principally the position each critic took on the future of the Jewish people. Although, as a faithful follower of Russian literary criticism, Gordon knew that in the cultural and political world in which he lived no neat separation between aesthetics and politics was even remotely conceivable, he somehow persisted in believing that his work could be evaluated purely on its literary merits. Thus, to a faithful friend who pointed out several factual errors in "The Tip of the Yud," Gordon testily retorted that such errors were incidental; after all, Heine had made egregious historical mistakes in his poetry, but these in no way lessened his poetic reputation.[26]

This attitude would not stand Gordon in good stead in the coming months, as his collected works were subjected to more and more rigorous criticism. At the end of August 1884, for example, Naḥum Sokolov published an extremely positive and rather sophisticated review of Gordon's collected works, praising both their style and content as unparalleled in the history of Hebrew verse. Sokolov greatly admired the poet and the poems, but felt it important to call into question Gordon's understanding of the nature of satire and his derogation of all the solutions to the plight of the Jews in Russia.[27] After reading this review, Gordon let loose a furious attack on his critic's youth and his ignorance. Sokolov, for his part, was taken aback by the vehemence of this reaction. In a letter to Gordon that has not previously been published, he retorted: I may be young but that does not necessarily make me wrong. I may not be a poet, but I may have ideas about poetry, and know that satire should not deal with the atypical, the unlikly, the unusual, but rather with the stereotypical, the expected, the known. Therefore, even if "The Tip of the Yud" is based on an actual occurrence, as Gordon maintained, it is misleading and potentially harmful, since it is based on an extraordinary, unexpected turn of events. More important, though:

> You take offence at me for saying that I could not find in your poems any clear doctrine, any system that points to a solution. This is true, and I still maintain this and will not be moved until you yourself point out to me what your solution is. For if I am to accept your claim in your last letter to me that your solution is "moderate reform" I still don't really know what reforms you are talking about. . . . Throughout your poetry you criticize religious orthodoxy, the enlightenment, even nationalism and the nationalists, but you never recommend any other answer or even hint at what the Jews should do.[28]

Not all of Gordon's critics would be so awed by his reputation or so contrite. In the summer of 1884 Gordon heard tell that *Ha-Meliz* was going to review his collected works and jauntily laughed off the idea of Zederbaum attempting to compose a critical piece on Hebrew poetry. Several months later, however, he discovered to his chagrin that the old publisher was not going to write the review himself but had assigned the task to Moshe Leib Lilienblum, the most formidable cannon in the nationalist camp. By this time, relations between Gordon and Lilienblum were cool at best: they had ceased corresponding since their differences of opinion seemed to be irreconcilable. But no truly harsh words had passed between them, either in public or in private. Gordon was therefore shocked and mortally wounded when, early in 1885, he first beheld in a special edition of *Ha-Meliz* the forty-eight-page "Review of the Collected Verse of Judah Leib Gordon" by Moshe Leib Lilienblum.[29]

This most sustained criticism of Gordon's work to appear during his lifetime was one of the most remarkable refractions of the tortuous twists in the cultural politics of Russian Jewry in the crucial years of the mid-1880s and demands careful explication. Lilienblum began with transparently patronizing praise: the "Friends of Hebrew" in the Russian capital ought to be complimented for publishing Gordon's verse, for he is better than all his predecessors. His poems are all pleasing and well crafted and lift their readers to the heights of emotion and sensitivity. As Gordon himself once put it in regard to another poet, he is a poet of the heart, not the head.

Indeed, the basic problem with Gordon, Lilienblum continued, is that he hearkens to his heart too much, allowing his emotions to overwhelm his brain. He succumbs all too easily to a highly fastidious aesthetic based on nineteenth-century European conceptions of beauty, against which he tests the reality of Russian-Jewish life. Whatever does not conform to this standard, he casts aside as ugly and degenerate. Gordon has never really been swayed by the regnant spirit of his age: while all the other Jewish artists passed through the various stages of Russian-Jewish intellectual development—the era of suffering and horrors under Nicholas I, the struggle for "assimilation" under Alexander II, the age of nationalism and reaction to anti-Semitism after 1881—Gordon remained constant in his zealous delicacy of spirit and mind, examining everything through the prism of refined European sensibility. In his writings before 1855 he made no mention of the horrors inflicted on the Jews by Nicholas's militarism; in the age of liberalization he found fault only with the rabbis and *melamdim* and the Codes of Law, never recognizing any of the legal impediments to Jewish success. Most amazing, the pogroms seem to have had no effect on him, for he has not written any good poems on the subject, only superficial and sarcastic little ditties.

Therefore, Lilienblum confessed, despite the admiration that I have for our major poet and our friendship over the last sixteen years, I unfortunately must say that I do not like all of Gordon's poems. I will not write about those that I do like— that is superfluous in this context; I will merely explain what I do not like. Crucial to this effort is the recognition that the notion of poetic license is preposterous and outdated. The ancient wisdom expressed by the medieval Hebrew poet Immanuel of Rome that the essence of poetry is its ability to construct fantasies and fancies has lapsed in our day, "when we have no need of *poets* to lie to us, and therefore readers today demand that poets speak only *truth* to them, truth in their depiction of life, truth in their understanding of reality, its causes and its chronology."[30]

With this literary credo articulated, Lilienblum worked his way through Gordon's four volumes, highlighting stanzas and statements that offended against "the truth," as he understood it, and therefore against art. Is there one poem in all of Gordon's oeuvre that praises anything Jewish? Lilienblum asked. One poem that reflects the Jews' creativity, their contributions to civilization, instead of their faults and errors? Does he say anything that would inspire the young to remain within the Jewish fold, rather than seeking enlightenment elsewhere? Gordon wants to spread enlightenment among the Jews, but he does not see the truth, which is that the Jewish masses do not need enlightenment, only basic literacy and some land to farm. He constantly harps on bringing the Jews in line with the time and the place in which they live, but never seriously explains why contemporary fashions are better than sacred traditions. In "Awake, My People!" he vastly overstated the possibilities for freedom even in the bright optimistic days of the 1860s; after 1881, this poem seems at best a sad joke. Why should Jews learn the language of the country in which they live? Aren't Jewish languages just as good? Why does Gordon urge his brethren to be "men in the streets and Jews at home," in other words, to conceal their Jewishness like contraband, as if it were shameful for a nineteenth-century European to be recognizable as a Jew? All his cries for a religious reform of Judaism are false to the core. If the Jews were a nation like all the nations, if they were living on their land in accord with their *Volksgeist,* their religious life would naturally follow suit and their youth would not run after other gods.

In general, no attempt to have Judaism conform to European standards and mores can succeed, for the simple reason that the Jews and the Europeans are of different biological mettle: the Jews are Semites and the Europeans are sons of Japheth to whom everything Jewish is, by nature, strange and repellent. Any attempt to recast Judaism in the spirit of Europe will, therefore, necessarily result in a hybrid that is simply not authentically Jewish. The only remedy to the prevalent religious crisis among the Jews, then, is their removal from Europe and their resurrection as a living people on their own soil.[31]

From this remarkable amplification of his previous views on religious reform— now adding a biological argument to the pragmatic, Palestinophilic stance he had previously maintained—Lilienblum went on to attack all the other basic planks of Gordon's ideology, as allegedly reflected in his poetry. Is it true that the *melamdim* are persecutors of the young, as Gordon and the other enlighteners always maintain? How long will Jewish authors retain his "fetishism," blaming everything on the poor teachers, the rabbis, the Talmud? Can't Gordon rise above these cliches to seek out the real reason for the sad plight of his people? Any wrongs committed by the teachers or rabbis must be understood not as a consequence of their own faults but of the conditions in which they find themselves—"just as all evil stems not from individuals, but from the society in which they live." Therefore, the realization has spread that to rectify the faults in Jewish life it is necessary to create a Jewish home in Palestine. But our poet insists that this goal must be predicated upon a prior religious reform of the Jews. Would that he and his friends would have opposed assimilation as heartily! In fact, those who advance emigration to America rather than the Land of Israel do so out of the hope that in America the Jews can assimilate completely.[32]

But Gordon is more complicated than the straightforward advocates of assimilation. He is, in effect, a man without beliefs. Now that the hopes and dreams that he cherished for decades have evaporated, he wallows in despair. Others were able to see the light after their ideals were crushed, but Gordon is too delicate, too fastidious, to bear the thought of Jews living in their own land without aping the beautiful exterior of European society. Would that he had been so fastidious in regard to the truth. His famous lines on the status of Jewish women in "The Tip of the Yud," for example, were far from true and accurate. His pitiful poem "My Sister Ruḥamah" was an utterly weak response to the pogroms. His "Flock of the Lord" was a pathetic restatement in verse of the attacks of the German assimilationists on Pinsker's pamphlet. A truly national poet should have raised his voice to proclaim solace and hope to his people, like the second Isaiah; Gordon, of all things, modeled himself after Zedekiah, a ruler with no political strategy save capitulation! In the contest between Zedekiah and Jeremiah, history has proven that the prophet, not the king, was right. How, then, can Gordon commit such foolishness to paper?[33]

He and the fawning Dubnov echoing him vilify Jeremiah and the ancient Jews for keeping the Sabbath, for not knowing that this quaint belief did not accord with European mores. But Jeremiah and his public, not Gordon and Dubnov, knew what was right for the Jews. Indeed, no other poem in Gordon's collection is as baseless as "Zedekiah in Prison," whose every line is utterly senseless. Perhaps the poet can be forgiven for this offence, since he wrote it while in prison and exile, not knowing whether he would ever be released. But while everyone has the right to write nonsense, no one has right to publish that nonsense, and it would have been much better had the poet buried this poem in his drawer.[34]

As the historians have amply demonstrated, no nation has ever followed its leaders blindly, against the direction dictated by its national ethos. On the contrary, leaders can only succeed if they hearken to the innate voice of their people. If they object to that voice, to that spirit, they are always doomed to failure and obsolescence. Therefore, when Gordon rails against the Oral Law, he does not understand that it was not foisted upon the Jews by the rabbis but developed within the Jewish national organism out of the people's intrinsic values and beliefs. In "Between the Lions' Teeth" he criticizes the Jews for not emulating Rome but fails to understand that the only area in which the Romans were superior to the Jews was in the art of death and destruction. Had Gordon himself lived through a pogrom in Odessa or Kiev in 1881, he would have realized that all his poems, all his short stories, all of his criticisms of the rabbis are useless and besides the point.[35]

He ought finally to learn the truth—that the fall of Judea and the destruction of the Temple resulted not from the actions and deeds of the rabbis and sages but from the "assimilationist enlighteners" like Josephus who loved Roman ways and were traitors to their people. If they had served the Jews rather than their enemies, the end would not have been the same.[36]

In brief, there is no way that someone who believes what Gordon does can be deemed a "national poet," as Dubnov calls him. What can that mean in the mouth of someone whose entire love for his people consists in the hope for its death as a national entity? A true "national poet" is

> one who seeks honor for his people as a vibrant nation, living its national life on its own soil, and not the life of wandering sheep living at the mercy of others, mimicking their rulers. It pains me to conclude that there is not even one hint in any poem of this sublime poet that testifies to his desire for the rebirth of his people![37]

Why has Gordon forgotten that all of the troubles that befell Israel were caused by the loss of its sovereignty? If Israel had remained on its own land, if it had lived a life there comparable to that of other nations, there would have been no room for characters like those Gordon created in "The Tip of the Yud." The lot of the Jewish woman would have been better; there would be a compassionate and wise Sanhedrin whose members were in touch with reality; there would be no need either for small-town rabbis insisting on the jots and tittles of obscure Rabbinic ordinances or for poems like those of Gordon. What the Jews need is not reform but the restoration of self-rule. Until such time, no religious reforms will help. Indeed, even Maimonides himself did not achieve his attempt at religious reform and ended in complete failure, for he, too, attempted to unite two radically different entities, the Torah of Israel, the sons of Shem, and the philosophy of the Greeks, the sons of Japheth. Judaism and Hellenism never were and never will be united as one.[38]

In sum, the Jews are lost until they mend their ways, but not through appeals to Gentile conscience and not through assimilation. "Mens sana in corpore sano," said the ancient wisdom: the Jews have first to heal their body, to make it healthy, united, independent. If they fail to do so, they forever will remain wandering bearers of the Mosaic faith, suffering without end, never attaining liberation. It is only to be hoped, Lilienblum concluded, that the *Collected Poetry of Judah Leib Gordon* has not yet been completed; that he will once more enrich Hebrew literature with many beautiful poems that will fight the right battle. If Gordon were to dedicate his unique and extraordinary talent to countering the enemies of the Jews and praising their collective talents; if he were to sing of the return of the Jews to Zion; if he were to unite the spirit of the Second Isaiah with that of Judah Halevi, then and only then would he justly be called "the national poet" of the Jews.[39]

To understand this extraordinary critique of Gordon's works it is necessary to delve rather deeply into its intellectual and ideological context. This has not yet been accurately done, despite the frequent citations of this review in the literature, which claimed in unison that Lilienblum here was quite simply translating into Hebrew the views of the Russian "nihilist" critic D. I. Pisarev.[40] In fact, in Lilienblum's critique of Gordon it is very difficult to identify any distinct resonances of that complex critic's idiosyncratic views on aesthetics or politics—his vehement opposition to the idealization of the masses, his self-description as a "Westerner," his belief that only an intellectual elite dedicated in absolute fealty to science could lead Russia to progress and salvation, his boundless derogation of all moral standards and literary creativity.[41]

Far more central to Lilienblum, and to the Russian-Jewish intelligentsia as a whole, were the two critics who, as mentioned above, together forged the essential catechism of the "progressive" Russian literary canon after the demise of Belinsky—N. G. Chernyshevsky and N. A. Dobroliubov. These two critics proceeded from a starting point very different from that of Pisarev. Totally committed to a very shallow conception of realism in art, they held that "[b]eauty is life; beautiful is that being in which we see life as it should be according to our conceptions; beautiful is the object which expresses life, or reminds us of life."[42] On this basis, they argued that the merit of a writer or an individual work of art depended exclusively on the extent to which it expressed not only reality but also the "natural aspirations" of a given epoch or nation. Dobroliubov in particular insisted that literature is but a "handmaiden whose importance depends on propaganda and ... who is judged by what she advocates and how."[43] Poetic license, flights of imagination, idiosyncratic representations of reality were but excuses for a decadent and bourgeois perversion of the meaning and goal of art. Literature is at all times to be judged solely by the extent to which it advances the sacred cause of revolution.

Even in the 1860s, a significant part of the Russian intelligentsia had serious doubts about this reductionist aesthetic. Turgenev, in a famous line, lambasted this view as "the still-born offspring of blind malice and stupidity."[44] By the 1880s, the avant-garde of the Russian literary intelligentsia had moved far beyond Chernyshevsky and Dobroliubov (or, for that matter, Pisarev), to a far more sophisticated understanding of the relation between art and reality.

But the Jewish intelligentsia in Russia—as virtually everywhere else in Europe—was always at least a generation behind the intellectual fashions of the hour. Thus, the voices of Dobroliubov and Chernyshevsky resounded heartily through the pages of Moshe Leib Lilienblum's writings, and nowhere more clearly than in his review of Gordon's collected works. It is not much of an exaggeration to say that everything in these forty-eight pages can be understood simply as an application to the Jewish world and to Hebrew literature of Chernyshevsky's and Dobroliubov's ideas. Lilienblum's determination to judge every poetic utterance by its historical or ideological "truth," even his sharp and relentless opposition of Jewish and European sensibilities and civilizations, are but plucked whole from the populist canon, transposed from Russian to Jewish particularism.

To be sure, Lilienblum and his cohorts did not appreciate the obvious irony of this ideological leap—that a "counterassimilatory" ideology was premised precisely on the assimilation of radical Russian mores and cultural values. Quite to the contrary, they frankly believed that they were advancing a purely Jewish, or even "Semitic," point of view. Indeed, the very adoption by Lilienblum and his colleagues of the terms "assimilation" and "assimilationist" to characterize all opponents of the Palestinian venture, regardless of their specific ideological persuasion, was a crucial step in the still unstudied development of Jewish political culture and ideological semantics in the late nineteenth century.

Judah Leib Gordon, of course, was not concerned with such issues when he read Lilienblum's review. Indeed, it took him almost an entire year to gather both the energy and the wit to respond in kind to Lilienblum's attack. In the interim, he tried to maintain a dignified silence, allowing others to counter what he regarded as Lilienblum's obvious errors of fact and grammar. The most Gordon did in this regard was to supply one of his nephews, a gymnasium student, with corrections of some of Lilienblum's mistakes, in order to make the point that even children could see through his arguments.[45]

In private, however, Gordon writhed in anger and in agony. He was certain that the main motivation of Lilienblum's attack was neither ideology nor aesthetics but personal pique, that Lilienblum was merely paid to do Zederbaum's evil bidding. But Gordon was genuinely shocked by what he considered to be the scandalously low level of Lilienblum's arguments, by the complete absence of any literary sensitivity or tolerance for poetic fancy. Behind Lilienblum's reductionism, Gordon was certain, there reeked "the smell of the study house."[46]

Almost immediately, Lilienblum's review became a true cause célèbre, as the Hebrew press in Russia and abroad was filled with articles either defending Lilienblum's review or attacking it.[47] Gordon confessed, only half in jest, that he feared that the debate over his poetry would endure as long as the controversy over Maimonides's views. I feel, he wrote to a friend, like a corpse lying in the coffin while the preacher prattles away a silly eulogy.[48] To remove himself from the direct center of the storm, in the early summer of 1885 he indulged himself in a trip to Vilna and Warsaw, where Hebrew literati like Naḥum Sokolov and David Frischmann—who led the charge against Lilienblum—arranged festive evenings to honor the visiting poet.

When he returned to Petersburg, however, reality confronted him once more. For the first time in many years he found himself without a secure income, as the young Barons Gunzburg had grown up and no longer needed a tutor. He garnered some extra income early that summer by agreeing to allow a collection of his lighthearted Yiddish poems to be published, but the total income from all of his literary efforts was not enough to support him and his wife.[49] For several months he tried to make ends meet, but to no avail. Finally, after much regret, he agreed to enter into discussions with Alexander Zederbaum about returning to edit *Ha-Meliz*. These negotiations were particularly complex, since the publisher knew that earlier that year Gordon had been the driving force behind a satiric pamphlet aimed at Zederbaum, mocking in unusually harsh tones the elderly publisher's disorganization, pretentiousness, and wooden prose.[50]

But both sides needed the other: Zederbaum knew that he had lost a goodly number of readers since Gordon left the paper and that its quality had taken a distinct turn for the worse; moreover, there were rumors that a competing Hebrew newspaper would be published in St. Petersburg, threatening the very survival of *Ha-Meliz*. Gordon, for his part, was even more reluctant than usual to consider collaborating with Zederbaum, since he feared that "people would say, with Zederbaum leading the pack, that Gordon, too, has his price," a prophecy that would come true all too soon.[51] But the financial pressure forced him to agree to return to *Ha-Meliẓ,* on the condition that he be officially appointed editor of the paper, with guarantees of editorial and financial independence. In early December 1885, he therefore returned to *Ha-Meliẓ,* and later that month received formal governmental approval as editor of the newspaper.

Gordon took to his editorial tasks with vigor and determination, picking up the issues and positions that he had articulated three years earlier. Without acknowledging in public the private, agonizing doubts he struggled with, he argued resolutely that the Haskalah had not failed, that the pogroms, the May Laws, even the mounting restrictions on Jewish access to educational institutions (which for Gordon was an even greater tragedy than the other two setbacks) did not in the least disprove the optimistic liberalism of the Enlightenment or faith in European civilization. In a series of strident editorials celebrating the centenary of the death of Moses Mendelssohn, Gordon pledged renewed allegiance to the tenets of the Jewish Enlightenment and to the dream of a fruitful integration of Judaism and European culture. Pointedly rejecting the basic premises of Peretz Smolenskin, Moshe Leib Lilienblum, and the other theorists of modern Jewish nationalism, Gordon insisted that Mendelssohn's legacy was still intact, that it was still possible to be "a full-fledged European in one's education, speech, deeds, and behavior, and at the same time a loyal Jew true to one's nation and one's faith."[52] Not only Mendelssohn but also one of the heroes of the Love of Zion movement fulfilled this definition—the recently deceased Sir Moses Montefiore was an enlightened Englishman who proudly served both his queen and the Jewish people by being veritably a model "man in the streets and a Jew at home."[53]

As before, it was in his series of pseudonymous feuilletons that Gordon spoke in his most fetching and complex voice. In the first of these pieces composed after his return, he presented his long-awaited response to Lilienblum's attack.[54] Addressing the audience he had abandoned for three long years, Gordon's semifictional alter ego confessed that much had changed in the Jewish world in the interim. Returning to the Jewish street after a long absence, he found himself accosted by armed guards "with Jewish faces, but dressed like Cossacks." At first he was thrilled by the sight of armed Jewish policemen, but his enthusiasm dimmed when they asked him to produce a document testifying to his nationalism. What's that, he queried, I don't understand the word "nationalism," I can't find it listed in the biblical Concordance or in any Hebrew dictionary. A nationalistic Jew, the "Hebrew Cossacks" answered, is one who loves his nation. Well, he retorted, I qualify; all my life I've demonstrated my love for my people. Not enough, replied the militia; you've got to have a document, a membership card, to prove that you're one of us. But you've got it all wrong, he explained. What you call nationalism has always been known simply as love for one's nation, something that is natural to every man and every Jew from birth. This love is congenital and unselfconscious; one doesn't strut about proclaiming this love, just as a beautiful but modest woman does not praise her own beauty to all she meets. But you have clothed this feeling in a new garb, which you simply borrowed from the nations around you. You have simply mimicked the Russian Slavophiles, who believe that true Russianness consists in rejecting the reforms of Peter the Great, celebrating the most absurd and repugnant peasant customs, retreating from Western culture into the isolation of

ancient Rus', and—not incidentally—ridding Russia of the Jews. These Slavophiles are no more patriotic Russians than their counterparts, the Westernizers,
who want to reform Russia in the spirit of Peter the Great and civilized European
norms.[55]

He continued:

> The split between the Slavophiles and the Westernizers exists between us, too, and
> separates me from you, my policemen. My love for my people is exactly the same as
> your nationalism. I, too, seek the salvation of the Jews, their redemption, and their
> return to their land. I, too, have worked in the past, work now, and will work in the
> future to make these dry bones live, albeit not with great alarms and trumpet sounds,
> and without any membership cards or rabbinical endorsements. However, I agree
> with the Russian Westernizers and say: Not in vain have we suffered so many trials
> and travails in our two-thousand-year exile, and labored mightily with so many other
> peoples to raise the level of human civilization. Now if we return to our land, we
> shall not do so empty-handed; we shall take with us some of the choice products of
> this good land in which we have lived, some of its wisdom, which pleases God and
> man, and plant these noble vines in the land of our forefathers. We will graft a foreign
> slip on the vine of Israel, to improve it and to adorn it; we will cause the beauty of
> Japheth to dwell in the tents of Shem.[56]

Thus, paraphrasing Genesis 10:27—"May God enlarge Japheth and let him dwell
in the tents of Shem"—Gordon seized on Lilienblum's opposition between the
"Semitic" Jews and the "Japhethic" Europeans and continued: You, on the other
hand, cry like the Israelites in the desert yearning for the glories of Egypt, weeping
"we will go with our garlic and our onions, we will return to whence we came. The
Enlightenment is deceitful and beauty vain, we are Asiatics and shall live as Asiatics!" You claim that any Jew who loves his people must love all its customs, no
matter how antiquated or absurd! Fine, you go your way and I'll go mine, and when
we both come to the place that the Lord decreed, I will tolerate you and you will
tolerate me. If you insist, I'll abjure any religious reforms, I'll excise everything
critical or bitter from my pack, and provide you only with honey-dipped sweets.
After three years of suffering and pain, now you'll get only jubilation and praise—
if that's what you want![57]

This complex pseudohomily delighted many readers but shocked many others—including Zederbaum, who unsuccessfully urged Gordon not to publish the
piece. But this feuilleton was a crucial linchpin in Gordon's approach to Jewish
journalism and Jewish politics throughout his second stint at *Ha-Meliz*. What he
was trying to do, in effect, was to maintain a delicate balance on the most important
issue of the day, the nascent Zionist movement. As before, he opposed the ideology
of Lilienblum and the other Jewish nationalists, now adding the rather damning
explanation that they were but Jewish versions of the Slavophiles. But he now tried
more carefully than before to distinguish between the ideology of the Lovers of
Zion and their actions and accomplishments. He had always maintained that the
Jewish colonization movement in Palestine was a worthwhile and even vital instrument of Jewish national regeneration. In addition, as he later confessed, he now
realized that in the preceding three years the Jewish settlements in the Holy Land
had made substantial progress, and it was therefore unwise to raise in public the

ideal of cultural modernization and religious reform as the essential precondition to Jewish national liberation.[58]

Thus, in the very next issue of *Ha-Meliz* after his feuilleton on the "Jewish Cossacks," he wrote an editorial attacking German-Jewish spokesmen who claimed that the Lovers of Zion were radical false messiahs dedicated to rescinding the emancipation of the Jews throughout Europe and gathering them all in Palestine. On the contrary, Gordon retorted, the colonists in Palestine were moderate pragmatists supported by such responsible parties as the Rothschilds and the Alliance Israélite Universelle, who represented absolutely no danger to the emancipation of the Jews in the West.[59] In his private correspondence—especially with the rich Jewish tea merchant Kalonymus Visotsky—he repeatedly denied that he was an enemy of the Palestinophiles. On the contrary, he asserted, he was drawn to their efforts and would always speak in favor of their drive to settle Jews in their ancient land, but he could not join their movement formally, since he could not become "a reactionary and fanatic who, like Lilienblum, would call on his brethren to renounce enlightenment, return to the ghetto, and teach their children to speak Yiddish."[60]

This attempt to steer a middle course between the Lovers of Zion and their opponents made Gordon few friends in either camp and quickly led to another eruption of the public controversy over his views. First Lilienblum responded angrily to Gordon's feuilleton, claiming that it distorted his views and those of the other Lovers of Zion.[61] Almost immediately thereafter, the minor Hebrew poet K. Shapiro published in pamphlet form a defense of Gordon's position, claiming that the poet totally rejected the proto-Zionist enterprise. Gordon was most unhappy with this pamphlet and responded angrily to it in an editorial in *Ha-Meliz,* which led to a retort by Shapiro, which in turn was answered by Gordon.[62] At the same time, Gordon wrote two new feuilletons aggressively countering Lilienblum's latest attack and several private letters defending himself against the charge that he was an antinationalist. By the middle of March 1886, Gordon confessed to a friend that all this literary bickering and ideological warfare had totally debilitated and depressed him; he began once more to hope against hope that he could be done with internal Jewish politics.[63]

But relief was nowhere in sight. Quite to the contrary, in the winter of 1886 a group of Hebrew writers less favorable to the nationalist cause than Gordon decided to publish in St. Petersburg a daily Hebrew newspaper expressing their views, to be called *Ha-Yom* (The Day). Soon thereafter, Naḥum Sokolov decided to follow suit and transformed his Warsaw Hebrew journal, *Ha-Zefirah,* into a daily. Sensing a trend, and desperately fearing the competition, Alexander Zederbaum decided to begin publishing *Ha-Meliz* on a daily basis rather than twice a week. Gordon strongly opposed this move, arguing that it was both unnecessary and unfeasible, but he was overruled by the publisher. There were now to be two daily Hebrew newspapers in the Russian capital![64]

On July 1, 1886, then, *Ha-Meliz* began to be issued six times a week, and Gordon found himself compelled to churn out an absurdly high number of articles every week, straining to fill the pages of his new daily newspaper. He knew that he could not sustain the quality of the paper at this pace, but to his readers he promised that the content and editorial posture of *Ha-Meliz* would not change: it would continue the course it had followed for the previous twenty-six years, supporting moderate religious and cultural reform, the importance of the spread of the Hebrew language, religious and national tolerance, loyalty both to the tsar and to God, and love of both Russia and the Land of Israel.[65]

The decision of *Ha-Meliz* to enter the fray of daily publication seems to have caused the staff of *Ha-Yom* great consternation, and one of its major contributors, David Frischmann, who had a year earlier written perhaps the most compelling rebuttal of Lilienblum's attack,[66] lashed out at Gordon in a vituperative piece that indirectly charged that he had sold his soul to the Lovers of Zion in order to become editor of *Ha-Meliz*.[67] Gordon laughed off this accusation as the figment of the imagination of a young, brash, and ambitious polemicist, not knowing that within the year Frischmann would expand on this accusation and begin yet another battle in the war of words over Gordon's views.

But through the rest of 1886 and most of 1887 Gordon was far too busy to pay heed to such matters, consumed as he was with his rather frantic attempt to fill the pages of *Ha-Meliz*. Day in, day out, he found himself writing at least one news summary and editorial, and often a book review or feuilleton as well. The pace was brutal, the quality of the result often unsatisfactory. But he continued to produce article after article on his favorite themes: the parallel tasks of enlightening the Jews of Russia and supporting the new colonies in Palestine; the parallel dangers of radical assimilation to the Diaspora and Orthodoxy in the Holy Land; the need for a moderate rabbinical seminary in Russia, devoted to *Wissenschaft des Judentums;* praise for the Hebrew Union College of Cincinnati and the American Reform movement's confirmation ceremony; the importance of Hebrew literature as the prime conduit of Jewish modernization. To these he added a new fear, that "Communists" were taking over the new Jewish settlements in Palestine.[68]

By the end of 1887, this work left Gordon drained both physically and emotionally, and certainly in no mood to get involved in any renewed ideological combat. Indeed, in a gesture of supreme fence mending, he even wrote to Lilienblum, praising a recent work and offering to renew friendly relations after the long lapse, an offer that Lilienblum accepted with glee.[69] But within a short time, Gordon found himself once more at the epicenter of an ideological quake: David Frischmann now more openly and vigorously repeated his charge that Gordon had traded away his integrity for money, that he had traduced his former beliefs and former colleagues by making peace not only with the Lovers of Zion but also their allies, the rabbis.[70]

Frischmann's piece led to a renewed frenzy of attack and counterattack, debating at great length, and with increased ire, Gordon's views on Jewish nationalism and the Palestinian movement. After Simon Bernfeld—a German-trained Galician-Jewish scholar who was currently serving as chief rabbi of the Sephardic community of Belgrade and whom Gordon respected a great deal—entered the fray, defending Gordon against Frischmann's charges while still characterizing him as a full-blown nationalist, Gordon felt compelled to pen to Bernfeld a long and candid letter that many have called his "spiritual testament," and which merits citation at length.[71]

Written on January 19, 1888, the letter began by thanking Bernfeld for exhibiting a sense of honor and honesty rare among his colleagues, but continued to explain that his defense of Gordon had itself seriously misrepresented the truth:

I hear the person who wrote to you (whom I take to be Sokolov) saying, "We all know that Gordon is an extreme nationalist," and you, too, say, "Gordon moved from one extreme to the next," and even, "I will not judge whether indeed Gordon changed his mind because of money." From this I learn three things: (a) I am considered by you and your friends—whoever they be—as an extreme nationalist; (b) that this nationalism is rejected by you; (c) that you deem it possible that I would change my opinions because of favors or money. Now, I shall never in my life respond to people like Kantor [the editor of *Ha-Yom*] or Frischmann, who turned on me for profit; even if thousands of their like pounce upon me I shall pay them no heed, for I shall not be judged by fools. But to those who defend me I must reveal my true thoughts, so that they can know whether the person they defend is worthy of their defense or is, in fact, dishonest.

Therefore know, my friend, that as much as you and your friends consider me a rabid nationalist, Lilienblum and the other nationalists regard me as an opponent, or at the very least as someone whose loyalties are in doubt, because of our differences of opinion over the meaning of "nationalism" and on settling Palestine.[72]

When I was a lad, Gordon continued, as a devout worshiper of the Lord I proclaimed in awe the Maimonidean profession of messianic faith: "I shall await him every day." But the son of David was not impressed by my awe and did not hasten to arrive. Meanwhile, I was transformed from a believer to a dreamer, my faith weakened, and I was no longer moved by the articles of faith. When my elders rushed to the prayer house, I remained in bed, sleeping and dreaming; and in my dreams I never ceased to hope for the redemption of the Jews and their return to Zion. But even then I knew that these were but impossible dreams; I knew that the nations of the world would never release the Jews from their bondage and that the Jews would remain all their days waiting for a miraculous salvation, never rebelling against their rulers. Thus, though I was depressed by each one of these obstacles to our redemption, somehow together they relieved my soul—since, after all, the negation of a negation yields a positive. I began to see that if the Jews would not rely on miracles and "postpone the end," if they would attempt to hasten their redemption with force, the nations around them would destroy them; and if the nations of the world would not prevent the Jews from returning to their land and living on their own, the Jews would destroy themselves, because in their servitude and decrepitude they lost their ability to rule themselves. Imagine what would happen to the Jews if the *Shulhan 'Arukh* would become their civil code and one of the obtuse rabbis a ruler! The rabbinate would consume the people!

Thus, I still fantasized about the return to Zion, he continued, but in reality realized this was a risky venture. In *Ha-Shahar* I wrote a small piece on the future of Israel, which was reprinted in 1876 by the apostate Brafman in the journal *Golos,* to represent me as declaring that I was Elijah come to herald the messianic king. Obviously, at the time this foolish statement led to nothing but levity, but apparently it did raise some doubts about me in the mind of the government; and when my brethren falsely slandered me in 1879 due to a dispute over our local rabbis, this article was brought up, and "*Golos* turned into *goles* [exile]."[73] Some time before this, when I was asked by the leaders of Anglo-Jewry to aid a philanthropic effort in Palestine in honor of Montefiore, I answered that since collecting money for such a purpose was politically complicated, I would only support their effort if they were considering establishing something larger and more substantial than ordinary charitable concerns, something like buying land in the Palestine in order to establish colonies that could later begin the revival of the nation. I told them that if they did this,

> I would doff European garb and don a sheepskin coat and wander through the hills of Judea blasting loud the shofar of redemption (everything that Brafman predicted), but that I would do so only on one condition: first, they must expel from Jerusalem and the other holy cities all the Jews living there, without exception, so that we could air out the place and get rid of the foulness and mold and restore the "air of the Land of Israel that makes wise."[74]

Thus, Gordon advised Bernfeld, long before the pogroms and before the rise of the Love of Zion movement, I was a lover of Zion in my dreams and never stopped being a Jewish nationalist, though my sort of nationalism was unacceptable both to the rabbis and to those who formally called themselves "Lovers of Zion." When Smolenskin and Lilienblum rebelled against European enlightenment, calling on the Jews to return to Asia, I was aghast: I had dreamed of the return to Zion all my life—but not in this way, before the people were prepared, before the land was rid of the spiderwebs that infested it. This notion pleased me when it was but a fantasy, a private dream, but when I saw it activated, I was shocked and dismayed and said: Woe unto us if the Lovers of Zion don't succeed, and woe unto us if they do! Then I wrote my two articles, "Our Redemption and Spiritual Salvation" and "Aid and Ezra," in which I expressed my view that emigration to Palestine is superior to emigration to America only if we improve ourselves and prepare the next generation in such a way that the redemption of our spirits would precede the liberation of our land. When I elaborated these thoughts, Lilienblum—the most extreme of the Lovers of Zion—argued against me by saying "Don't confuse the issues," that redemption and spiritual salvation are two separate issues, that physical redemption must come first and then spiritual salvation will follow naturally. I did not agree with him and didn't trust his promise, but what could I do? I decided to keep my mouth shut and my ears open; I was not an opponent of the colonization of Palestine, but neither was I as active in its regard as I, more than they, wanted me to be.[75]

The Lovers of Zion did not truly understand my point of view and proclaimed that I was an "enemy of Zion" and a nonnationalist. The first to denounce me in this way was Lilienblum, who, in his review of my collected poems, declared that not one of my poems called on the Jews to return to their land. But this was preposterous, since all of my poems were written before the pogroms, when the idea of the return to Zion was buried in the minds and hearts of either believers or dreamers and the time had not come to give it life. In 1883, when I went to the baths at Marienbad, I stopped in my hometown, Vilna, and was met by the local Lovers of Zion, who berated me for being an opponent of the colonization of the Land of Israel. I explained to them, as above, that I was not an "enemy of Zion," that I loved Zion but was silent in my love for want of knowing what to say, since I did not believe in perfect faith in the possibility of the return and was not satisfied by the way in which it was organized. They answered that for a person like me, silence was tantamount to opposition and that it is impossible to fight two battles at once; therefore, they said, it is vital to implant in the people the love of Zion so that they could rise from their slumber and act.

I decided then to take part in this effort, first in secret and then perhaps in public, if it turned out that the labors of the Lovers of Zion were not in vain. In Marienbad I convinced Kalonymous Visotsky to become a Lover of Zion and also discussed the matter with Baron Gunzburg, who told me that from Marienbad he was going to Paris, where he would consult with Rothchild and would do whatever Rothchild did. Gunzburg didn't keep his promise, and I did not raise the matter with him again.

When I returned to edit *Ha-Meliz* in 1885, I frequently spoke positively about the settlement of the Holy Land and informed readers who were secure in the Diaspora about the needs of our brethren in Palestine—and I did all this without any ulterior motive, with no expectation of compensation, contrary to what my accusers say, for *Ha-Meliz* was entirely under my control, and if I had wanted to oppose the colonies no one could have withheld my wages. I should add that in the last issue of 1885, I explained in my feuilleton my thoughts on the issue of nationalism, which was then confounding our writers. I distinguished between different kinds of nationalism, between the pure, refined nationalism in which I believe and the foul and impure nationalism of the yeshivah students and their supporters. From all of this, you and your friends can conclude that there is no truth to the claims of my accusers that I changed my mind at all, or especially not that I changed my mind because of money. Those who at first thought me an opponent of the Palestinian colonization were wrong, and those who consider me a fanatic Palestinophile are wrong too. Now, as then, I try to stay attuned to events, to what the hour demands, and what is of use to the Jews I support as much as is in my power.[76]

Finally, Gordon wrote, two other things are claimed by those who accuse me of moving from one extreme to the other. The first regards my relations with Zederbaum. It is an open secret that I wrote the pamphlet against Zederbaum and gave it to be published to the very same Frischmann, who now considers me deceitful for working with Zederbaum after saying all those nasty things against him. But everyone knows that precisely the opposite is true, that Zederbaum hired me even though he knew that I had written the pamphlet and indeed planned to write another one, detailing even more graphically his crookedness and inability to run a newspaper. I did not change to suit him, but he changed because of me, which is a much greater accomplishment. Frischmann also accuses me of cosying up to the rabbis after I have fought them all my life; that is a libel, pure and simple, as anyone can see from my recent articles.

This, Gordon concluded, is what I wanted you to know, so that you could understand me. You may show this letter to Sokolov to convince him of my innocence as well, but "you are not permitted to publish this letter or any part of it until thirty days after my death. I remain your trusted friend until thirty days before you can publish these words."[77]

In retrospect, with access to his published writings and correspondence through the years, it appears that in this torturously defensive letter Gordon was being only slightly disingenuous in representing himself as more consistent in regard to the return to Zion than he actually had been. But apart from some small factual details, this letter did not contain much that was new or revealing about Gordon's views on nationalism and Zionism but merely summed them up in tones both wistful and dolorous. When Bernfeld finally did publish this epistle—not thirty days, but two years after Gordon's death, in 1894—once more a storm of controversy was unleashed over Gordon's views, this time led by Orthodox opponents of the Lovers of Zion who used Gordon's words as evidence that the movement as a whole was antitraditionalist and by those who refuted his claims that it was he who converted Visotsky to Zionism[78]

In January 1888, to be sure, Gordon had no inkling that the epistle would be printed in the not-too-distant future. But he would soon know that on one issue raised in the letter to Bernfeld he had most certainly been wrong: he had not turned Alexander Zederbaum into a publisher to his liking. Within nine months, the two would once again have a tumultuous falling-out that resulted in Gordon's quitting *Ha-Meliz,* and Jewish journalism, for good. Deprived of his mouthpiece and his public role, Gordon would once more, and now without cease, hover on the brink of disillusionment and despair.

12

Conclusion
1888–1892

On September 1, 1988, Judah Leib Gordon resigned as editor of *Ha-Meliz* for the second and last time. Issuing a daily newspaper in Hebrew had severely drained his health, but the primary cause of his departure was his ongoing fury at Alexander Zederbaum. At the end of August, the publisher had set out on a trip to Istanbul to investigate the Ottoman authorities' closing of Palestine to Jewish immigration, and had left *Ha-Meliz* in the hands not of Gordon, the editor, but of a minor assistant. Incensed and repelled by this snub, Gordon summarily resigned from the newspaper and refused even to read Zederbaum's frantic cables begging him to reconsider.[1]

By now Gordon was convinced, once and for all, not only that Jewish journalism in Russia was at a dead end but also that all his travails, and those of his comrades-in-arms, had been traduced by a conspiracy of malevolence and charlatanry. The Russian government had finally and utterly discredited itself in his eyes by introducing strict Jewish quotas in educational institutions and by expelling Jews from important positions in the legal profession and civil service. The Jewish intelligentsia was bankrupt, in his view, split between nationalists urging the Jews back to the ghetto and assimilationists oblivious to their people's needs. Even the debate over Palestine was now at a standstill, as the Love of Zion movement languished in desuetude and inactivity.

To friends and correspondents Gordon bemoaned his overwhelming feelings of lassitude and dejection. He considered returning to Vilna for a period of rest and spiritual refreshment, but felt too weak to make the trip.[2] To a young author using the pen name Sholem Aleichem, Gordon wrote a series of letters, at once warm and despondent, epitomizing his state of mind at the time. Praising the young writer's talents but bemoaning his decision to dedicate himself to a Jewish cultural renaissance in Yiddish, Gordon wrote (in Russian as well as Hebrew): You master the Russian and Hebrew languages, how can you then devote yourself to creating a culture in our wretched dialect? If your muse expresses itself only in Yiddish, go on and indulge yourself, but it would be sinful if you would decide to raise your children in that tongue. That would be like forcing them to promenade down Nev-sky Prospect in tattered rags and worn-out shoes. Indeed, the very effort to revive Yiddish as a language of art and culture is but "an ugly symptom of the spread of reaction among us," a repudiation of the efforts of the last two or three generations to enlighten the Jews of Eastern Europe.[3]

On the personal level, as well, Gordon confronted even greater misery than before, in a most unseemly denouement of his long-lived clash with Alexander Zed-erbaum. When Gordon resigned from *Ha-Meliz*, the first part of a new collection of his short stories had already been printed on the paper's presses in order to be sent to its contributors as a holiday bonus. After Zederbaum returned to St. Peters-burg from his travels, he advised his readers that they would not suffer in the least from Gordon's departure, except that they would not receive the promised collec-tion of his short stories, since he had reneged on his commitment to deliver the rest of his work to *Ha-Meliz*. In a furious open letter Gordon refuted this charge, claiming that the agreement about the stories had lapsed with his resignation from the paper. Zederbaum retorted by charging Gordon with financial dishonesty and intellectual fraud. As Gordon had predicted years earlier, Zederbaum now accused the famous poet and ideologue of the Enlightenment of selling his soul for lucre, of reversing his previous opposition to the Love of Zion movement in order to keep his job at *Ha-Meliz*. Enraged, Gordon lashed out in a brutal diatribe against Zed-erbaum that not only denied this accusation but also detailed, over nine lengthy installments in a Warsaw Hebrew journal, Zederbaum's pitiful ignorance of Hebrew, his intellectual buffoonery, and his fraudulent financial chicaneries. Zed-erbaum, for his part, responded in an equally long and scabrous series of articles repeating his denunciation of Gordon. So unpleasant was this public fracas that a group of Odessa Hebrew writers issued a public call for its cessation, as an ugly embarrassment to the Jewish literary world.[4]

By late 1889, then, Gordon had descended into an all but interminable malaise. Having severed his ties to the organized world of the Jewish intelligentsia in Russia, he was faced now with no spiritual succor and no steady income. Rather gratefully, he took up an offer made to him by a longtime supporter, the publisher Ilia Efron, who, together with the famous Brockhaus firm of Leipzig, had recently begun work on a Russian version of the classic Brockhaus encyclopedia. Gordon was entrusted with much of the administrative work of the *Entsiklopedicheskii slovar'*, and with editing the articles on matters of Jewish import.[5] To intimates in Russia and abroad he poured out his soul in eloquent descriptions of his hopelessness and wrath. Don't try to convince me to return to the battlefield of Jewish politics, he declared, for the war is lost, the cause betrayed, the illness incurable. Never will I write in Hebrew again, he told many friends; now I shall write only from left to right.[6]

For the next year, Gordon worked on the Russian encyclopedia and steadfastly maintained his self-imposed estrangement from Hebrew journalism and Jewish public affairs. Throughout all of 1890, his total output in Hebrew was but a handful of private letters and one short dedicatory poem. By the middle of the next year, however, he was forced to rethink this voluntary retirement, as he faced the gravest personal crisis of his life, a persistent intestinal ailment that failed to respond to medical treatment. When several physicians advised him that surgery was needed, though perhaps too late to help, he traveled to Berlin for an operation by a renowned surgeon. After a month's recuperation in the German capital, he returned to St. Petersburg with the knowledge that the surgery had not succeeded in stemming the spread of what was by now recognized as cancer. When he was strong enough to leave his bed, he returned to work at the encyclopedia but found little there to occupy him and less solace, for the project had advanced well beyond its initial phase and required little of his talents, as even the Judaica articles were being handed over to a new sort of expert, the university-trained scholar.

In the past Gordon would have responded to this last rebuff with venom and rage. Now, recognizing that his days were numbered, he retreated into quiet resignation. Sensing that one day the demise of his life and his era would be of interest to historians, he began, after the lapse of many years, to keep a diary and to record some memoirs of his youth and days of glory. He even tried his hand again at writing Hebrew poetry, producing some unusually modest verses, including one poem in favor of emigration to America that once again provoked much criticism and anger on the part of the Lovers of Zion. At the same time, he briefly toyed with the idea of collaborating in the publication of a new Hebrew journal supporting the colonists in the Holy Land. In his journal, day after day, he mulled over the strange fate of the Jews in Russia and abroad, repeating the litany of his lifelong faith. "Why can't a Jew be a man like all men, and a lover of Zion a lover of the world?" he asked himself once more, convinced to the end that his hoped-for synthesis was possible.[7]

To the minor Hebrew poet M. M. Dolitsky, who had been among the Jews recently expelled from Moscow and was now on his way to a new life in America, Gordon wrote, in mid-July 1892, what would turn out to be his last poem:

> Why do you weep, poor wanderer, why do you wail,
> On leaving a land that has ejected you from its midst?
> I, too, am leaving a land
> Which has rejected me, but my soul is at peace. . . .
>
> You go on your way, to life—go and do battle,
> Here on my bed I shall end my fight.
> And you and I shall both not regret
> The dreams that you will dream and that I dreamed in my day.
>
> It was not false hopes that I saw in my dreams
> And neither will you be deceived by lies;
> Therefore, like me, do not fear the grave:
> Here is my pen, arise and take my place![8]

Less than two months after completing this poem, on September 4, 1892, Judah Leib Gordon succumbed to cancer at the age of sixty-two.

His funeral, held two days later, was a grand affair for the Jews of the Russian capital. As *Ha-Meliz* recorded in great detail (not mentioning, of course, its recent attacks on the deceased), a large crowd gathered to accompany Gordon to his eternal rest with great dignity, and many wreaths of flowers were strewn on his coffin, which was preceded along its way by the cantor and choir of the main synagogue of St. Petersburg. At the cemetery, eulogies were delivered in Hebrew, Russian, and German and telegrams were read from admirers in Vilna, Minsk, Riga, Moscow, and Odessa. Memorial meetings were held later in many of these cities, with the commemoration in Gordon's hometown being perhaps the most fitting. In the synagogue of the Vilna Jewish intelligentsia, which was the closest thing in the Pale to a "liberal" house of worship, a substantial crowd gathered to mourn its departed native son. As was the case at other such gatherings, Gordon was lionized in Russian and in Hebrew as the greatest Hebrew poet of the nineteenth century; only in Vilna, however, did the cantor intone his prayers for the eternal rest of the soul of the deceased to the accompaniment of an organ, recently installed to modernize this "dignified" house of worship. The honoree doubtless would have approved.[9]

Almost immediately after Gordon's death, Hebrew authors, critics, and litterateurs began to debate his poetic legacy. For decades thereafter, in Odessa and St. Petersburg, in Berlin and Vienna, in Jerusalem and Tel Aviv, the arguments raged and the tempers flared. Was Gordon a literary genius or a hack? A brilliant lyricist or but a clever publicist? A poetic innovator or merely a talented philologist? The deliberations over Gordon's place in the pantheon of Hebrew creativity followed all the tortuous twists and turns of Jewish literary and cultural politics in the twentieth century, as each generation read Gordon's verses through the new aesthetic and ideological filters of its age.[10]

Similarly, in the years after his death devotees of virtually every Jewish political movement in Eastern Europe, and later in Palestine, invoked Gordon's heritage, even while summarily rejecting the essential articles of his severed faith. Jewish socialists, Revisionist Zionists, and Labor Zionists all insisted that Gordon would have sympathized with their mutually antagonistic causes.[11]

More justifiably, Gordon's legacy has been linked to one of the most influential Russian-Jewish thinkers in the next generation, 'Ahad Ha'am, who himself noted his debt to Gordon in his famous essays arguing against the mainstream of the Zionism movement. But Gordon was not simply, or even essentially, a precursor of Cultural Zionism. Gordon's personal religious beliefs were by no means so radical or agnostic as those of his younger colleague and, as has been demonstrated above, Gordon viscerally rejected the alpha and omega of 'Ahad Ha'am's intellectual enterprise, the application of the rhetoric of modern European nationalism to the Jewish case. Most fundamental, Gordon's enthusiastic and undying commitment to the Western model of acculturation and emancipation was profoundly at odds with 'Ahad Ha'am's basic political premise, that Western European Jewry was marked by "slavery within freedom." Nonetheless, of course, there were broad lines of continuity between 'Ahad Ha'am's immensely influential critique of Herzlian Zionism and Gordon's earlier arguments regarding the Love of Zion. More subtly, in addition, it may well be that through the intermediacy of 'Ahad Ha'am, Gordon's objections to the statist aspirations of modern Jewish nationalism continued to be espoused by a small stream of intellectuals within (if often at the margins of) the Zionist movement who were committed to a liberal religious sensibility—men such as Judah Magnes.[12]

At the same time, outside the Zionist camp followers of Simon Dubnov's Diaspora Nationalism and the Jewish members of the Russian Constitutional-Democratic party repeated Gordon's insistence on the twinning of Jewish emancipation and the victory of Russian liberalism, even as they abandoned his belief in the centrality of Hebrew culture to Jewish life.

More broadly, if far more elusively, it can be argued that Gordon's views on the type of religious reform necessary for and appropriate to East European Jews were far more prescient than those of his opponents. Not, to be sure, that any such religious revolution occurred in Russia proper; that was far from possible, given the political and cultural climate that prevailed. But the religious profile ultimately embraced by the majority of Eastern European Jews who emigrated to America— in large measure, the "moderate reform" of the Conservative movement, heir to the Breslau tradition—was precisely the type of synthesis between modernism and tradition preached by Gordon throughout his adult life. At the very least, historians of American Jewry ought to consider the tentative hypothesis that the religious revolution of American Jews was not the product solely of the processes of Americanization and the preachings of a German-Jewish elite, but that there was, for want of a better term, an innate East European approach to the reform of Judaism that was stymied at home by social reality but realizable in conditions of political freedom and cultural pluralism. Such an indigenous East European approach to the reform of Judaism—articulated, for one, by Judah Leib Gordon—was self-consciously moderate in its demands, insisting equally on the primacy of the Talmud, the Hebrew language, and the return to Palestine and on the legitimacy of reconciling Judaism with Western culture, technology, and mores.

In the end, too, it can be argued—as it was at the beginning of this study—that although the Haskalah per se gradually lost its following among the Jewish intelligentsia in Russia and Poland, the quest of Judah Leib Gordon and his colleagues for the religious, educational, and social reform of the Jews did not die out even in Eastern Europe, but continued to dominate the lives of the millions of Jews who straddled the gulf between traditional Judaism and the modern world.

But whether or not the Haskalah was buried along with Judah Leib Gordon, his death surely marked the end of an era. The unique amalgam of Hebrew Enlightenment and liberal politics that was born in Berlin in the mid-eighteenth century and reached its peak in St. Petersburg over a century later could not survive the gloomy morass that confronted the Jews in fin-de-siècle Russia. Gordon's unbridled faith in the cultural, religious, and political rejuvenation of the Jews in the bosom of a humane and liberal Russia gave way to more "realistic" dreams as the crisis of Russian Jewry continued into a new reality and a new century.

Notes

Abbreviations Used in Notes

AZJ *Allgemeine Zeitung des Judentums*
'Igerot Y. Y. Weisberg, *'Igerot Yehudah Leib Gordon,* vols. 1–4 (Warsaw, 1894)
KP *Kitvei Yehudah Leib Gordon: Prozah* (Tel Aviv, 1960)
KS *Kitvei Yehudah Leib Gordon: Shirah* (Tel Aviv, 1956)
Klausner Yosef Klausner, *Historiiah shel ha-sifrut ha-ʿivrit ha-ḥadashah,* vol. 4 (Jerusalem, 1953)

Chapter 1. Introduction

1. "Le-mi 'ani ʿamel," KS 27. All translations from the Hebrew, Russian, Yiddish, and German are by me, unless otherwise noted. In translating the substantial amount of poetry cited in this volume, I have attempted to remain as close to the simple meaning of the original without striving either for literalness or for an approximation of rhyme and meter. Variances in spelling of names occur when transliterating the original languages.

2. See his letter to Y. Y. Weisberg in *'Igerot* 4, 333–335, and to Sh. Bernfeld in *Reshumot* 4 (1926), 374–375.

Chapter 2. From Vilna to Enlightenment

1. Czeslaw Milosz, *Native Realm: A Search for Self-Definition,* trans. Catherine S. Leach (Berkeley, 1981), 92.

2. The following sketch of the Vilna Gaon elaborates on my entry, "Eliyyahu Ben Shelomoh Zalman," in *The Encyclopedia of Religion,* ed. Mircea Eliade (New York and London, 1987), vol. 5, 98–100. For the most recent scholarship on the Gaon, see I. Klausner, *Ha-Ga'on Rabbi 'Eliyahu mi-Vilna* (Jerusalem, 1969); Ḥ. H. Ben Sasson, "'Ishiuto shel ha-Gr"a ve-hashpaʿato ha-historit," *Zion* 31 (1966), 39–86, 197–216; I. Etkes, "Ha-Gra"a ve-ha-haskalah: tadmit u-meẓi'ut," *Perakim be-toledot ha-ḥevrah ha-yehudit bi-yemei ha-beinayim u-vaʿet ha-ḥadashah, mukdashim le-Prof. Yaʿakov Katz* (Jerusalem, 1980), 192–217.

3. Louis Ginzberg, *Students, Scholars and Saints* (Philadelphia, 1928), 135.

4. The sources on the Gaon's opposition to Hasidim are collected in Mordekhai Wilensky, *Ḥasidim u-mitnagdim,* 2 vols. (Jerusalem, 1970).

5. I. Etkes, *R' Yisra'el Salanter ve-reshitah shel tenuʿat ha-musar* (Jerusalem, 1982), 65; Gedalyahu Alon, "The Lithuanian Yeshivas," trans. by S. Leiman in *The Jewish Expression,* ed. Judah Goldin (New York, 1970), 448–464; and Shaul Stampfer, "Shalosh yeshivot lit'aiyot ba-me'ah ha-19," unpub. Ph.D. dissertation, The Hebrew University of Jerusalem, 1981.

6. See my *Tsar Nicholas I and the Jews: The Transformation of Jewish Society in Russia, 1825–1855* (Philadelphia, 1983), 49–96.

7. The following biographical information is based, unless specifically noted, on Gordon's own account in his partial memoirs "ʿAl nehar kevar," in KP 277–290.

8. See his note in KP 289.

9. This scene is described in the introduction to his Russian memoir of his arrest, "Tiurma i ssylka," first published in *Perezhitoe* 4 (1913), 1–45, translated into Hebrew in KP 291–308.

10. See his caustic comments in his additions to his memoirs, KP 347.

11. For example, see Klausner, which is invaluable for its biographical and bibliographical information; and, in English, the charming if dated work by Shalom Spiegel, *Hebrew Reborn* (New York, 1930).

12. *Tsar Nicholas I and the Jews,* 97.

13. See the hitherto unpublished letter of Mikhl Gordon, written on July 3, 1868, in manuscript in the Judah Leib Gordon Archive, National and University Library, Hebrew University of Jerusalem, File 4°761, letter 2.

14. KP 274–275, 347–348.

15. KP 277.

16. Letter to A. B. Luria, *'Igerot* 1, 82.

17. See my *Tsar Nicholas I and the Jews,* 97–122.

18. See below, chapter 10.

19. "Ha-'Ahavah," reprinted in *Shirei Mikha"l* (Tel Aviv, 1954), 203–206.

20. See Dan Miron, "Rediscovering Haskalah Poetry," *Prooftexts* 1 (1981), 297–298.

21. Letter to Shneur Sachs, reprinted in ibid., 253–255.

22. KS 317.

23. See, especially, his story "Keviẓat ha-derekh," reprinted in KP 141–158.

24. Letter to Miriam Markel-Mazessohn, March 6, 1871, *Ha-ʿOlam* 25 (1936), No.4, 71.

25. "ʿAl korḥakha 'atah ḥai," KS 12.

26. *Entsiklopedicheskii slovar',* vol. 24a, 525–526; *Evreiskaia entsiklopediia,* vol. 12, 739; *Encyclopedia Lithuanica,* vol. 4, 176–178.

27. On the dowry, see Klausner 317; the poem in memory of his father-in-law is "Hah, ki ne'esaf 'ish ha-ḥesed," KS 304

28. Shaul Ginzberg, *Historishe verk,* vol.1 (New York, 1937), 130.

29. "'Aḥarei mot," KS 313–314.

30. "Hoi 'aḥ!" KS 321.

31. KS 322.

32. KS 324–325.

Chapter 3. The Beginnings of a Career

1. See *Tsar Nicholas I and the Jews,* 183–188.

2. The best survey of Russian-Jewish history in this period is Iulii Gessen, *Istoriia evreiskogo naroda v Rossii,* vol. 2 (Leningrad, 1927).

3. Jacob S. Raisin, *The Haskalah Movement in Russia* (Philadelphia, 1913), 11.

4. For differing interpretations of the pre-1855 Haskalah, see Israel Zinberg, *History of Jewish Literature,* trans. and ed. Bernard Martin (Cincinnati, 1978), vols. 11 and 12, and my *Tsar Nicholas I and the Jews,* 109–122.

5. Paul Miliukov et al., *History of Russia* (New York, 1969), vol. 3, 6.

6. The details on Gordon's family are from his official police record preserved in the Shaul Ginzburg Archives, Manuscript Division, The Hebrew University of Jerusalem, $4^0$1281 A, file 20/5. Interestingly, however, the dates of the births of his children do not always correspond to the more accurate dates given in his correspondence. On Gordon as secretary of the Jewish community of Ponevezh, see the report on a fire there signed by him in *Ha-Maggid* 2 (1858), No. 32, 127–128.

7. "'Adonai 'al mayim rabim," attributed to 1855, KS 10.

8. "David u-Varzillai," KS 95–98.

9. Reprinted in KS 53–87.

10. KS 53–54.

11. For a formidable recent analysis of this work, see Dan Miron,"Bein takdim le-mikreh—shirato ha-'epit shel Y"L Gordon u-mekomah be-sifrut ha-haskalah ha-'ivrit," *Meḥkarei Yerushalayim be-sifrut 'ivrit* 2 (1983), 154–185.

12. See below, chapter 7.

13. KS 63.

14. KS 91.

15. Y. Ḥ. Brenner, "'Azkarah le-Yalag," in *Kol Kitvei Y. Ḥ. Brenner,* vol. 7 (Tel Aviv, 1928), 137.

16. AZJ 22 (1858), No. 6, 76.

17. Ibid., 77.

18. See his letter reprinted in *Ha-Maggid* 2 (1858), No. 39, addendum 1.

19. Judah Leib Gordon Archives, Letteris File, Letters No. 1, 7, 9.

20. "Me-'erez Lit'a," *Ha-Maggid* 1 (1857), No. 36, 42.

21. On the history of this claim and debate, see Jacob Katz, *Out of the Ghetto* (Cambridge, Mass., 1973).

22. "Divrei shalom ve-'emet," *Ha-Maggid* 2 (1858), No. 13, 49–50.

23. The second installment of the article is in ibid, No. 14, 53–54.

24. Ibid., 54.

25. See, for example, Klausner 319.

26. "Kol me-'erez Rusiyah," *Ha-Maggid* 2 (1858), No. 34, 135; No. 35, 138–139; No. 37, 146–147; "Kol 'anot," ibid., No. 43, 171. The apology is in the last article.

27. "Davar yom be-yomo," KP 242.

28. See, for example, his poem "Rabat to'elet hi 'esh okhelet," later called "Ha-be'erah," in *Ha-Maggid* 2 (1858), No. 32, 128.

29. See the introduction to the first edition (Vilna, 1859), xxiv. Thus, the dating of the composition of the fables in Miron, "Bein takdim le-mikreh," 188, is slightly misstated. Gordon's fables have recently been studied in an exhaustive work by Janine Strauss, *Yehudah Leib Gordon, Poète hébreu (1830–1892): Son oeuvre de fabuliste* (Paris, 1980). This work, which devoted over four hundred pages to a detailed analysis of the one hundred fables, is eminently successful in discussing the linguistic and generic aspects of its subject, but less so in regard to the context of the fables and their broader ramifications. As a result, some of the subtler thrusts of Gordon's satire are missed.

30. 'Igerot 1, 55–56.

31. See, for example, the multiple use of this argument in the first major treatise of the Russian Haskalah, Isaac Ber Levinsohn, *Te'udah be-yisr'ael* (Vilna, 1828).

32. 'Igerot 1, 6.

33. Ibid., 14–15.

34. Ibid., 16.

35. Ibid., 17. Incidentally, the fact that this confession of a strategy to evade the Russian censor could be printed in a book that itself passed the approval of a censor in June 1894, during a far more repressive period in Russian and Russian-Jewish history, speaks volumes about the nature of tsarist censorship.

36. "Kab'a me-'ar'ah ve-l'a kor'a me-'igr'a," (Pesaḥim, 113).

37. "Ha-dag ha-katon ve-ha-dayag," KS 193. On Gordon's Judaization of foreign folk material, see the interesting, if somewhat romanticized, essay by Shaul Tchernichovsky, under the pseudonym Ben Gutman, "Gordon be-tor memashel," *Ha-Shiloaḥ* 13 (1904), 244–251.

38. "Ha-akhbarim yaḥdav yamtiku sod," KS 199–200.

39. See the English rendition of "The Boy and the Schoolmaster" in James Michie, trans., *La Fontaine: Selected Fables* (New York, 1979), 26–29.

40. "Ha-na'ar ve-ha-zaken," first edition of *Mishlei Yehudah,* 35–37. In the later version, reprinted in KS 190, Gordon amended the ending to correspond with contemporary developments, changing "Impetuous ones!" to "Reformers of the world!"

41. AZJ 24 (1860), No. 27, 462.

42. AZJ 24 (1860), No. 9, 133.

43. *'Igerot* 1, 64–65.

44. Ibid., 115–116.

45. See, for example, his depressed letter on his twenty-eighty birthday, in Judah Leib Gordon Archives, Letteris file, Letter 62.

46. "Shenei yamin ve-laylah 'eḥad be-malon 'orhim," first published in Odessa in 1870, reprinted in KP 3–16.

47. "'Ereẓ ḥadashah," KS 36–38.

48. "Derekh bat 'ami" was first published in 1861 in the Vienna Hebrew periodical *Kokhvei Yiẓhak,* No. 26, 55–57. At the end of the poem Gordon signed it, in "Poh navi zeh 'asher bi-Lithauen"—"here, in my dwelling place in Lithuania," a pun on Ponevezh. Clearly, since Gordon left Ponevezh in October 1860, this poem must have been written before then. However, in his collected works (KS 18–19), this poem is preceded by the curious comment "Written in 1864–5, and first published in *Kokhvei Yiẓhak* 26." Gordon—or the editor of the collection—had obviously confused matters considerably. The substantial difficulty of dating Gordon's poems correctly cannot be resolved perfectly; I have accepted Gordon's own attributions as accurate unless they are contradicted by clear external evidence, as in this case. If a date of composition cannot be determined, I have based my analysis on the date of publication, clearly noting the difference. Unfortunately, other works on Gordon, even the best among them, do not maintain this distinction and, therefore, frequently confuse the order and development of his works.

49. AZJ 24 (1860), No. 18, 271.

50. AZJ 24 (1860), No. 31, 462–463.

51. On Shavli, see *Entsiklopedicheskii slovar',* vol. 39, 88–90; *Evreiskaia entsiklopediia,* vol. 15, 900–901; *Encyclopedia Lithuanica,* vol. 5, 133–135.

52. *'Igerot* 1, 69.

53. Ibid., 69 and 73–74.

54. AZJ 25 (1861), No. 12, 168–170.

55. Ibid, 169–170.

56. AZJ 25 (1861), No. 11, 153.

57. AZJ 25 (1861), No. 13, 185; *Ha-Meliẓ* 1 (1861), No. 26, 461–462; *Razsvet* 1 (1861), No. 44, 702.

58. *Raszvet,* loc. cit.

59. See his reconstruction of these events in his memoirs reproduced in KP 309–311.

60. *Razsvet,* loc. cit.

Chapter 4. "Awake, My People!"

1. See his letter of April 20, 1860, published in *Razsvet* 1 (1861), No. 52, 831.

2. *'Igerot* 1, 74.

3. Ibid.

4. On *Razsvet,* see S. L. Tsinberg, *Istoriia evreiskoi pechati v Rossii* (Petrograd, 1915), 29–61; Moshe Perlmann, "*Razsvet* 1860–1861, the Origins of the Russian-Jewish Press," *Jewish Social Studies* 24 (1962), 162–182; idem, "Notes on *Razsvet* 1860–61." *Proceedings of the American Academy for Jewish Research,* 33 (1965), 21–50; and Alexander Orbach, *New Voices of Russian Jewry* (Leiden, 1980), 22–42.

5. See note to "'Al d'a b'a bakhin'a!," KS 289.

6. Ibid.

7. "Drevne-evreiskii iazyk u russkikh evreev," *Sion* 2 (1861), No. 17, 265–269.

8. Ibid., 267.

9. "'Al har Zion she-shamem," KS 11–12.

10. KS 17–18.

11. For examples of this interpretation, and for fascinating, if idiosyncratic, musings on Gordon's line, see Dov Sadan, *Be-z'etkha u-ve-'ohalekha* (Israel, 1966), 9–50.

12. See below, chapter 11.

13. "'Erez Bavel ha-'atikah ve-hahameha," *Ha-Zefirah* 1 (1862), No. 21, 23, 24, reprinted in fuller version in *Ha-Shahar* 2 (1870), 241–260; "O znachenie nekotorykh imen' sobstvennykh v Talmuda," *Sion* 2 (1862), No. 40, 628–629.

14. *'Igerot* 1, 83.

15. Ibid., 76.

16. On the Polish Uprising of 1863, see, most recently, Norman Davies, *God's Playground* (New York, 1982), vol. 2, 347–368, and Piotr Wandycz, *The Lands of Partitioned Poland* (Seattle, 1974), 155–179.

17. AZJ 27 (1863), No. 46, 714–716.

18. Ibid., 715.

19. Ibid. Compare this argument with the approach taken by Gordon himself in a speech he made on Coronation Day in Shavli, as reported in the correspondence from Shavli in *Russkii invalid* 50 (1863), No. 199, 853. Obviously, under these circumstances Gordon could not express himself so freely as he did on the pages of the *Allgemeine Zeitung.*

20. Ibid., 716.

21. Ibid.

22. *'Igerot* 1, 90.

23. Y. L. Rosenthal, *Toledot hevrat marbei haskalah be-yisra'el be-'erez Rusiyah* (St. Petersburg, 1890), 24–26.

24. KS 12–15; V. A. Zhukovskii, *Izbrannoe* (Leningrad, 1973), 31–35. On Zhukovskii's elegy, see Irina M. Semenko, *Vasily Zhukovsky, Life and Work* (Boston, 1976), 17–19.

25. Thomas Gray, "Elegy Written in a Country Churchyard," *The Poems of Thomas Gray* (London, 1937), 73–74.

26. KS 13–14.

27. *'Igerot* 1, 102–103.

28. See below, chapter 6.

29. KS, unpaginated introduction.

30. Klausner 333–334.

31. *Shirei Yehudah* (Vilna, 1868), vii–viii.

32. Ibid.

33. On Kovner, see Klausner 139–175 and the curious biography by Max Weinreich, *Fun beyde zaytn ployt* (Buenos Aires, 1955).

34. *'Igerot* 1, 100–101.

35. *Ḥeker davar* (Vilna, 1865), 11.

36. *'Igerot* 1, 100.

37. Letter reproduced in Yiddish translation by Weinreich, 218–220.

38. Miron, "Bein takdim le-mikreh," 129.

39. Cited in Isaiah Berlin, *Russian Thinkers* (New York, 1978), 150.

40. V. Belinskii, "Pis'mo k N.V. Gogoliu," in his *Stat'i i retsenzii* Moscow, 1971), 438–447. I follow here the rendering by Sir Isaiah Berlin in his well-known article cited above, 172–173.

41. See, for example, the introduction to the Soviet edition of Belinsky's critical works cited in note 39, Mark Poliakov, "Podvizhnik russkoi literatury," 5–19.

42. Berlin, 160–182; Andrzej Walicki, *A History of Russian Thought* (Stanford, 1979), esp. 139–142.

43. Berlin, 179–180.

44. KS 87–94.

45. Gittin 57b. I have followed here the translation by Maurice Simon in the Soncino Talmud (London, 1936).

46. "Bein shinei 'arayot," *Shirei Yehudah,* 1–2.

47. Ibid., 10.

48. Miron, "Rediscovering Haskalah Poetry," 300. Uncharacteristically, however, Miron in this article did not mark the important differences between the early and later versions of this poem, thus calling into question some of his major conclusions and characterizations of the development of Gordon's verse.

49. KS 103–107.

50. *Shirei Yehudah,* 23.

51. *Shirei Yehudah,* 23–24.

52. See Louis Ginzberg, *Legends of the Jews* (New York, 1928), vol. 4, 43–47, and vol. 6, 202–204.

53. Ibid., 24.

54. "Ha-'ishah vi-yladeha," ibid., 62–67.

55. Ibid., 62.

56. *The Second Book of Maccabees,* trans. S. Tedesche, ed. Solomon Zeitlin (New York, 1954), 169, Gittin 57b. See the fascinating study by Gerson David Cohen, "Maʿaseh Ḥannah ve-shivʿat baneha be-sifrut ha-ʿivrit," *Sefer ha-yovel li-khvod Mordekhai Menaḥem Kaplan,* Hebrew volume (New York, 1953), 109–122.

57. *Shirei Yehudah,* 67.

Chapter 5. Religious Reform I

1. *Entsiklopedicheskii slovar',* vol. 32A, 826–827; *Encyclopedia Lithuanica,* vol. 5, 389–390; *Evreiskaia entsiklopediia,* vol. 14, 795.

2. *'Igerot* 1, 103.

3. *Ha-Karmel* 5 (1866), No. 48, 308.

4. *Kol Mevasser* 6 (1866), No. 11, 171–173, mispaginated in the original.

5. Ibid.

6. There is no scholarly study of Gordon's Yiddish verses. For a recent journalistic appraisal, see Ḥayim 'Orlan, "Yalag ke-meshorer be-yidish," ʿ*Al ha-mishmar* January 15, 1982, 7. I am grateful to Dr. Jacob Kabakoff for this reference.

7. *Ha-Karmel* 6 (1866), No. 1, 1.

8. *Ha-Karmel* 6 (1866), No. 5, 33.

9. Ibid.

10. Ibid., 34.

11. Ibid.

12. See below, chapter 10.

13. *Ha-Karmel* 6 (1866), No. 14, 106.

14. Ibid.

15. *Ha-Karmel* 6 (1866), No. 11, 83–84.

16. *Ha-Karmel* 6 (1866), No. 14, 109.

17. "Rashei ʿam-ha-ʾarez," *Ha-Karmel* 6 (1866), No. 17, 129.

18. *Russkoe prilozhenie k "Ga-Karmel,"* 6 (1866), No. 28, 121–122.

19. Ibid., 122.

20. *Ha-Karmel* 6 (1866), No. 33, 257–258.

21. *ʾIgerot* 1, 106.

22. The first edition bears the censor's stamp from May 31, 1867, and the year of publication of 1868.

23. KP 142–145, attributed by Gordon to Nissan 1867; first published in *Ha-Shaḥar* 2 (1870), 164–168.

24. Gittin 57a.

25. KS 142–143.

26. Ibid., 145.

27. *ʾIgerot* 1, 108–109.

28. See my *Tsar Nicholas I and the Jews,* ch. 4 and 5.

29. *ʾIgerot* 1, 108.

30. On Zederbaum, see the works cited by Tsinberg and Orbach, passim. As is well known, Zederbaum was the grandfather of Iulii Martov, the leader of the Mensheviks. See Israel Getzler, *Martov: A Political Biography of a Russian Social Democrat* (Cambridge, England and Melbourne, 1967).

31. *ʾIgerot* 1, 111–112; see also the unpublished letters from Zederbaum to Gordon in the Gordon Archive, National and University Library, Jerusalem.

32. Ibid.

33. "Der kolisher indik," reprinted in *Sikhes khulin* (Vilna 1899), 62.

34. "ʾAḥarit simḥah tugah," KP 17–77.

35. Klausner 447–448. For a recent analysis, see Israel Bartal, "Ha-lʾo yehudim ve-ḥevratam be-sifrut ʿivrit ve-yidish be-mizraḥ ʾeiropah bein ha-shanim 1856–1914," unpub. Ph.D. dissertation, The Hebrew University of Jerusalem, 1980, 18–23.

36. KP 63.

Chapter 6. Religious Reform II

1. *ʾIgerot* 1, 134 and 163, and his letters to Miriam Markel-Mazessohn, reprinted in *Ha-ʿOlam* 24 (1936) No. 38, 656; No. 40–41, 707; *Ha-ʿOlam* 25 (1936), No. 1, 15.

2. *Ha-Karmel* 7 (1869), No. 41, 309–310, and *Ha-Maggid* 12 (1869), supplement, 20–21.

3. A. B. Ehrlich in *Ha-Maggid* 12 (1868), No. 28, 223; No. 29, 231; No. 30, 247–248; Z. H. Jonathansohn in *Ha-Meliz* 8 (1868), No. 6, 48.

4. "Ve-samaḥta be-ḥagekha," KS 145–148, first published in *Ha-Shaḥar* 2 (1870), 197–202; "Paḥad ba-laylah," *Ha-Meliz* 9 (1869), No. 45, 318–320.

5. *Ha-Maggid* 12 (1869), No. 37, 295.

6. On Brafman, see Shaul Ginzburg, *Meshumodim in tsarishn Rusland* (New York, 1946), 65–79.

7. Ibid.

8. "Evreiskie bratsva," *Den'* 1 (1869), No. 27, 433–436; No. 28, 452–454. Gordon referred to this piece in *ʾIgerot* 1, 144, and in his memoirs in KP 311.

9. See below, chapter 9.

10. *Den'* 1 (1869), No. 27, 435.

11. Ibid. See also below, chapter 10.

12. Ibid., No. 28, 454.

13. See his letters to Miriam Markel-Mazessohn, *Ha-ʿOlam* 24 (1936), No. 36, 621, and No. 37, 638.

14. David Philipson, *The Reform Movement in Judaism* (New York, 1931), 284–328; Michael A. Meyer, "Ha-sinodim ha-yehudiim be-Germaniah ba-maḥazit ha-sheniiah shel ha-meʾah ha-teshʿa-ʿesreh," *Meḥkarim be-toledot ʿam yisraʾel ve-ʾerez yisraʾel* 3 (1974), 239–274.

15. *Hatʾot neʿurim,* reprinted in M. L. Lilienblum, *Ketavim ʾotobiografiim* (Jerusalem, 1970), vols. 1 and 2.

16. *Ha-Meliz* 8 (1868), No. 13, 16, 18, 21, 24, 25, 27, 29.

17. *Ha-Meliz* 9 (1869), No. 8–12.

18. Ibid., No. 9, 68.

19. Ibid., No. 12, 91.

20. On *He-Ḥaluz,* see Klausner 56–105.

21. On Lilienblum, see Klausner 190–300.

22. *Ha-Levanon* 6 (1869), especially No. 20–24, 31–49, each of which contains at least one, and often two, articles attacking Lilienblum. See, too, Yaʿakov Halevi Lifshiz, *Zikhron Yaʿakov* (Kovno, 1924), vol. 2, 72–116.

23. Lifshiz, op. cit. The only scholarly work to deal with this controversy in any detail in not very satisfactory: Gideon Kazenelson, *Ha-milḥamah ha-sifrutit bein ha-ḥaredim ve-ha-maskilim* (Tel Aviv, 1954).

24. This correspondence was published in an excellent edition by Shlomo Breiman, *'Igerot M. L. Lilienblum le-Y. L. Gordon* (Jerusalem, 1968).

25. See ibid., 76–82.

26. "Be-zekhutan shel ha-rabanim," *Ha-Meliz* 9 (1869), No. 47, 328–329.

27. Ibid.

28. "Be-zekhutan shel ha-rabanim, maʿaneh le-Daniel Bagar," *Ha-Levanon* 7 (1870), No. 4, 25–27, and No. 5, 33–35.

29. *'Igerot* 1, 147.

30. Lifshiz, 106.

31. See below, chapter 7.

32. *'Igerot* 1, 147.

33. Ibid., 148.

34. Ibid., 144.

35. Ibid., 154–155.

36. Ibid., 157, where "foi" is spelled "fois." It is unclear whether the error was made by Gordon or by the editor of his letters.

37. "Binah le-toʿei ruaḥ," *Ha-Meliz* 10 (1870), No. 30, 224–225; No. 31, 233–235; No. 32, 239–241; No. 33, 251–225; No. 35, 267–268; No. 36; 273–275; No. 39, 288–289; No. 41, 305–306; No. 42, 313–314.

38. Ibid., 233.

39. Ibid., 240.

40. Ibid., 252.

41. Ibid., 234.

42. Ibid., 289.

43. *Ha-Shahar* 2 (1870–1), 154–156; reproduced in *'Igerot* 2, 172–174.

44. Ibid.

45. See, for example, Klausner, 346–349.

46. David Gordon, "Davar be-ʿito," *Ha-Maggid* 12 (1869), No. 27–33.

47. See below, chapters 9 and 10.

48. See Ismar Schorsch, "Zacharias Frankel and the European Origins of Conservative Judaism," *Judaism* 30 (1981), 344–354.

49. See the relevant texts in Rivkah Horowitz, *Zekhariah Frankel ve-reshit ha-yahadut ha-pozitivit historit* (Jerusalem, 1984), 111–122; for a Zionist reading of these texts, see idem, "Raʿayon ʿazmaʾut ha-yehudim be-ʾereẓ-yisraeʾl le-R' Zekhariah Frankel bi-shenat 1842," *Kivunim* 6 (1980), 5–25.

50. See below, chapter 7.

51. *'Igerot* 1, 155–156.

52. First published in *Ha-Shaḥar* 2 (1870–1), No. 8, 353–354.

53. See, for example, the classic statement by Shalom Spiegel, *Hebrew Reborn* (Cleveland, 1962), 186–187.

Chapter 7. St. Petersburg: Culture and Politics

1. See Sidney Monas, "The Dream of the Suffering Horse," afterword to Fyodor Dostoyevsky, *Crime and Punishment* (New York, 1968), 537–538.

2. For the best review of the demographic dynamics of Russian Jewry in the nineteenth century, see Simon Kuznets, "Immigration of Russian Jews to the United States: Background and Structure," *Perspectives in American History* 9 (1975), 35–124.

3. Jacob Lestchinsky, *Dos yidishe folk in tsifern* (Berlin, 1922), 73–75.

4. For the best available description of Jewish St. Petersburg, see Shaul Ginzburg, *Amolike Peterburg* (New York, 1944); Iulii Gessen, "Sankt Petersburg," *Evreiskaia entsiklopediia*, vol. 13, 936–950; and Judah Leib Gordon's own history of the community, "K istorii poseleniia evreev v Peterburge," *Voskhod* 1 (1881), No. 1, 111–123, and No. 2, 29–47.

5. There is as yet no reliable scholarly work on the Gunzburg family. The most substantive information can be gleaned, inter alia, from the following works: *Evreiskaia entsiklopediia* (St. Petersburgh, n.d.), vol. 6 525–534; Henri Sliosberg, *Baron Horace O. de Gunzbourg, sa vie et son oeuvre* (Paris, 1935); David Maggid, *Sefer toledot mishpaḥat Ginzburg* (St. Petersburg, 1899); Shaul Ginsburg, "Di familie Baron Ginzburg: drei doyres shtadlones, tsedoke un haskole," in his *Historishe Verk* (New York, 1937), vol. 2, 117–162; Sh. L. Tsitron, *Shtadlonim* (Warsaw, n.d.), 334–376.

6. See, now, Arcadius Kahan, *Essays in Jewish Social and Economic History* (Chicago, 1986).

7. Rosenthal, *Toledot ḥevrat marbei haskalah,* vol. 1, 82, and, on Gordon's activities as secretary of the society, I. M. Cherikover, *Istoriia Obshchestva dlia rasprostraneniia prosveshcheniia mezhdu evreiami v Rossii* (St. Petersburg, 1913), vol. 1, passim.

8. David Feinberg, "Zikhronot," *He-ʿAvar* 4 (1959), 20–36.

9. Rosenthal, 83–84.

10. "Be-ẓeiti mi-Telz," KS 28.

11. "Obzor sovremennoi evreiskoi literatury," *Evreiskaia biblioteka* 1 (1871), 342–373; 2, 474–486.

12. Ibid., 342.

13. Ibid., 343; see note of editor objecting to this disregard of medieval Hebrew poetry and philosophy.

14. Ibid., 346.

15. Ibid., 348.

16. Ibid., 349.

17. Ibid., 350.

18. Ibid., 353.

19. Rosenthal, 93.

20. *Report Presented by Sir Moses Montefiore, Bart.,* . . . *Upon His Return From His Mission to St. Petersburg, August, 5632–1872* (London, 1872), 16–17; for mention of Gordon, see 18. This report is reproduced with omissions in L. Loewe, ed., *Diaries of Sir Moses and Lady Montefiore* (London, 1890), vol. 2, 247–254. See also Gordon's description of his arrangements for Montefiore's visit and his meeting with Sir Moses, "Ra'iti 'et penei Montefiore," KP 280–282, and his address-poem to the British notable in KS 288–289.

21. Rosenthal, 90ff, and Cherikover, 157ff.

22. Cherikover, 124, 129, 151.

23. See Gordon's report on the activities of the society, "Peʿulat vaʿad ha-ḥevrah le-harbot haskalat benei yisra'el be-'ereẓ Rusiyah bi-shenat 1874," *Ha-Maggid* 19 (1875), No. 33, 287; No. 34, 297; Cherikover, 157–158; and Rosenthal, 113–115 and passim.

24. *Golos* (June 1873), No. 164.

25. "Ponevole zapozdavshii otvet gazete "Golos," *Evreiskaia biblioteka* 4 (1873), 440.

26. See his letter to Mikhl Gordon in *'Igerot* 2, 192.

27. See his letter to his publisher, reproduced in KP 1–2, and Klausner 362.

28. See the unpublished letter from Crémieux to Gordon, on stationery of the Alliance Israélite Universelle, dated August 20, 1874, in the Shaul Ginzburg materials, Rivkind Archive, National and University Library, Hebrew University, 4°1281A, file 18/9.

29. *Piatiknizhie Moiseevo v evreiskom tekste i doslovnom russkom perevode dlia evreev* (Vilna, 1875), unpaginated introduction.

30. Rosenthal, 108–111.

31. On the internal friction surrounding this compendium, see Moshe Perlmann, "L. O. Levanda and J. L. Gordon: Levanda's Letters to Gordon, 1873–5," *Proceedings of the American Academy for Jewish Research* 35, (1967), 139–185.

32. "Pegishoti ʿim Y. Brafman," KP 311–313.

33. Ia. B.[rafman], "Iezuity iudeistva," *Golos* (1876), No. 117, 2.

34. Ibid.

35. Lev Gordon, "Mirovozzrenie talmudistov," *Golos* (1876), No. 156, 2–3.

36. Ibid., 3.

37. Ibid.

38. Ibid.

39. Ia. B[rafman], "Iezuity iudeistva," *Golos* (1876), No. 216.

40. *'Igerot* 2, 197.

41. This is a complicated story that requires detailed exposition. In 1877, an anonymous sixteen-page pamphlet entitled *Die jüdische Frage in der orientalischen Frage* was published in Vienna by the publishing house run by Peretz Smolenskin. This pamphlet, issued soon after the start of the Russian-Turkish War, argued that with the inevitable dissolution of the Ottoman Empire, Palestine be turned into a Jewish state under the auspices of Britain. The anonymous author argued that the "Jewish Question" was a purely national, rather than religious, question, that the nationality of the Jews was completely separate from their religion, and that therefore the Jewish state to be established in Palestine ought to have a clear and distinct separation of church and state. The idea of such a state, the author insisted, was eminently practical and practicable in the immediate future, as the only solution to the Jewish problem.

In 1947, the noted historian N. M. Gelber—who had discovered the pamphlet in the Vienna archives in 1922 while working on the Jewish Question at the Congress of Berlin—published the original text of the pamphlet along with a Hebrew translation and attributed the pamphlet to none other than Benjamin Disraeli—*Tokhnit ha-medinah ha-yehudit le-Lord Bikonsfild* (Tel Aviv, 1947). Gelber made this attribution on the basis of the following source. The Austrian minister Leo von Bilinsky claimed in his memoirs that after reading Theodor Herzl's *The Jewish State,* he gave the Zionist leader's book to Johann Freiherr von Chlumecky, a noted Austrian politician. Chlumecky responded: "Herzl's plan for a Jewish state is devoid of any originality. It is likely that he read the pamphlet *The Jewish State in the Eastern Question* by Disraeli that he—Chlumecky—translated into German at the request of the English ambassador in Vienna, and published anonymously in Vienna" (Gelber, 35). The attribution of this pamphlet, and this plan, to Disraeli, as part of his overall schemes in the infamously convoluted debates over the so-called Eastern Question in British politics at the time, was thereafter disputed by several of Disraeli's biographers.

In 1958, the Israeli bibliographer Gedaliah Elkoshi found in Peretz Smolenskin's correspondence to Judah Leib Gordon a letter written in 1877 which began:

> In regard to your pamphlet in the German language, I tell you that I have read it with great interest, even though in some matters I disagree with you, especially in regard to the Turkish Empire, which in your mind is soon to disband, but which is not so, since perhaps the end of the Russian Empire (as it is now constituted) will come before that of Turkey, and that is just and to be hoped by all, since if justice reigned in Russia even half as much as in Turkey (even before the Constitution) its inhabitants would be fortunate. But in general, I found your ideas to be true and worthy of publication [G. Elkoshi, "Zeror 'igerot shel Perez Smolenskin 'el Yehudah Leib Gordon," *Kiryat Sefer* 34 (1958) 250].

On the basis of this fragment, Elkoshi triumphantly published an article in the Israeli Labor Party daily *Davar* entitled "The Program was Y. L. Gordon's!" Elkoshi's basic point, beyond the coincidence of dates, was that the thrust of the pamphlet was identical to that of Gordon's 1870–1871 article about the messianic idea censored from *Ha-Meliz* and published in Smolenskin's *Ha-Shahar* and to Gordon's ideas on Zionism as expressed in his editorials in *Ha-Meliz* in 1881. Elkoshi continued:

> In these articles Gordon expresses his nationalist credo, which was political-secular in its essence, and its goal the revival of the nation in the Land of Israel on the basis of secular European culture, through a thorough separation of church and state (*Davar,* 1 August 1958, p. 6).

Elkoshi's article led to a defense by Gelber of the attribution to Disraeli, and then to a long and rather nasty exchange of letters between the two scholars in the pages of *Davar,* in which ad hominem attacks were interspersed with overt political disagreements and blatantly incorrect characterizations of Judah Leib Gordon.

As often occurs with such acrimonious scholarly debates, both sides vastly overstated their cases—and both sides were probably wrong. Most important, it is clear that Elkoshi's claim that Gordon wrote this particular pamphlet is insupportable, based as it is on a combination of the flimsiest sort of historical conjecture and ideologically motivated misreading of sources. What is certain from Smolenskin's letter is that in 1877 Gordon did indeed write a German pamphlet on the imminent downfall of the Ottoman Empire; but both internal and external considerations militate persuasively against the identification of Gordon's lost pamphlet with *Die jüdische Frage in der orientalischer Frage:*

1. First and most important, as discussed above, Gordon vehemently disagreed with the notion—already circulating in the late 1870s—that a Jewish state be established in the Land of Israel *before* the Jews had undergone cultural and religious reform. Time and time again he insisted, first in private and then in public, that mass Jewish colonization in Palestine (not to speak of the formation of a Jewish polity) be conditioned upon the *prior* religious reform of the Jews. At no time did Gordon believe in or advocate the position of the author of *Die jüdische Frage* that a Jewish state in Palestine be based upon the separation of church and state or that the religious and national aspects of Jewishness are separable. Quite to the con-

trary, both in the 1870s and in the far more contentious 1880s, Gordon insisted to the end that the religious and national attributes of Judaism were ineluctably intertwined and could not be separated by an act of will or deliberate obfuscation. (See below, Gordon's critique of Leon Pinsker's *Autoemancipation*.) Thus, on this basis of ideological matters alone, the attribution to Gordon of this pamphlet is contrary to all the evidence and must be rejected.

2. Moreover, as discussed below, Smolenskin in the late 1870s himself vehemently disagreed with the notion of establishing a Jewish state in Palestine. Had the pamphlet mentioned in his letter to Gordon contained such a notion, how could Smolenskin then have said that he found Gordon's ideas to be true?

3. As will be discussed at length in chapter 11 below, at the end of his life Gordon wrote a "spiritual testament" in which he defended himself against the accusation that he had been an opponent of the Love of Zion movement. In this letter he elaborated on his various activities in support of Jewish colonization in Palestine, but did not mention writing a proposal for a Jewish state in Palestine, an argument that would have clinched his self-defense. Since Gordon instructed his correspondent that this letter be held in confidence until thirty days after his death, there is no reason whatever to suppose that Gordon would have had any reason to conceal his authorship of a proto-Zionist pamphlet. The fact that even here he did not mention such a pamphlet strongly supports the conclusion that he did not write one.

4. Finally, as mentioned above, the pamphlet was published during the Russo-Turkish War of 1877–1878, when tensions between Russia and England over the fate of the Near East—including the Holy Land—were at the very center of international tensions. It is impossible to conceive of Gordon, the secretary of the St. Petersburg Jewish community, a loyal subject of the tsar, and a savvy politician, writing a pamphlet directly in contravention of Russian war aims, advocating the ceding of Palestine to England, and sending such a seditious pamphlet to Austria for publication there in German. On the other hand, it is very possible to conceive of Gordon writing a different pamphlet, promoting the dissolution of the Ottoman Empire, the only matter alluded to in the letter to him by Smolenskin.

In the end, this does not mean that Gelber's attribution of the pamphlet to Disraeli is unassailable; on the contrary, it is fraught with many grave difficulties. Although this matter is far beyond the considerations of this study, the most likely hypothesis is that Chlumecky's claim that Disraeli wrote such a pamphlet was part and parcel of the furious diplomatic cat-and-mouse game that characterized and inflamed the Near Eastern issue at the time in which Disraeli's putative Jewishness was certainly a live issue. In any event, whoever wrote this pamphlet, it most certainly was not Judah Leib Gordon.

42. "Sha'ah 'ahat shel korat ruah," KP 285–290.

43. Ibid., 288.

44. Ibid.

45. Ibid., 246.

47. "Kozo shel yud," first published in *Ha-Shahar* 7 (1875), No. 10, 565–573; No. 11, 635–645; No. 12, 713–719; reproduced in KS 129–140, where a misprint or error from the previous collected works is repeated: the poem is dated "Marienbad, in the month of 'Av, 1878" rather than 1876. The expression "Kozo shel yud" is used in the Talmud: see Menahot 29a and Rashi's commentary on that page.

47. KS 129.

48. Ibid., 130.

49. Ibid., 133.

50. Ibid., 135.

51. Ibid., 138.

52. Ibid., 139–141.

53. For a review of the critical literature on "Kozo shel yud," see the excellent recent article by Ben-Ami Feingold, "'Kozo shel yud'—'anatomiah shel satirah," *Mehkarei Yerush-*

alayim be-sifrut 'ivrit 2 (1983), 73–77; for a perceptive and informative survey of the criticism of Gordon in general, see Shmuel Verses, *Bikoret ha-bikoret* (Tel Aviv, 1982), 11–33.

54. Feingold, 77–103.

55. KS 138.

56. Letter to Miriam Markel-Mazessohn, reproduced in *Ha-'Olam* 24 (1936), No. 37, 637–683.

57. Ibid., No. 40–41, 707.

58. KP 2.

Chapter 8. Exile

1. See his letters in *'Igerot* 2, 204, 237, 242, and 258.

2. The stories were: "Ba-'avur na'alayim," *Ha-Meliz* 14 (1978), No. 10, 201–203; No. 11, 220–223; and "Ha-me'urav be-da'at," written in 1878 according to a letter of that year, *'Igerot* 2, 252 but published only in *Ha-Meliz* 16 (1880), No. 26, 545–550; No. 27, 565–570; No. 30, 629–634; No. 31, 645–650; and No. 32, 665–670. The prose poems were entitled "Mizmorei Yehudah" and published in *Ha-Shahar* 9 (1887 [sic!]) 104–107; the fable was "Ha-sa'ir ha-mishtaleah," ibid., 215–218. The Russian translations of the Tish'a Be-'av lamentations were apparently never published; on their composition, see *'Igerot* 2, 216.

3. The first three parts of "Shenei Yosef ben Shim'on" were published in *Ha-Shahar* 10 (1880), No. 1, 27–37.

4. *'Igerot* 2, 215.

5. Ibid., 231.

6. "Ba-'alot ha-shahar," *Ha-Shahar* 9 (1878–1879), No. 1, 3.

7. Ibid., 4–5.

8. V. Stasov, "Po povodu postroiki sinagogi v S. Peterburge," *Evreiskaia biblioteka* 2 (1871), 453–473.

9. "V kakom stile dolzhna byt' postroena sinagoga v Peterburge?" *Razsvet* 1 (1879), No. 5, 188–191; see Stasov's response to Gordon in No. 10, 384–385.

10. For the best account of the rabbinical controversy, see Shaul Ginzburg, "Y. L. Gordon's arest un farshikung," in his *Historishe Verk* (New York, 1937), 123–129.

11. The following account is based, unless otherwise noted, on Gordon's memoirs of his arrest and exile, posthumously published in their original Russian as "Tiurma i ssylka," *Perezhitoe* 4 (1913), 1–43; these memoirs were later translated into Hebrew in KP 291–308.

12. "Tiurma i ssylka," 23. In a later autobiographical snippet entitled "Divrei ha-sitnah," he claimed that the fifth charge did not refer to the revolutionary Gordon but read: "You dishonestly run the affairs of the community, and embezzle its funds" (KP 284).

13. *'Igerot* 2, 261.

14. See entry on Pudozh in *Entsiklopedicheskii slovar'*, Vol. 50, 767–768.

15. "Lebenzon i Levinson," *Russkaia starina* 25 (1879), No. 9, 159.

16. See *'Igerot* 2, 276–277, and Klausner 371–372.

17. "'Al nehar kevar: ha-yaldut ve-ha-shaharut," first published in *Reshumot* 1 (1918), 69–96.

18. *"Rahamei-'em,"* first published in the 1889 edition of his stories, reprinted in KP 99–104.

19. See note in KP 99.

20. The text of this letter was printed as an appendix to "Tiurma i ssylka," *Perezhitoe* 4 (1913), 45.

21. Ibid., 36.

22. Ibid., 43.

23. Shaul Ginzburg, "Y. L. Gordon's arest un farshikung," 123n.

24. *'Igerot* 2, 255.

25. Ibid., 266–267.

26. Ibid., 270; on this scandal he later wrote the poem "Ha-bat ha-shovevah," KS 48.

27. "A. B. Lebenson, ego literaturnaia deiatel'nost' i ego znachenie dlia russkikh evreev," *Evreiskaia biblioteka* 8 (1880), 163.

28. Ibid., 166.

29. "Zidkiyahu ve-vet ha-pekudot," KS 98–101.

30. On Zedekiah, see, inter alia, II Kings 24:4–20; 25:1–20; Jeremiah 27:1, 29:3, 31:9–11, 38:5, 39:1–7, 44:30, 51:59, 512:1–7; I Chronicles 3:15; II Chronicles 36:12.

31. The Hebrew reads: "Bi-meẓudat Lit'a yisaditiha/ U-ve-Pudash hiẓavti delateha," unmistakably recalling I Kings 16:34—"Be-yamav banah Ḥi'el bet ha-'eli 'et Yeriḥoh ba-'Aviram beḥoro yisdah u-vi-Seguv ẓe'iro hiẓiv deletaha."

32. KS 98.

33. Ibid.

34. Zedekiah had ordered the liberation of the slaves of his kingdom, an act that in Gordon's mind may well have been evocative of the emancipation of the Russian serfs, the greatest accomplishment of Alexander II.

35. Ibid., 99.

36. Ibid., 348, which is missing some of the original German interpolations, which can be found in earlier editions of his collected works. See, e.g., *Kol shirei Yehudah Leib Gordon* (St. Petersburg, 1884), 179–180.

Chapter 9. Pogroms and the Crisis of Jewish Liberalism

1. Marc Bloch, *The Historian's Craft* (New York, 1953), 193.

2. For the latest, and most sophisticated, treatment of this problem, see Jonathan Frankel, *Prophecy and Politics: Socialism, Nationalism, and the Russian Jews, 1862–1917* (Cambridge, England, 1981).

3. For the most cogent exposition of this point of view, see Yakov Letschinsky, "Di yidishe imigratsie in di Fareinikte Shtatn," in E. Tcherikover, ed., *Geshikhte fun der yidisher arbeter-bavegung in di fareinikte Shtatn* (New York, 1945), vol. 1, 27–40, esp. 29–32.

4. For the most lucid discussion of the emigration of Russian Jews to America, see Simon Kuznets, "Immigration of Russian Jews."

5. E. Tcherikover, "Revolutsionere un natsionale ideologies fun der rusish-yidisher intelegents," in his *Geshikhte,* vol. 2, 149–157. For a critique of this point of view, see Frankel, 50–51.

6. Frankel, 5, 47–48.

7. There is as yet no acceptable scholarly analysis of Smolenskin's life and ideas. The best attempt at a biography is Klausner, vol. 5, 15–268, which suffers from the usual problems of Klausner's nationalistic and anachronistic approach. See also Frankel, index, and Charles Freundlich, *Peretz Smolenskin: His Life and Thought (A Study of the Renascence of Jewish Nationalism)* (New York, 1965).

8. See Frankel, 82.

9. On David Gordon, see Carol Diament, "Polemics of Rebirth: David Gordon and Proto-Zionism, 1858–1886, unpub. Ph.D. dissertation, Yeshiva University, 1983.

10. See Yosef Salmon, "David Gordon ve-ʿiton Ha-Maggid: Ḥilufei ʿemdot le-le'umiut ha-yehudit 1860–1881," *Zion* 47 (1982), 145–164.

11. See Tscherikover, "Revolutsionere un natsionale ideologies," and Frankel, 28–48.

12. On *Razsvet,* see also S. L. Tsinberg, *Istoriia evreiskoi pechati v Rossii v sviaze s obshchestvennymi techeniiami* (Petrograd, 1915), 237–246.

13. Once more, there is unfortunately no first-rate modern study on Lilienblum. Klausner 190–300 is the most thorough chronological and bibliographical survey; see, too, Shlomo Breiman's introduction to his edition of Lilienblum's autobiographical works, *Ketavim 'oto-biografiim* (Jerusalem, 1970), 7–74, and his introduction to his edition of the correspondence between Lilienblum and Gordon, *'Igerot M. L. Lilienblum le-Y. L. Gordon (Jerusalem, 1968), 9–61.*

14. Tsinberg, op. cit., 248; on Russian anti-Semitism, see Shmuel Ettinger, *Ha-'antishe-miut ba-ʿet ha-hadashah* (Tel Aviv, 1978), 145–190.

15. "Hitbonenu me'od u-re'u," *Ha-Meliz* 16, No. 1 (April 1 1880), 1–7; "'Ani yashen ve-libi ʿer," ibid., 4–6; "Be-mishkenot Yaʿakov be-hul," ibid., 18–20.

16. For an excellent analysis of Gordon's most important feuilleton series, see now Shmuel Verses, "'Zelohit shel palyaton' ve-samemaneha—ʿal 'omanut ha-feleton shel Yehu-dah Leib Gordon," in *Mehkarei Yerushalayim be-sifrut ʿivrit* 2 (1983), 105–125.

17. See especially his editorial "Lefanim ve-l'o le-'ahor," *Ha-Meliz* 16, No. 7 (May 13, 1889), 127–130.

18. "Be-mishkenot Yaʿakov be-hul," ibid., No. 8 May 20, 1880, 158 and No. 10, (June 3, 1880), 201.

19. "Be-mishkenot Yaʿakov be-hul," ibid., No. 3 (April 15, 1880), 60; No. 10 (June 3, 1880), 200; No. 28 (Oct. 14, 1880), 295–296; "Moze 'ani—'et ha-'ishah," ibid., No. 32 (Nov. 11, 1880), 663–672.

20. Letter to Z. Kaplan, *'Igerot* 2, 282–283, and Mikhl Gordon, ibid., 299.

21. "Ve-ha-hokhmah me-'ayin timaze," *Ha-Meliz* 17, No. 1 (January 6, 1881), 7.

22. Ibid., 3.

23. "K istorii poseleniia evreev v Peterburge," *Voskhold* 1, No. 1 (January 1881), 118–119.

24. "Melekh tipesh," *Ha-Meliz* 17 No. 9 (March 3, 1881), reprinted in KP 117–121.

25. "Ha-melekh met, yehi ha-melekh!" ibid., No. 10 (March 10, 1881), 187–192.

26. David Gordon, "Nidhei-yisra'el," *Ha-Maggid* 25, No. 7 (Feb. 16, 1881), 51–52.

27. KS 312; letter to Z. Kaplan, *'Igerot* 2, 308–309.

28. "Literaturnia letopis': Obozrenie drevne-evreiskoi literatury i zhurnalistiki," *Voskhod* 1, No. 4, sovremennaia letopis', 29.

29. Ibid., 29–30.

30. S. M. Dubnow, *History of the Jews in Russia and Poland* (Philadelphia, 1918), vol. 2, 250–251. For the original reports on this and other pogroms, see G. Ia. Krasnyi-Admoni, *Materialy dlia istorii antievreiskikh pogromov v Rossii* (Petrograd-Moscow, 1923), vol. 2.

31. Yehudah Slutsky, "Ha-gi'ografiiah shel peraʿot 5641," *He-ʿAvar* 9 (1962), 16–26; I. Michael Aronson, "Geographical and Socioeconomic Factors in the 1881 Anti-Jewish Pogroms in Russia," *The Russian Review* 39 (January 1980), No. 1, 18–20. A recent work has appeared on the pogroms: Stephen M. Berk, *Year of Crisis, Year of Hope: Russian Jewry and the Pogroms of 1881–1882* (Westport, Conn., 1985).

32. Aronson, 20–31, and Hans Rogger, *Jewish Policies and Right-Wing Politics in Impe-rial Russia* (Berkeley and Los Angeles, 1986), passim.

33. *'Igerot* 2, 314.

34. Dubnow, 260.

35. Ibid., 259.

36. See Frankel, 57–58, and sources cited there.

37. N. M. Gelber, "Di rusishe pogromen onheyb di 80ker yorn in shayn fun estraykhisher diplomatisher korespondents," *Historishe Shriftn* 2 (1937), 469.

38. Ibid.

39. "Be-mishkenot Yaʿakov be-hul," *Ha-Meliz* 17, No. 19 (May 19, 1881), 401.

40. Ibid., 402.

41. Letter from Mikl Gordon to J. L. Gordon, dated May 24, 1881, in Judah Leib Gordon Archive, National and University Library, Hebrew University of Jerusalem, File 4°761.

42. *'Igerot' 2, 315.*

43. "Be-mishkenot Ya'akov be-ḥul," *Ha-Meliẓ* 17, No. 20, 423–426.

44. Translated by Arthur Hertzberg in his *The Zionist Idea* (New York, 1970), 169.

45. See his editorial "Bin ba-davar ve-haven ba-mar'eh," *Ha-Meliẓ* 17, No. 20 (May 26,) 405–410.

46. "Se'arot Teman," ibid., No. 22 (June 9, 1881), 454.

47. Ibid.

48. "'Aḥarit ha-za'am," ibid., 455–456.

49. Ibid.

50. "Ḥalom be-'aspamya," ibid., No. 25 (June 30, 1881), 520–521.

51. See studies cited in note 31 above.

52. "Naḥamu, naḥamu 'ami," *Ha-Meliẓ* 17, No. 29 (July 28, 1881), 605–660.

53. Ibid., 608.

54. Ibid., 611.

55. See above, chapter 5.

56. Hertzberg, 169–170.

57. See B. Ẓ. Dinur, "Tokhniotav shel 'Ignatiev le-pitron she'elat ha-yehudim, u-ve'idot neẓigei ha-kehilot be-Peterburg be-shenot 5641-2," *He-'Avar* 10 (1963), 37–82.

58. "Be-mishkenot Ya'akov be-ḥul," *Ha-Meliẓ* 17, No. 31 (August 11, 1881), 666.

59. Ibid.

60. Reprinted in KP 78–92.

61. Ibid., 78.

62. See above, chapter 5.

63. KP 92.

Chapter 10. The Battle Over Zion

1. For the fullest reports on this evening, see A[dolf] L[andau], "Skromnoe torzhestvo," *Voskhod* 1 (1881), No. 11, 24–40; and Alexander Zederbaum, "Ḥagigat ha-yovel," *Ha-Meliẓ* 17, No. 43 (November 3, 1881), 863–866.

2. "Be-ne'arenu u-vi-zekenenu nelekh," *Ha-Meliẓ* 17, No. 44 (November 10, 1881), 884–886, reprinted (in uncensored version) in KS 30–31.

3. *Yudishe folksblat* 1, No. 5 (October 29, 1881), 77–79.

4. Letter to G. Sirkin, *Nedel'naia khronika Voskhoda* 22 (1902), No. 38, 31; see, too, his letter to Z. Kaplan in *'Igerot* 3, 6–9.

5. "Literaturnaia letopis'," *Voskhod* 1 (1881), No. 10, 21.

6. *'Igerot* 3, 9–10.

9. Ibid., 10.

10. "Ẓeloḥit shel palyaton," *Ha-Meliẓ* 17, No. 14 (April 14, 1881), 271–274, reprinted in KP 200–202.

11. Dinur, "Tokhniotav," 27. See also the excellent treatment of this episode in Frankel, 75–77 (which, however, confuses Dr. Isaac Orshansky with his brother Ilia).

12. Ibid.

13. See his memoir in KP 313–314.

14. On the previous adventure, see KP 311–313.

15. See their letter reprinted in Krasnyi-Admoni, 526.

16. See Frankel, 68–69.

17. "Be-mishkenot Ya'akov be-ḥul," *Ha-Meliẓ* 18, No. 6 (February 9, 1882), 110.

18. "Mefuzar u-meforad," ibid., No. 7 (February 16, 1882), 113–116.

19. "Ge'ulatenu u-fedut nafshenu," ibid., No. 12 (March 22, 1882), 211.

20. Ibid., 212.

21. Ibid., 213.

22. Ibid., 215.

23. Ibid.

24. "'Ezrah ve-'Ezr'a," ibid., No. 13 (April 6, 1882), 233–239.

25. "'Ein me-'arvin she'elah be-she'elah," ibid., No. 14 (April 12, 1882), 258.

26. "Simu dim'atenu ba-nod," ibid., 262.

27. Ibid.

28. *'Igerot* 3, 16.

29. *'Igerot* 4, 425.

30. "Be-mishkenot Ya'akov be-ḥul," *Ha-Meliz* 18, No. 24 (June 22, 1882), 488–491.

31. Ibid., 490–491.

32. Reprinted in KP 202.

33. Ibid., 205.

34. "Popytki religioznyi reform u evreev," *Voskhod* 2 (1882), No. 7–8, 1–29.

35. Ibid., 16–17.

36. Ibid., 17.

37. Ibid., 17–81.

38. Ibid., 19.

39. "Literaturnia letopis'," *Voskhod* 2 (1882), No. 7–8, 87–89.

40. Ibid., 89.

41. Ibid., 94–95.

42. "'Eder 'adonai," KS 31–32.

43. Shabbat 54b.

44. KS 32.

45. Ibid.

46. *Perezhitoe* 3 (1911), 392–339.

47. The literary supplement was called *Migdanot;* "'Aḥoti Ruḥamah" was published there on pp. 5–6, and was reprinted in KS 31.

48. KS 31.

49. Ibid.

Chapter 11. Attack and Despair

1. *'Igerot* 2, 23–25.

2. A Sh. Friedberg, "Le-ma'an ha-'emet," *Ha-Meliz* 35 (1895). No. 125, 3–4. See also his memoir of Zederbaum in *Sefer Ha-Shanah* (1900), 238–53.

3. "Ve-z'ot le-Yehudah," *Ha-Shahar* 10 (1880 [sic!]) 455–467.

4. Ibid., 466–467.

5. *'Igerot* 3, 38–93.

6. "Dikdukei 'aniot," *Ha-Meliz* 19, No. 31 (April 25, 1883), 487–490.

7. "Sha'aruriah mi-koẓo shel yud," *Ha-Maggid* 27 (1883), No. 19, 148–149. This concluding accusation alluded to God's instructions to Elijah the Prophet to condemn King Ahab and Queen Jezebel for their conspiracy to murder Naboth the vineyard owner: "Go down and confront King Ahab who [resides] in Samaria. He is now in Naboth's vineyard; he has gone down there to take possession of it. Say to him, 'Thus said the Lord: Would you murder and take possession? Thus said the Lord: In the very place where the dogs lapped up Naboth's blood, the dogs will lap up your blood too.'"

8. "Teshuvah le-var nash," *Ha-Meliz* 19, No. 41 (May 29, 1883), 656–658.

9. "'Ahoti ne'eshamah," *Ha-Shahar* 11 (1883), No. 7, 403–407.

10. *'Igerot* 3, 40.

11. Ibid., 52.

12. Ibid., 70.

13. *Kol shirei Yehudah Leib Gordon, yeshanim gam hadashim* (St. Petersburg, 1884).

14. Reprinted in KS, unpaginated introduction "Me'et ha-mozi'im le-'or."

15. Ibid.

16. KS, unpaginated introduction "Me-'et ha-mehaber."

17. KS 106–117.

18. KS 148–166.

19. Ibid., 166.

20. Ibid., 33.

21. Ibid.

22. *'Igerot* 3, 81.

23. Ibid., 75.

24. S[imon] D[ubnov], "Literaturnaia letopis': Evreiskii Nekrasov," *Voskhod* 4 (1884), No. 7, 43.

25. See his *Kniga zhizni* (Riga, 1934) 1, 172.

26. *'Igerot* 3, 84.

27. See his review in *Ha-'Asif* 1 (1884), 211–217.

28. Letter of September 28, 1884, in Judah Leib Gordon Archives, National and University Library, Hebrew University of Jerusalem, File 4°761, Sokolov file. Gordon's letter to Sokolov has apparently not been preserved.

29. "Bikoret le-khol Shirei Yehudah Leib Gordon," reprinted in *Kol kitvei Moshe Leib Lilienblum* (Odessa, 1912), vol. 3, 26–78.

30. Ibid., 31.

31. Ibid., 36.

32. Ibid., 40.

33. Ibid., 50–51.

34. Ibid., 56.

35. Ibid., 59–60.

36. Ibid., 61.

37. Ibid., 63.

38. Ibid., 67–86

39. Ibid., 74.

40. See, for example, Klausner 274.

41. For the most intelligent analyses of Pisarev in English, see Andrzej Walicki, *A History of Russian Thought from the Enlightenment to Marxism* (Stanford, 1979), 209–215; and Isaiah Berlin, *Russian Thinkers* (New York, 1978), index.

42. Quoted in Walicki, 192.

43. Ibid., 206.

44. On Turgenev's views, see, inter alia, Leonard Schapiro, *Turgenev: His Life and Times* (New York, 1978), 141–162.

45. *'Igerot* 3, 105.

46. Ibid.

47. See Klausner 278–283 for most extensive treatment and references.

48. *'Igerot* 3, 140.

49. Ibid., 125.

50. This pamphlet was *Tefah meguleh* (St. Petersburg, 1885), published under the name of Y. H. Mezah.

51. See *'Igerot* 3, 144–148, and below, chapter 12.

52. "'Arba'ah ḥarashim ke-ve-maḥazeh," *Ha-Meliz* 21, No. 96, (December 23, 1885), 1603–1606.

53. Ibid.

54. "Ẓeloḥit shel palyaton," ibid., No. 93 (December 12, 1885, 1505–1510, reprinted in KP 214–217.

55. Ibid., 216.

56. Ibid.

57. Ibid., 216–217.

58. See below, letter to S. Bernfeld.

59. "Lo re'i zeh ke-re'i zeh," *Ha-Meliz* 21, No. 94 (December 16, 1885), 15 23–25.

60. *'Igerot* 3, 162; see also his previous letters to Visotsky, ibid., 131–132, 149.

61. "Berur devarim," *Ha-Meliz* 22, No. 1 (January 3, 1886), 4–8.

62. See *"Gilui da'at,"* ibid., No. 2 (January 6, 1886), 30; Shapiro's "Mikhtav galui le-h' Yalag," ibid., No. 5, (January 17, 1886), 78–79; and Gordon's "Teshuvati be-ẓidah," ibid., 79.

63. *'Igerot* 3, 167.

64. Ibid., 154, 195–196.

65. "Ḥadash mal'e yashan," *Ha-Meliz* 22, No. 61 (July 1, 1886), 785–789.

66. See Klausner 278–283.

67. David [Frischmann], "'Otiot porḥot," *Ha-Yom* 1 (1886), No. 123, 3; see Gordon's response in *'Igerot* 3, 185.

68. See "'Akhsanyah shel torah," *Ha-Meliz* 22, No. 107 (September 4, 1886), 1377–1379; "Sefer ha-ḥayim," ibid., No. 118 (September 17, 1886, 1489–1495; "Ḥeshbon ha-nefesh," ibid., No. 121 (September 23, 1886), 1521–1524; "Ḥerut yisra'el," ibid., 23, No. 76 (April 2, 1887), 791–793; "Ka'asher pitarnu—ken hayah," ibid., No. 112, (May 22, 1887), 1175–1178.

69. See Shlomo Breiman, *'Igerot Moshe Leib Lilienblum le-Yehudah Leib Gordon* (Jerusalem, 1968), 196–197, 227.

70. See his attacks against Gordon reproduced in *Kol Kitvei David Frischmann* (Warsaw, 1914), vol 5, 141–170, and Klausner 394–397.

71. *'Igerot* 4, 245–250.

72. Ibid., 246.

73. Ibid., 247.

74. Ibid., 248.

75. Ibid.

76. Ibid., 249–250.

77. Ibid., 250.

78. See Breiman, 60–61.

Chapter 12. Conclusion

1. See his "Ha-Ẓa"v le-minehu," *Ha-Ẓefirah* 16 (1889), No. 14, 55.

2. Letter to I. Friedlaender published in *Voskhod* 22 (1902), No. 49, 33–34.

3. See his letters to Sholem Aleichem reprinted in ibid., No. 40, 24–27, and in *'Igerot* 4, 310.

4. On this controversy, see Klausner 407–409.

5. See his letters in *'Igerot* 4, 322–324, and in *Voskhod* 22 (1902), No. 49, 34–53. Volume 41 A(82) of the *Entsiklopedicheskii slovar'* contains photographs of the contributors to the encyclopedia, including that of Gordon.

6. *'Igerot* 4, 334; *Reshumot* 4, 374–375; and above, chapter 1.

7. "Davar yom be-yomo," KP 325.

8. "Le . . . Mehaḥem Dolitsky," KS 300–331.

9. See *Ha-Meliẓ* 34 (1892), No. 202–204, for notices of Gordon's death and funeral; *Voskhod* 12 (1892), No. 40, and Y. Y. Weisberg, *Yehudah Leib Gordon ve-toledotav* (Kiev, 1893), for descriptions of memorial meetings.

10. For the most informed survey, see Shmuel Verses, "Shirat Yalag be-mivḥan ha-dorot," in his *Bikoret ha-bikoret* (Tel Aviv, 1982), 11–100.

11. See Ben-Ami Feingold, "Yalag be-perspektivah historit," *M'oznaim* 54 (1982), 3–4.

12. See 'Aḥad Ha'am, *'Al parashat derakhim* (reprint, Tel Aviv-Jerusalem, 1948), 4–5; and Arthur A. Goren's forthcoming article, "Spiritual Zionists and the Dilemma of Statehood, 1942–1948."

Bibliography

This is the first full-length scholarly biography of Judah Leib Gordon in any language. The two most noteworthy previous biographical sketches of Gordon were: the long chapter on him in Yosef Klausner, *Historiiah shel ha-sifrut ha-ʿivrit ha-hadashah,* vol. 4, Jerusalem, 1953, 301–466, which is extremely useful, especially for bibliographical purposes, but is severely tainted by Klausner's self-acknowledged ideological biases; and Abraham Benedict Rhine, *Leon Gordon: An Appreciation,* Philadelphia, 1910, which was written in 1902 as a thesis for the rabbinical degree at the Hebrew Union College and is now utterly dated and of no scholarly value.

There exists no complete bibliography of works by and about Judah Leib Gordon, and indeed such an undertaking would result in a small book on its own, given the number of sources involved. My own running count of Gordon's published works—necessarily incomplete due to the loss of some materials and the inaccessibility of others—runs to approximately two thousand individual items and fills forty-two single-spaced typed pages. A comparable list of works about Gordon, if feasible, would probably be even longer.

As a result, what follows is by no means a complete bibliography of works by and about Judah Leib Gordon, but a compendium of three distinct types of sources used in the writing of this book. The first is a short list of archival collections consulted; the second is a guide to bibliographies on the published works of Gordon, and a list of his works cited in this study; and the third is a list of other works cited in the notes to this book.

Archival Documents

Jerusalem
Jewish National and University Library. Judah Leib Gordon Archives, Collection 4°761. Letters of 264 correspondents to Gordon.
Schwadron Collection of Autographs and Portraits of Jews. Twenty-two letters by Gordon to various correspondents.
Rivkind Archive–Saul Ginzburg Collection 4°1281. Four documents regarding Gordon.

New York
YIVO Institute for Jewish Research. Tcherikower Archive F. 757, nos. 90, 91. Two letters by Judah Leib Gordon.

Works by Gordon

A. Bibliographies: There have been many attempts at producing bibliographies of Gordon's Hebrew works. The following are the most useful and complete: for a list of the various editions of Gordon's books and letters published until 1950, see Yosef Klausner, *Historiiah shel ha-sifrut ha-ʿivrit ha-ḥadashah,* vol. 4 (Jerusalem, 1953), 412–413. On Gordon's articles in Hebrew see Yoḥanan Pograbinski, "Bibliografiiah shel ma'amarei Yehudah Leib Gordon," *Kiryat Sefer* 8 (1931), 248–262, and his "Nosafot le-ʿBibliografiiah shel ma'amarei Y. L. Gordon'," *Kiryat Sefer* 9 (1932–1933), 250–257; these articles engendered a response by G. Elkoshi, "Nosafot ve-tikunim le-bibliografiiah shel ma'amarei Yalag be-ʿivrít," *Kiryat Sefer* 21 (1944–1945), 61–64, with an exchange of letters between Pograbinski and Elkoshi in ibid., 215–216. For Gordon's letters not included in his collected correspondence, see Avraham Yaʿari, "ʿIgerot Yehudah Leib Gordon she-l'o nikhlelu be-koveẓ 'igerotav," *Kiryat Sever* 37 (1962), 380–398.

B. The following editions of Gordon's works, in chronological order, have been used in this study:

'Ahavat David u-Mikhal. Vilna, 1856/7.
Mishlei Yehudah. Vilna, 1860.
Shirei Yehudah. Vilna, 1868.
ʿOlam ke-minhago. Odessa, 1868; Warsaw, 1874.
Kol shirei Yehudah Leib Gordon. 4 volumes. St. Petersburg, 1884.
Sikhes Khulin- lider in der folkshprakhe. Warsaw, 1886.
Kol kitvei Yehudah Leib Gordon. Odessa, 1889.
'Igerot Yehudah Leib Gordon, ed. Y. Y. Weisberg. 4 volumes in 2 books, Warsaw, 1894.
Kitvei Yehudah Leib Gordon: Shirah. Tel Aviv, 1956.
Kitvei Yehudah Leib Gordon: Prozah. Tel Aviv, 1960.

C. The following articles and letters (in alphabetical order), not included in the collected works listed above, have been cited in this study:

"A. B. Lebenson, ego literaturnaia deiatel'nost' i ego znachenie dlia russkikh evreev." *Evreis-kaia biblioteka* 8 (1880), 160–177.
"ʿAḥarit ha-zaʿam." *Ha-Meliẓ* 17 (1881), No. 22, 455–458.
"ʿAkhsanyah shel torah." *Ha-Meliẓ* 22 (1886), No. 107, 1377–1379.
"ʿArbaʿah ḥarashim ke-ve-maḥazeh." *Ha-Meliẓ* 21 (1885), 1603–1606.
"Be-mishkenot Yaʿakov be-ḥul." *Ha-Meliẓ* 16 (1880), No. 1, 18–20; No. 3, 58–60; No. 8, 157–158; No. 10, 200–202; No. 28, 295–296; *Ha-Meliẓ* 17 (1881), No. 19, 401–402; No. 20, 423–426; No. 31, 664–666; *Ha-Meliẓ* 18 (1882), No. 6, 109–112; No. 24, 488–491.
"Be-zekhutan shel ha-rabanim." *Ha-Meliẓ* 9 (1869), No. 47, 328–329.
"Binah le-toʿei ruaḥ." *Ha-Meliẓ* 10 (1870), No. 30, 224–225; No. 31, 233–235; No. 32, 239–421; No. 33 251–252; No. 35, 267–268; No. 26, 273–275; No. 39, 288–289; No. 41, 305–306; No. 42, 313–314.
[Correspondence] *Allgemeine Zeitung des Judentums* 24 (1860), No. 18, 271.
[Correspondence] *Allgemeine Zeitung des Judentums* 24 (1860), No. 27, 410.
[Correspondence] *Allgemeine Zeitung des Judentums* 24 (1860), No. 31, 462–3.
[Correspondence] *Allgemeine Zeitung des Judentums* 25 (1861), No. 11, 153.
[Correspondence] *Allgemeine Zeitung des Judentums* 25 (1861), No. 13, 185.
[Correspondence] *Allgemeine Zeitung des Judentums* 27 (1863), No. 46, 714–717.
[Correspondence] *Ha-Karmel* 6 (1866), No. 14, 106.
[Correspondence] *Ha-Maggid* 2 (1858), No. 32, 127–128.
[Correspondence] *Ha-Meliẓ* 1 (1861), No. 26, 461–462.
[Correspondence] *Razsvet* 1 (1861), No. 44, 702.

[Correspondence] *Razsvet* 1 (1861), No. 52, 831.

"Dikdukei 'aniot." *Ha-Meliz* 19 (1883), No. 31, 487–490.

"Din ve-ḥeshbon 'al ha-va'ad le-'ezrat ha-re'evim be-Telz." *Ha-Karmel* 7 (1869), No. 41, 309–310. Reprinted in *Ha-Maggid* 12 (1869), No. 15, 20–21.

"Divrei shalom ve-'emet." *Ha-Maggid* 2 (1858), No. 13, 49–50; No. 14, 53–54.

"Drevne-evreiskii iazyk u russkikh evreev." *Sion* 2 (1862), No. 17, 264–269.

"'Erez Bavel ha-'atikah ve-ḥaḥameha." *Ha-Zefirah* 1 (1862), No. 21, 167–168; No. 23, 183–184; No. 24, 190–192; reprinted in fuller version in *Ha-Shahar* 2 (1870, 241–260.

"'Ezrah ve-'Ezr'a." *Ha-Meliz* 18 (1882), No. 13, 233–239.

"Evreiskie bratsva."*Den'* 1 (1869), No. 27, 433–436; No. 28, 452–454.

"Ge'ulatenu u-fedut nafshenu." *Ha-Meliz* 18 (1882), No. 12, 209–216.

"Gilui da'at." *Ha-Meliz* 22 (1886), No. 2, 30.

"Ḥadash mal'e yashan." *Ha-Meliz* 17 (1881), No. 25, 517–522.

"Ha-melekh met, yeḥi ha-melekh!" *Ha-Meliz* 17 (1881), No. 10, 187–192.

"Hashmatah." *Ha-Shahar* 2 (1870–1871), 154–156.

"Ha-Za"v le-minehu." *Ha-Zefirah* 16 (1889), No. 14, 55; No. 15, 59–60; No. 16, 62–63; No. 17, 67–86; No. 18, 71–72; No. 19, 75; No. 20, 79; No. 21, 82–83; No. 22, 25; No. 23, 91–92.

"Ḥerut yisra'el." *Ha-Meliz* 23 (1887), No. 76, 791–793.

"Heshbon ha-nefesh." *Ha-Meliz* 16 (1880), No. 1 1–7.

"Ka'asher pitarnu—ken hayah." *Ha-Meliz* 23 (1887), No. 112, 1175–1178.

"K istorii poseleniia evreev v Peterburge." *Voskhod* 1 (1881), No. 1, 111–123, No. 2, 29–47.

"Kol 'anot." *Ha-Maggid* 2 (1858), No. 43, 171.

"Kol me-'erez Rusiyah." *Ha-Maggid* 2 (1858), No. 34, 135; No. 35, 138–139; No. 37, 146–147.

"Lashon giptit la-'ivrim." *Migdanot* (St. Petersbury, 1883), 16–23.

"Lebenzon i Levinson." *Russkaia starina* 25 (1879), No. 9, 159.

"Lefanim ve-l'o le-'aḥor." *Ha-Meliz* 16 (1880), No. 7, 127–130.

[Letters to Miriam Markel-Mazessohn]. *Ha-'Olam* 24 (1936), No. 36, 621; No. 37, 637–638; No. 38, 656; No. 40–41, 707; 25 (1936), No. 1, 15.

[Letter to Sh. Bernfeld]. *Reshumot* 4 (1926), 374–375.

[Letter to I. Friedlaender] *Voskhod* 22 (1902), No. 49, 33–35.

[Letters to Sholem Aleichem] *Voskhod* 22 (1902), No. 40, 24–27.

[Letter to G. Sirkin] *Nedel'naia khronika Voskhoda* 22 (1902), No. 38, 31.

"Literaturnaia Letopis': Obozrenie drevne-evreiskoi literatury i zhurnalistiki." *Voskhod* 1 (1881), No. 1, sovremennaia letopis', 17–35; No. 10, 19–36; *Voskhod* 2 (1882), No. 7–8, 79–95.

"L'o re'i zeh ke-re'i zeh." *Ha-Meliz* 21 (1885), No. 94, 1523–1525.

"Me-'erez Lit'a," *Ha- Maggid* 1 (1857), No. 36, 42.

Mirovozzrenie talmudistov. 3 volumes, 1874–1876 (edited by Gordon).

"Mirovozzrenie talmudistov" *Golos* 14 (1876), No. 156, 2–3.

"Moze 'ani—'et ha-'ishah." *Ha-Meliz* 16 (1880), No. 32, 663–672.

"Naḥamu naḥamu 'ami." *Ha-Meliz* 17 (1881), No. 29, 605–611.

"O znachenie nekotorykh imen' sobstvennykh v Talmuda." *Sion* 2 (1862), No. 40, 628–629.

"Obzor sovremennoi evreiskoi literatury." *Evreiskaia biblioteka* 1 (1871), 342–373; 2 (1871), 474–486.

"Pe'ulat va'ad ha-ḥevrah le-harbot haskalat benei yisra'el be-'erez Rusiyah bi-shenat 1874." *Ha-Maggid* 19 (1875), No. 31–35.

Piatiknizhie Moiseevo v evreiskom tekste i doslovnom russkom perevode dlia evreev. Vilna 1875 (edited by Gordon with an introduction).

"Ponevole zapozdavshii otvet gazete 'Golos'." *Evreiskaia biblioteka* 4 (1873), 435–444.

"Popytki religioznyi reform u evreev." *Voskhod* (1882), No. 7–8, 1–29.

"Sefer ha-ḥayim." *Ha-Meliẓ* 22 (1886), No. 118, 1489–1495.
"Simu dim'atenu ba-nod." *Ha-Meliẓ* 18 (1882), No. 14, 260–263.
[Speech on opening of girls' school in Tel'shi.] *Russkoe prilozhenie k "Ga-Karmel"* 6 (1866), No. 28, 121–122.
Tefaḥ meguleh. St. Petersburg, 1885 (published under the name of Y. H. Mezaḥ).
"Teshuvah le-var nash." *Ha-Meliẓ* 19 (1883), No. 41, 656–658.
"Teshuvati be-ẓidah." *Ha-Meliẓ* 22 (1886), No. 5, 79.
"Tiurma i ssylka." *Perezhitoe* 4 (1913), 1–45.
"V kakom stile dolzhna byt' postroena sinagoga v Peterburge?" *Razsvet* 1 (1879), No. 5, 188–191.
"Ve-ha-ḥokhmah me-'ayin timaẓe." *Ha-Meliẓ* 17 (1881), No. 1, 1–7.

Other Works Cited in This Study

Alon, Gedalyahu. "The Lithuanian Yeshivas." In Judah Goldin, ed., *The Jewish Expression.* New York, 1970, 448–464.
[Anonymous review of *'Ahavat David u-Mikhal.*] *Allgemeine Zeitung des Judentums* 22 (1858), No. 6, 76–77.
Aronson, I. Michael. "Geographical and Socioeconomic Factors in the 1881 Anti-Jewish Pogroms in Russia." *The Russian Review* 39 (1980), 18–31.
Bar Nash. "Sha'aruriah shel koẓo shel yud." *Ha-Maggid* 27 (1883), No. 19, 487–490.
Bartal, Israel. "Ha-l'o yehudim ve-ḥevratam be-sifrut 'ivrit ve-yidish be-mizraḥ 'eiropah bein ha-shanim 1856–1914." Unpublished doctoral dissertation, The Hebrew University of Jerusalem, 1980.
Belinskii, Vissarion. *Stat'i i retsenzii.* Moscow, 1971.
Ben Sasson, Ḥaim Hillel. "'Ishiuto shel ha-Gr"a ve-hashpa'ato ha-historit." *Ẓion* 31 (1966), 39–86, 197–216.
Berk, Stephen M. *Year of Crisis, Year of Hope: Russian Jewry and the Pogroms of 1881–2.* Westport, Conn., 1985.
Berlin, Isaiah. *Russian Thinkers.* New York, 1978.
Bloch, Marc. *The Historian's Craft.* New York, 1953.
Brafman, Jacob. "Iezuity iudeistva." *Golos* 14 (1876), No. 117, 216.
Breiman, Shlomoh, ed. *'Igerot Moshe Leib Lilienblum le-Y. L. Gordon.* Jerusalem, 1968.
Breiman, Shlomoh. [Introduction to his edition of Moshe Leib Lilienblum] *Ketavim 'otobiografiim.* Jerusalem, 1970, 7–74.
Brenner, Yosef Ḥaim. "'Azkarah le-Yalag." *Kol kitvei Y. Ḥ. Brenner,* vol. 7. Tel Aviv, 1928, 124–175.
Cherikover, I. M. *Istoriia Obshchestva dlia rasprostraneniia prosveshcheniia mezhdu evreiami v Rossii.* St. Petersburg, 1913.
Cohen, Gerson David. "Ma'aseh Ḥannah ve-shiv'at baneha be-sifrut ha-'ivrit." *Sefer ha-yovel li-khvod Mordekhai Menaḥem Kaplan.* New York, 1953, 109–122.
Davies, Norman. *God's Playground.* 2 volumes, New York, 1982.
Diament, Carol. "Polemics of Rebirth: David Gordon and Proto-Zionism, 1858–1886." Unpublished doctoral dissertation, Yeshiva University, 1983.
Dinur, Ben Ẓion. "Tokhniotav shel 'Ignatiev le-pitron she'elat ha-yehudim u-ve'idot neẓigei ha-kehilot be-Peterburg be-shenot 5641-2." *He-'Avar* 10 (1963), 37–82.
Dubnov, Simon. *Kniga zhizni.* 3 volumes, Riga, 1934–1940.
Dubnov, Simon. "Literaturnaia letopis': Evreiskii Nekrasov." *Voskhod* 4 (1884), No. 7, 20–43.

Dubnow, Simon. *History of the Jews in Russia and Poland.* 3 volumes, Philadelphia, 1918.

Ehrlich, A. B. [Review of *Mishlei Yehudah*]. *Allgemeine Zeitung des Judentums* 24 (1860), No. 9, 133.

Ehrlich, A. B. [Review of *Shirei Yehudah*] *Ha-Maggid* 12 (1868), No. 28, 233; No. 29, 231; No. 30, 239–240; No. 31, 247–248.

Elkoshi, Gedaliah. "Ha-tokhnit haytah shel Yalag!" *Davar,* August 1, 1958, 5–6.

Elkoshi, Gedaliah. "Ḥidat ha-tokhnit 1877." *Davar,* September 5, 1958, 5–6.

Elkoshi, Gedaliah. "Ẓeror 'igerot shel Pereẓ Smolenskin 'el Yehudah Leib Gordon." *Kiryat Sefer* 34 (1958), 117–261.

Encyclopaedia Lithuanica. 6 volumes, Boston, 1970–1978.

Entsiklopedicheskii Slovar'. 86 volumes, St. Petersburg, 1890–1907.

Etkes, Immanuel. "Ha-Gr"a ve-ha-haskalah: tadmit u-meẓi'ut." *Perakim be-toledot ha-ḥev-rah ha-yehudit bi-yemei ha-beinayim u-va-ʿet ha-ḥadashah mukdashim le-Prof. Ya'akov Katz.* Jerusalem, 1980, 192–217.

Etkes, Immanuel. *R' Yisra'el Salanter ve-reshitah shel tenuʿat ha-musar.* Jerusalem, 1982.

Ettinger, Shmuel. *Ha-'antishemiut ba-ʿet ha-ḥadashah.* Tel Aviv, 1978.

Evreiskaia entsiklopediia. 16 volumes, St. Petersburg, 1906–1913.

Feinberg, David. "Zikhronot." *Ha-'Avar* 4 (1959), 20–36.

Feingold, Ben-Ami. "'Koẓo shel yud'—'anatomiah shel satirah." *Meḥkarei Yerushalayim be-sifrut ʿivrit* 2 (1983), 73–103.

Feingold, Ben-Ami. "Yalag be-perspektivah historit." *M'oznaim* 54 (1981–1982) No. 3–4, 45–50.

Frankel, Jonathan. *Prophecy and Politics: Socialism, Nationalism, and the Russian Jews, 1862–1917.* Cambridge, England, 1981.

Freundlich, Charles. *Peretz Smolenskin: His Life and Thought (A Study of the Renascence of Jewish Nationalism).* New York, 1965.

Freidberg, A. Sh. "Le-maʿan ha-'emet." *Ha-Meliẓ* 35 (1895), No. 128, 3–5.

Friedberg, A. Sh. "Zikhronot ʿa"d ha-'Erez." *Sefer Ha-Shanah* 1 (1900), 238–253.

Frischmann, David. *Kol kitvei David Frischmann,* vol. 5. Warsaw, 1914.

Gelber, N. M. "Di russishe pogromen onheyb di 80ker yorn in shayn fun estraykhisher diplomatisher korespondents." *Historishe shriftn* 2 (1937), 466–496.

Gelber, N. M. *Tokhnit ha-medinah ha-yehudit le-Lord Bikonsfild.* Tel Aviv, 1947.

Gessen, Iulii. *Istoriia evreiskogo naroda v Rossii.* 2 volumes, Leningrad, 1927.

Gessen, Iulii. "Sankt Peterburg." *Evreiskaia entsiklopediia,* vol. 13, 936–950.

Getzler, Israel. *Martov, A Political Biography of a Russian Social Democrat.* Cambridge, England Melbourne, 1967.

Ginzberg, Louis. *Legends of the Jews.* 6 volumes, New York, 1928.

Ginzberg, Louis. *Students, Scholars and Saints.* Philadelphia, 1928.

Ginzburg, Shaul. *Amolike Peterburg.* New York, 1944.

Ginzburg, Shaul. *Historishe verk.* 3 volumes, New York, 1937.

Ginzburg, Shaul. *Meshumodim in tsarishn Rusland.* New York, 1946.

Gordon, David. "Davar be-ʿito." *Ha-Maggid* 13 (1869), No. 27–33.

Gordon, David. "Nidḥei yisra'el." *Ha-Maggid* 25 (1881), No. 7, 51–52.

Goren, Arthur A. "Spiritual Zionists and the Dilemma of Statehood." Forthcoming article.

Gray, Thomas. *The Poems of Thomas Gray.* London, 1937.

Haʿam, ʿAḥad. *ʿAl parashat derakhim.* Tel Aviv–Jerusalem, 1948.

Ha-Levanon 6 (1869), No. 20–24, 31–49—articles against Gordon.

Ha-Meliẓ 34 (1892), No. 202–204—notices of Gordon's death.

Hertzberg, Arthur. *The Zionist Idea.* New York, 1970.

Horowitz, Rivka. "Raʿayon ʿaẓma'ut ha-yehudim be-'erez yisra'el le-R' Zekhariah Frankel bi-shenat 1842." *Kivunim* 6 (1980), 5–25.

Horowitz, Rivka. *Zekhariah Frankel ve-reshit ha-yahadut ha-pozitivit historit.* Jerusalem, 1984.

Hurvitz, Shaul. "'Aḥoti ne'eshamah." *Ha-Shaḥar* 11 (1883), No. 7, 403–406.

Iskr . . . skii, Aleksandr. [Correspondence from Shavli.] *Russkii invalid* 50 (1863), No. 199, 853.

Jonathansohn, Z. H. [Review of *Shirei Yehudah*]. *Ha-Meliẓ* 8 (1868), No. 6, 42.

Kahan, Arcadius. *Essays in Jewish Social and Economic History.* Chicago, 1986.

Katz, Jacob. *Out of the Ghetto.* Cambridge, Mass., 1973.

Kaẓenelson, Gideon. *Ha-milḥamah ha-sifrutit bein ha-ḥaredim ve-ha-maskilim.* Tel Aviv, 1954.

Klausner, Israel. *Ha-Ga'on 'Eliyahu mi-Vilna.* Jerusalem, 1969.

Kovner, Avraham Uri. *Ḥeker davar.* Vilna, 1865.

Krasnyi-Admoni, G. Ia., ed. *Materialy dlia istorii antievreiskikh pogromov v Rossii.* 2 volumes, Petrograd–Moscow, 1923.

Kuznets, Simon. "Immigration of Russian Jews to the United States: Background and Structure." *Perspectives in American History* 9 (1975), 35–124.

La Fontaine, Jean de. *La Fontaine: Selected Fables,* trans. James Michie. New York, 1979.

Landau, Adolf. "Skromnoe torzhestvo." *Voskhod* 1 (1881), No. 11, 24–40.

Lebensohn, Micah Yosef. *Shirei Mikha"l.* Tel Aviv, 1954.

Lestchinsky, Jacob. "Di yidishe imigratsie in di Fareinikte Shtatn." In E. Tcherikower, ed., *Geshikhte fun der yidisher arbeter-bavegung in di Fareinikte Shtatn,* vol. 1. New York, 1945, 27–40.

Lestchinsky, Jacob. *Dos yidishe fold in tsifern.* Berlin, 1922.

Levin, Y. L. "Seʿarot Teman." *Ha-Meliẓ* 17 (1881), No. 22, 450–455.

Levinsohn, Isaac Ber. *Teʿudah be-yisra'el.* Vilna, 1828.

Lifshiẓ, Yaʿakov Halevi. *Zikhron Yaʿakov.* 3 volumes, Kovna, 1924.

Lilienblum, Moshe Leib. "Berur devarim." *Ha-Meliẓ* 22 (1886), No. 1, 4–8.

Lilienblum, Moshe Leib. "Bikoret le-khol shirei Yehudah Leib Gordon." Reprinted in *Kol kitvei Moshe Leib Lilienblum,* vol. 3. Odessa, 1912, 26–78.

Lilienblum, Moshe Leib. "'Ein meʿarvim she'elah be-she'elah." *Ha-Meliẓ* 18 (1882), No. 14, 258–259.

Lilenblum, Moshe Lieb. *Ḥat'ot neʿurim.* Reprinted in his *Ketavim 'otobiografiim,* ed. Sh. Breiman. Jerusalem, 1970.

Lilienblum, Moshe Leib. "Obshche-evreiskii vopros i Palestina." *Razsvet* (1881), No. 41, 1598–1599; No. 42, 1638–1642.

Lilienblum, Moshe Leib. "'Orḥot ha-Talmud." *Ha-Meliẓ* 8 (1868), No. 13, 16, 18, 21, 24, 25, 27, 29.

Lilienblum, Moshe Leib. "Nosafot le-''Orḥot ha-Talmud'." *Ha-Meliẓ* 9 (1869), No. 8–12.

Luzzatto, Samuele David. [Letter to Gordon.] *Ha-Maggid* 2 (1858), No. 39, 195.

Maggid, David. *Sefer toledot mishpaḥat Ginẓburg.* St. Petersburg, 1899.

Meyer, Michael. "Ha-sinodim ha-yehudim be-Germaniah be-maḥaẓit ha-sheniiah shel ha-me'ah ha-19." *Meḥkarim be-toledot ʿam yisra'el ve-'ereẓ yisra'el* 3 (1974), 239–274.

Miliukov, Paul, et al. *History of Russia.* 3 volumes, New York, 1968–1969.

Milosz, Czeslaw. *Native Realm: A Search for Self-Definition,* trans. Catherine S. Leach. Berkeley, 1981.

Miron, Dan. "Bein takdim le-mikreh—shirato ha-'epit shel Y"L Gordon u-mekomah be-sifrut ha-haskalah ha-ʿivrit." *Meḥkarei Yerushalayim be-sifrut ʿivrit* 2 (1983), 127–197.

Miron, Dan. "Rediscovering Haskalah Poetry." *Prooftexts* 1 (1981), 292–305.

Monas, Sidney. "The Dream of the Suffering Horse." Afterword to Fyodor Dostoyevsky, *Crime and Punishment,* New York, 1968, 529–542.

Montefiore, Moses. *Diaries of Sir Moses and Lady Montefiore,* (ed. L. Loewe. 2 volumes, London, 1890.

Orlan, Ḥayim. "Yalag ke-meshorer be-yidish." ʿ*Al ha-mishmar,* January 15, 1982, 7.

Orbach, Alexander. *New Voices of Russian Jewry.* Leiden, 1980.

Perlmann, Moshe. "L. O. Levanda and J. L. Gordon: Levanda's Letters to Gordon, 1873–5." *Proceedings of the American Academy for Jewish Research* 30 (1967), 139–185.

Perlmann, Moshe. "Notes on Raszvet 1860–61." *Proceedings of the American Academy for Jewish Research* 33 (1965), 21–50.

Philipson, David. *The Reform Movement in Judaism.* New York, 1931.

Pinsker, Leon. "Pis'mo dra. L. S. Pinskera k L. O. Gordonu." *Perezhitoe* 3 (1911), 392–393.

Raisin, Jacob S. *The Haskalah Movement in Russia.* Philadelphia, 1913.

Report Presented by Sir Moses Montefiore, Bart., . . . Upon His Return From His Mission to St. Petersburg, August, 4632–1872. London, 1872.

Rogger, Hans. *Jewish Policies and Right-Wing Politics in Imperial Russia.* Berkeley and Los Angeles, 1986.

Rosenthal, Y. L. *Toledot ḥevrat marbei haskalah be-ʾereẓ Rusiyah.* 2 volumes, St. Petersburg, 1886–1890.

Sadan, Dov. *Be-ẓ'etkha u-ve-ohalekha.* Israel, 1966.

Salmon, Yosef. "David Gordon veʿiton Ha-Maggid: Ḥilufei ʿemdot le-le'umiut ha-yehudit 1860–1882." *Ẓion* 47 (1982), 145–164.

Schapiro, Leonard. *Turgenev: His Life and Times.* New York, 1978.

Schorsch, Ismar. "Zacharias Frankel and the European Origins of Conservative Judaism." *Judaism* 30 (1981), 344–354.

Semenko, Irina M. *Vasily Zhukovsky, Life and Work.* Boston, 1976.

Shapiro, K. "Mikhtav galui le-h' Yalag." *Ha-Meliẓ* 22 (1886), No. 5, 78–79.

Sliozberg, Henri. *Baron Horace O. de Gunzbourg, sa vie et son oeuvre.* Paris. 1935.

Slutsky, Yehudah. "Ha-gi'ografiia shel peraʿot 5641." *Ha-ʿAvar* 9 (1962).

Smolenskin, Peretz. "Ve-z'ot le-Yehudah." *Ha-Shaḥar* 10 (1880 [sic!]), 455–467.

Sokolov, Naḥum. "Sedeh ẓofim." *Ha-ʾAsif* 1 (1884), 211–217.

Speigel, Shalom. *Hebrew Reborn.* New York, 1930.

Stampfer, Shaul. "Shalosh yeshivot lit'aiyot ba-me'ah ha-19." Unpublished doctoral dissertation, The Hebrew University of Jerusalem, 1981.

Stanislawski, Michael. "Eliyyahu Ben Shelomoh Zalman." *The Encyclopedia of Religion,* ed. Mircea Eliade. New York and London, 1987, vol. 5, 98–100.

Stanislawski, Michael. *Tsar Nicholas I and the Jews: The Transformation of Jewish Society in Russia, 1825–1855.* Philadelphia, 1983.

Stasov, V. "Otvet g. L. Gordonu." *Razsvet* 1 (1879), No. 5, 384–385.

Stasov, V. "Po povodu postroiki sinagogi v S. Peterburge." *Evreiskaia biblioteka* 2 (1871), 453–473.

Strauss, Janine, *Yehudah Leib Gordon. Poète hébreu (1830–1892): Son oeuvre de fabuliste.* Paris, 1980.

Tcherikover, E. (= Cherikover, I. M.) "Revolutsionere un natsionale ideologies fun der rusish-yidisher intelegents." In his *Geshikhte fun der yidisher arbeter-bavegung in di Fareinikte Shtatn,* vol. 2. New York, 1945, 138–202.

Tsinberg, S. L. (= Zinberg, Israel) *Istoriia evreiskoi pechati v Rossii v sviazi s obshchestvennymi techeniiami.* Petrograd, 1915.

Tsitron, Sh. L. *Shtadlonim.* Warsaw, n.d.

Verses, Shmuel. *Bikoret ha-bikoret.* Tel Aviv, 1982.

Verses, Shmuel. "'Zeloḥit shel palyaton ve-samemaneha—ʿal 'omanut ha-feleton shel Yehudah Leib Gordon." *Meḥkarei Yerushalayim be-sifrut 'ivrit* 2 (1983), 105–125.

Volfson, Moshe David. "Be-zekhutan shel ha-rabanim: ma'aneh le-Dani'el Bagar." *Ha-Levanon* 7 (1870), No. 4, 25–27; No. 5 33–35.

Voskhod 12 (1892), No. 40—notices on Gordon's death.

Walicki, Andrzej. *A History of Russian Thought.* Stanford, 1979.

Wandycz, Piotr. *The Lands of Partitioned Poland.* Seattle, 1974.

Weinreich, Max. *Fun beyde zaytn ployt.* Buenos Aires, 1955.

Weisberg, Y. Y. *Yehudah Leib Gordon ve-toledotav.* Kiev, 1893.

Wilensky, Mordekhai. *Ḥasidim u-mitnagdim.* 2 volumes, Jerusalem, 1970.

Zederbaum, Alexander. "Bin ba-davar ve-haven ba-mar'eh." *Ha-Meliẓ* 17 (1881), No. 20, 405–410.

Zederbaum, Alexander. "Ḥagigat ha-yovel." *Ha-Meliẓ* 17 (1881), No. 17, 863–866.

Zhukovskii, V. A. *Isbrannoe.* Leningrad, 1973.

Zinberg, Israel. *Di geshikhte fun der literatur bay yidn.* 9 volumes, New York, 1943; translated into English and edited by Bernard Martin, *History of Jewish Literature,* 12 volumes, New York, 1978.

Index